Two F
PUBLISI

A Daily Guide to Live by Faith
Even When Life Throws You a Curve

NEXT VERSE

HAL KITCHINGS

An imprint of Two Penny Publishing
twopennypublishing.com

For information about the author, book events, or interviews,
please contact the author representative at:
info@twopennypublishing.com

Library of Congress Control Number: 2021923598

Hardback ISBN: 978-1-950995-59-2
Paperback ISBN: 978-1-950995-58-5
Also available in Ebook

Printed in the United States of America
F I R S T   E D I T I O N

ENDORSEMENTS

"If you have committed to spending time in God's word every day but you need some help fulfilling that goal, I highly recommend the devotional book *Next Verse* by my dear friend Dr. Hal Kitchings. Not only does this reader-friendly work provide a plan for reading through the entire Bible in a year, but in it, Dr. Kitchings also provides daily applications for life from one section of each day's reading. I have known Hal since he served as the Student Minister of a church that I pastored in the 1980s. I have watched him mature as a man of God and a minister of the gospel for over three decades. His applications of key Bible passages each day come from a life that has realized the value of trusting what God has said in His word for those times when life throws you a curveball. So, I urge you to step up to the plate and take a swing at applying God's word to your life daily with some solid coaching from a godly and gifted pastor, Dr. Hal Kitchings!"

Ken Alford
Former President of the Florida Baptist Convention and Former
Chairman of Trustees of the Southern Baptist Convention's North American Mission Board

"Hal Kitchings has written an excellent day-by-day devotional book. He has written this devotional easy enough for a new believer to comprehend and deep enough for a more mature believer. *Next Verse* is a great new resource for those who are developing consistent time alone with the Lord."

Michael Catt
Founder of the Refresh Conference and Executive Producer of Sherwood Pictures

"*Next Verse* is a virtual tour of the Bible led by a seasoned guide. Using this book, you'll be able to read through the Bible in a year—or at your own pace—with Hal's reassuring insights for each day. In our era of accelerating evil and accumulating problems, we need a book like the Bible and a Pastor like Hal Kitchings!"

Robert J. Morgan
Teaching Pastor at The Donelson Fellowship Church and Best-Selling Author

To My Grandchildren

LIVING BY FAITH

YOU ARE NOT MEANT TO BE ALONE. From the very beginning, we see a triune God. In Genesis 1:26 the word *us* shouts the doctrine of the Trinity: God the Father, Son, and Holy Spirit. We certainly know this from what many call the Great Commission in Matthew 28:18-20. You know, the one that says...*baptizing in the name of the Father, Son, and Holy Spirit.* And there are other verses in the Old and New Testament we could point to for this foundational doctrine of the Christian faith.

God has no desire for you to go through life by yourself. He wants a relationship with you. Spending time with Him daily in Bible study and prayer is key. We see in our daily reading that He didn't want us to be alone so He made Eve for Adam. (It doesn't mean you have to be married, but if it's God's will, He will bless the union in Him through the marriage relationship.) He wants you to find people whom you can share life with. He wants you to find a church that fits so you can be in a small group. Do you have one? The church is His idea and it's irreplaceable. Fellowship with other believers is paramount for consistency throughout this year. No one knows what the future holds, but we do know who holds the future. A good friend of mine often says "No one should fight the fight alone." He's right. God demonstrated this from the beginning. Live by faith today...

5

DAILY READING:
Genesis 3:1-4:26; Matthew 2:13-3:6
Psalm 2:1-12; Proverbs 1:7-9
Focal Passage: Genesis 3:1

LIVING BY FAITH

THE ENEMY WANTS TO CAUSE YOU TO DOUBT. Don't let him. He's used this method since the garden, when he caused Eve to doubt God's Word. So be aware, but not afraid. Prepare by studying God's Word. You need to know what it says to not be fooled. Remember, the truth will set you free!

The devil wants you to doubt your salvation. He wants you to doubt your worth. Rick Warren once said, " You are not who you think you are. You are not who others think you are. You are who God says you are." And He doesn't have "accidents." He creates people and if you know Him, He has a purpose for your life. Don't let Satan deceive you into thinking you are not capable because of your past sins, your IQ, or your non-spiritual lineage. The Christ in you is bigger than all of those things.

You are an overcomer as a child of God. Keep reading the Bible. Keep journaling what He's teaching you. (Don't write a book. Just jot notes of truth.) Apply it one day at a time. Win the day! And stop engaging in "stinkin thinkin!" (That's not the way you spell those words.) You may even need to follow a dream this year that God gave you years ago. If God gave it to you, don't doubt it! Live by faith today...

LIVING BY FAITH

WHAT MIGHT BE SAID OF YOU WHEN YOU ARE NO MORE? We know what was said of Enoch. It's as if he was walking down a road one day talking with the Lord, then all of a sudden God decided to talk with him face to face. Can you imagine? But what greater statement could be made than it being said *(twice)* "Enoch walked with God." And then there's old Noah. You know, the one who built the ark before ever seeing rain. Though not perfect (ONLY Jesus reached perfection), the scripture says he walked with God, also. He stood out during his era as a man blameless and righteous.

I have preached a message about the various types of funerals I believe people have. 1. Dreadful. This is the person who never put their faith alone in Christ and everyone knows it. 2. Doubtful. This is where the individual claimed to know God, though there was little evidence. (The family left behind usually suffers through this one, too.) 3. Delightful. This is the one where the person died knowing the Lord and living for him. Translated-he walked with God. (No, this person wasn't perfect either. Only Jesus.) 4. Wasteful. This is a deathbed conversion experience. I believe someone can trust Jesus during their last days, or hours, or even minutes. And I believe, based on the thief on the cross in the New Testament, that person will be with God in paradise. I just think it's a shame. Think of all the fruit that could have been produced from this one life if they had been totally surrendered to Jesus. It's a saved life, but somewhat of a wasted life. Please don't be that guy or gal.

Don't miss the purpose of your life. Know Jesus by doing what you're doing today. Read the Bible and apply it to your life. Obey God, by faith. Fear Him and be willing to be ridiculed. I'm sure Noah was. God will bless you, your family, your friends, your colleagues, and your classmates; even your funeral can have an impact. There's nothing greater to be said of you at the end of your days, than what was said of Enoch and Noah. Walk with God. Live by faith today...

LIVING BY FAITH

THE BEST KIND OF OBEDIENCE IS QUICK OBEDIENCE. It's not always that we don't know what God wants us to do, it's that we'd rather not do it. In our passage today we see Peter, Andrew, James, and John follow Jesus. Jesus asked them to do something major. This was no little decision. They were being asked to leave their family and familiar surroundings to follow Jesus. Jesus did not lay out their entire future. They left *immediately*. They were quick because this was Jesus and there was nothing vague about it. And if you read ahead, you will find they had no regrets.

What's Jesus calling you to do? Is it salvation? The Bible says today is the day of salvation. You don't have to think about this one. Jesus came. Jesus lived perfectly. Jesus died for your sins. Jesus rose from the grave and is alive. You can admit your sins and follow Him. Don't delay this decision, folks. Don't try to "clean yourself up." Trust Him by faith and He'll do the cleaning as you allow Him to be Lord (boss).

Is there something else Christ has called you to do or be? Is it clear? Have you seen it through scripture readings, prayer, circumstances, wise counsel, and the prompting of the Holy Spirit? If so, don't delay. Is it full-time vocational ministry? Is it moving? Is it breaking off an engagement? Is it changing jobs? He will NOT call you to do something then leave you "hanging." My lifetime verse is 1 Thessalonians 5:24 because it constantly assures me that He'll help me accomplish what He's called me to. "The one who calls you is faithful, and He will do it." He'll do the same for you, no matter what it is or how overwhelming it may appear. Live by faith today...

LIVING BY FAITH

WE CANNOT GO TO THE MOUNTAIN UNTIL WE HAVE BEEN IN THE VALLEY. Today you read the greatest messages by the greatest preacher who ever lived. Known as the Sermon on the Mount, Jesus begins by delivering what we know as the Beatitudes. They set forth how men and women are to live as Kingdom people. Tony Evans said we could call them antibiotics from God's pharmacy to aid life transformation. I like that.

Jesus begins with what's essentially needed to experience transformation. A transformation from the inside, not the outside. To be **poor in spirit** is to be dependent on God – every moment of every day. Sometimes it takes a while for us to get there. Sometimes it takes a dark time for us to get there. God is patient. But He longs to have a close relationship with us, and He will do whatever it takes for us to finally get it. He does not want to see us just on Sundays or occasionally during the week. He wants to visit with us moment by moment. He wants to be our life. He wants us to have joy during this life so we will be fulfilled and be salt and light.

Don't waste your pain. Use it for Him. Don't be cocky, be confident in Him. He works in and through you as you depend on Him. Please don't wait on a "dark time" to learn this lesson. Use the difficulties in life you've already been through as lessons of dependency. But if something is around the corner, know you can depend on Him. He will see you through! Be blessed! Live by faith today...

LIVING BY FAITH

STOP MAKING PROMISES. Jesus is not keen on us making flippant promises. Some type of oath on our part shouldn't be used to convince someone we are telling the truth. God wants us to speak the truth—period. It's one thing to be a child and make promises on the playground. It's another to be a believer and follow up statements with "I promise!" Please don't be that type of person. Much damage can be done.

We were reminded yesterday of the importance of being a peacemaker. This is **not** the same as a peacekeeper. A peacekeeper will often stretch the truth in order to please or "keep the peace." Did I mention how much damage this does? Yes, I did. It hurts the cause of Christ all the while trying to "keep the peace," even if it is supposedly being done "in the name of Christ." Psalm 5:6 from yesterday's reading says, *"You destroy those who tell lies; bloodthirsty and deceitful men the Lord abhors."* See, He's not keen on this practice.

As you grow in truth by reading and practicing God's Word, you will be less likely to make promises. Keep reading. Keep applying what you are reading. And for heaven's sake, stop making promises! Say "yes" to Jesus. Say "yes" to truth from God's Word. Say "yes" to whatever you know is a "yes" and "no" to whatever you need to say is a "no." Live by faith today...

DAILY READING:
Genesis 16:1-18:19; Matthew 6:1-24
Psalm 7:1-17; Proverbs 2:1-5
Focal Passage: Genesis 18:14

LIVING BY FAITH

IT MAY BE TOO HARD FOR YOU, BUT IT IS NOT TOO HARD FOR GOD. Living by faith is exciting because it entails doing things we cannot do by ourselves. In other words, if God doesn't show up, we look like idiots! Ever been there? I have. I have felt God call me to do some things in my life that looked ridiculous to some. Yes, living by faith is never boring!

God told Sarah she was going to be pregnant and have a son. She laughed and God reminded her **nothing is too hard for Him.** He was right. (He is always right.) And she was shown that regardless of human boundaries, God has none. We must remember, He set the boundaries. (Go back to Genesis for a reminder.) He can do whatever He wants, with whomever He wants, whenever He wants. He's God. He's faithful!

Be sure not to live your life of faith like you would if you were on your own. You are not. If you are a believer, the Holy Spirit lives inside of you. If you sense He's leading you to do something that may seem radical, do it. What's the worst thing that can happen? You "failed" doing something sacrificial because you did it out of love for Jesus. He's sovereign. Trust Him. You only live once and once is enough if we do things out of obedience to God. Your life is but a vapor.

What are you thinking about right now? Does it involve a step of faith? FANTASTIC! Maybe this is the year! Live by faith today...

LIVING BY FAITH

YOU WILL NOT GO TO PRISON FOR WORRYING, BUT YOU WILL BE KEPT FROM ENJOYING ALL THE PLACES GOD HAS FOR YOU TO ENJOY. Living freely for Jesus provides much freedom. When we try to live the Christ-life and worry at the same time, it's disastrous. God does not want His children to be burdened about daily life. There's always going to be something on this side of heaven. Our world is depraved. We are sinful. Stuff happens! And worry makes it worse. How do I know? Because I am a worrier. I've struggled with this for years. I read once that if you want to know how to deal with worry, ask a worrier. I'm not sure about that, but I do have some experience. God continues to provide healing for me. We are all a work in progress.

I had one guy tell me that his grandmother said that if you worry as a Christian, you are basically calling God a liar. Wow! That's strong, isn't it? Another guy told me that it's like sitting in a rocking chair. It makes you feel like you're doing something, but you're going nowhere. Worry is a sin. We may not go to prison, but we'll miss out on the daily joy God has for us in this world. He came to give us life—abundant and free!

Birds do their thing and God takes care of them. He died for us. There's no need to think He's on vacation while we're down here struggling with *whatever*. He doesn't take vacations. Consider what's concerning you and pray about it. If you can plan to prepare for whatever it is that's ruining your day, do it. And follow through! BUT if you can't do anything about it, after you pray, shout! Shout for joy because your God is up to something good. That's His nature. Don't forget that. Enjoy your freedom in Christ and go places—places He intends for you to explore and enjoy. Live by faith today...

LIVING BY FAITH

SACRIFICES PRODUCE GREAT VICTORIES. Never underestimate what God will do when you obey—especially sacrificially. The story of Abraham's willingness to sacrifice his son, Isaac, is pregnant with meaning. But the reality is that when we sacrifice, we see clearly. Abraham saw the ram after he did what God asked. Surely it was there prior! Our vision is clouded when we hesitate to follow through on God's directions for our lives.

We tend to pause when God speaks. Now if it's something fairly simple, we may do it quickly. But if it's perhaps somewhat inconvenient or requires sacrifices on our part, look out! We may justify why God is "wrong." We may pretend we didn't hear it. We may come up with any number of reasons for not obeying. If so, it's costly! And it usually involves hurting others.

You probably won't be asked to sacrifice your son on the altar today, but that does not mean you will not be tested. God has His divine ways of testing each of us. He does so to help us mature. Tests are given to students to help, not hurt. (It doesn't always feel that way, does it?) God will not go against His character. He is love. If you sense He is asking you to make a sacrifice of some kind, do it. It may be a job. It may be money. It may be a friendship. Whatever it is, it will probably hurt. If you're wounded, God will heal you! You may need to go ahead and obey and stop overthinking it. Live by faith today...

Genesis 23:1-24:51; Matthew 8:1-17
Psalm 9:13-20; Proverbs 3:1-6
Focal Passage: Proverbs 3:5-6

LIVING BY FAITH

JUST BECAUSE YOU DO NOT UNDERSTAND YOUR PATH, DOES NOT MEAN IT IS NOT THE RIGHT ONE. Do you ever feel as if you are doing your best to understand God's direction, but it seems futile? Me too. Maybe you are exactly where you need to be. Maybe God is increasing your faith. He wants every compartment of our hearts and lives. That takes time. We tend to hold on to certain aspects of our lives.

The word *trust* could be translated "to lie down." I lie down on my bed, without hesitation, because I fully trust it. When we don't understand why our job went away, why our relationship with our children seems difficult, why our neighbor keeps tossing our cat, we lean into Jesus even more. If not, we may go astray due to the trial. That, my friend, can be costly! Ramp up your prayer life. Perhaps missing a meal or taking a break from social media for the purpose of consecrated prayer is the answer? (The Bible calls for fasting, at times.) It may be necessary. God wants OUR UNDIVIDED ATTENTION.

When the Bible uses *with all our heart* here, it means "completely." Our heart can be deceitful in all its ways. Our own understanding cannot sustain us. Out of the heart is the wellspring of life.

So, pray and get God's Word in your life, because when we **know** Him, our **paths** are made straight. That does not mean perfect. It means we'll see God removing obstacles along the way. Pay attention, and be amazed. Alternatively, not seeing how God will resolve your situation may be exactly where He wants you—for now. Live by faith today…

LIVING BY FAITH

DON'T FORGET THE FIRST WAVE WHEN THE SECOND ONE APPROACHES. Jesus was patient with the disciples. They were on a boat in the midst of a storm. Jesus was sleeping. They were scared. They woke Him up and He calmly asked them a question about their faith. Then He calmed the storm. Jesus still amazes me. He woke up from a dead sleep, did a miracle, and challenged the disciples. I don't believe I would have been so nice to the guys, especially after what they had already experienced with Christ. He had already done miracles. They saw them. So, what was a storm to Jesus? Besides, He was in the boat! Come on, guys!

Wait a minute… I do the same thing. You do the same thing. We all do the same thing. Let's not think ill about these boys so quickly. God has worked in my storms and yours. The waves sometimes overwhelm me, but He has always rescued me at just the right time. How foolish of me to think there wouldn't be another one and another one. I'm not in heaven yet. So He wants me to remember His faithfulness time and time again. Then I'm not as fearful and I don't panic, like the disciples did.

Jesus may not be "in the boat" with me, but He's in me. The Holy Spirit resides in the believer. Jesus even told the disciples how good it'd be when the Spirit comes. He's in us. He's with us. He's got us. Don't forget your own waves and what happened after the storm was over. Live by faith today…

LIVING BY FAITH

JESUS DID NOT COME TO EARTH TO "HANG OUT" WITH RELIGIOUS PEOPLE. That statement is usually difficult for two types of people: religious and non-religious. Religious people can make the mistake of thinking their good deeds qualify them for heaven. They often have a type of haughtiness about them due to their misunderstanding of their works-based faith. Non-religious people often think they have to be good to be accepted into heaven. Not true. Both groups are wrong. (We will see this when we get to the story of the Prodigal Son.) Salvation is based on faith alone.

Jesus demonstrates how to live. He spent much time with the disciples. We certainly need to spend time with fellow believers. The church is a hospital for sinners, not a country club for saints. Some church members forget this. We find in our reading of the gospels that Jesus spent time with lost people (non-religious folks). And today we read the classic statement about His primary reason for coming to earth. Not to make religious people feel comfortable, but uncomfortable. He met the sinners where they were and offered them a better life—a life in relationship with Him. It doesn't get any clearer or any better than that.

Who are you hanging out with these days? Do you have a church family to share with, grow with, serve with, and worship with? I hope so. Do you spend any time with those "outside" the church? I hope so. Jesus would want you to. If you and I do not intentionally, regularly, connect with those who have no hope, we missed Jesus' daily life. Connect with lost people. Love them. Be real. Watch how God will use you. Live by faith today…

LIVING BY FAITH

JESUS WOULD NOT LOOK AT WAL-MART SHOPPERS LIKE WE SOMETIMES DO. I am fairly certain you have been to Wal-Mart. I'm also fairly certain you've been during a busy season of the year. Furthermore, I'm fairly certain you get frustrated at times by certain individuals or groups. Am I right? Regardless, I do. I can go to Wal-Mart or other places and get "put out" with certain individuals. It can be because of their rude behavior. It may even be because of their sense of entitlement. I just find myself at times thinking, "How can this person be this way?"

Jesus loved everyone. He never would go to Wal-Mart ready to "pick people apart" due to their behavior. If there was someone there acting odd, or rude, or whatever—he'd have compassion. Why can't I be more like Him? Maybe I forget what it's like to be a non-believer. (Why wouldn't I act like the unapologetic sinner that I am?) Maybe I forget not everyone was raised in a Godly home, wonderful church, and loving community. Maybe the person has not grown spiritually in their faith? Maybe it's me more than them? I want to see people like Jesus did. Don't you?

Jesus didn't hide in a cave with His disciples. He got out into the community where people were—all kinds of people. When He saw those who were hurting, He had compassion for them. He realized they had no Godly guidance. He compared them to lost sheep. Sheep are dumb. They must have a leader, or they will hurt themselves. Such is the case with people. We are dumb sinners. We need a leader. And the first and foremost leader should be Jesus. He's the only one who loves us unconditionally and sees our sinful state with a loving eye. When He "eyeballs" us, He knows our life can be better if we'll only turn our eyes to Him. Live by faith today...

LIVING BY FAITH

HOW ARE WE SUPPOSED TO ACT LIKE A SNAKE AND A DOVE AT THE SAME TIME? This passage has always intrigued me. I've seen plenty of snakes in my lifetime. I've also seen many doves. They are opposite, yet Jesus says we are to act like both of them. Jewish people thought serpents were evil creatures. They saw them as crafty, guileful, artful, or sly. Jesus was basically saying the believer should be wise. Wisdom comes from God and the Bible says we are to pray for it. It's not knowledge. It is thinking like God would think. And a dove strikes us as beautiful, gracious, and loving. We are to allow Jesus to help us be both so we will have an impact on our culture.

Jesus knew we would live in this world but wanted to be sure we knew how not to be of this world. Living our daily lives brings us in contact with some mean folks. It can be hard not to "strike back." We don't have to be a "pushover," but we do have to be Christlike in our reactions. Jesus wasn't a sissy. But He never sinned. Only as we continue to get to know Him will we be able to know how to lovingly and shrewdly deal with mean folk we come in contact with.

I've been dove hunting numerous times. I know, right now I sort of feel bad about it too. I am not an avid outdoorsman or shooter. The few times I've picked doves up after shooting them, they seemed so harmless... soft... and kind. Anyway, they help us know what Jesus is speaking of here in the focal passage. Besides, the dove is prevalent in the Old Testament and the New Testament. I guess we might call them biblical birds. Oh well, be gentle, gracious, and appropriately "soft," in your relationships. Jesus says we can be all those things. Live by faith today...

LIVING BY FAITH

FEAR OF MAN HAS TO BE ONE OF THE GREATEST HINDRANCES TO FULFILLING GOD'S WILL. I believe this to be true. The Bible confirms it. It's human to want to be liked. It's tempting to please man over God, so others won't give us a hard time. I get it and have fallen many times. But we must understand that when we sign up for God's team, He's the Head Coach. He calls the shots. We may not like it, but He never asks us to do anything or to not do something without a heart of love. It would go against His character.

I believe we can still have friends when we obey God. We may lose a few, even though deep down they probably respect us. God puts others in our lives along the way. They often help us fulfill our destiny. I had some friends who are no longer with us, who wasted their lives pleasing others. They will **never** get another chance. Love people but love them enough to please God. They won't forget you because there aren't many out there who live this way.

The Bible says that bad company corrupts good character. Love everyone, but don't go on vacations with everyone! Be salt and light, but don't get in the same "salt shaker" with them when you don't need to be. Don't be the light, late at night, in places where you shouldn't be. Know the difference. Keep getting to know Jesus intimately and He'll help you. It can be the difference between fulfilling your purpose in life and wasting it. Live by faith today...

LIVING BY FAITH

LOSING CAN BE WINNING IN THE CHRISTIAN LIFE. Jacob wrestled with a "strong man" and lost. It was the best defeat of his life. It was a "representative" from God and it obviously doesn't matter exactly who it was. What matters is that Jacob was never the same. That's what happens when we are broken. It's not fun. It's just necessary to be emptied of self and filled with the Spirit to fulfill our destiny.

Have you been broken? Have you had an experience that you couldn't "fix?" I have. I was in my forties serving as a pastor of a church. I sensed God released me from my assignment and decided to resign. I was broken. I'd always had "success" in ministry. Not this time. Not in the way we typically measure success. But it was an experience that changed me. I didn't change my name, but it would have been an ideal time to go by my given name instead of my nickname. Harold means strong leader. I became a stronger leader after being broken. I have a long way to go, but that experience took me to another level. Why? I learned that God wants me to totally depend on Him. Education, experience, abilities, and gifts are all good, but they are nothing without being intimate with Jesus. He alone helps us through our sudden "fights" in life that we may face.

I was assigned this particular passage to preach on in a seminary preaching class. I was terrified! Not only did I have to preach in front of my peers, but I also had to preach this unique passage. I didn't totally understand the context then. I do now. Maybe it was providential. Please know that God is real, and He knows what He's doing. If you are being "whipped" in life, surrender. He'll give you a "limp" that will bless you beyond measure. Live by faith today...

LIVING BY FAITH

THERE IS A DIFFERENCE BETWEEN COCKINESS AND CONFIDENCE. Cockiness is everywhere. It's in Hollywood or your local grocery store. People who display a prideful attitude can be on the playing field. You know, that guy interviewed after catching the winning touchdown pass who makes sure everyone knows he's the reason for the victory. It's cockiness—a manner that depends on self. It is a person who has not learned that God, not him, is God. Cockiness is totally opposite of Jesus. Talk about someone who could have been cocky but was not. He was and is perfect. No, He was not cocky, He was confident. There's a difference...

Confidence comes from brokenness. (See yesterday's focal passage.) Once we are carrying a wound from realizing our total dependence on Christ, we never "walk" the same. Our walk is with Him, not against Him. It is with Him, not out in front of Him. It is with Him, not way behind Him. And that brings confidence in who we are in Him. It's like David in the Old Testament, who we will read about. He was confident because God had been with him when he fought the lion and the bear. Why wouldn't God be with him in fighting Goliath, the biggest giant he'd ever faced? That is God-ordained confidence. God wants that for all His children. Like David, we can step up to the battle line and say *bring it on*, you giant of a problem!

Meekness is a fruit of God-confidence. It's strength—bridled. Like a broken horse. Meekness is not weakness. It's a person walking in confidence because he is walking with Jesus in an intimate relationship. If I had known this or practiced this earlier in my life, I would have been a much better person, student, friend, relative, and athlete. Hold your head high; God is with you and stands ready to help you do things beyond you. Live by faith today...

LIVING BY FAITH

HERE WE HAVE THE ONE SIN THAT WILL KEEP A PERSON OUT OF HEAVEN. It is called blasphemy of the Holy Spirit. The Holy Spirit convicts us of our sinfulness. If we do not admit our sin and confess Jesus by faith as our only redeemer, we will spend eternity in hell when we die. It is the truth. It is the reality of a just and merciful God. No one would want to go before an unjust judge in this world. Why would we want anything less from the God of the universe? It's humanity's fault, not God's fault. We saw this when we studied Adam and Eve. It will be further confirmed when we reach our study in the book of Romans. God does not send people to hell; people go there if they refuse to put their faith in Jesus alone for salvation.

Contrary to what many believe, suicide does not send one to hell. Adultery does not send one to hell. Homosexuality does not send one to hell. There are various levels of consequences due to sin. BUT the only sin that sends a person to hell is rejecting Jesus as your personal Savior. Please don't do it. There's no second chance.

Sometimes it seems death comes in waves. This has been one of those weeks. Three people I knew died. Two of them are in heaven simply because they admitted their sin and put their faith alone in Jesus. One is in hell due to not accepting Christ. It's heartbreaking. Could I have done more? Perhaps. I hope to learn from it. I can still see his face from the last time I saw him… though, it will never happen again. I'm thankful for those whom I have shared the hope we have in Christ with. Every moment and every person is precious. The Bible declares that today is the day of salvation. Maybe this is your day. Pay attention to whom God brings across your path today. His face may reveal no hope and a need for a friend who cares enough to tell him about Jesus. No matter how bad this person has been, the only sin that will keep him out of heaven is rejecting Jesus. It could be a divine appointment. Live by faith today…

DAILY READING:
Genesis 39:1-41:16; Matthew 12:46-13:23
Psalm 17:1-15; Proverbs 3:33-35
Focal Passage: Genesis 41:16

LIVING BY FAITH

I PUT THIS VERSE ON A BOTTLE FULL OF DIRT ONE TIME. I was pastor of Morrison Heights, in my hometown of Clinton, Mississippi. The church needed to relocate due to growth. There were numerous reasons from a human perspective it could not be done. It would be costly. Not everyone was "on board" with the decision. What would we do with the old property? The list goes on, but I will stop here. Then there were reasons why we should relocate, that I sensed were of God. I felt it was my responsibility to lead the church toward the initial steps of relocation. But, who was I to finally say to a group of leaders, "As your Pastor, I believe God's will is to relocate so we can expand for Kingdom purposes?"

The focal passage was my primary text when preaching to the congregation about what I sensed. I explained how Joseph was asked to do something that he knew he couldn't do, but that God could certainly do. He had interpreted dreams before, but he knew the God he feared, who was always with him—good times and bad—would not fail him. So, for the church to take on this huge step of faith, I had to be sure we all knew that it was bigger than us. Only by God's grace could HE help us relocate. And God did it. It was a process, but we voted to relocate, found the property, paid for it, and had a service on the dirt before I was called back to Florida to pastor. The Sunday I preached on this verse, people could pick up a small bottle of dirt with the text typed on it during the response time after the message. It was to be a visual reminder of what God can do... and to pray.

When I go home to Clinton, Mississippi, I usually drive by the church on the Interstate and say to myself, *Thank you, Lord.* I couldn't do it. Church members couldn't do it. But GOD did it!

What's He calling you to do that you can't do? It's not likely that it's to interpret a dream for someone. But it could certainly be a dream ordained by God that depends on your obedience. God didn't leave you down here just for "small things." He is a big God and He ordains big plans for His people. Surrender it to Him. Make sure it accomplishes Kingdom purposes. Be sure you're not doing it for selfish reasons. And if you don't have a God-ordained dream, pray for one. If you already do, it's not if it's coming, it's *when.* Live by faith today...

LIVING BY FAITH

WHAT ARE SUCH UGLY COWS DOING IN THE BIBLE? They were part of Pharaoh's dream that Joseph interpreted. They represented seven years of famine that Egypt would experience after seven great years of abundance. The phrase *"I had never seen such ugly cows"* was a revelation of how awful it was going to be.

We all have some "ugly cows" during our lifetime. Seasons of difficulty come to us all. When Job was questioned by his wife about his season of heartache he replied, "You're talking like an empty-headed fool. We take the good days from God—why not also the bad days?" (Job 2:10 MSG) Jesus, the Son of God, certainly experienced both. If we think one day everything is going to be perfect during our time on earth, we are just as "empty-headed" as Job's wife.

The story of Joseph we have been reading demonstrates the various seasons of life. Joseph certainly had his share of both. What an amazing man of God! But the Lord was with Joseph. He will be with you, too. Be wise like Joseph, to be prepared for whatever may come your way. Know God, now. Obey what you understand His will for your life to be, now. Then you will be better prepared for all of life and God will use you to help others. Sometimes the help for others will be immediate; other times, it may be delayed. But rest assured, your pain will be used for good if you will allow it to be. Jesus was perfect and they crucified Him. But He didn't stay dead. He arose so that we might have life. He will help you rise from your absolutely *ugly cow* days and use them for good. Let Him. Live by faith today...

LIVING BY FAITH

GODLY MEN WEEP SOMETIMES. Have you ever heard the expression "Big boys don't cry?" It's a lie. This unfortunate misinformation has kept many a man from expressing his God-given emotions. It certainly would be abnormal for a grown man to cry over scratching his arm, barely breaking the skin. I get it. But God has given us a heart. When we experience hurt or joy over something significant, it's natural to cry. Joseph did twice in today's readings. The scripture we focused on follows an earlier time of weeping. Joseph had been through a lot. He certainly wasn't a sissy boy. Some would say he'd easily earned the title of a "man's man" in today's vernacular. It's no wonder he cried—his heart hurt due to his brothers treating him like dirt, even tossing him in the dirt once. He had been betrayed by others, too. Folks, he'd had years of difficulty and now was seeing God's redemption before his very eyes. He cried.

I was fortunate to be raised by a dad who expressed his emotions. (Yes, there were a few times he used anger in the wrong way. Haven't we all?) He openly wept in front of his family. There were times his heart was stirred, and he cried. I recall going to his office as a young adult and him telling me that he loved me. He had tears in his eyes. I'm not sure what was going on that day, but he openly wept as he once again expressed his unconditional love for me. (As far as I know, I had not done anything wrong at that time.) I will never forget that moment.

Guys, we can learn much from females. They tend to express their love for others more readily than we do. Just because we are males does not mean we cannot do the same. If God moves you to tears at the right time, for the right reason, let it go—weep. Jesus did. And He was fully God and fully man. Maybe, just maybe, you'll shed a tear soon because you should. God can use it in your life, and possibly others. Live by faith today...

LIVING BY FAITH

ARGUING HAS ACCOMPLISHED VERY LITTLE IN MY LIFETIME.

As I reflect over the years, I see little productivity from arguments I participated in or started. I wasted time—mine and theirs. Plus, arguments can even lead to temptations. For example, if you find yourself losing an argument, you may be tempted to strike a blow. This certainly wouldn't be a good witness. And it could lead to possible long-term damage to a relationship. It's just not good. Good discussions for understanding or clarification can be productive. That's not what arguing is. When one argues, the purpose is mostly counterproductive.

Joseph had become a lot wiser through the years than when he was younger. During his adolescence, he was somewhat of a braggart. His brothers didn't respond favorably, hence a major reason he was tossed in a pit years earlier. Now he was providing wise counsel to his brothers. He knew the core of who they were from years earlier. He had heard them argue about what to do with him. He did not want them to waste time after such a positive reunion arguing over "spilled milk." They could have easily gotten off track and even wallowed in their sinfulness from the past. Joseph wanted them to press on…

Are you argumentative? Don't rush past this question. Think about it. Maybe even ask someone who knows you well if you are. Dig deep if you are, because it can hurt your life's purpose and many other people. Life is too short for that possibility. Do you find yourself often engaging in arguments? I know a guy… bless his heart, he seems to always be looking for an argument. One day I finally told him to stop it. Just stop it. If he wanted to talk about Jesus or life in general, fine. But if he wanted to continue talking about a useless topic of discussion over and over again, I was done. We don't talk much anymore. But I love him. Don't be that guy or gal. Discussions can be fine. Explaining our beliefs can be biblically sound. Arguing is detrimental. Try to avoid arguments and see what happens. Live by faith today…

Genesis 46:1-47:31; Matthew 15:1-28
Psalm 19:1-14; Proverbs 4:14-19
Focal Passage: Psalm 19:1-4

LIVING BY FAITH

THE HEAVENS PREACH A SILENT SERMON THAT SHOUTS
GOD'S GLORY. God reveals Himself. All we have to do is open our eyes. There
are two types of revelation. One is *special revelation* and consists of Jesus and the
Bible. The other is *general revelation*. General revelation is the way people all over
the world can know about God. He is the creator of the universe. Creation shouts
that there is a God. There is only one who could do such an amazing, glorifying job.
Just look up. The amazing sunsets always remind me of how awesome God is.

Common sense reveals that the sky, the trees, the mountains, and the seas were
created. Every watch has a watchmaker. That just makes sense. And we have a
conscience. This, too, reminds us of how God works in us to reveal His existence.
These realities are confirmed in the first few chapters of Romans. We shall soon read
for ourselves.

Have you ever heard the statement *"Well, what about the guy in Africa who's
never heard of Jesus?"* You probably have. Maybe you've wondered too? The God of
the heavens, the Lord Jesus Christ, would never allow someone to go to a Godless
hell with no way of knowing Him personally. That's not His character. He shouts
I AM HERE through creation. He declares His glory continually. When a person
responds to the light he is given, rest assured that God will provide more light. And
what greater light in the world shines day by day for everyone to see than the sun?
God can, and will, and has, used the sun to lead people to The Son—Jesus. There's
no other way to Him but through Him. No, you don't have to "park your brain" to
believe in Christianity. It makes sense. Maybe today you'll see a rainbow or a sunset.
Regardless, thank God for His revelation... both types. Live by faith today...

LIVING BY FAITH

SOMETIMES I FEEL HOW THE DISCIPLES MUST HAVE FELT AT TIMES— LIKE A DOOFUS. Today we were reminded that even the disciples didn't always understand the words of God. (Jesus was fully God and fully man as He came to redeem the world.) Jesus was giving them a "heads up" concerning the religious leaders of the day. They didn't get it. They thought He was referring to something they thought they had done. What they had done was not an issue when Jesus was around. They never went hungry. If they forgot to bring the bread to eat, He'd make some more. Not a problem. They were WAY OFF from what He was talking about. Have you ever been "way off" from understanding the truth of God's Word? I have. Most of the time it was because I just had not fully understood the context of the passage. Or I had not been confronted with a particular theological issue before. Regardless, I find comfort in this passage. If you ever feel like a doofus, you're in good company. The disciples didn't know all there was to know about all there was to know, either.

After graduating from college, I went on to receive Master's and Doctorate Degrees, by God's grace. I still don't know all there is to know about God's Word. Sometimes I feel like the more I know, the more I realize I don't know. Don't be discouraged when you come across a Bible reading or question that you don't understand. Take the time to study the text or belief and God will surely give you the answer. If not, trust Him. Christianity is based on faith. One day the fog will clear, and we will know as the original disciples know now that they are in heaven.

Never allow your lack of knowledge to cause you to stop growing in your faith. The only way to know more is to grow more. Never allow someone to cause you to feel lesser due to your lack of understanding. Jesus is patient with us, just like He was with the original disciples. We are all on a journey and we all are at different levels for various reasons. I did not start growing in my faith until my later teen years. Trust where you are now and don't worry if you ever feel like a doofus. Be encouraged by the disciples' lack of understanding at times. They literally walked with Him. Live by faith today…

LIVING BY FAITH

THE BEST WAY TO HURT THOSE WHO HURT YOU IS TO NOT HURT THEM. Allow God to use the energy you would use to nurse your wounds to be more like Him. Jesus forgives us. Think about all we've done to hurt Him in His holiness. Joseph was much like Jesus, yet he was a sinner like us. He used the abuse his own brothers had poured upon him for Godly purposes. He understood God's sovereignty. He didn't waste the pain. He didn't become bitter. He became better. Others benefited greatly due to the way he handled his hurt.

God transformed Joseph's heart. All he went through caused him to lean into God more and more. And the Lord was with Joseph. That is why he didn't hurt his brothers at this juncture in his story. Listen, he was hurt because they thought he would hurt them now that their dad was dead. Wow! What character! What integrity! That's what God can do with all of us when we get hurt. He can use it to soften our hearts. Oh, we will get hurt. I have. You have. All God's children have. But remember you are here to fulfill a mission. God's mission.

Stay in the battle. When your family of origin hurts you, let it go. When someone in your church family hurts you, suddenly and unexpectedly, take it to Jesus in prayer. When a friend you thought was a good friend hurts you, learn from it. This is one of the most difficult aspects of life I have gone through so far. I cannot tell you I have been victorious through all my hurtful episodes in life. But I can tell you God's grace has been sufficient and progress is being made. The same can happen for you. Let this remind you not to hurt others. Let this remind you that if you allow Jesus to be Lord (boss) of your life, you'll still have others hurt you. Let this remind you that God can absolutely catapult you to another level spiritually if you use that hurt from others for good. Many lives will be saved. Because in essence, that's what you'll be doing by not turning bitter. Use it for good. Live by faith today...

LIVING BY FAITH

DON'T BE ODD FOR GOD BUT BE OPEN TO GOD SPEAKING THROUGH SOMETHING ODD. The last thing we need is to act odd for God. There's enough of that in our world. People need to see that we are sinners saved by grace, not sinners saved to make Jesus look like a religious freak. Jesus was real. Jesus was authentic. We need to be the same. Be like Jesus.

Moses probably thought his lot had been cast. He was eighty years old and working the fields for his father-in-law. Things changed quickly. He saw a bush on fire, yet not burning up. That's odd. He went to check it out and God spoke to him through a burning bush. (There were a lot of unusual occurrences in the Old Testament, don't you think?) God's ways aren't our ways. Out of nowhere, during Moses' ordinary day God revealed His extraordinary plan for his life.

I believe God's primary way of speaking to us today is through the Bible. I believe He also speaks through people, the Holy Spirit, and circumstances. But it may come at odd times. I've stopped on the side of the road numerous times to write on a napkin. Some of my sermons came from these notations. (I didn't say they were good; I'm just saying that's where some came from.) When you sense God is "giving you a word," pay attention, like Moses. If that means making a notation, make a notation. (It doesn't have to be on a napkin.) If it means getting up in the middle of the night to pray, get up and pray. If it means something is on your mind and it's confirmed to be from God because all of a sudden someone else talks about it out of nowhere, pay attention. If it means praying for someone at an unusual time while you're with them, do it. It may even mean telling someone you want to let them know you love them when they aren't expecting it. Hey, it may mean sharing the gospel with a stranger as you stand in line at Wal-Mart. No, it's probably not going to be a bush on fire. But if it's God, you will be on fire for God when you see how He blesses your obedience. What if Moses had not paid attention? Pay attention today, especially to something out of the ordinary. God may be in it. And your day will go from ordinary to extraordinary. Maybe even for the rest of your lifetime. Live by faith today...

DAILY READING:
Exodus 4:1-5:21; Matthew 18:1-22
Psalm 22:19-31; Proverbs 5:15-21
Focal Passage: Exodus 4:10-12

LIVING BY FAITH

GOD WILL NOT CALL YOU TO SPEAK IN FRONT OF PEOPLE AND NOT GIVE YOU THE WORDS TO SAY. I have identified with the expression that He cares more about our availability than our ability. He knows who we are and how we are wired. He made us. He reminds Moses of this fact in our text today. Moses was not confident in his speaking ability. How could he possibly be the one chosen by God to lead people if he stuttered? Because God called him. That's all that matters. The character of God is not to call us to speak in public and leave us speechless. He is not going to embarrass us. That's not His character. He uses weak vessels to accomplish great feats for Him. Just say yes. Don't be a *nacho* man, like Moses. (You know, "God, I'm *nacho* man!")

I know God called me to preach. You know how I am sure? Because I was shy growing up and never wanted to talk in public. I won "Male Camper" of my youth group one summer. The first thing you do if you receive this award is speak to the church family in a camp service upon returning. Do you know what I said? Exactly! I'm *nacho* man! They gave me the plaque and gave the speaking assignment to someone else. When I sensed God calling me to preach, I was concerned about speaking. So, when I speak, I can assure you, I know who's doing it. I cannot. He can. Moses could not. God could and He did. He will use us if we make ourselves available. And He will even cause us to enjoy it. That's the kind of loving, incredible God we serve. I love Him for that. Don't you?

Don't try to talk God out of what He's called you to do. He will use your insecurities for good. He will cause others who knew you "way back when" to be amazed at what He's done in and through you. They will have no doubt that God is real. Find out what God has called you to do. Do it to the best of your ability. But realize it's your *availability* He wants most. He'll take care of the rest. Live by faith today...

LIVING BY FAITH

THIS VERSE IS BEING READ ALL OVER THE WORLD RIGHT NOW. Psalm 23, written by David, is the "go-to" chapter in the Bible for death. I have heard it read over and over again during funerals or at graveside services. And for obvious reasons. At the time of this writing, basketball legend Kobe Bryant had just died tragically in a helicopter crash. Along with him were his oldest daughter and seven other people. It is amazing to watch how a basketball player is making national news. People all over the world have been touched in some way. Countless thousands are reading or will read what I call the "funeral passage," and may likely focus on our focal verse. Even non-believers will read this scripture due to its popularity during difficult days—mainly during a time of grief. I'm praying God will use this time for good and for the saving of many lives.

The rod was used by David, the Shepherd boy, to beat wild animals that would attack sheep. God knows His sheep by name. If He needs to stop an attack, He will. He has ultimate power. Be comforted. The staff was used by David to guide sheep and even pull them back from harm. God guides His children. When we suddenly find ourselves grieving over the death of a loved one, He will help us navigate our newfound path. Our divine Shepherd has power and grace. His grace is sufficient. Not before we need it, but *when* we need it. If He needs to use the hook in the staff to "jerk us back," due to the heat of a tragedy, He'll do it. Trust Him.

Kobe's wife and three other daughters are walking a new path now. They've never been down it before. They need God's power to help them know where to go from here without their strong leader in the home. They need God's grace to pull them from their darkest hour to future blessings. God can use their story for His glory. He can do the same for you. Will you let Him? He's the Good Shepherd and He knows when His sheep are going through a dark time. He specializes in bringing them out and bringing them through to the other side. Live by faith today...

LIVING BY FAITH

I KNOW A BLIND LADY WHO CAN SEE BETTER THAN MOST.
There is a lady in a church I've pastored, we'll just call her "Jane" (because that's her name), who is legally blind. She is humble. God gives grace to the humble. She has experienced much grace and gives graciously. Though she does not have many worldly possessions, nor would be considered one who stands out, I think she will be in the *front lines* in heaven. This verse says that those that stand out on earth won't necessarily stand out in glory. It's not necessarily the wealthy, it's those who have sacrificed much for Kingdom purposes.

Mrs. Jane regularly brings my wife and me snacks. They are not just any snacks. These snacks are our favorites. She also gives us gift cards. These aren't gift cards to expensive restaurants. That's why they are even more meaningful. She always gives us Christmas gifts with "spending money" for the holiday season. This past Christmas she made something for both of us in an arts and crafts class. Did I mention she can barely see? The gifts are treasures, just like she is.

I wish I could see like her. She sees past her limitations. She sees past her past failures and insecurities. She sees past wounds from her family. How can she do this? I mean, she rarely complains. Why? Because she sees Jesus in everything. He is the total embodiment of love. She loves with her entire being and gives graciously. Sounds a lot like Jesus, doesn't it? I want to see like Mrs. Jane. She sees better than most of us. Don't assume the wealthy on earth or well-known on earth will be first in line in heaven. I'm thinking Mrs. Jane will be toward the front with 20/20 vision. She will receive her reward in heaven. Let's be sure we always keep in mind what's most important to Jesus. Live by faith today…

LIVING BY FAITH

GO WATCH AN ANT AT WORK, JUST NOT A FIRE ANT. Actually, if you are brave or have a high pain tolerance, you may want to go watch a fire ant. I wouldn't. I'd just go watch another species of ant work. It's biblical to watch an ant. The Bible is so practical. God knows what He's doing. He made the ant. He made us. He knows how and when to connect the two. That's what's going on in the verse today. Ants are constantly at work. Laziness is not in their DNA. But being a slacker can be a temptation for people. Some people struggle with this issue more than others. There's no place for it as a Christian. When we justify being lazy, we are doing that—justifying being lazy. It is a sin.

Life is short. We have a purpose to fulfill—a Kingdom purpose. Being lazy on a daily basis means we do not maximize our time. We need to build disciplines into our daily schedule that fit our calling. Start with spiritual disciplines, like prayer and Bible study. Know your strengths and use them daily. Build systems into your work week that allow you to focus. Read about leaders who have worked hard at perfecting their craft. Find a mentor in your career path and learn from them as much as possible. Make sure they work hard, yet are balanced. (Perfectionists and workaholics are not recommended.) Discover what disciplines must be mastered to be most successful in your field. Do that. Do those things until they become as natural as brushing your teeth in the morning. (If you don't brush your teeth when you wake up, you may want to start there.)

No one who was successful in the Bible was lazy. Study them and you will see. No one successful in history was lazy. Read about them and see for yourself. Certainly, no star athlete just practiced when they were supposed to. They practiced when they weren't supposed to. Go the extra mile. Every child of God has a calling and it's important to die knowing you lived with daily passion in your life's ministry. Know your niche and get after it! I've read somewhere that if you love what you do, you won't work a day in your life because you'll be doing what God gave you a passion for. What a blessing to know you have a purpose for being here. Allow that to fuel your work ethic. Live by faith today...

DAILY READING:
Exodus 12:14-13:16; Matthew 20:29-21:22
Psalm 25:16-22; Proverbs 6:12-15
Focal Passage: Matthew 20:29-34

LIVING BY FAITH

DON'T LET THE CROWD KEEP YOU FROM SEEING YOUR PURPOSE. The crowd in the passage didn't want Jesus to be bothered by two blind men. He was on His way to Jerusalem to complete His mission. This didn't stop Jesus. People are His mission. What we think Jesus should be doing is often not what Jesus thinks He should be doing. Remember that. Our ways just aren't like His. He's God and we are not. We shouldn't be surprised that Jesus paused. He seemed to always pause for hurting people. Usually at the most inopportune times, too.

The two guys did not allow the jeers of the crowd to keep them from crying out to Jesus. They were desperate. They had faith. They were broken. When one is desperate, faith-filled, and broken beyond repair, you cry out to the only one who can heal your brokenness. Nothing else matters! Many people continue to struggle to see all that Jesus wants for them because they are too scared to cry out to Him. Maybe it's pride. Maybe it's fear of man. The reality is it is sin that keeps them from admitting their need for Christ. He looks for people like these guys. He can't wait to clear up the blindness of man due to sin. What about you? Have you cried out? Maybe you have cried out for salvation. Good! What about during your sanctification? Maybe you've hit a blind spot? Cry out right now. He can't wait to hear from you. Perhaps it's been a while. Do not postpone this God-ordained moment.

I believe one of the biggest regrets people will have is listening to the crowd. Don't do it. It never results in anything positive whatsoever. Besides, people are looking for someone to follow. They need to see those whose confidence is in Jesus. It will make them think twice about continuing to follow others instead of God. Relish the opportunity! Be passionate about it. It's going to be great and you will be on your way to accomplishing your ultimate God-given purpose. When you fear God you will be less likely to fear anything! And others will be more likely to follow your example instead of wasting time pleasing others. Live by faith today...

FEBRUARY 1

DAILY READING:
Exodus 13:17-15:18; Matthew 21:23-46
Psalm 26:1-12; Proverbs 6:16-19
Focal Passage: Exodus 14:13-16

LIVING BY FAITH

GOD OFTEN SPEAKS LOUDEST THROUGH THE SILENT PAUSE.
I learned years ago in preaching class that people tend to listen better during a pause. Think about it. Better yet, observe the next preacher you hear. See if he uses "the pause." When someone is speaking and suddenly there is silence, it tends to get the audience's attention. Now, the guy may not say much before or after, but those listening will listen during that moment. Sometimes I think it's because they think the preacher forgot where he was in his message. I hate when that happens! It's happened to me several times.

The Israelites were scared. Even though they had seen God do miracles, they were afraid this particular "hard place" was too much for Him. Ha! Fear makes us act foolish. The folks were upset with Moses and had lost their way. That's what happens when we focus on our challenge instead of our God. Moses finally told them just to pause. Stand still. God was going to do something. That's hard for me. I like to move. I can't stand still long. My family says I'm hyper. Surely not! Regardless, there are times I pause. I can listen to God more intently. Maybe you need to pause. Perhaps you've been asking "why" too much? God can handle our whys. But often we just need to ask "what?" "What is it you are saying, God?"

Don't stand still too long. Shortly after "the pause," God implored Moses to get moving. We do need to know when to "put feet to our prayers." And we need to know what exactly God wants us to do when we move forward. Moses did exactly what God said, and it worked. When we act in faith, like Moses did by holding up the rod, we move forward. God works and we often question why we were so paranoid in the first place. He is always faithful! Pray. Pause. Move. God may be about to open up a path you never dreamed of before. Live by faith today…

FEBRUARY 2

DAILY READING:

Exodus 15:19-17:2; Matthew 22:1-33
Psalm 27:1-6; Proverbs 6:20-26
Focal Passage: Exodus 15:24

LIVING BY FAITH

IF YOU LEAD, SOME WILL GRUMBLE. This happened to Moses, one of the greatest leaders of all time! When he died it was said of him that there was no one like him. God had just used this leader to lead the children of Israel onto dry land. The enemy perished. It was amazing! They even danced and sang afterward in celebration! But shortly after, they grumbled. Wow! How soon we forget.

Leaders who want everyone to like them will have a miserable life. It can't be done. All through these chapters in Exodus we see Moses was grumbled against. It wasn't just this one incident. My goodness, Jesus was perfect, and He was crucified! He was the best of the best in leadership. Actually, He was the best of the best in everything! Don't you love Jesus? Yeah, me too.

All through the scriptures, we see leaders being railed against at times. Nehemiah, David, and Joseph, just to name a few. Take a glance at history. And President of the USA! Man, they never win! Someone will always be at their throat. Coaches. Teachers. CEOs. And believe it or not, Pastors. I know. You're shocked. Listen, there's a lot more good than bad that comes with the call of being a pastor. But I can assure you, there will always—always—be someone complaining. Let me give you a few tips: Lead anyway. Pray on the spot. Look to the scriptures for examples of how to respond. Read about leadership. Take it as a positive because the only way not to receive a complaint is to do nothing or say nothing. Remember that sheep are stupid. And never forget, we are all sheep! Lord help us lead and have no regrets! Live by faith today...

FEBRUARY 3

DAILY READING:
Exodus 17:8-19:15; Matthew 22:34-23:12
Psalm 27:7-14; Proverbs 6:27-35
Focal Passage: Exodus 17: 10-13

LIVING BY FAITH

OUR BATTLES ARE WON BY LIFTING OTHERS. If we are living a selfish life, we are losers. We really are. And we are certainly not helping others win. Moses was leading. Joshua and others were literally fighting a major battle. Whenever Moses's arms grew tired from providing strength and direction for the battle, he had others lift his hands. This ministry of Aaron and Hur made all the difference in the world. The battle was won. Moses succeeded. And "no-names" were the key. There are no "no-names" in the economy of God. Everyone counts.

For battles to be won here on earth, we need each other. God did not make us to be alone the majority of the time. We need company. The best days are spent with God's people. It is when we are around other brothers and sisters in Christ that we receive the support we need. If Moses needed it, I sure need it. You probably do, too. Don't fight your battles alone. Rest assured, God knows your heart and sees everything. If you encourage others, He will encourage you through others. It happens every time.

I have a long way to go in the ministry of encouragement. I do know that when I have encouraged others, I feel fulfilled. It makes sense. Why? Because it's biblical—this ministry of encouragement. So, make it a practice. Be sensitive to people God puts around you who need you to help them fulfill their purpose. Keep the BIG PICTURE in mind that if it gets in the way of your TO-DO list, God will help you make up the time. Trust Him! He's all about others. He wants us to be all about others. Never, ever, underestimate how God will use your encouragement for Kingdom purposes. Who knows, the one He is bringing to mind right now may be your greatest accomplishment on this side of heaven. Live by faith today...

DAILY READING:
Exodus 19:16-21:21; Matthew 23:13-39
Psalm 28:1-9; Proverbs 7:1-5
Focal Passage: Matthew 23:27-28

LIVING BY FAITH

IF YOU ARE EVER SAID TO BE LIKE A WHITEWASHED TOMB, IT'S NOT A COMPLIMENT. Jesus often called the Pharisees out for being so religious. Religion does not make you right with God. It's basically man's way of trying to be right with God. Only Jesus makes us right with God. He is the bridge to God due to our sinfulness. If Jesus called out religious folks in His day, I am sure He would in our day. He does through the scriptures. This one is an example.

Whitewashed tombs refer to painting tombs white, so they look very beautiful on the outside. But on the inside, they were still full of ugly, dry, dead bones. No matter how nice the outside of a grave looked, it was still wretched—putrid on the inside. Jesus doesn't have a lot of nice things to say about fakes. These leaders of religion in His day had wicked motives and desires. Jesus knew it. He called them out. He challenged them.

Jesus came to do away with religion. That's why He was so upset when religion tried to make Him look like a fake. Jesus loved the Father. He loved people—all kinds of people. He exemplified what a relationship with the Father looked like. And He spoke of love. He didn't let rules keep Him from setting people free. He was authentic. The next time you visit a graveyard and see nice, pretty, white tombstones, take time to do your own spiritual evaluation. Are you religious? Are you a fake? Do you say and do the right things, but are miserable? Pharisaic people participate in a church service depressed when they walk in and are worse when they walk out. So, are you walking with Jesus in a relationship, reflecting His love? Do you attend church for show or for worshipping Jesus alone? Think about it. Pray about it. Enjoy your freedom in Christ, not a dead religion of some sort. Live by faith today...

FEBRUARY 5

DAILY READING:
Exodus 21:22-23:13; Matthew 24:1-28
Psalm 29:1-11; Proverbs 7:6-23
Focal Passage: Exodus 23:4-5

LIVING BY FAITH

IF YOU ARE GIVEN THE OPPORTUNITY TO HELP A DONKEY OUT, DO IT. The Israelites were given clear instructions to relate to all people honestly and fairly. There were to be no exceptions! No one was to be treated with favoritism. Favoritism does not reflect God properly. He has no favorites! He loves everyone! It doesn't matter what the color of their skin is. It doesn't matter what type of accent they have. It doesn't matter what they've done. It doesn't matter how bad their family tree appears to be. It just doesn't matter. And it certainly doesn't matter what a person may have done to us. We are to forgive. Even if we think the person is somewhat "donkey-like" we are to try to do good by them.

So, your "enemy" may not have a donkey. Their donkey which likely doesn't exist will probably not get stuck in a ditch or cul-de-sac in your neighborhood. The donkey of someone you really despise, in the flesh, will not likely be carrying an overbearing load. But the person may be under a heavy load at some point. God wants us to look for opportunities to help someone we're at odds with for all the days of our lives. We're to try to do good by all, until the day we die.

The body of Christ will be hurt by the body of Christ. Someone is going to hurt our hearts along the way. We will hurt others. We are depraved. There is no perfect church! The Church is the people of God. It's happened. Study the Bible. It's going to happen. Study church history. It's happened to me. It's happened to you if you've lived long enough. What do we do? We look for opportunities to minister. Maybe it's ministering somehow when the person you struggle with has a death in their family. Maybe it's helping them out if they lose their job. If it's a toxic person, do it anyway. It doesn't mean you have to go on family vacations together. Be wise. Help a donkey out as soon as possible! Live by faith today…

DAILY READING:
Exodus 23:14-25:40; Matthew 24:29-51
Psalm 30:1-12; Proverbs 7:24-27
Focal Passage: Matthew 24:36-44

LIVING BY FAITH

JESUS WILL RETURN ONE DAY, SO FOCUS ON WHAT MATTERS MOST. Eschatology—the study of end times—has never been a great passion of mine. That does not mean I don't believe in the return of Christ. I do. That does not mean I don't believe in Bible prophecy. I do. That does not mean I don't believe that a believer could adopt a certain view concerning the return of Jesus. I do. That does not mean I break fellowship with other believers if they have a different view than I do of how it will all play out. I just believe what's most essential is that a believer believes Jesus will return. I guess I'm what some describe as "pro-second coming." I'm for it!

In our verses today, Jesus said that the Father knows. He indicates that we are not to focus on details but focus on today. We are to make the most of our Kingdom purposes each and every day. Don't waste time! Be balanced. Let others know about what Jesus has done so they might be ready if Jesus returns in their lifetime. Live your purpose. Stay balanced. Don't focus on end times so much that you don't accomplish God's priorities for your life every day. Study the book of Revelation. God will honor it. Study other passages about the return of Christ. But don't go overboard. I've known people who only want to talk about eschatology. They sort of make me uncomfortable. Please don't be that guy!

If anything, this passage and others should make me more passionate about sharing the gospel with the lost. It should make me want to know for certain what God has called me to be and do. It should make me prioritize my family, not insist they determine which view they are to have about the second coming. Don't be ashamed to not know all the details. Let the words of Jesus encourage you concerning the study of end times today. Live by faith today...

DAILY READING:
Exodus 26:1-27:21; Matthew 25:1-30
Psalm 31:1-8; Proverbs 8:1-11
Focal Passage: Matthew 25:21

LIVING BY FAITH

LITTLE IS BIG IN GOD'S ECONOMY. We are to be good stewards of what God has given us. This certainly means of our time, our God-given abilities, and our resources. We are not to waste our time trying to understand why we may or may not have as much as others. It really doesn't matter in the big picture—God's big picture. We are to make the most of what we have.

The older I am, the more I realize how "little is big." For example, I work with people every day. I see church members and staff members up close and personal. As I observe people, I've started to pay close attention to the little things. Do they respect authority? Do they show up early for meetings? Are they kind to strangers? Do they speak or minister to people who can do absolutely nothing for them? You see what I mean? Little is big!

Christians will give an account of how we've lived with what we've been given. Scripture calls this the "judgment seat of Christ." We will be rewarded or not rewarded based on our daily lives. It matters. And it's been my experience that those who pay attention to little things in life typically are the ones that God uses to do "big things" in life. When we are faithful to what God has called us to be and do, whatever that may be, He allows us to be a part of something big. Don't underestimate your role in life. Live by faith today...

FEBRUARY 8

DAILY READING:
Exodus 28:1-43; Matthew 25:31-26:13
Psalm 31:9-18; Proverbs 8:12-13
Focal Passage: Matthew 26:6-11

LIVING BY FAITH

MINISTERING TO THE POOR IS IMPORTANT, BUT NOT THAT IMPORTANT. Jesus makes it very clear that worshipping Him is most important. Whether it's privately or publicly, He blesses the praise of His people. The disciples were appalled that Jesus would allow this woman to "waste" such an important perfume on Him. How dare Jesus do such a thing! (How dare the disciples do such a thing—mainly Judas.) Jesus defended the woman and called her action "noble." Although we are clearly to minister to and care for the poor, our primary worship and dedication is to Jesus Christ. If not, our motives could be impure—like Judas' motives. Good works on the outside do not automatically mean Jesus has done a work on the inside. Judas and others we read about demonstrated this reality.

Are you seeing what's important in the Christian life? Devotion to Jesus. Worshipping Jesus. Being "sold out" to Jesus. Having a relationship with Jesus. Everything else in life flows from our intimate relationship with Him. God wants us to notice and care for *invisible* people. Jesus certainly did. They need to be shown the love of Christ. But we must not do so at the expense of our daily walk. If so, we can lose the joy of ministry. Live out of the overflow, like this lady.

The woman wanted to give her best to Jesus. She had the opportunity of a lifetime to express her overwhelming devotion to Him. She took advantage of it, though others misunderstood. Would you do that? Would I? Do we? Do we have such an intimate relationship with Christ that we look forward to giving Him our best? It is not likely to be a bottle of our best cologne or perfume, but it can be our best—whatever that may be at any given moment. Live by faith today...

DAILY READING:

Exodus 29:1-30:10; Matthew 26:14-46
Psalm 31:19-24; Proverbs 8:14-26
Focal Passage: Matthew 26:20-25

LIVING BY FAITH

FAKE LEADERS HAVE BEEN HANGING AROUND GENUINE JESUS FOLLOWERS FOR QUITE A WHILE. Don't be shocked. Now, not everyone we may think is a fake, is a fake. Be careful. But please know that Judas' true colors finally surfaced. The same is true for others who pretend to be followers of Jesus. Just give it time. God will "call them out" like He did in the passage, and they will eventually suffer the consequences. It just may take a while, and we may or may not see it.

I grew up watching a television show called *Leave It to Beaver*. It was family-oriented and there was a guy named Eddie Haskell who hung out with young Beaver and his older brother, Wally. This teenager was a fake. He pretended to like others and be part of the gang—a good gang—but he was ridiculously a rascal. He was what some would call a professional schmoozer. He was slick! And he sort of made me sick, just watching and listening to him on TV. He was a mess. Always up to no good.

Judas was the original Eddie Haskell. He had been up to no good for a while, but he finally revealed himself, the true person he had always been. He just played along with the other disciples when he questioned whether Jesus had picked the right one who would betray Him. And he was one of the original disciples, no less. We shouldn't be surprised, yet disappointed, when *Eddie* (Judas) shows up in a deacons meeting, or staff meeting, or your small group Bible study. Don't be fearful or paranoid, just be aware. Allow the person to bring you to your knees in prayer. Use their deceitfulness to "check your heart" and even be used to "call them out" at times. (Do so biblically, if you are called to exercise some type of church discipline.) I have seen the damage a fake leader in a church can do to the body of Christ. It is not pretty or fun. But it is not insurmountable. Jesus handled it up close and personal. Learn from Jesus. Follow His directives. Live by faith today...

DAILY READING:

Exodus 30:11-31:18; Matthew 26:47-68
Psalm 32:1-11; Proverbs 8:27-32
Focal Passage: Matthew 26:50-54

LIVING BY FAITH

WHAT SEEMS RIGHT AT THE TIME, MAY NOT BE RIGHT AT THE TIME. I've always chuckled inside at this one disciple who whacked the high priest's servant's ear off. (We will discover it was Simon Peter as we continue reading the other gospel accounts.) I know. It's a very serious moment in the life of Christ. I just tend to think it's, well, interesting. I guess I see myself doing the same...I hope. Well, maybe not. Jesus said he shouldn't have done it. Peter knew He didn't need his help. I mean, he'd seen Him do miracle after miracle. I guess he should have known He could have called down 10,000 angels, huh? He chose not to do so in order to fulfill His purpose for coming to earth. This was a major step in the process of redeeming us all.

I've acted somewhat like a vigilante myself through the years. Haven't you? What seemed to be the right thing for me to do as a believer ended up not being the right thing to do as a believer. It was done in the flesh. That's actually what happened here in our text today. Peter was acting based on what he thought was the right thing to do. When we take matters into our own hands, people get hurt. We may not cut someone's ear off, but we may hurt the cause of Christ. It may take years for the wound to heal, all because we "struck a blow" because we were impatient or too aggressive.

As we study the life of Christ, we know timing really is everything. We must give God time to do His will, not ours. We must know when to act. We must know when to stay still or remain silent. Like Peter, just because we are close to Jesus doesn't always mean we will act like Jesus. So we learn. We learn from Peter. We listen better. We don't react as much as we act—as Christ would. And we humble ourselves when we act in the flesh. We learn. We ask God to help us always do what He'd want us to do, at the right time. His time. Live by faith today...

FEBRUARY 11

DAILY READING:
Exodus 32:1-33:23; Matthew 26:69-27:14
Psalm 33:1-11; Proverbs 8:33-36
Focal Passage: Exodus 32:1

LIVING BY FAITH

THIS FELLOW MOSES LOVED HIS *SHEEP* REGARDLESS OF THEIR CONTEMPT. The NIV says the children of Israel referred to Moses as "this fellow." Can you believe it? This is Moses! He has led them through numerous difficult situations. He has explained God and His directives due to his overwhelming love for his people. He has gone up to the mountain to receive incredible instructions for years to come. What do they do? They refer to him as... *this fellow!*

God used Moses' time of shepherding to prepare him for leading God's people. Sheep are dumb. Sheep need directions. Sheep need loving discipline. Sheep need a shepherd. Moses was well equipped to dismiss name-calling or a lapse of memory. He returned from receiving the Ten Commandments to discover just how crazy "sheep" can be in a short amount of time. He was upset. I would be too! But he actually pleaded with God to give them another chance. (I'm not sure I'm there yet.) God relented, yet disciplined them, in time, for their disobedience. He's merciful and just. He responds to genuine repentance, without abandoning His character. He's God.

So, how can we become more like "this fellow?" Know God face to face. Abide in Him. Learn from our past mistakes. Realize God never wastes any part of our journey. Love God, love people. Accept our responsibility for operating at a higher level than normal. Maybe realize we've come too far in our journey to let go of God or His people. And maybe you put a porcelain sheep in your room or office to be reminded of who you lead. I put one in my office several years ago. It is a constant reminder that the people I lead don't always act very smart. It's a reminder that I too, am a sheep. We must abide in the Chief Shepherd! "This fellow" Moses did. Live by faith today...

DAILY READING:
Exodus 34:1-35:9; Matthew 27:15-31
Psalm 33:12-22; Proverbs 9:1-6
Focal Passage: Matthew 27:21-22

LIVING BY FAITH

MY NAME IS NOT HAL, HAROLD, OR TRIBBLE, IT'S BARABBAS.
My grandfather, Atley Asher Kitchings, named his second son, my dad, after his favorite professor. He attended Southern Seminary in Louisville, Kentucky. He was greatly influenced by a man named Dr. Harold Tribble. So, after naming his first son Atley Asher, Jr., he decided to name my dad Harold Tribble Kitchings. I am Harold Tribble Kitchings, Jr. I've always gone by Hal, so, there'd be no confusion when people called the house to speak with Harold. My one and only boy, Harold Tribble Kitchings, III, goes by Trey. Trey named his son, who was born on this very day, Clayton Scott Kitchings. (I'm believing Clayton will do even greater things for God's Kingdom purposes than all of us!)

With all of that background on my family name as a backdrop, you need to know I believe I am Barabbas. Jesus took his place. Jesus took my place. Jesus took your place. I guess we could all go by the name, Barabbas, huh? What a blessing!

We will soon discover, in the Gospel of Luke, that Barabbas was a rebel and a murderer. In other words, he was a wretched sinner. So am I. So are you. We are all wretched sinners needing a redeemer. A sin is a sin. There are various consequences. But we are all in need of a savior. That savior is Jesus, the savior of the world. Do you know Him? Have you trusted Him as a substitute for your sin? If so, thank Him. He has transformed your purpose for living. If not, why not today? My grandson was born today. Today is a good day to be born again. Allow your substitute for your sin to take over. Surrender your life to Him. It will be the greatest decision you will ever make, *Barabbas*. Live by faith today...

FEBRUARY 13

DAILY READING:
Exodus 35:10-36:38; Matthew 27:32-66
Psalm 34:1-10; Proverbs 9:7-8
Focal Passage: Exodus 36:2-7

LIVING BY FAITH

GOD'S PEOPLE WERE SO GENEROUS THEY HAD TO BE TOLD TO STOP. Moses had commissioned God's people to use their gifts and offerings for building the tabernacle. The Lord had given them wisdom. Their wisdom and generosity were so great, they were told to stop. Can you imagine? Actually, we should imagine…

Imagine if we prayed for wisdom. We will discover in our study of scriptures that we are to pray for wisdom. So, we can be wise. Wisdom basically means we think more like Jesus than thinking in the flesh. It's supernatural.

Imagine if we so faithfully gave our tithes and were good stewards of all our financial blessings. If so, we would be quick to respond to opportunities to give offerings. Offerings are opportunities to give beyond our tithe to the Lord's work. Churches have various offerings. They can be for expanding mission endeavors. They can be used for building facilities for future generations. Some churches use offerings for church planting. Imagine what can be done for Kingdom purposes if God's people are wise stewards and respond quickly and overwhelmingly to giving opportunities. WE should imagine and pray God does it in our local churches.

Using our imagination does not have to stop after childhood. Keep using it for the glory of God! Imagine what can happen. Live by faith today…

DAILY READING:
Exodus 37:1-38:31; Matthew 28:1-20
Psalm 34:11-22; Proverbs 9:9-10
Focal Passage: Matthew 28:18-20

LIVING BY FAITH

BE SURE THE GREAT COMMISSION DOES NOT BECOME THE GREAT OMISSION IN YOUR LIFE. Jesus left the disciples with their marching orders. He did not focus on their "weak knees" during the days leading up to His death. He did not major in how difficult it would be to accomplish His instructions. He simply let them know their responsibility now that the greatest miracle ever had been accomplished—the death, burial, and resurrection. What an opportunity. What a responsibility.

Nothing has changed. Present-day disciples of Christ are to go. That's action. We are to make disciples. That's an investment in people. God loves all people. We are to do the same. A disciple is a learner. We are to invest in people all over the world teaching them to follow Christ daily. Those who have a relationship with Christ are to be baptized as an act of obedience. This is an outward expression of an inward experience. They are not to be ashamed as they are immersed in front of witnesses. While doing so, a reminder for all is the blessed trinity – the Father, Son, and Holy Spirit. The investment to influence other believers goes on until Jesus returns, during the good days and the bad days. He promises to be with us all the days of our lives. We need Him. As you perhaps celebrate Valentine's Day today, never forget that He's counting on us to share the essence of love. What an opportunity. What a responsibility.

We will be discovering the essence of love, reflecting redemption, as we continue our journey through the scriptures. *This is real love—not that we loved God, but that He loved us and sent His Son as a sacrifice to take away our sins.* Live by faith today…

DAILY READING:
Exodus 39:1-40:38; Mark 1:1-28
Psalm 35:1-16; Proverbs 9:11-12
Focal Passage: Mark 1:9-11

LIVING BY FAITH

IF BAPTISM WAS NOT IMPORTANT, JESUS WOULD NOT HAVE TAKEN THE TIME TO BE BAPTIZED. He took the time. Jesus is the Son of God. He came to redeem us due to our sinfulness. Every moment was precious. That being said, He never wasted a second during His time on earth. He took the time to be baptized. This sends a loud message to His followers—take the time to be baptized.

Jesus wanted to identify with sinners. I mean, that's why He came. He came to save sinners. He wanted to be distinguished as THE Son of God! No one else was like Him or ever will be the one true Messiah. He was baptized for you. He was baptized for me. Shouldn't we take time to be baptized for Him?

The ministry of the Son of God begins with this amazing affirmation from God the Father. We are able to see the Trinity—Father, Son, Holy Spirit—at work here. What a moment! We, too, should desire to please our Heavenly Father. If we are His children due to putting our faith in Him alone, He is Lord (Boss). We want to do what the "Boss" says. He wants us to follow His Son. Jesus was baptized.

This marks the official launching of Jesus' ministry on earth. Think about it… Maybe the reason some Christians aren't "launching" into their ministry is because they haven't been baptized. It could be they know it's an important next step in their faith journey and they hesitate to go further because they haven't taken this initial step of identifying with Christ. Is that you? Be baptized sooner than later! You'll be glad you did, and your example could influence others to do the same. Live by faith today…

DAILY READING:
Leviticus 1:1-3:17; Mark 1:29-2:12
Psalm 35:17-28; Proverbs 9:13-18
Focal Passage: Mark 1:35

LIVING BY FAITH

PERHAPS THIS IS THE *SECRET* TO OUR WALK WITH THE LORD. I think so. Jesus often got up early and went to a solitary place to pray. If He did, why would we not think it is the fuel for our daily walk? Our journey in Christ requires God's power. Prayer is powerful! Only God knows what difference this time alone with the Father accomplished for our redemption plan.

Jesus didn't come to build a crowd. His priority was not being *the miracle man*, though He was. He came to preach the good news. He came to "set the captives free." He came to set Kingdom priorities. Time alone in prayer is a Kingdom priority. Is it with you?

Jesus found a place early in the morning. I was taught to do the same years ago. It is a part of my daily routine. I have no regrets. And on those rare occasions I miss, I pick it back up the next day. I don't "beat myself up." There's freedom in Christ. I meet with Him because He's Lord—Boss. I meet with Him because He alone is faithful. I meet with Him because it's the most important relationship I have. Strong relationships take time. I meet with Him because He tells us to abide. If I meet with Him on Sundays only, I'm just paying Him a visit. I meet with Him because He is my best friend. As the old spiritual song goes—He never failed me yet! He won't! He won't fail you either. Are you meeting with Him regularly? Perhaps alone? In the morning? In a quiet place? Meeting with Jesus as regularly as you brush your teeth in the morning. It's that important. It's more important. Jesus came to show us how to live daily. Here's the *secret*. Walk with the Lord daily, preferably early in the morning, talking with Him. Oh, and be sure to listen, also. Live by faith today…

FEBRUARY 17

DAILY READING:
Leviticus 4:1-5:19; Mark 2:13-3:6
Psalm 36:1-12; Proverbs 10:1-2
Focal Passage: Mark 2:15-17

LIVING BY FAITH

SHOULD A HOLY MAN HANG OUT WITH A HOODLUM? Why of course! Jesus did. He is the holiest of the holiest. It drove the religious folks of the day nuts. They couldn't understand. Jesus made it plain. Sick people need a doctor. Sinners are sick. We are all sick sinners. The religious people were, too. They just didn't like to think so. They were focused on their religiosity. They felt Jesus needed to do the same. The audacity of them to think they knew the purpose of God!

Jesus was willing to meet people where they were. We should do the same. Sure, it may be a little uncomfortable. That's ok. I can remember being uncomfortable around good Christian people that I didn't know well. Can't you? People that don't know Christ need to know Him. And they need to know Him from those that know Him personally—via a relationship. Not a religion. How will they know if they don't know through us? Remember, that's what the Great Commission is all about. (Matthew 28:18-20)

Lost people should probably not be our closest friends. They should be our friends. We need to be examples. We should not be "odd for God." We should be ambassadors for God. There's a difference. A big difference.

Go out of your way to meet the unchurched. Talk with them about life in general. You don't have to ask if you can pray for them during the first few conversations. Be yourself. Find out their interests and talk about those things. If you go out of town, bring them back a gift of some kind. Be kind to them. Encourage them. Everyone needs an encouraging word. Remember their birthday. You don't have to approve of their lifestyle, whatever it may be, to love them like Jesus. Represent Him well. They need a touch from the great physician—Jesus. Live by faith today...

DAILY READING:
Leviticus 6:1-7:27; Mark 3:7-30
Psalm 37:1-11; Proverbs 10:3-4
Focal Passage: Psalm 4

LIVING BY FAITH

WHEN YOU ARE LIVING OUT OF THE OVERFLOW, YOU RECEIVE WHAT YOU WANT. Sounds radical, doesn't it? It is. Delighting ourselves in the Lord means abiding in Him. As we grow in our understanding of God and His Kingdom purposes, we want what He wants. Make sense? Sure it does. That doesn't mean it's easy, it just means it's right. We fight the flesh, but as we grow in Christlikeness, we grow in wanting what Jesus wants.

God wants to bless us. He doesn't want to hide His will for us. Sometimes we think He might, but He doesn't. The more we seek Him, the more content we are in our daily lives. We should rest in this reality. He doesn't play "hide and seek" with us. If we don't know what to do, what do we do? We seek Him more. Maybe we fast AND pray? Maybe we get wise counsel? Maybe we have a personal retreat? Maybe we talk with a Christian counselor? Maybe we understand the value of waiting? I know, I don't like this one either.

Delighting in Him is the key. Do we look forward to worshipping Him daily and on weekends? Or do we just "visit" Him when it's convenient? Are we clued into His purpose for our lives right now? Or do we just do what we have to do to get by? Do we practice what we know is God's will? Prayer. Worship. Fellowship, for example. Or do we just do those things occasionally? I'm afraid it's not so much that we don't know God's will as it's that we don't put Him first. Delight in Him and watch how your "wanter" changes. We want what He wants. Live by faith today...

DAILY READING:

Leviticus 7:28-9:6; Mark 3:31-4:25
Psalm 37:12-29; Proverbs 10:5
Focal Passage: Mark 3:31-35

LIVING BY FAITH

IF YOU LOVE JESUS, YOU WILL LISTEN TO HIM MORE THAN YOUR MAMA. It's true. The focal passage today says as much. Jesus's mother and brothers were outside wanting to chat with Him. He felt He needed to keep teaching. We don't know exactly what they felt was so vital that they interrupted His teaching. Maybe they felt He had "gone too far" with His newfound ministry at the time? Maybe they were going to ask Him about something they had heard that was bothersome? Maybe they just wanted to know if He was going to be home the next day for a family meal? I don't know. You don't know. We don't know. If we needed to know, we'd know.

Jesus used this moment to make sure that His followers knew He must be Lord. Another word for Lord is boss. Disciples of Christ submit to God's agenda. True followers want nothing more than to be about Kingdom work. Following God's will comes before any other relationship—even a wonderful mom. He had one. Maybe you have or had one? I did.

One time my mom came to me questioning why I would leave my hometown, where she lived, to move back to Florida to pastor. Do you know what I told her? I told her I was simply doing what she and my dad had taught me. They taught me to follow Jesus. They even taught me the great hymn *I Have Decided to Follow Jesus*. On this particular occasion, God helped me say these things to my loving mom appropriately. You know what she did? She changed the subject. She was the sweetest lady, but she was also a mess at times during her later years. She knew not to say anything else. If I was telling the truth, which I was, she knew I had no other choice, even if she was my mama.

What are you supposed to do today? Don't allow your mom, dead or alive, to keep you from following God's will. Live by faith today...

DAILY READING:
Leviticus 9:7-10:20; Mark 4:26-5:20
Psalm 37:30-40; Proverbs 10:6-7
Focal Passage: Mark 5:18-20

LIVING BY FAITH

NEVER UNDERESTIMATE THE POWER OF TESTIFYING AT HOME. Jesus had radically changed this man. He had quite a reputation. It wasn't good at the time. Let's just say he was a wild man! Not anymore. He had met Jesus and looked at things differently now. (That's what occurs when we meet Jesus.) He wanted to "hang out" with Christ. Actually, he begged Jesus to allow him to follow Him elsewhere. I would, too. I mean, he probably thought he could learn some things from Jesus. He could, but Jesus felt otherwise about his direction. He told him to go home and testify about his change and God's mercy in his life. He did and it greatly impacted those that knew him before his radical change. That's what happens. When Jesus comes into our lives, people see the change and it brings further glory to God.

One of the greatest legacies we can leave is at home. They know us. And when Jesus becomes Lord, they see the difference. Our demeanor changes. Our priorities change. Our generosity changes. Our friends change. I mean, everything changes! God will use our change to change others. That's the way it works. If God calls you to go home, go. I did twice and it was some of the greatest years of my life. No regrets! That' doesn't mean it was easy. It means it was God's will and He blessed it. He always blesses obedience.

Has Jesus radically changed you? He can. He will. And others will be amazed. If people at home see the changes, you are on your way to leaving a legacy. Live by faith today…

DAILY READING:

Leviticus 11:1-12:8; Mark 5:21-43
Psalm 38:1-22; Proverbs 10:8-9
Focal Passage: Mark 5:25-34

LIVING BY FAITH

ARE YOU BUMPING AGAINST JESUS OR BOWING TO JESUS? There is a big difference. Jesus knows all. He knows when people are simply bumping against Him. The disciples didn't know. Jesus did. The disciples didn't understand. Sometimes we can't distinguish between those interested in Jesus and those genuinely following Jesus. Not so with Jesus. He let the disciples know that He knows. He wanted to know who touched Him. A desperate lady touched Him because she believed He was her only hope for healing. She was absolutely correct! Jesus healed her—all of her. Jesus heals the entire person. The word "healed" translated *well* means complete or whole. It's often used as the same word, saved. Salvation took place that day. She exemplified great faith. And she was willing to go public. Going public demonstrates our true belief.

She was desperate. She fell at the feet of Jesus. She did this unashamedly in public. Are you willing to do that? Have you ever been desperate enough to bow to Jesus? Privately? What about publicly? We see a fantastic demonstration of humility from this woman. She had probably exhausted all resources. Unfortunately, that's what often occurs today. We exhaust all resources before finally bowing to Jesus for help. He's fine with it. He would prefer us to do so sooner than later. We just need to do it before it's too late. He's waiting patiently.

What's up with you today? Are you facing an insurmountable situation in your life? Have you bowed today? If not, hit your knees as soon as possible. Cry out to Him. Share your heart. He loves for us to seek Him first. No bumping. Only bow. Live by faith today...

DAILY READING:
Leviticus 13:1-59; Mark 6:1-29
Psalm 39:1-13; Proverbs 10:10
Focal Passage: Mark 6:4-5

LIVING BY FAITH

WHAT MIGHT WE MISS DUE TO OUR LACK OF FAITH? We will probably never know this side of heaven. Sometimes I think we whiz past the truth of this passage. We only stop long enough to think negatively of Jesus's hometown folks or use this to say we can't minister at home. Yes, we hope we would have recognized Jesus as the Messiah. And it's not easy ministering where you grew up, but we're not Jesus. As I mentioned in an earlier devotional, ministering where I graduated from high school and college was one of the greatest blessings of my life. That didn't mean it was easy. So, don't use this verse as a proof text to not serve at home if God's calling you to do so.

Don't we lack faith from time to time? Sure we do. Just like the people whom Jesus encountered in our passage today. It's not that Jesus couldn't do more. His power is unlimited. It's that they refused to trust Him. It seems they took Him too lightly. That never works to our advantage. Jesus is God. God works miracles. God loves to do things in and through us that bring Him glory. He uses ordinary people like us to do extraordinary things through us.

I'd rather burn out than rust out. (I'm not promoting burning out here.) I've often said I'd rather fail at doing something I sense God wants me to do that will utterly fail without His intervention than succeed at doing the mundane. That's everywhere. Let's dream big. Let's ask God to show us what to do in the days ahead that stretches our faith. Let's not worry about what people in our hometown think. I don't know about you, but I don't want a conversation in heaven one day about all that God had for me to do if I'd only trusted Him. I pray to God you and I are not the cause of God not doing more because we were fearful or hesitant to obey. Let's live each day as if it's our last. One day it will be. Live by faith today...

DAILY READING:
Leviticus 14:1-57; Mark 6:30-56
Psalm 40:1-10; Proverbs 10:11-12
Focal Passage: Mark 6:34

LIVING BY FAITH

JESUS SEES US AS VULNERABLE SHEEP THAT NEED DIRECTION.
He's right. I can't imagine living my life without Him. I stumble enough with Him.
I cannot imagine what my journey would have been like on my own. I need Him.
You need Him. Everyone needs Him. Some don't realize it, yet. Or maybe they do,
they just don't want to allow Him to provide direction.

When I see the word COMPASSION, I pause. That's a good word. It is a kind
word. It is a loving word. It is a Jesus word. Here Jesus saw people like sheep and
had compassion. That means His heart hurt for us with overwhelming love. Sheep
are known to be dumb. Sheep are known to have no sense of direction. Sheep are
known to be defenseless. If all of these characteristics are true, which they are, sheep
need help. If not, life will be short-lived and miserable at best. Something for all of
us to ponder today. Where would we be without Jesus? Where would our world be
without Jesus? In worse shape, whether everyone realizes it or not. It's bad, but not
as bad as it would be without Jesus and His followers.

Find a directionless sheep today and take them to Jesus. Cry out to the Good
Shepherd today if you feel vulnerable right now. Go find a herd of sheep with a
good under-shepherd to join, if you don't already have one. Maybe even find a stinky
sheep out there on the street and give them a meal or glass of cold water. We are all
sheep and we need Jesus—The Chief Shepherd. Live by faith today...

FEBRUARY 24

DAILY READING:
Leviticus 15:1-16:28; Mark 7:1-23
Psalm 40:11-17; Proverbs 10:13-14
Focal Passage: Leviticus 16:20-22

LIVING BY FAITH

I'VE NEVER SEEN A MORE BEAUTIFUL GOAT IN ALL MY LIFE. Here we find a picture of what happened on the Day of Atonement. A priest would confess all the sins of the Israelites over the head of a goat and then drive it into the wilderness, symbolically bearing their sins away. The word "scapegoat" might come to mind here. We think of this word when a person or group is made to take the blame for others. In this biblical context, the goat would take the sins of the people away. The goat was released into the wilderness never to return. Jesus has fulfilled this biblical "type" in that He paid for our sins once and for all. The Israelites had to do this once a year. Not so, for a person who has put their faith in Christ alone. Because *that* is a one-time experience.

What a beautiful picture of redemption! Jesus has dealt with the pollution of sin and the burden of sin has been removed—forever. Since our sins have also been sent away, spiritually, we cannot lose our salvation. Hallelujah! The scapegoat isn't coming back tomorrow or the next day or the next to return to us all the sins we thought were gone. If we have trusted Jesus Christ alone as Savior, our sins have been removed "as far as the east is from the west."

Watching the goat being led away served as a very vivid reminder to the Israelites that their sins had been removed and atoned for. Ordinances like the Lord's Supper and baptism are our reminders. Of course, if you need to buy a porcelain goat and put it in your house or find a picture of one to remind you daily of what Jesus has done, do it. We are free in Christ! This is a good reminder as we are walking through all the rituals of Leviticus. I don't know about you, but I'm glad I live on "this side" of the cross. Live by faith today…

DAILY READING:
Leviticus 16:29-18:30; Mark 7:24-8:10
Psalm 41:1-13; Proverbs 10:15-16
Focal Passage: Leviticus 18:21-23

LIVING BY FAITH

HOMOSEXUALITY IS SANDWICHED BETWEEN SACRIFICING KIDS AND HAVING SEX WITH AN ANIMAL. Let this sink in for a moment or two. In a day and age when being gay is accepted by so many, we need to know what scripture says. Here we find today that it's **detestable**. This means *deserving to be detested; abominable; hateful*. Now, lest you think I'm a "gay-basher," let me be quick to say that adultery and other sexual sins are addressed as wrong in this chapter. I'm just being sure we know the Bible does speak of homosexuality as sin here and in other passages throughout the Old and New Testament.

Sin is a sin. We are all sinners. Consequences vary. The thought of someone sacrificing their child for an idol is fairly foreign to most of us. And the thought of having sex with an animal is as well. So, when did the other become more common? When did we start agreeing, in some cases, with the world's standard of what's ok and what is not? The next time someone asks you "where is that in the Bible?" concerning the sin of homosexuality, perhaps these three verses should be your "go to?" Think about it. Pray about it. There's a reason some people struggle with this sin. Recognize their struggle. Point them to the truth. Love them with the love of Christ. Pray regularly for them. Remember, Jesus met people where they were and offered hope for a better life. He wants us to do the same.

God set prohibitions early on for His people. Sexual relations have always been of value to our creator. He alone knows what's best. We can trust God's holy statutes and disregard pagan customs in order to save ourselves from devastating consequences. God wants us to be different than the world. Not only does it save us from having to dig ourselves out of a deep hole, it also causes the world to see we are different. There's a reason. Jesus. He's the hope of the world! Live by faith today...

DAILY READING:

Leviticus 19:1-20:21; Mark 8:11-38
Psalm 42:1-11; Proverbs 10:17
Focal Passage: Mark 8:34-35

LIVING BY FAITH

STRADDLING A FENCE HURTS, NO MATTER WHO YOU ARE. I grew up straddling fences while playing in my neighborhood. We played hard and a little fence never stopped us from reaching our destination. But there was this one time… when I was in high school a group of us went to the State Fair. Someone in the group (I'm sure it wasn't me) had the bright idea of jumping the fence instead of paying to get in. (Yes, I know you're surprised, but I'm sure it wasn't my idea.) So, we jumped the fence. We all considered ourselves great athletes so the fact that it was a very tall fence didn't bother us. We saw it as a challenge. We loved to compete with one another. This is a fence-straddling I'll never forget. I wish I could tell you it was because my conscience bothered me for years. But, it was actually because it hurt being at the top of that big ole fence. No number of jumping fences prepared me for this one. Yes, I'll never forget it.

Jesus doesn't want us to straddle the fence. Not only does He want us to live honestly and not cheat to get into the State Fair, but symbolically He doesn't want us to straddle the fence. It hurts. It hurts you and me as people. He wants us to be followers, not just fans. A fan just shows up every now and then or when it's convenient. A follower seeks to follow Jesus every moment of every day. Not just when it's convenient. It won't be. You follow Him when you experience pain and rejection. Because you will sometimes.

Those who have trusted Christ, but still hold on to certain areas of their life are straddling the fence. It hurts. And it hurts the person's witness for Christ. There's no way for a straddler to experience abundant life or enjoy eternal reward later. It's not worth it. It's a wasted life. Get off the fence!

If you lose your life here, you are allowing Jesus to be Lord (Boss). You say no to your fleshly desires and yes to Jesus—one day at a time. You pursue His Kingdom matters and freely identify with Him and His family. You experience intimacy with Christ in this life and enjoy even greater rewards in eternity. So, if you're hurting because you are straddling the fence, you have been reminded of what to do. Live by faith today…

DAILY READING:
Leviticus 20:22-22:16; Mark 9:1-29
Psalm 43:1-5; Proverbs 10:18
Focal Passage: Mark 9:23-24

LIVING BY FAITH

WHEN YOU DOUBT, YOU CAN PRAY ABOUT THAT TOO. Here was a dad who believed in Jesus. He had already demonstrated a significant measure of belief by bringing his possessed boy to Him. The disciples were unable to heal him. Maybe that's why he asked Jesus to heal him with a question mark. Jesus quickly let him know all things are possible by His reply. *If you can?* Actually, I love this portion of scripture. I picture Jesus grinning at the man with a loving, confident look with the response. Sort of like, "Hello, if I can? Bro, I'm God!" I know, that's probably not very pastoral. I'm just telling you what I think every time I read verse 23.

So, the dad admits his belief but was brutally honest about his unbelief. What a dad! His boy witnessed his authenticity at this critical moment. And he was being humble in front of God. He was asking for help with his doubts. He asked Jesus to help him. We can, too.

Are you doubting the healing of your son? Tell it to Jesus. Are you doubting your retirement plan? Tell it to Jesus. Are you doubting your significance? Tell it to Jesus. Are you doubting your job security? Tell it to Jesus. Are you doubting a doctrine in the Bible? Tell it to Jesus.

Jesus longs for us to be honest. He responds to authenticity. This is the epitome of who He is. So the next time you believe, but doubt, pray about it. Trust me, He will not send down lightning from heaven. How do I know? Because I'm still here! Live by faith today...

DAILY READING:
Leviticus 22:17-23:44; Mark 9:30-10:12
Psalm 44:1-8; Proverbs 10:19
Focal Passage: Mark 9:38-41

LIVING BY FAITH

WE MUST BE CAREFUL ABOUT BEING OVERLY CRITICAL OF THE PASTOR ON TELEVISION. Have you ever been flipping channels and landed on a preacher preaching? Probably. Next question… Have you ever stopped to listen to him preach? Probably. At least once. I have. I don't always agree with everything they say. I don't always like their hairstyle or the way they dress. As a matter of fact, sometimes I think to myself, "he sure isn't a Southern Baptist." I know. How arrogant! So were the disciples. They just didn't know it, evidently. They did after this conversation with Jesus.

Contrary to what some of us think, Jesus was not a Southern Baptist. Neither was John the Baptist. (It's ok. You can still go to sleep tonight, my fellow Southern Baptist friends.) The disciples thought they were an elite group of guys. Now, they were unique, and we thank God for them. But they were not the only ones who had the gospel of Jesus Christ. No group or denomination is exclusive. Jesus makes it clear one cannot work for Him and against Him at the same time. The name of Jesus is the key. The real Jesus. The Jesus of the Bible. The Jesus who was fully God and fully man. The Jesus who lived a perfect life, died on a cross for our sins, and was raised on the third day. The Jesus who sits at the right hand of the Father interceding on our behalf. The Jesus who longs for an intimate relationship with us—us sinners. That Jesus. Yes, that incredible Jesus. Don't you love Jesus? He's one of a kind! No one is like Him!

When I was growing up, I'd often ask my dad about different denominations or religions. He'd always start with Jesus. He'd say something like this, "Hal, we have differences, but the main thing is Jesus." It's that simple. So, I try really hard not to be too vocal about televangelists or TV preachers. It's hard sometimes. But God uses all of us. He spoke through a donkey, for heaven's sake! It's the message of the gospel that saves, not the messenger. Next time you're in a group at church and someone starts bashing someone who has a certain hairstyle you dislike, be careful. I know some Southern Baptists who have weird hairstyles, too. Live by faith today…

Leviticus 24:1-25:46; Mark 10:13-31
Psalm 44:9-26; Proverbs 10:20-21
Focal Passage: Mark 10:13-16

LIVING BY FAITH

JESUS VALUED CHILDREN BECAUSE OF THEIR IMPACT ON ALL OF US. Jesus loved people. He certainly loved children. Here we see Him demonstrating His undying love for them. The disciples didn't get it. Sometimes we don't get it. Yes, they can be hyperactive. Yes, they can be immature. Yes, they can be demanding. But they are children. Those are often normal characteristics of children. That's why parents and adults are parents and adults. We are to teach them. We are to coach them in all things. We are to model life for them.

Yesterday we had "potato day" at the church where I pastor. We hand out free potatoes to our community on the corner of our property. We've seen God use this ministry in numerous ways through the years. We had a first yesterday—one of our children actively participated. Her parents were present and allowed her to engage with our community. She was so trusting of everyone. I mean it was wholehearted and with such humility. I have scenes in my mind that I think I'll treasure forever. What precious moments! Not one person refused to take potatoes or smiled while doing so. Children have a way about them that impacts.

Jesus wants all of us to come to Him with total trust and humility. We can't get there any other way. To be prideful, like the Pharisees we keep reading about, and think it's our own righteousness that makes us right with God, is wrong. It's never worked and will never work. We are to humbly trust Jesus with our whole hearts. When we do, He assures us of heaven and heavenly impact here on earth. People see the difference and they're more likely to accept our love. Live by faith today...

DAILY READING:

Leviticus 25:47-27:13; Mark 10:32-52
Psalm 45:1-17; Proverbs 10:22
Focal Passage: Mark 10:42-45

LIVING BY FAITH

THOSE RECEIVING TROPHIES IN HEAVEN WILL LOOK DIFFERENT THAN THOSE RECEIVING TROPHIES DOWN HERE. We are accustomed to the rich and famous receiving trophies here on earth. We are used to seeing great athletes receive medals during the Olympics. What we're not used to seeing down here are rewards being given on a regular basis to servants. Yes, I know it happens. I know about the Nobel Peace Prize. But it's not like it's going to be in heaven.

Jesus made sure the disciples understood, that what they understood, was misunderstood. Whoever wants to be rewarded in heaven must be a suffering servant. Those who are slaves to Jesus are considered great. Greatness equals servanthood! We serve others by loving them no matter what they can do for us. As we continue reading the New Testament, we will discover that God created us for good works. And that the body of Christ is to serve one another. Jesus doesn't ask us to do something He wasn't willing to do. He was the ultimate example of a suffering servant.

We must experience pain to get to a better place. We must endure pain willingly, depending on Jesus moment by moment. As we fall more in love with Him through this pain, we fall more in love with people. And we serve them naturally and lovingly. That is greatness! Whom will you serve naturally? Don't worry about being rewarded down here. God will pass out rewards in heaven for His glory. Now, that's worth living for! Live by faith today...

LIVING BY FAITH

BEING STILL HAS NEVER BEEN EASY FOR ME. When I see children who have the wiggle worms, I identify with them. I have difficulty staying still. It's a discipline I've learned over the course of time, but it doesn't come naturally. What about you?

Our passage today says to be still. The psalmist encourages and comforts God's people with the knowledge that God would help them with their battles. He would defend them against their enemies. There is a time to be still. They certainly needed to do their part, but they needed to understand God would do His part. He always does. No need to worry about the battles being faced. He is God and He knows what they need when they need it. The same is true for us.

We live in tumultuous times. There are always battles being fought somewhere. Yes, they may be overseas, but they can still impact us. Some battles rage in the homes of people. Even God's people have trials and tribulations with family units. What do we do? Be still. It does not mean you shouldn't work for peace. It just means we should take time to be at peace with our God. He longs to hear from us. He wants to remind us of His precious promises.

Make being still a priority. It needs to be a regular part of our daily lives. Not just when we're in the battle. It needs to be when we're on the mountaintop. Steady yourselves by stillness. It doesn't matter if you're wired like me—sort of hyper, be still. God will help you. He has helped me do this. It makes all the difference in the world. Live by faith today…

LIVING BY FAITH

NO MATTER WHAT TRICK YOU MAY TRY TO PULL ON JESUS, HE WILL AMAZE YOU IN THE END. Here they go again… messing with Jesus. The Pharisees just never seemed to give up, did they? They were determined to try to put an end to Jesus. They pulled every trick in the book to try to ruin His reputation. It never worked. You can't trick Jesus. He wins. He won. When we are on His team, we win. So, don't be shaken by those who think they are winning in a way contrary to Jesus' teachings. It's only a matter of time before they will be exposed.

Boy, they thought they had Him on this one. Jesus let them know it's right to support the government. When the government is functioning well it supports those living under its rules in various ways. Our commitment to the state is not our only commitment. The greater commitment is to God's Kingdom work. His authority is greater because it's comprehensive. And His has no mistakes. You support the one without neglecting the other. Jesus was wise in His answer. They were amazed! We are always amazed at how Jesus never fails. His ways don't break down during a crisis. And those guys were certainly in the midst of a crisis. Jesus was making these men look bad, even though they kept trying to prove how good they were, and how good others must be. Jesus can't be tricked!

Has someone bent the rules on you recently? Maybe you've been hurt by a good person? Perhaps a friend—one you thought was a friend—has tricked others into thinking you are a bad person? Don't get on their level. Allow Jesus to set them straight. He will. They will be amazed. And you will, too. You'll find out one day how it all turned out. Trust Him. Live life by His rules, not theirs. Tricking Jesus doesn't work. Lots of "good" folks have tried through the years. Live by faith today…

DAILY READING:
Numbers 4:1-5:31; Mark 12:18-37
Psalm 48:1-14; Proverbs 10:26
Focal Passage: Mark 12:24-27

LIVING BY FAITH

WE WILL NOT TURN INTO ANGELS IN HEAVEN. One of my favorite movies is a classic shown around Christmastime. It's called *It's A Wonderful Life*. I almost feel like I must watch it every December to get in the mood. My favorite character is Clarence. Clarence is an angel. (I don't want to share too much about the movie in case you haven't watched it yet.) There is a certain scene in the film which portrays him finally getting his wings. I've always thought most people who think humans turn into angels in heaven probably received their belief from this flick. Maybe not.

Maybe it's because of misinterpreting our focal passage today. Jesus corrected the Sadducees' faulty belief system. He let them know fairly quickly they didn't really know the scriptures, otherwise they would not be confused. Jesus pointed back to the Old Testament to help them realize their faulty theology. He let them know that in heaven it will not be like it is on earth. Although heaven is somewhat of a mystery, we know enough to know we will be similar to one big happy family. We'll be spiritually alive and a great big extended family. That's hard for us to wrap our minds around totally, but if you're in a church family, you understand to a point.

Jesus lets them know we will be like angels. Not in the very essence of an angel, but in that they don't marry. We won't either. That's the point. No one will be married, and no one will be having babies. There's no procreation in heaven.

Next time someone asks if their loved one is an angel now that they have died and are in heaven, point to this scripture. Tell them they won't be called "Clarence" either. Live by faith today…

Numbers 6:1-7:89; Mark 12:38-13:13
Psalm 49:1-20; Proverbs 10:27-28
Focal Passage: Mark 13:10

LIVING BY FAITH

NOW YOU KNOW WHEN JESUS WILL RETURN. I remember as a child asking my dad questions about the Bible. The older I get, the more I recall doing so. He was also so good about handling my questions. I was curious. One of my questions was about Jesus' return. All I remember him simply saying was Jesus would return after everyone all over the world heard the gospel message. That was it. He didn't pull out any charts to explain the various views. He didn't tell me what view of eschatology he embraced. He simply answered the question and we moved on.

I don't recall him telling me chapter and verse, but here it is. Maybe that's why I don't get all "worked up" about prophecy. Jesus never did. He said to trust the Father. And He focused on sharing His message and loving people. Sounds good to me. As a matter of fact, I personally believe if someone believes Jesus is returning, which I do, the person would spend the majority of the time sharing the gospel. In other words, if someone has a passion for the return of Christ, that individual should naturally have a burden for lost people. Their time would be spent on meeting people where they are and telling them about Jesus. Don't you think?

As far as the charts and various millennial views… that's fine. I'm just going to focus on sharing the gospel and fulfilling my purpose the best I can. If I can trust Jesus with my eternal destiny, I can trust Him with the details of His second coming. I believe it's all going to pan out in the end. Live by faith today…

DAILY READING:
Numbers 8:1-9:23; Mark 13:14-37
Psalm 50:1-23; Proverbs 10:29-30
Focal Passage: Numbers 8:23-26

LIVING BY FAITH

IS FIFTY THE BIBLICAL RETIREMENT AGE? I don't think so. But someone could potentially make a case for it being an age of transition. What's happening in our passage is a gracious provision for aging men. A number of males had God-given responsibilities which were physically demanding. They had various temple assignments. Some were responsible for Passover preparations. God gave instructions to allow them to transition to less taxing jobs so as not to bring defilement to the nation. It provided a graceful exit which would fit their next season of life. In this case, fifty was an age of transition.

At the time of this writing, I am hanging on to my fifties. It's hard, but I've been successful so far. I am pastoring a church in St. Petersburg, Florida that I love. God has given me a love for the city, too. I have no idea how much longer I will be here, but at my age, I could be in for a transition even before my "retirement." If so, God will make it clear and it will not mean I'm retiring. I've still got a good ten years or so left in me as long as my health holds up. I have a good model.

Dr. Jim Futral just transitioned to "retirement." He's over seventy years old! He's been a mentor of mine for decades. Even though he's no longer the Executive Director of the Mississippi Baptist Convention, he's still got years of ministry left in him, based on all indications. So even though he's "retiring," he's not really. He's transitioning to another role in ministry. And we see this transitioning through various seasons of life is biblical. It's OK. God blesses it.

Maybe you're approaching a transition age? Maybe you're experiencing a forced transition? Regardless, it's ok. God is your ultimate provider. Seek Him. Obey Him. Be open to His ways, which are often different than ours. His plan is always best. Live by faith today...

LIVING BY FAITH

IN SPITE OF A CLEAR CALL FROM GOD AND EXPERIENCING MIRACLES, MOSES HAD DARK DAYS. If you've been called by God, you will have days or seasons which are difficult. You've read enough of the Bible to know this to be true. We all know Moses heard the voice of God speaking through a burning bush. We all know God has moved in and through him in miraculous ways. And here we find him crying out to God because he's so discouraged. Answering God's call on your life doesn't mean everything is going to be perfect, because we are not perfect, and the people we serve with are not perfect. We are all sheep. And we all know sheep aren't the brightest bulbs in the box, although they're not all baaaaaad.

Moses was fulfilling his call to lead the children of Israel. It was not easy for any of them. Moses cried out to God because they were grumbling about food. They were being crybabies. Moses was the under-Shepherd. God was the Shepherd. So God was really in charge. Sometimes that's easy to forget. He forgot due to his discouragement, but God heard his prayer. He answered his prayer. He reassured him. That's our God. He doesn't expect us to be able to handle everything that comes our way while fulfilling our call. That's His job. He uses dark moments to remind us of His faithfulness.

If you are called to lead people, you will have times of discouragement. It goes with the territory. They will say and do things that will absolutely cause you to think you're going to lose your mind. As a matter of fact, you may if you don't seek God and wise counsel. Allow God to do a deeper work within you during these dark days. Pray. Fast. Trust. Take some time off. But don't do something you'll regret. Remember that help is on the way. God has ways of bringing people alongside you in ministry. Watch for those who are competent, trustworthy, and filled with the Holy Spirit. You aren't meant to fulfill all God has for you to do here on earth by yourself. It's called the Church. God's people help us fulfill God's will. Live by faith today...

DAILY READING:
Numbers 11:24-13:33; Mark 14:22-52
Psalm 52:1-9; Proverbs 11:1-3
Focal Passage: Numbers 12

LIVING BY FAITH

WE ARE TO MARRY PEOPLE OF FAITH REGARDLESS OF RACE.
Yes, that's what was going on here. Moses' siblings were challenging his authority. They decided to use the "race card" to do so. Moses married a lady from Cush—now Ethiopia. Moses, of Jewish descent, married a descendant of Noah's son Ham, through Cush. She was of African descent. Obviously, she had embraced the one true God, like her husband, Moses. Yes, marriage is to be faith-based, not race-based as some believe. The Lord's response clearly proves this truth. God was UPSET that Miriam and Aaron criticized Moses' marriage to an African woman!

Moses did nothing wrong here. Miriam and Aaron were in the wrong. God punished them for their wrong. And without Moses' plea for grace, the consequences of their sin would have been worse. We see the humility of Moses in this chapter. God greatly uses humble people. God greatly punishes those who see color instead of character. I think we will one day realize the truths of our text today. We will see how God has punished racial prejudice. We will also see how gracious He's been in spite of our racial prejudice.

Should one seek to marry a person with a different ethnicity no matter what it may cost? No. I don't think so. I think if one is to marry, one should seek to marry a person sold out to faith in Jesus, no matter the cost. Not everyone should marry. But if one does, he or she should intentionally marry a believer. If the believer has a different skin color or accent, so be it. Do not allow your culture, family, or friends to allow you to miss God's best for your life. Don't even allow a misguided preacher to cause you to stumble over this one. Your life is not their life. You will be responsible for following God. I will too. We can't blame anyone for our disobedience. Regardless of how difficult it may be to move beyond our wrong beliefs, we must. All we have to do is follow the example of Moses and not the example of his siblings. And remember what happens when we are cultural Christians instead of biblical believers. Live by faith today…

LIVING BY FAITH

BLESSINGS FROM GOD DON'T COME WHEN WE JUST OBEY HIM WHEN CONVENIENT. I've been a fan of Caleb for many years. My wife and I planned on naming our second boy Caleb. We didn't have a second boy. We had a girl. And in a real sense, she's like a Caleb, just not by name.

Caleb had a different spirit. His attitude was not like others. Most people have the herd mentality. They go with what others say or do without regard to what God may want them to say or do. Not Caleb. We see from scripture that even though others saw challenges, Caleb saw opportunities. Even though others were fearful, Caleb was faithful. Even though others were guided by the crowd, Caleb was guided by conviction. That's what it means, in essence, to have a different spirit from others.

You don't have to be a jerk or cocky. You just have to be confident in who you are in Christ. You must allow Him to put *stuff* in you on a regular basis in order to think differently. You're not going to get this just by going to church on Sundays. God wants you to know Him. God wants to meet with you during the week. God wants you to be like Caleb. Caleb will be loyal to those in authority and supportive when others aren't. Caleb will cause others to think twice before rolling with the herd. Caleb is the one God wrote about as an example. (Would you be one?) Caleb was blessed because of his undying loyalty to God and His ways.

Caleb types have the kind of vision I heard defined this way years ago… a mental picture of what could be fueled by the conviction of what should be. You see it? Good. Be God's man or woman in season and out of season. Live by faith today…

LIVING BY FAITH

THIS CURTAIN TEAR WAS LIKE NONE OTHER. Have you ever had a tear? Maybe it was a tear in a shirt or your pants. Perhaps you've even had a curtain tear while you were hanging it. Well, there's never, ever, been a tear like this one! This tear in the temple curtain symbolized Jesus had achieved what He came to do. Jesus made it possible for us to have direct access to God. It is called the Priesthood of the believer. You know all those rules and regulations you've been reading about in the Old Testament? No more, my friend! No more! Hallelujah!

Jesus provided our redemption. He has provided the atonement for our sins. We can now come into the presence of the one and only Holy God. We don't need another human being, a high priest, a priest of any kind, a goat, a lamb, NOTHING! As the old hymn goes, Jesus paid it all and all to Him we owe! Jesus Christ, the God-Man, is our great high priest who willingly gave Himself for our sins once and for all. It's over, baby! Turn out the lights! Enjoy the freedom we have in Christ to live a life of obedience out of love. My, my, it makes wading through all those verses on the law worth it. Doesn't it? It just makes our redemption all the sweeter!

So the next time you encounter a tear, may it remind you of what Jesus has done. No need to get upset, no matter how inconvenient it may be. Just take a moment to say HALLELUJAH! Maybe take a moment to sing the old hymn mentioned? Maybe just smile and go on. Live by faith today...

DAILY READING:
Numbers 16:41-18:32; Mark 16:1-20
Psalm 55:1-23; Proverbs 11:7
Focal Passage: Numbers 16:41

LIVING BY FAITH

GOD'S PEOPLE CAN BE FICKLE EVEN WHEN THEY HAVE SEEN THE GLORY OF GOD. It's hard to believe, but it's true. The Israelite community blamed Moses and Aaron for the death of God's people. I know, it's laughable. But in essence, we see it all the time. Think about it... Tragedy happens and it's someone's fault. Someone always has to be the scapegoat. When God's people respond this way, it is costly. It hurts the witness of the church. It hurts those in authority who have accepted the call to lead the church. It just leaves a bad taste all the way around.

God is holy. His character does not allow for open rebellion. The Israelites were reaping the consequences of their sin. The people were casting blame on the ones who had given their lives to try to protect them. It's sad, isn't it? It's incomprehensible, isn't it? It's heartbreaking, isn't it? It makes you sort of mad, doesn't it? (Well, it does me.)

Please be careful not to blame your leader who is trying to follow the will of God. Don't cast stones. Go to the cornerstone—Jesus—and pray about your concerns, if you have any. Allow God to handle things which may be hard to reconcile in your own mind. Your leader sees the big picture. If you've never sat in his chair, do not think you understand. You don't. Has he always been arrogant? Self-serving? Be careful, folks. You do not want to have regrets down the road and your church certainly doesn't want to one day say... *you know, I wish we had handled that differently.*

Any time I think I have it tough, I try to remember Moses and Aaron. They **really** had it tough. What I've been through and you've likely been through is nothing compared to these guys. Move forward. Let it go. Trust God. Learn from the past. Following the example of Moses in most cases will assist you in leading God's way. And remember the times in life when you truly saw the glory of God revealed in the past. It will help you in the present and future. Live by faith today...

LIVING BY FAITH

DOING WRONG ON THE WAY TO DOING RIGHT IS WRONG.
I'm right. How do I know? First, because of our passage today. Moses was on the way to doing right. God had given specific instructions to him and was going to graciously use him to perform a miracle. Moses channeled his anger in the wrong way. Instead of speaking to the rock, he struck it twice and acted like the water came out of the rock due to him. Not good! He disobeyed the specific instructions of almighty God and then tried to receive the glory. God punished him. It was a steep punishment that "fit the crime."

The judgment pointed to the Lord's holiness. Moses **and** Aaron had failed to honor God's holy character in this part of this amazing story. They both would suffer. After all they had done and would do, they received their just punishment. It could have been worse. We've certainly read worse so far.

The second reason I know I'm right is because I'm guilty. I've done wrong on the way to doing right. I remember needing to discipline my children when they were young and being too harsh. That's doing wrong on the way to doing right. I have gotten frustrated with God's people and my body language didn't communicate love even when I knew I needed to speak with them about various issues. I could share other examples, but I'll stop here. Can you relate, my friend? Sure, you can! Next time, let's think twice before we act wrong on the way to doing what's right. The consequences are never, ever good. Just think about what happened to Moses. If need be, think about what's happened to me at times over the years. Better yet, think about what's happened to you when you did wrong on the way to doing right. No fun, is it? Live by faith today...

DAILY READING:
Numbers 21:1-22:20; Luke 1:26-56
Psalm 57:1-11; Proverbs 11:9-11
Focal Passage: Numbers 21:4-9

LIVING BY FAITH

WHEN PANIC OCCURS, KEEP YOUR EYES ON JESUS. There are times in life when people panic. It may be understandable. In this case with the Israelites, it was totally understandable. They had once again reverted to their favorite complaint. *Why have you led us up from Egypt to die in the wilderness?* And it cost them dearly! Their lack of faith brought on poisonous snakes which bit them and caused death to a number of them. It was God's way of disciplining them for their lack of faith. They admitted their sins and reached out for help. God was gracious, once again, and provided a way for them to live. Moses made a bronze snake and all they had to do was look at it to live.

They demonstrated faith in God by looking at the bronze snake. It provided a way for them to be saved from death. Many years later, Jesus compared the lifting up of the bronze snake to His being lifted up on a cross as a cure for the world's sin problem. It is a fabulous picture of the necessity of looking to the Lord Jesus Christ in faith to be saved. What a story! What a Savior!

Sometimes there will be panic due to a perceived worldwide problem or actual catastrophes. Use good judgment. Seek God for wisdom. Follow His instructions and the instructions of those who are Godly leaders. Be sensitive to those in places of authority. God often works through them as well. But please don't panic. Fear is not of God. Trust Jesus. Look to Him, especially when others are in a state of panic. This can be a wonderful opportunity to share the love of Jesus. It shows our Redeemer lives and we trust him—regardless! It will be noticed and make a noticeable difference in whether or not you lose your joy. Watch out for snakes and as always... Live by faith today...

LIVING BY FAITH

GOD MAY BLOCK YOU IN AN ODD WAY TO KEEP YOU FROM DOING SOMETHING DISASTROUS. Balaam was an unusual prophet for sure. He sent mixed signals. God's spokesperson should never send mixed signals. It hurts more than helps. God used Balaam's donkey to keep him from disobeying. Yes, I know most of the time we talk about how if God can speak through a donkey, He can speak through anyone. Boy, do I know that! But sometimes we miss another truth here. God will graciously keep us from doing something really stupid at times. He loves us so much He will go to unusual measures to stop us from hurting ourselves, others, or His Kingdom purposes.

God knows more than you and I. Even when we think we know for absolute certain God is calling us to do something, how He does it and when He does it is up to Him. We **must** trust Him! Maybe, just maybe, you are being "blocked" from going down a path. Maybe, just maybe, someone or something unusual is actually keeping you from going down that path. God knows and He's not trying to trick you. He is not the author of confusion. Satan is. So don't be confused. When you are not sure, pause. Keep praying and seeking wise counsel. God will make a way, so don't create a way yourself and end up hurting yourself. It's costly!

Always remember the message more than the messenger. Yes, God has certain requirements for those who preach and teach. (It's not perfection.) But never leave God because His messenger acts or seems donkey-like. I have seen many people "leave" God or His Church due to the goofiness of His spokesperson or people. Please don't do it! God speaks through sinners. It's His message, not the messenger's. Keep your eyes on Jesus and His way. His way, not ours, is always the best way. Live by faith today...

LIVING BY FAITH

STAY FAR AWAY FROM SORCERY. Throughout the Bible, we see it's never God's will for us to seek direction from omens. Balaam had a bad habit of doing so. Here he does not, and he relies on God's direction alone. He had the Spirit of God on him due to his obedience not to resort to sorcery as at other times and uttered a poetic tribute to God's hand of blessing on Israel in the following scriptures.

It's best to distance yourself from anything which hints of being demonic in nature. When I was growing up, we had a Ouija Board in the house. We didn't know any better. We do now. Regardless of whether or not you think it's OK, I suggest you not own one or play the game. It's not wise. We know a lot more these days about demonic activity that should help us with this issue.

Having the spirit of God is paramount to an abundant life. God's desire is that we have a relationship with Him. When we admit our sin, believe on Jesus, and put our faith in Him alone, we start the journey. As we grow, we seek His face in prayer and read His Word. Staying close to Him gives us the abundant life He offers. This does not mean we won't have problems. This means we will know how to deal with them. God is our source. We need no other source—certainly not any type of demonic source.

Stay away from sorcery. Encourage others to do the same. When you find yourself being exposed in any way, run. If you are watching TV and a commercial comes on which hints of the demonic, change the channel. Don't look at horoscopes. We don't need them! God does not give us the spirit of fear. Trust Him! Don't live in fear or let the enemy cause you to gradually slip off into a slippery slope you don't need to be involved in. **Stay far away today and every day!** Live by faith today...

LIVING BY FAITH

ANY FORM OF THE NAME ANN WILL GET MY ATTENTION MORE THAN OTHERS. Today's daily reading had lots and lots of names. The one which stood out to me the most was Anna. You see, my mama was named, Patricia Ann. She went by Ann. She was beautiful on the inside and outside. I know. You think I'm prejudiced. I'm really not. If you knew her, you'd know I'm not prejudiced. I saw pictures of her from days gone by and she really was a pretty lady. And as far as her inward beauty... wow! She glowed. She had some of the characteristics of Anna. Now that you know why Anna initially got my attention more than all the names we read (some we'd never heard of, much less able to pronounce), let's consider how she's described.

She was old. I didn't say it. That's what the Gospel of Luke says. The older I get, the more I realize old is not a bad word. It's good for numerous reasons. What are they? Well, you young folks will see when you get old. That's not the main purpose of this writing... but I will leave you with this. A person who has walked closely with God for a long period of time knows Him when He appears. You think about that.

She was from the tribe of Asher. The Asher clan was strong. Do your research. My grandfather on my dad's side was named, Asher. I did a sermon once on the name. It's a powerful name and clan. Your clan matters. If you think you are from a "bad" clan, change it.

She worshipped God daily. That was the key and that's our key to knowing Jesus. We spend time with Him in prayer and Bible study regularly and consistently. When we do, we know it's Him when He shows up in various ways and places. He's recognizable. He's not foreign.

She was thankful. People who stand out with joy are grateful. It's for every day. Be thankful.

She spoke about Jesus. It wasn't forced. It was natural. Jesus conversations come naturally when we regularly worship Him. We speak about Him to others because we can't hold it in. Live by faith today...

80

LIVING BY FAITH

KNOCK A HOME RUN FOR GOD. My dad died shortly after I was ordained into the gospel ministry. He asked me before the ordination council meeting if I understood why we even had ordination in our local churches. At the time I said something like, *"Well, I think it's more men's idea than God's."* He immediately let me know that was not true! He was so glad we discussed this prior to the council meeting. Now I understand. I believe ordination is God's idea and here is an Old Testament passage which certainly indicates this truth.

Joshua was already known by the Israelites and others as a well-respected, humble leader. He was also known as a close associate of Moses. He had an incredible record of bravery. All he lacked was the public stamp of approval from the Lord through a ceremony in which Moses would symbolically transfer leadership to a worthy man of God. This is why Moses and other leaders of God laid hands on him. This is exactly why we ordain those called of God to ministry. It's a symbolic ceremony of approval from those who know the candidates, and believe God has used them in the past and are ready for God to use them in the future.

When I was ordained, I have a memory of what only one man said to me. It wasn't my dad or other men I loved and respected. It was the Mayor of Clinton, Mississippi at the time. His name was Billy Ray Smith. (I always loved and respected him, too.) When he laid hands on me, he whispered in my ear, *"Knock a home run for God."* He knew I played baseball in high school and college. He knew I would identify with the statement as a way to motivate me. He knew I wasn't a home run hitter. But he knew I could do my best to serve God faithfully all the days of my life, and leave the results up to Him. I'm still trying. What about you? Knock a home run for God. God calls us to serve Him until the day we die. Live by faith today...

LIVING BY FAITH

EVEN IF YOU FACE A PANDEMIC DISEASE AND MUST BE
ISOLATED FROM OTHERS, YOU STILL HAVE JESUS. At the time of this
writing, we are facing the Coronavirus pandemic. It's unprecedented and no one
knows the end result. Precautions are being made and social distancing is common.
Who knows, I may have to keep my distance from my wife Kellie before this is over.
She may enjoy that. Not for long though, she is very attracted to me. (Remember,
keep your sense of humor during a crisis. It's important!) But I can still spend
time with Jesus. He longs for an intimate relationship with us. If one of the worst
things that can happen is that we have to keep our distance from loved ones, we can
draw near to Him like never before. And when life goes back to normal, it won't be
normal. It will be abnormally better!

This Psalm is so appropriate for a time of crisis. HE is our rock. HE is our
fortress. We can trust in Him at all times. And then those last two verses concerning
two things: *God is strong, and God is loving.* What better way to start your day, or end
your day, or finish your devotional reading than with these verses! Wow! God's got
you. God's got me. God's got us. I sort of feel like what we'll read later this year
from the Apostle Paul... whether we live or die, we want to bring honor to Christ.

A crisis situation is not a time to be fearful. It's not a time to worry. It's a time
to be faithful. God uses unusual situations to use us in unusual ways. THINK of
ways to minister to those you may not normally think about. And if you are not
facing a crisis right now, still think of someone who may need a touch of some kind
from you. Toilet paper is at a minimum at the time of this writing. Toilet paper
to someone would be great in some cases. That's likely not the case for us now, so
maybe just a gift card of some kind would be more appropriate. Allow tough times
to draw you nearer to God and closer to acting like Him. He was all about loving
others. Be strong. Be loving. Live by faith today...

Numbers 30:1-31:54; Luke 4:1-30
Psalm 63:1-11; Proverbs 11:20-21
Focal Passage: Luke 4:22

LIVING BY FAITH

IF PEOPLE TALK DOWN TO JESUS, THEY WILL TALK DOWN TO YOU. Have you ever had someone talk down to you? I have. I don't like it. Ok, now, have you ever talked down to someone else? Yeah, me too. I don't like it and I am sure the person I did it to didn't appreciate it either. So, now that we have this established...

When Jesus' public ministry began, people were amazed. They should have been. He was absolutely the most amazing person who has ever walked this earth! Some tried to reconcile how He could be so incredible by directly or indirectly talking down to Him. You know, something like, *Hey man, this is Joseph's son, chill. There's nothing special about him.* It didn't faze Jesus. You know why? HE knew who He was! Do you?

You are a person God has created. God desires to have a close relationship with you. He wants to make sure you know who you are. You are a unique, never-before-created person with a one-of-a-kind purpose. Though you may have a well-known dad, grandad, or son, that is not who you are. You may even be known due to your job or team. That is not who you are. You may even be known as a kind soul, that is not who you are. You are, whether you've realized it or not, a person God created and He wants to know you intimately via a relationship with Him through Jesus.

Why all this? Because when someone talks down to you, you need to know who you are. That way, though it may sting a little, it won't destroy you. No one defines you. God does. So, don't let the one who talks down to you, for whatever reason, ruin your day or your identity. Try to handle it right and press on with who you are in Christ and what your call in life is. It's just a reminder that when someone tries to get you down, Jesus is there to lift you up. Live by faith today...

LIVING BY FAITH

YOU CAN BE EXCEPTIONAL OR NOT, THE CHOICE IS YOURS.
Caleb and Joshua were exceptional. Following their story reminds us, like others, that they had choices to follow God. They obeyed. Others did not. God reminded some of the people who were not following Him wholeheartedly that their choices from the past reaped negative benefits. It could happen again. I heard this statement years ago which rings true here: "People make choices and choices make people."

What does it take to stand out for God? How do you become an MVP (Most Valuable Player) for God's army? Well, if we pause to consider a few characteristics from Caleb and Joshua, we have a pretty good idea. One, they listened and obeyed. Some of us just listen. That's not obeying. I can listen and hear my wife ask me to clean the dishes. What I do with this information determines my future—well, sort of. These two guys obeyed because they believed God spoke truth and loved them. They didn't think God was being selfish, or rude, or unkind. They realized His character and trusted Him. Two, they lived by faith. They "saw" what others did not see. That's faith. Believing in what God says, even when you can't see it at the time. Three, they didn't follow the crowd. They stood out from the crowd. They didn't allow others to intimidate them in how they were going to live their lives. That's critical to being different.

So, are you exceptional? Am I? We need to always put truth into our lives. We need to obey what we know is God's Word and will. We need to realize we may not see it at the time, but we do it because Christianity is all about living by faith. And we decide ahead of time that we will not be crowd-followers. If you and I do these things, we will be exceptional. Not for our benefit, but for God's glory. There's a big difference. Live by faith today...

LIVING BY FAITH

WHEN JESUS IS IN THE HOUSE, EVERYTHING CHANGES. This is one of my favorite passages in the entire Bible! I love preaching this text to folks. It's a picture of what happens when a church allows Jesus to be the primary focus. Everything changes in the life of a church when Christ is Lord over everything. So often we allow our programs to become the priority over the person of Jesus. There's nothing wrong with programs, but they should not become more important than Jesus. Remember, the church is His Church. I don't care if you're the Pastor, the Youth Pastor, a founding member, etc. The Church is the Church of Jesus Christ! Amen. Hallelujah!

Jesus drew people from all walks of life. He was authentic. He was fully God and fully man. There was and is no one else like Him. People wanted to hear what this miracle worker had to say. So, when the boys arrived with their limited friends and couldn't get in the house, they got creative. (Creativity has a place in the church today, by the way.) They created a hole in the roof, unlike our roofs today, and lowered their friend right smack dab in the middle of the church service. I love it! Use your imagination and you can picture it. Jesus didn't rebuke them. I sort of feel like He smiled at these brothers. He certainly was pleased. He healed the guy, blessed them all, and folks left the worship service amazed because they had never seen anything like this before! That's the stuff that happens when Jesus is in the house!

What changed? The religious people get upset over their preferences and leave empty. People with all kinds of troubles find the great physician—Jesus. Church folks get pumped and tell others about what Jesus is doing in their lives and the life of their church. Others follow the example of those who see things differently. Faith is being sure of what you do not see. Convictions start taking the place of preferences. FAITH changes everything! It's not just theological jargon. It's truth. It's reality. It's what God honors. It's what you need today. It's what I need every moment of every day. Live by faith today...

LIVING BY FAITH

JESUS DID NOT COME TO EARTH TO JUST HANG OUT WITH RELIGIOUS FOLKS. Jesus connected with people. He met people where they were and shared how they could be in a better place. Some listened and obeyed. Some just listened. I think we get that.

Once again, the religious leaders of the day, called Pharisees and teachers of the law, were uptight about Jesus' lifestyle. He was not like them. He was actually not like them at all. His priority was not legalism. He came to fulfill the law, not spend every moment of every day looking religious and speaking in a way most people couldn't understand. He came to love everyone. He came to give hope to the most wretched sinners people could think of. Levi was one of those. Jesus met him where he was, and the man was changed. He was so excited he threw a party. Now remember, he was a new believer. That meant there were some "wild folks" at this gathering. (Doesn't that make you chuckle? It does me.) So, because of this, the religious types questioned his association with those at the gathering. They just didn't understand his mission, nor their real one. People are more important than rules and regulations. If rules get in the way of loving on lost folks, there's something wrong.

Jesus found ways to connect with those who didn't know Him personally. He spent time with the disciples and other believers. That's not an issue. We need each other as the Church. But we can't go live in a cave. We must be salt and light. We need to intentionally find ways to get to know and share with those who won't go to church with us. Do you do that? If so, God bless you in your ministry and journey. If not, please start today. You will not be sorry. It will bless others and bless you. Get creative. Start working out at a gym where others work out. Start eating at the same restaurant to have the same waiter over and over. Get gas at the same place. Join a club which has the same interest as you. Bottom line, connect with people who don't know Christ. Follow the example of Jesus. Have the smell of dirty sheep on you in the end. Religious people will hate it. Jesus will love it! Live by faith today…

DAILY READING:
Deuteronomy 2:1-3:29; Luke 6:12-38
Psalm 67:1-7; Proverbs 11:27
Focal Passage: Deuteronomy 3:26-28

LIVING BY FAITH

THERE COMES A TIME WHEN WE SPEND MORE TIME
INVESTING IN OTHERS WHOM GOD HAS CALLED TO DO WHAT
WE DO. We all have a different calling from God. Every calling is vital for
Kingdom purposes. As a believer, what has God called you to do? God called me
to be a pastor. I was taught years ago that I should always have someone younger
than me to invest in, someone my age to share with, and someone older than me to
put "stuff" into me. I've tried. At least one time during my journey I think I failed
somewhat, and it cost me. Practice these things no matter what God has called you
to do. I heard pastor Johnny Hunt say one time that all he wanted on his epitaph is
OTHERS. That's good… and that's what is going on here in our focal text.

Moses now needed to focus more on others—mainly his protégé, Joshua. You
see, by investing more time in Joshua, he was investing in others long term. Joshua
would lead the children of Israel into the Promised Land due to Moses' disobedience.
(Remember that passage?) God allowed Moses to view the land from a distance
but stuck with His discipline of Moses from earlier in the journey. Friend, God is
perfect. His judgment alone is always spot on. He is merciful and He is just. What
a God we serve!

Joshua, mentioned for the third time in Deuteronomy, would lead sooner
than later now, and enable the Israelites to enter the land. What an incredible
responsibility. And even though he had learned much from Moses already, he needed
more. God instructed Moses to put more time into Joshua in preparation for his
eventual role of being the leader. He was the man for the job! So Moses encouraged
him and strengthened him. Can you imagine being on the receiving end of being
blessed by Moses like that? Wow, what a gift of preparation for Joshua!

IF we are following God's call on our lives, we need to be encouraging and
strengthening others. Are we? If not, let's get on it today! If we are, as we grow
older and more seasoned, we need to start investing more in those who come behind
us. If you don't know who that is, pray. Pray God clearly shows you and get to work.
They will be used in a greater way and others will be blessed. Our investment in
people is never a waste! Live by faith today…

LIVING BY FAITH

A GODLY SPIRITUAL HERITAGE DOESN'T JUST HAPPEN ACCIDENTALLY. I thank God for those who trust Jesus as their personal savior who had no spiritual influence from family. It happened in the Bible and it happens today. I have often said I should be a lot better person than I am due to my Godly Christian heritage. My parents and grandparents were intentional with me. They made it a priority to teach me the Bible and have me involved in a local church. Why? Because they were familiar with our verse today and others in the Bible that encourage parents and grandparents to teach biblical truth to children.

Moses was reminding the new generation of Israelites of their opportunity to influence other nations. It was going to happen automatically. It was going to happen when they saw they were genuinely different. Others needed to see their God was unlike other gods. In order to do so, they dare not forget what they'd been taught and even seen. Humans naturally will tend to forget the goodness of God's mercy, and drift. One way to protect them from this was to teach God's ways to their children. Teaching them kept them involved in God's Word as well as helped their kids know God's ways. It helped everyone! It made a difference in the adults, their children and grandchildren, and pagan nations. It was and is a win for everyone!

When you dig deep into the meanings of these words, you find there's a consistent lifestyle involved. For example, my mom and dad taught us and others God's truths. But they didn't leave their knowledge in their heads. They lived these truths because they had landed in their hearts. They had a heart for God too, and it showed in their daily lives. They were not "odd for God." They were overjoyed with God. This is what I mean... They had joy, which is a fruit of the Spirit. It comes from knowing and abiding in Jesus. They were the same at church as they were at the mall or a game. No, they weren't perfect. No human is, which is why we need Jesus. But it was not a formality or an effort to look good. It was just who they were. That goes a long way in influencing children.

Parents, grandparents, be real. Know God and let Him be known. Talk to them naturally about Kingdom matters as you walk through life. Take God seriously, but don't take yourself too seriously. They long for authenticity. Live by faith today...

LIVING BY FAITH

WHEN JESUS SAYS SOMEONE IS THE BEST MAN EVER, WE BETTER PAY ATTENTION. John the Baptist was not the founder of the Southern Baptist Convention. As a matter of fact, he was not responsible for any Baptist denomination. Furthermore, he was not associated with any religious organization. He was the forerunner of Jesus. And here Jesus says there was none like him—ever. What a statement! It demands our attention.

John the Baptist let others know someone was coming who would change everything. We can do the same. We can tell others about Jesus. When we have experienced Him personally, He changes everything! He changes our daily lives. He changes our eternal destination.

John the Baptist stood out. He was in a sense a "wild man." The way he dressed and what he ate was not like everyone else. He didn't care. You read his story and realize he did not have the herd mentality. He was willing to swim upstream. He was his own man. Why? Because he was God's man. God's man doesn't care to be a clone. He only wants to be what God made him to be.

John the Baptist was humble around Jesus. Humility is a Godly characteristic. The Bible lets us know we should be humbled by Christ. John was not a proud man. And when he met Jesus, he went to a whole other level. The same will occur with you and me. When we meet Jesus personally and really get to know Him, He humbles us. We are less and less proud. We are confident in who we are in Christ. Not prideful.

Jesus lets us know we too can be great. How? By being identified with Him. He became the one and only God-man, THE GREATEST of all time! When we associate ourselves with Him by faith alone, we too can be great because we are on His team. Live by faith today...

LIVING BY FAITH

THE VALUE OF WOMEN IN MINISTRY IS IMMEASURABLE.

Women played a vital role in the life of Jesus and His ministry. The verses we're focused on make it clear. He even calls them by name. The roles of men and women are different. No matter what we think or believe, it is true. That makes neither gender better than the other. God created both male and female and said it was good. He makes no mistakes! And both genders are vital for Kingdom work.

The twelve disciples were His core group. Many women traveled with them and supported the work of Christ. These women had been touched in various ways by the ministry of Jesus. Jesus had rescued them from sin and healed many from sicknesses. They were totally surrendered to following Him. Make no mistake, the effectiveness of Jesus' earthly ministry was significant due to the female followers who added a special influence not otherwise felt.

As I think of women who have assisted me in ministry through the years, I rejoice. I won't name names, but I will list some specific ministries. Some prayed. They prayed regularly and specifically. They gave gifts. They were not expensive gifts. Often, they were gifts they had made themselves. They equipped others. They knew the vision I was trying to accomplish with those who taught God's Word and they helped. They protected me. Have you ever noticed how a mama bear protects her cubs? Yeah, that's the kind of protection I'm talking about. It was almost like my mom or sisters were around. These women were spirited and if you said something about me, they would attack. I thank God for them!

If you are a woman of God, please allow these women in the text today to be an encouragement. Keep doing the ministry God has led you to do. If you're not in active ministry right now, maybe it's time. Sure it is! Live by faith today...

Deuteronomy 9:1-10:22; Luke 8:4-21
Psalm 69:19-36; Proverbs 12:2-3
Focal Passage: Luke 8:19-21

LIVING BY FAITH

NEVER LET YOUR MOMMA, YOUR SISTER, OR YOUR
GRANDPAW SLOW YOU DOWN. Some interpret this passage in a way which
almost makes Jesus seem insensitive to His earthly family. That's not what's going on
here. All one has to do is read what He said about His mom when He was on the
cross. He made sure, even in the midst of excruciating pain, that John the beloved
disciple was going to pay close attention to her after His death. No, this text simply
shows that God must be first. Lordship means we allow God to be our boss. He
alone rules. He alone is to call the shots in our lives.

God's children listen to God's Word and obey. They don't merely listen. The
book of James will remind us of this truth soon enough. I always hoped my two
children obeyed me over time primarily because they loved me. That is the ultimate
compliment for a parent. And God desires that we realize He asks us to do things
or not do things due to knowing what's best. He loves us. That's why He has
boundaries for us, even when we don't like them or don't understand them.

My wonderful dad died when I was twenty-seven years old. I had not started
pastoring at that point in my journey. I've often wondered if he'd agree with some
of the decisions I've made through the years as a pastor. I'm pretty sure he wouldn't.
I've also thought if I'd have made some of the decisions I've made if he had lived.
Why? Because I would have likely asked his opinion on major ones. Would my
love for him have caused me to make decisions that weren't what God would have
wanted? I hope not. I'll never know. The reality is whether our family is alive or not,
we must follow what we understand to be God's will for our lives. They don't stand
before Judge Jesus on our behalf one day. We do. Love your family, but love Jesus
more. Live by faith today…

LIVING BY FAITH

JUST LIKE THE DISCIPLES, MAYBE WE'RE THE ONES WHO
REALLY NEED TO WAKE UP? The disciples were in the midst of a storm. They
had heeded the words of Jesus to get in a boat to go to the other side of a lake. Then
all of a sudden, a storm which scared them to death came up out of nowhere. (Ever
had that happen? Sure you have... a literal storm and a "storm" in life.) God sends
trials to us because He has something bigger for us to experience. Its end result is
always good! Sometimes we have storms just because of life. Yes, bad things can
happen to good people.

So, Jesus is taking a nap. (Here's your text for taking a nap, guys.) The disciples
were so terrified, they woke Him up. (I would have thought twice about waking
Jesus up from a nap. What about you? I guess it shows how scared they were.) They
were like, *"Lord, have mercy on our souls, we're gonna die up in this boat while on this
lake,"* (my paraphrase). How soon we forget that Jesus is "in the boat." He hadn't left
them, and He's not going to leave us when we have a storm. What will it take for us
to finally get it? Jesus calmed the storm and reassured the disciples.

Instead of thinking Jesus is asleep during our trial because we feel like our
prayers are hitting the ceiling, we need to wake up. Jesus is still on His throne and
He wants to take our storm and use it for His glory. He desires us to stay calm. Not
because we've got this. But because He's got this! Wake up and think of times in the
past when He was faithful during your testing or trials. Wake up and take advantage
of the resources He's given you. Wake up and realize this is an opportunity to show
a watching world you really mean what you say—Jesus is Lord! Wake up to an
opportunity which may never come in this form again. And don't forget to be in awe
of what He does during your storm. Our fear of Him causes us to
be prepared for the next time a storm suddenly comes our way. What a Savior! Live
by faith today...

LIVE BY FAITH

HERE WE HAVE AN OLD GEEZER'S TEXT. A geezer is defined as *"an odd or eccentric man."* I'm thinking it could be a woman, too. (Please don't tell my wife I mentioned this.) Regardless, when we are in our later years, God can still use us for His glory. (I was taught years ago in seminary that later years means fifty plus. Don't shoot the messenger. I'm just telling you what I was taught. Besides, I'm one of you.) The Psalmist was evidently a geezer when he wrote these words. And he was still being used by God.

Though the Psalmist had experienced various trials and tribulations, he was confident God would use him in the days ahead. God had already used troubled days in the past to strengthen, correct, and even develop him. Sound familiar, fellow geezers? Absolutely! That's what our sovereign Lord does with all His children. Just as the writer of this Psalm wanted to influence the next generation with the reality of how God can use difficulties of all kinds for good, we should do the same. As long as we have breath and our right mind (well, you know what I mean) we need to invest in the younger generation as much as possible. This can mean befriending them. It can mean communicating truth to them. It can mean encouraging them every opportunity you have. It can mean many things. Pray about it and then do it, if you're not already. Your investment in the younger generation will outlast your life. That's leaving a legacy, my friend!

The main reason I'm writing this devotional book is because of my grandchildren. I want them to be able to read about how Jesus has impacted my life. I want them to know of my own struggles and how God rescued me. I want them to understand their spiritual heritage and the trust they've been given to carry it on in their unique way. I want them to know "Big H" (my grandpa name) loves them and desires for them to love Jesus with all their heart, soul, and mind.

Let's do this for the young folks, geezers! It's the least we can do during the fourth quarter of our lives. Live by faith today…

LIVING BY FAITH

EASTER IS ON THE WAY. Easter celebration falls on different weekends each year. Regardless, this passage is where Jesus shares His true identity to the disciples. He had already given a number of hints leading up to this point. For example, we will discover in the days ahead that He had predicted the "destruction of the temple" of His body. This was a statement about His suffering and death.

It was God's plan that He suffer, be rejected by Israel's leaders, be killed, and then be raised the third day. Easter in a nutshell. This was an announcement that Easter was on the way. They did not fully understand His predictions about His death and resurrection until after it occurred. It was hard for them, and others, to let go of thinking the Messiah would come as a ruling, conquering, political figure, and force. That was man's way. This was God's way. A suffering servant who would take away the sins of the world.

This is the crux of Christianity. This is what makes a follower of Christ different than others. This is why we celebrate in such a phenomenal way on Easter Sunday. It's the reason to celebrate! Nothing can stop believers from doing so. Even this year during the Coronavirus pandemic, people will celebrate, they just won't do it the same way. For the first time in American history, groups will not gather on the campuses of their churches, they will gather with families online.

Nothing can stop Easter! They couldn't stop Him then and they cannot stop Him now. Are you celebrating Easter? Believers do so every day. He is alive! Is He alive in you? Has He brought you from death to life? He wants to and He can if you will surrender to Him. Admit your sin. Believe He is the Son of God who lived a perfect life, died on the cross, and is alive today. He will change your life. Things sometimes change in ways we don't expect. He does not! Live by faith today...

APRIL 1

DAILY READING:
Deuteronomy 18:1-20:20; Luke 9:28-50
Psalm 73:1-28; Proverbs 12:10
Focal Passage: Luke 9:28-31

LIVING BY FAITH

IT IS NOT FOOLISH TO BELIEVE IN THE RESURRECTION OF JESUS CHRIST. Adrian Rogers once said, "The Bible says a fool says in his heart there is no God, and April Fool's is his holiday." It's true. Jesus' inner circle of disciples was able to witness an amazing scene. But don't miss that Moses and Elijah were talking about Jesus's death, resurrection, and ascension, which would open the door to salvation. Believe by faith in what Jesus came to do and accomplish. It would be foolish not to. Maybe you don't believe or maybe you know someone who doesn't believe.

Pastor, lawyer, apologist, and friend Dr. Frank Harbor developed an acrostic to help bridge unbelief to belief. He uses the word **R-A-M-P.** (Get it? A ramp helps one to get from one side to another. Brilliant!) It would be foolish on my part to say I have remembered everything I've read or heard. I have not. But I have been able to keep this one stored in my mind. Here it is:

- **Resurrection:** Jesus was raised from the dead. NO other religion can make this claim.

- **Archeology:** Archeologists continue to make discoveries that support scriptures.

- **Miracles:** Miracles were performed by Jesus and His disciples to solidify He was God.

- **Prophecies:** Prophecies that have been fulfilled verify the truth of Christ and the Bible.

You and I may be fooled by some folks today. We may even have fun fooling some others. But let's not be a real fool. Believe in Jesus. He's the answer to **everything!** Live by faith today...

DAILY READING:
Deuteronomy 21:1-22:30; Luke 9:51-10:12
Psalm 74:1-23; Proverbs 12:11
Focal Passage: Deuteronomy 22:5

LIVE BY FAITH

GOD HAS NEVER APPROVED OF A MAN DRESSING LIKE A WOMAN OR VICE VERSA. This is a clear prohibition of the gender distinctions God designed from the beginning. There has never, ever been a time in history where it was okay for a man to intentionally dress like a lady. There has never, ever been a time in history where it was okay for a woman to intentionally dress like a man. It's just not right in God's eyes. Just because a section of our society approves of this does not make it right. Again, it's not biblical, and please don't think just because it has become somewhat the norm in some parts of the world that it's now okay.

Men and women bear the image of God. He specifically created us to be distinct, as well as complementary toward each other. Gender confusion clearly breaks this down. It is saying, to a Holy God, *you have made a mistake in how you made us and we're taking care of it our way.* Make no mistake, through this entire chapter we read that purging evil is the norm. Sin is serious. The consequences are catastrophic. God is holy.

What, for example, would cause a man to want to dress like a woman? 1. The person may not be a Christian. Why wouldn't a lost person act lost? 2. The person may consider whatever is popular, even by some who claim to know God, to be okay. It could be the "herd mentality," or poor theology. 3. Maybe, just maybe, it's a weakness and the person is absolutely miserable because he or she knows it's a sin. As Christians, we must stand for truth, with the love of Christ. Meet people where they are and help take them to where they need to be in every way possible. Someone with this issue likely needs Christian counseling at some point. Help them. And always remember, but for the grace of God... Live by faith today...

DAILY READING:
Deuteronomy 23:1-25:19; Luke 10:13-37
Psalm 75:1-10; Proverbs 12:12-14
Focal Passage: Deuteronomy 23:10

LIVING BY FAITH

ARE WET DREAMS AN ABOMINATION AGAINST A HOLY GOD?
When the Bible mentions emissions several times, it's referring to wet dreams. That's the only thing it could be referring to. It happens to young men and older men. It can actually happen to men in between those two age groups. The Old Testament law was very strict and ceremonial. I am fairly certain we've learned this in recent readings. Bodily discharges for men and women were addressed. We are not bound by these directives today.

A man who has a wet dream is not "unclean." In other words, I do not believe it is a sin. The issue is what takes place in the mind. No one can control what they dream about. Even last night I literally dreamed I was a part of killing a wild hog. This was not like any wild hog in the wild. It was more like the hog on *Lion King*. It spoke. We sliced it up and it was over. Was it something I came up with? No. I come up with some crazy stuff, but not that. I'm telling you, some dreams are nuts. Some are not. Some are funny. Some are fine. Guys, it's not a sin to dream about crazy stuff. It is an opportunity to examine our hearts and minds. If we are putting things in our minds which are not of God, stop it. It could have an impact on your thought life, which could relate to dreams. If you find yourself inflamed by lust, confess it to the Lord. If you need to ask for help or discuss this with someone, do it sooner than later. You will not be the first one to do so. You will not be the last one to do so. This issue has been around for a long time. Bottom line, we continue to see the holiness of God. He wants nothing to do with sin, and He desires that we go out of our way to keep our hearts and minds pure. We are to be holy as He is holy.

Before closing, I want to suggest something to parents. Pray about when to discuss sexual matters with your children. Don't go "old school" and give them a book with stick figures in it to explain the "birds and the bees." Back in the day, I think parents thought they were even being radical by doing so. (I know mine did.) I spoke with my son. My wife Kellie spoke with our daughter. I'm not saying it was perfect timing or what the ultimate result was. I just know it's better for us as parents to do this rather than social media or friends. Live by faith today...

APRIL 4

LIVING BY FAITH

WE HAVE A CHOICE EVERY DAY ABOUT HOW FRUITFUL OUR DAILY WALK WITH JESUS WILL BE. This passage is so simple, so familiar, and yet, so overlooked. It should not be. It is the key to fruitful Christian living. It's another abiding passage. It's another key to bearing the fruit of the spirit, which is the goal of Christianity. Mary understood the goal. We find her throughout scripture at Jesus' feet. When we find one constantly at the feet of someone, we recognize humility. We automatically see submission. We see one who is teachable. That's often lacking in today's society. Let's always remain teachable until the day we die. Let Jesus be our primary teacher. Jay Strack says, "Leadership begins at the feet of Jesus." And as believers, we lead someone, whether we know it or not. Better that we lead more like the greatest leader ever than whatever we might be able to offer in our strength.

Martha, Martha, Martha. I can just visualize this scene. I think Jesus had a smile on His face when He called her out. Don't you? I think He was just reminding her not to let ministry activity take precedence over opportunities to spend time with Jesus. Ministry should be done out of the overflow of our time alone in Bible study and prayer or it can become routine. We can burn out and do things in the flesh. We lose our joy and passion. People can even see the emptiness by which we do ministry. It's not a good look. Jesus reminds us today to seek ye first the Kingdom of God. When we do, **everything** turns out better.

Let's not kick Martha to the curb. She's valuable for all of us. We need to do what God has called us to do. If your gift is service, serve. If it's exhortation, exhort. If it's teaching, teach. Whatever it is, do it! But do **not** forget where your fuel comes from. Your energy and motivation come from your personal walk with Jesus. From spending time alone with Him. From not forgetting that we do what we do to bring glory to Him and not ourselves. That is all. Live by faith today...

APRIL 5

DAILY READING:
Deuteronomy 28:1-68; Luke 11:14-36
Psalm 77:1-20; Proverbs 12:18
Focal Passage: Luke 11:29-32

LIVING BY FAITH

THERE'S NO NEED FOR A SIGN FROM JESUS TO HELP YOU BELIEVE. I dare say we probably have all wished for some type of sign from God. You know, when making a decision. Lord, if you will just... (fill in the blank). Folks, that's not faith. Faith is being sure of what we hope for and being certain of what we do not see. What else does God have to do? Nothing! This passage tells us.

Demanding some sort of sign is nothing new. How many times have you heard someone say they need to see God with their own eyes do something miraculous in order to believe? Often, I imagine. Again, that's not faith. It's a lack thereof, and that's not what Christianity is based on. Saving faith is believing Jesus is the son of God. He lived a perfect life. He died on a cross for our sins. He rose again three days later and is alive. If we put our faith in Him alone, we have salvation.

Jonah was a picture or a "type" of Christ, as some would describe his story. He was in the belly of a whale for three days. He was spit out and then he preached. His message, not the man, saved people. Gentiles in Nineveh believed Jonah, though he performed not one miracle. How much more should those in Jesus' day believe Jesus was the Messiah! He performed miracles and was the greatest miracle of all because of His death, burial, and resurrection.

There's no need for a sign. Study historical accounts of Jesus. Believe in what the Bible says. Look at what He's done in the lives of others through the years. Many have died a martyr's death because of their belief in Him as the Son of Man. Folks, it takes more faith to not believe, than to believe. Please don't demand a sign. And please help those who want a sign to see that the greatest sign has already been performed. Live by faith today...

DAILY READING:

Deuteronomy 29:1-30:20; Luke 11:37-12:7
Psalm 78:1-31; Proverbs 12:19-20
Focal Passage: Luke 11:39-41

LIVING BY FAITH

JESUS WASN'T A FAN OF PAYING MORE ATTENTION TO THE OUTSIDE THAN THE INSIDE. And HE sure let folks know it, especially the religious teachers of the day. You know, those who major in rules and regulations without regard to the primary importance of the heart relationship with Christ. We still have those types today. We must remember our passage today too, so we don't slip into legalism. We don't do good things to look good in the sight of God and others. We do good things because our heart is being transformed and it comes more naturally.

The Pharisees were greedy. Greed displays a hard heart. These law abiders excelled in misplaced focus. An example is given right here in our passage today. They were trying to make Jesus feel bad about not washing His hands due to a ritual, and yet they couldn't care less about being generous. This is always a sign of the heart. Johnny Hunt says, "You're never more like Jesus than when you're giving." God wants us to look like Him more than the world. We must be careful not to get it backward. Love Him. Out of love for Him, you do right by His standards alone. They're in the Bible.

How we handle our possessions reveals major truths about our relationship with Christ. Do we tithe? We should. It's biblical to give a tithe to your local church. Do the percentages. Read the scriptures. There's nothing that has deleted this wonderful principle for a Christ-follower. Do you give offerings? That's above and beyond. What a sweet time to be able to bless ministries or people in need. Please don't miss this blessing. You will not believe how God will bless it. Try it. I double-dog dare you. Live by faith today...

DAILY READING:
Deuteronomy 31:1-32:27; Luke 12:8-34
Psalm 78:32-55; Proverbs 12:21-23
Focal Passage: Deuteronomy 31:7-8

LIVING BY FAITH

WHEN YOU HAVE THE OPPORTUNITY TO ENCOURAGE A LEADER IN FRONT OF HIS FOLLOWERS, DO SO. Do you realize what just happened? Moses was turning over to Joshua the responsibility to lead the children of Israel into the Promised Land. Technically, he didn't have to say a word. But he did. And he did it in front of everyone. He encouraged his protégé, Joshua, to take the helm and do so with great courage. He let him know the Lord would be by his side every step of the way. Everyone heard Moses encourage Joshua.

There may be a time soon when you have a chance to encourage a leader. Maybe it will be today or tomorrow? If not, it will come one day. Don't miss it! Be a blessing. Encourage them in some way. If possible, remind them of God's faithfulness, even when they face unforeseen challenges in the days ahead. Let them know God has providentially prepared them for this moment in their lives.

Those who lead have followers. Some of them may follow, appropriately. Some may not. Some may not realize how fortunate they are to have such a leader. If possible, tell them. If possible, remind them. Maybe they need to know the leader of the past was a blessing, but the leader of the present can be too. Sometimes people get stuck in the past. We all must press on with new leaders for new experiences. And when you can bless the leader in front of his followers, it makes a world of difference. Do it every chance you get. Wouldn't you want someone to do that for you?

When God calls someone to lead, He will not leave them. The Lord is with you and me as we accept various responsibilities that lie ahead. <u>Be strong and courageous</u>. Live by faith today...

APRIL 8

LIVING BY FAITH

I FIND THESE WORDS COMFORTING ON THE ANNIVERSARY OF MY DAD'S DEATH. I've lived longer now without my dad than with him. In some ways, it's hard to believe. Though dead, he still speaks. The reason is that he had a relationship with Christ and spoke the Word of God to me. Not just because he was my pastor growing up, but because he lived it outside the pulpit. He knew it would be my lifeblood for the entirety of my life on earth. He loved God and he loved people.

While writing this devotional during the current Coronavirus pandemic, I suddenly received a call from an elderly member. It was through an app I put on my phone several months ago due to international travel. I had almost forgotten I had it. Anyway, that's how she got in touch with me. Odd as it seems, I decided to answer even though I usually don't take calls during my study hours unless it's an emergency. Do you know why I took it? Exactly! Because I wanted to honor my dad this day. I thought, what would Big Harold do? He'd answer it. He was the greatest pastor ever! (I know, I may be a little prejudiced.) I'm so glad I took the call because I left the conversation encouraged by this sweet Godly lady.

The Lord had instructed Moses and Joshua to write down a song in this chapter in order for the people to remember their journey with God. This song warned them of the perils of idolatry and the blessings of obedience. God had been so merciful to them and they did not want to forget the lessons from their past. The song had four major divisions—each one vital.

These final words before Moses' death were essential to their future. He made sure they realized that the Word of God is the life of God's people. As believers, the Word communicates truth like no other as we walk this journey we call life. It is our life. It is active and sharp. Biblical application is our spiritual food. My dad understood and he made sure throughout life that I did, too. He wasn't perfect. Neither was Moses. Daddy reminded me of Moses in ways. But the one that stands out the most is that if he were giving a speech prior to his death like Moses did in front of Joshua and God's people, he'd likely say the same thing. God and His Word will always be with you. Live by faith today...

APRIL 9

Deuteronomy 33:1-29; Luke 13:1-21
Psalm 78:65-72; Proverbs 12:25
Focal Passage: Luke 13:1-5

LIVING BY FAITH

BIBLICAL REPENTANCE IS A MATTER OF LIFE AND DEATH.
Please do not underestimate the need to repent. It is necessary for salvation. It is necessary for spiritual growth for believers. So it's a matter of life. One of those reasons takes care of eternal life. The other takes care of abundant life. Have you repented—biblically? Are you repenting on a regular basis as a Christian? Life is brief and should be lived God's way. If not, the consequences are devastating.

Some people let Jesus know how wicked Pilate was. Maybe due to wanting Christ to say something about him? He instead took the opportunity to focus on the need for everyone to repent. Regardless of position or stature, repentance is necessary to be in a right relationship with God. Repentance is turning from sin and self to Jesus alone for salvation. It's a type of inner desire to turn from one's old wicked life to a new life in Christ. He cleans us up through the sanctification process here on earth. It cancels divine judgment and the terrible consequences of eternal life without trusting Jesus. And if a believer does not live in a state of repentance, he will have a temporal judgment which leads to negative consequences. In other words, we should keep short accounts as we spend time alone with Christ in prayer and Bible study. Talk with Him about your shortcomings and know He loves to hear your heart and blesses repentance in this way.

Easy believism is not biblical repentance. Head knowledge doesn't make one a believer. It is clear in scripture because the demons believed but didn't know Him personally. Don't be duped by the enemy or the world. Know Christ. Know His Word. Repent and live! Live by faith today...

DAILY READING:
Deuteronomy 34:1-Joshua 2:24; Luke 13:22-14:6
Psalm 79:1-13; Proverbs 12:26
Focal Passage: Joshua 1:5

LIVING BY FAITH

THE SAME GOD WHO WAS WITH YOUR MENTOR WILL BE
WITH YOU. Dr. Howard Hendricks once said a man should have three individuals
in his life: a Paul, a Barnabas, and a Timothy. He was explaining the value of having
an older mentor, a brother (one of similar age), and a younger man to invest in and
build up. As mentioned a few days ago, my dad died when I was twenty-six years
old. He was indeed my primary mentor. How would I make it without him? I was
just getting started in full-time ministry. I learned God would be with me. He gave
me a peace during the time of his death. He reassured me in the days following.
He still does.

After discovering no one would ever be like Moses, who knew the Lord face to
face and who God used to perform miraculous signs and wonders, Joshua received his
marching orders. Folks, we may have to follow a great person, but not Moses. But
our focal passage shows us God was going to be with his successor also. God didn't
want Joshua to be like Moses. He didn't need a Moses now. He needed a Joshua.
And Joshua was a fantastic leader and man of God. Please don't miss this!

When a mentor dies (and it may be a father, a father figure, or someone else God
placed in your life who influenced you), do not panic. Remember the charge given
to Joshua. Be strong and courageous. Why? Because God is and will be with you
all the days of your life. If not, it won't be because He moved. It will be because *you*
moved. Remain close to Jesus and He will be your primary source of encouragement.
He will also put others in your life along the way to help. No, they won't be like
the mentor who died. They will be used in different ways. And in the sovereignty
of God, you will be blessed. Others will be, too. It will be very similar to Joshua.
March on, my friend. That's what your mentor would want you to do. Live by
faith today...

DAILY READING:
Joshua 3:1-4:24; Luke 14:7-35
Psalm 80:1-19; Proverbs 12:27-28
Focal Passage: Luke 14:7-14

LIVING BY FAITH

DO NOT SEEK AN IMPORTANT POSITION, LET THE POSITION SEEK YOU. Those were the words of Dr. Ted Traylor many years ago. I was serving in my first pastorate and attending my first state convention of Florida Baptists. Several guys were running for President of the state convention, and I asked for Ted's advice on one particular guy. He shared his thoughts about who was running and mentioned that one of the leading candidates had a perception of seeking the position. He looked at me and in so many words said, *"Hal, it's always best to let a position seek you instead of you seeking a position."* I totally understood what he was saying. It actually sounded like advice my dad would have given me. I've noticed through the years that Ted has lived that way. He's been nominated for numerous important positions in our Southern Baptist Convention, as well as the Florida Baptist Convention. Someone always went to him for permission to nominate him, not the opposite.

The Pharisees were always exalting themselves. Jesus was teaching them, and others, the importance of humility. When we live with an eternal perspective, an earthly position of notoriety means absolutely nothing. (Most don't care and probably only your mom will remember.) Humility brings glory to God. That's the trophy we want as believers. But those who directly or indirectly attempt to bring recognition to themselves will lose in the end. In other words, that guy may win here, but he's a loser long-term. I think when we reach eternity, we may all be surprised at what was valuable. Let's regularly check ourselves to be sure we're not acting pharisaical.

What's an indication? How do we know if one is truly humble or if we are? Jesus tells us in the last few verses. Do we treat everyone with dignity? Who do we think of inviting to an important event? Is our first "go-to" the well-known person in our community or is it one of the "least" in our community? I think what Jesus was trying to teach and regularly exhibited was this: Do things for "the least of these" with no regard for recognition. If so, I think we're making progress toward genuine humility. Live by faith today…

DAILY READING:
Joshua 5:1-7:15; Luke 15:1-32
Psalm 81:1-16; Proverbs 13:1
Focal Passage: Luke 15:8-10

LIVING BY FAITH

TODAY IS A DAY THAT WILL GO DOWN IN HISTORY AS—THE CORONA EASTER. Never before in my lifetime or in the history of America have we not gathered together for worship on Easter Sunday. Some churches have had sunrise services for decades, as well as their regular worship service on Easter. Not today. Today the majority of churches are submitting to the authorities who have issued a quarantine. Though it's not ideal, most have gotten used to the idea. Adjustments have been made and more people will hear the gospel via social media than ever before. For this, I give praise to a sovereign God! May He do what only He can do. May history record this Easter as being like none other, besides the original!

With that being said, what if only one person comes to faith in Christ today? What if after all the advertising, all the money spent on media upgrades, all the hype, and all the expectations have gone through the roof, only one person is born again? According to our passage today, <u>it will be worth it and reason enough to celebrate</u>! The principle being taught by our Lord in this chapter is that God goes to great lengths to see salvation and restoration take place—great lengths! The woman found the lost coin and told her friends and neighbors to rejoice. And then we find the angels rejoice when just one person—one person—is born again. Wow, what a Savior! What a wonderful story! What a timely reminder!

I hope and pray many come to Christ today as I preach a message that I have literally entitled, *"The Corona Easter."* But if only one person puts their faith in Jesus Christ as a result of what we do online today with music, video testimonies, prayer, and the message—Hallelujah! Thank you Lord, for a gentle reminder for today. Thank you that this reminder works every day of our lives. May we be faithful to share the gospel message in the power of your Spirit today as we have divine appointments. Live by faith today...

DAILY READING:
Joshua 7:16-9:2; Luke 16:1-18
Psalm 82:1-8; Proverbs 13:2-3
Focal Passage: Joshua 8:1

LIVING BY FAITH

WHEN SOMEONE ON YOUR TEAM HURTS THE CAUSE OF CHRIST, GOD HAS A PLAN. The Israelites were defeated at Ai due to the sin of Achan. Joshua put the sentence of death on him and his children. They all were involved in sinful actions. It was in accordance with God's commands at the time. God is holy. Sin is serious. Achan willfully, intentionally, disobeyed a clear prohibition and was responsible for the deaths of thirty-six innocent men. It was all so he could enrich himself with a few trinkets. What a price to pay! As someone has said in the past, *"Sin will take you farther than you want to go, keep you longer than you want to stay, and cost you more than you want to pay."*

If you are a part of the family of God, someone will let you down. It happens. Sometimes it's us. (May this be a reminder that it doesn't need to be us.) WHEN someone in your church sins, it will hurt their immediate family. It will hurt the church family. It will hurt the family of God at large. Suffering will take place. Consequences will come sooner or later. God doesn't wink at sin. He never has and we're discovering that reality as we're reading the Bible through this year. If we have a relationship with Jesus, we are forgiven. And just like in the Old Testament, He is patient and gracious. But we must never forget He is just and merciful. He must punish sin.

The Lord tells Joshua to press on in spite of the hurt Achan caused. If you've ever been hurt by someone on the team, you get it. Joshua is told to not be afraid or discouraged. God promises victory and He keeps His promises. Joshua did move on and God did provide a glorious victory. He will do the same for you and me. Yes, it can be discouraging. You can even wonder what you may have done wrong. Examine your heart but move on. Jesus is Lord and we must let our relationship with Him be first. He has us here for a purpose and we can't allow someone to distract us. Time is short. God's got this. You've got this because He's got you. Move on and know the best is yet to come. Live by faith today...

APRIL 14

DAILY READING:
Joshua 9:3-10:43; Luke 16:19-17:10
Psalm 83:1-18; Proverbs 13:4
Focal Passage: Luke 16:19-31

LIVING BY FAITH

I PREACHED ON THIS PASSAGE THE FIRST TIME I EVER
PREACHED ON A SUNDAY MORNING. I was serving in my first full-time
position after graduating from seminary. I was the Youth and Activities Minister at
Daniel Memorial Baptist Church in Jackson, Mississippi. The Pastor was Dr. Byron
Malone. (He preached my ordination sermon and I preached his funeral message. I
loved him and will forever be grateful for the influence he had and continues to have
on my life.) Dr. Malone saw something in me I had not fully realized at the time.
He saw the potential of me one day transitioning to be a Senior Pastor. Without my
knowledge, he started preparing me. One way was to allow me to preach. He had
let me preach on a Sunday night and now I was preaching on a Sunday morning.
He let me select my text. I chose the one you just read. At the time, it had gripped
me for some reason. (It still does.) Jesus was speaking on the subject of hell. I was
realizing it really was a place for those who died without a relationship with Christ.
I believed it. My upbringing taught me about the doctrine of hell. I just had never
taken the time to think about it much. I was thinking about it then and I just
decided to preach on the subject. I've never forgotten it, not only for obvious reasons
but also because I lost my place once in the middle of the sermon. I drew a blank
and everyone knew it. I admitted it, chuckled along with everyone else, and God
graciously helped me find my place to continue.

I believe we find a number of realities in this passage. The doctrine of hell
is biblical. If someone dies without putting their faith in Christ alone for their
salvation, they will go to hell. God does not send someone to hell. There are no "do-
overs." There is a chasm which cannot be adjusted for anyone—*anyone*. Wealth does
not get one to heaven. Good works do not get one to heaven. Neither does being a
sorry rascal, nor being dirt poor, for that matter. One's faculties are intact in eternity.
The lost man in our text was now "praying" and now had a "burden" for lost people—
mainly his family members. I know, it's sad. And he could only cry out in torment
(great discomfort) every moment of every day because he could somehow visualize
them one day joining him. God lets us know the power of the Bible. Jesus let him
know God's Word was powerful enough to bring them to the saving knowledge of
Jesus Christ. Isn't that amazing? Absolutely! Live by faith today...

DAILY READING:

Joshua 11:1-12:24; Luke 17:11-37
Psalm 84:1-12; Proverbs 13:5-6
Focal Passage: Proverbs 13:5-6

LIVING BY FAITH

TODAY WE FOCUS ON WHAT COULD BE CALLED *THE BOOMERANG PASSAGE.* What does a boomerang do? You toss it and it comes back to you. And if you're not careful, it will hit you in the face. That's exactly what our focal passage is about today. If we are not real, authentic, straight shooters, we will pay some day. It may feel like there's been a "pass," but being fake is costly.

Do you loath lying? Good. That's probably because you believe Jesus is the way, the truth, and the life. And you walk closely with Him. Therefore, you cannot stand being around fakes for very long. Listen, Jesus had some harsh words for fakes in His day. The religious leaders of the day were fakes and He called them out—often. Now, be careful if you sense you have identified someone who is not a person of integrity. Check yourself. Be sure as you talk with God about this matter that you look in the mirror. Afterward, if you sense your hunch was true, that the person doesn't seem to be totally true, take action. Only God can let you know exactly what that means based on the situation. Chances are as you continue to pray for the person, you distance yourself for an indefinite period of time. It's hard. It hurts. But if it is indeed wickedness, you have no other choice.

What is righteousness, anyway? How can we know if we're walking closely with Jesus? Well, the fruit of the Spirit. Read about them. Examine each one closely. Our goal as a believer is the authentic bearing of the fruit of the Spirit. Listen, do we encourage others naturally? Do we look out for those who have little when no one is listening or watching? Or do we spend more time being critical of everything and everybody? Those are also things to consider. Let's be real. Authenticity is not just a word made popular in recent years

It's been around for thousands of years. When we're real, it comes back to us in a good way. If we are not, it also comes back—but not in a way we'd prefer. God speaks truth and He always keeps His Word. Live by faith today...

DAILY READING:
Joshua 13:1-14:15; Luke 18:1-17
Psalm 85:1-13; Proverbs 13:7-8
Focal Passage: Joshua 14:6-13

LIVING BY FAITH

THERE ARE TWO WAYS TO FINISH STRONG IN YOUR LATER YEARS OF LIFE. I think we could build a case for Joshua 13 and 14 being called *Encouraging Chapters for Old Folks*. Why? Because we find in Joshua 13, God describing Joshua as very old and still having work to do. Then we find his old buddy Caleb, reminding him of God's promise from way back. He was old, but still had his memory when it came to the things of God. Here we have two old Godly buddies still going strong. (If you think you're an old geezer today, this should put some spring in your step.)

Caleb followed his convictions. Not his preferences, his convictions. Convictions come from God by having a close relationship with Him. When Jesus becomes your primary source for all of life, you live on a path that brings glory to Him. It's a good path because He does not want to ruin your life or confuse you in any way. His ways are best, even if you don't understand them. The reason Caleb is described as one following God wholeheartedly is that he didn't separate his life into two categories. God wasn't a part of his life. God was his life. If you compartmentalize your walk with God, you are missing it and will not finish strong. No one retires from God. He is your life until death. Caleb was simply following God's will, even in his later years.

Caleb lived confidently. He was not being cocky here. He had God-confidence. Verse 12 from our focal passage says, *"the Lord helping me."* In other words, he was proclaiming that God would bless him because He said He would. And he was reassuring everyone it would ultimately be because of God being his source of strength. Older people need to live confidently because they're doing things in the strength of the Lord, not their own strength. Some don't have much strength. That's ok. God still has you here for a reason. Don't wane. Don't put your head down. Wake up and walk forward in God's strength. Be sure people see it's because you are a child of God and He still has you here for a reason. Live by faith today...

DAILY READING:
Joshua 15:1-63; Luke 18:18-43
Psalm 86:1-17; Proverbs 13:9-10
Focal Passage: Psalm 86

LIVING BY FAITH

DAVID—A MAN AFTER GOD'S OWN HEART—DEMONSTRATES HOW TO TALK WITH GOD. I say "Talk with God" because so often we just talk without listening to God. Remember that. Meditating on God's Word or His goodness is not strange. It's biblical. Don't allow some odd eastern mystic to cause you to miss out on a way to connect with God Almighty. Talk. Listen. Meditate. Take a walk in nature. Sing. Listen again. Read some more of His Word. Look closely at this passage today.

We should not be intimidated to pray to our heavenly Father. Just as we should come with awe and respect, we should not come hesitantly to pour out our heart to Him. David does pour out his heart. He appeals for help and makes sure his sins are laid bare. He reminds himself of God's character. God alone is the one true God who is like **no other.** David realizes the need for singular focus. A mind divided with other loyalties works against us. David talks with God about some ruthless people in his life. (Have you ever had ruthless people in your life? Live for Christ long enough and you will be able to identify them. It happens. Let it be a badge, not a burden.) And David talks about Moses and how God was available to him during all his life experiences. You see, God was available for David, too. He is available for you. He is available for me. That's who God is and why prayer is so vital to the life of a believer. Just open up your heart. Talk with Him. Share your great love with Him. Pray praises for His attributes which are like none other. It's going to be good and will bless you.

I thought about encouraging you to just read this entire Psalm aloud by yourself somewhere. As a matter of fact, I think I will. Please get alone somewhere and just read this prayer aloud. It'll do you good. It did me good. Follow the example of a man who had a heart for God. Talk with God. Live by faith today...

DAILY READING:
Joshua 16:1-18:28; Luke 19:1-27
Psalm 87:1-7; Proverbs 13:11
Focal Passage: Luke 19:1-10

LIVING BY FAITH

ZACCHAEUS WAS A WEE LITTLE MAN WITH SOME TALL
LESSONS. Every time I hear or read that name, the song begins in my head. I
was taught a children's song about Zacchaeus years ago that had a catchy jingle.
(Maybe you're already singing it?) It begins by calling him a wee little man. He was,
according to scripture. But we find some tall lessons in his biblical account.

God looks at the heart. He uses short people, tall people, large people, etc.
Never allow your size or looks to determine whether or not you can be used by God.
I mean, all you have to do is read the focal passage. What was pointed out about his
size ended up being to his advantage. Isn't that just like God? He constantly shows
us He will take what seems like a disadvantage and use it for His advantage. So, old
Zach was not a popular man. Not because of his height, but because of his heart.
He was a wretched sinner. He stole from folks and got away with it at the time. He
obviously stooped below his public status by climbing a tree. This was a good sign. It
indicates humility. He wanted to see this one who everyone was talking about. And
Jesus saw him. I love that! Jesus saw him. You see, Jesus sees people we may not see.
He selects people out of a crowd who may be "overlooked." Jesus invites Himself
to his house and Zacchaeus gladly welcomes Him into his home. It changed him.
Zacchaeus showed his heart change because he immediately started making plans to
make things right with people. He demonstrated genuine repentance.

The religious types in the passage did not like it. They were accusatory toward
Jesus once again. They were all about the law. Jesus was all about grace. They were
all about holy huddles. Jesus is all about opening up the huddle for hoodlums. He
came to heal sick people. Zach was sick. The religious people were sick. You are
sick. I am sick. We are sick in our sinfulness. We all must admit our sin, repent,
and believe on Jesus. That's why He came. And it changes our heart. Over time,
we should look a lot more like Christ than our fleshly selves. Spiritually speaking,
we should grow "taller" over the course of our life due to our relationship with Jesus.
That's where it starts—a relationship—just like it did with the wee little man. Live
by faith today...

DAILY READING:
Joshua 19:1-20:9; Luke 19:28-48
Psalm 88:1-18; Proverbs 13:12-14
Focal Passage: Luke 19:45-46

LIVING BY FAITH

WHEN A CHURCH HAS SO MUCH GOING ON THAT PRAYER IS SECONDARY—ADJUST. When I pastored Morrison Heights Baptist in Clinton, Mississippi, I had a lot going on and so did the church. I had a young wife and two children and was working on my doctorate. Morrison Heights was running about a thousand in attendance and we were not what Tom Rainer calls "the simple church." We had numerous ministries all through the week and were constantly considering adding to that number. We had a prayer ministry and a yearly prayer conference. That did not mean prayer was a top priority. It was helpful, no doubt. I cannot imagine where we would have been without it. But prayer did not permeate the church. It was secondary to all our activities.

Jesus let us know in our passage today that replacing prayer with activity is not good. Furthermore, He has no tolerance for "activity for profit." It's obvious the church back then had abandoned its primary calling. Jesus' Words—*"My house will be a house of prayer."*—leaves no room for discussion. Case closed. Prayer should permeate <u>everything</u>. It's a priority for God's church!

In the middle of all that was going on as a young pastor, a seminary buddy invited me to join him for a prayer conference. I immediately declined. Why? Because I had so much going on, of course! He persisted and because I had read the book *"Fresh Wind, Fresh Fire"* that was popular then, I went in spite of my busy schedule. Jim Cymbala wrote the book. His church, Brooklyn Tabernacle, was sponsoring the event. It was a game-changer for me and Morrison Heights. I came back with a renewed passion to make prayer a priority. I turned Wednesday nights into a **real** prayer meeting. Seriously, we prayed the entire time after opening up with scripture. Also, we had a prayer time during the Sunday morning services **every** week. As far as I'm concerned, it was the key turning point for my ministry there. Over time, God started doing what only He could do. Never, ever, replace prayer with activity. It will limit you and/or your church's Kingdom impact. Live by faith today…

DAILY READING:
Joshua 21:1-22:20; Luke 20:1-26
Psalm 89:1-13; Proverbs 13:15-16
Focal Passage: Joshua 22:5

LIVING BY FAITH

DON'T RELAX TOO MUCH. Life is full of ups and downs. It will always be this way on this side of heaven. When you have a good season, don't relax too much. Let me explain. I am not talking about vacation or recreation. Those are important to maintain balance. I am talking about when you have been on the mountaintop or you've had a fairly non-eventful time in your life. That is not the time to stay where you are in your relationship with God. He always wants us to pursue Him. It's not a bad thing. It's a good thing. It's actually a *very* good thing.

With land acquired and battles won, Joshua gives direction for the future. But he is very clear about how to enjoy the future. He did not want the people of Israel to forget God. He loved God and loved them. He recognized his responsibility to share a vision that would bring glory to God and protect them from drifting. Joshua wanted them to leave a spiritual heritage. D.A. Carson once said *"... the worst possible heritage to leave with children: high spiritual pretensions and low performance."*

What did you see in the verse today concerning how to accomplish this? I see love. It is what Jesus said when asked about the greatest commandment. He said to love God with all your heart, soul, and mind. When we genuinely love someone, we are loyal to them even when we don't understand them. We serve them to the best of our ability without regard for recognition. And we do these things knowing the person is depraved. God is perfect. It should be natural, but if we drift from holding fast to Him, it won't be. And He loves us way too much to let us continue going down the wrong path. Let's be reminded today, as Joshua reminded followers in his day—don't relax too much. Serve Him with all your heart and soul. Live by faith today...

DAILY READING:
Joshua 22:21-23:16; Luke 20:27-47
Psalm 89:14-37; Proverbs 13:17-19
Focal Passage: Joshua 23:9-11

LIVING BY FAITH

NEVER FOCUS ON THOSE AGAINST YOU WHEN YOU ARE FOLLOWING GOD'S WILL. Have you ever heard the saying, *"God plus one equals a majority?"* It is true, isn't it? But sometimes it's hard to live out. We have a tendency to allow those against us to be our focus, instead of the God who is for us. If we are living a faith-filled life, we will have opposition. God's ways often disrupt the understanding of others. They don't always get it. Maybe they do, but they don't want to "go there" themselves. Regardless, be careful not to allow those not happy about your direction in life or leadership to make you miserable.

Joshua was old. He knew his time on earth was limited. He let the people know God had done great things. Not him. God. So when God is fighting for us, we need not worry about the number of folks against us. No matter if it's a few or quite a few. When we are on God's team, running His plays, we win. The odds are always in our favor. Trust Him with what that looks like. You may not even totally grasp that reality until you reach heaven. Or it may be years from now. Those whom Joshua had led for so many years, and with so many victories, needed to keep their eyes on God. If not, they would be defeated because they kept looking over their shoulders at those against them.

I have been guilty of paying too much attention to my distractors. Not so much in friendships, but in leadership. Let me explain. As a Pastor, you will automatically have distractors along the way. Some don't like what you preach or how you preach. Some may not think you have a pastor's heart. And then some do not like your leadership style. It's too strong. It's too weak. Do you see where I'm going? Unless you sit in the Pastor's chair, you will never fully understand. I didn't. Now, there's a lot more good than bad in the life of a Pastor. But you can focus more on those not liking who you are or what you're doing. Sometimes I have confronted them. Sometimes I have not. Sometimes I have worried about them—even if it's a small number or just one person. Worry is a sin. In all these years, it's never been beneficial to focus on the ones against me. I've learned to try to make things right, if possible. If not, I've learned to move on in the grace of God, with those in favor of what God's doing. Trust me, it works out much better. Live by faith today…

DAILY READING:
Joshua 24:1-33; Luke 21:1-28
Psalm 89:38-52; Proverbs 13:20-23
Focal Passage: Proverbs 13:20

LIVING BY FAITH

DO YOU LOOK MORE LIKE YOUR MOM, DAD, OR CLOSE FRIEND? Most people who knew my mom say I favor her. But what I'm talking about here is not appearance. I'm talking about what this verse is speaking of. Whom do we look like internally? Whom do we act like? We likely act more like the person or persons we spend the most time with. Sure, parents have an influence. They have a huge influence on who we become. But so do peers. Parents need to be careful about letting their children run freely with whomever. It may cause long-term damage. The Bible even says bad company corrupts good character. The Bible also shows us that as we read about the Old Testament and the New Testament people.

Foolish people act foolishly. If we spend a lot of time with them, their foolishness will rub off on us. It's natural. So, let's say you are making a decision. It can be about something small or large. And let's say you ask your foolish friend whom you have been spending a lot of time with for advice. It's human nature to ask close friends their thoughts on decisions being made. They are unlikely to give you Godly advice. So, if you are presently spending too much time with those not walking closely with the Lord, you need to rethink whom you allow into your inner circle of friendships. And if you were influenced by foolish folks in years gone by, just remember it may take a little time to get that junk out of your head. Foolish friends may give you the green-light to go further into your foolish direction. Be careful!

Wise people act wisely. If we spend time with those who walk closely with God, they will rub off on us. Their actions will show up in our actions. Their words and even body language may show up. If they are a lot like Jesus, so be it. And if you are in need of Godly counsel, they are right there at your fingertips. Be wise. Find the wise ones. Pray for God to show you who they are. Ask if you can spend some time with them. They will make all the difference in the world in who you turn out to be. And who you turn out to be will impact your family, friends, church, and colleagues. Wise people will help you make wise decisions, and you will be more likely to be accused of looking like the person God intended you to look like all along. Live by faith today...

DAILY READING:

Judges 1:1-2:9; Luke 21:29-22:13
Psalm 90:1-91:16; Proverbs 13:24-25
Focal Passage: Proverbs 13:24

LIVING BY FAITH

IF YOU ALLOW YOUR CHILD TO BE KING, GOD'S KINGDOM WILL SUFFER. That's a strong statement, isn't it? So in this verse, the writer is not promoting physical abuse. It is not some sort of a license to treat your child like a punching bag. Quite the opposite. A rod refers to discipline that is reasonable for the behavior exhibited. It promotes good behavior for the future. To wink at the child as if he was cute is a wink toward evil. To let things go will be costly. It doesn't matter how busy you are or how weak your parents were with behavior modification. Children need discipline that will help alter their poor behavior and produce good behavior. Now, as the child grows into teen years, the punishment will look different. But there still need to be consequences while the child is under our roof.

If you take your child to church, that's good. If you do devotionals in the home, that's good. If you listen to Christian music in the home on a regular basis, that's good. All of these practices are good and I've not mentioned others. But if you do these things without properly disciplining your child or children, you are setting them up for failure as adults. I've watched a lot more children who were loved enough by their folks and were disciplined succeed in life than the opposite. Sure, it's no guarantee. But it's God's way for building His Kingdom purposes. There is a natural order of alignment under authority. If it's broken, the home will be broken. Be strong parents. God will give you what you need one day at a time. And your child will love you for it in the long run. Why? Because you demonstrated love God's way. Allowing children to be king is the popular way—not the biblical way. It shows weakness or downright laziness on the parent's part.

If your child runs with other children who have parents who allow their kids to run amok, it will constantly create turmoil in your home. What am I getting at? Some of this is unavoidable and that's ok because we need to be salt and light. But I want to encourage you to position your child to be around other like-minded families. The ideal place to find these is in a local church. Please make sure your church family is a high priority for your own family. You will not regret it! Some of my greatest memories from growing up occurred because of the people and ministries of the churches that helped raise me. Live by faith today...

DAILY READING:
Judges 2:10-3:31; Luke 22:14-34
Psalm 92:1-93:5; Proverbs 14:1-2
Focal Passage: Judges 3:31

LIVING BY FAITH

SHAMGAR WENT FAR AND SO CAN YOU. It was a Sunday night. I was Student Pastor at Morrison Heights Baptist, in Clinton, Mississippi. My pastor, Dr. Ken Alford, asked me to preach for the evening service. I selected this passage in the Old Testament. I have always gravitated toward scriptures that churchgoers may have never stopped long enough to consider before. Also, I had recently read a devotional by one of my favorite authors, Chuck Swindoll, about Shamgar. So, I stood up to preach with my Bible in one hand and a homemade ox goad in the other, that I pulled out as a surprise visual at just the right time. Since that evening, I have preached on this passage, and Judges 5:6 many times, in many churches over the years. I also discovered numerous others had written or preached on Shamgar as well. The ones who further influenced my understanding of this powerful passage were E.V. Hill, Bob Pitman, and Jay Strack.

God desired the Israelites to let Him be boss, King, Lord of their lives, during this era of biblical history. For about three hundred years or so, when they would start doing what was right in *their* own eyes, they'd cry out to God for help. He would graciously appoint a judge (leader) to rise up and rescue them. Sometimes it was a "nobody" from "nowhere." Shamgar fit that description. I believe our witness can travel far if we follow the example of old Shamgar. 1. God did what Shamgar could not do. He could not follow a great leader like Ehud, the second judge, that accomplished so much good. Furthermore, his dad was evidently a well-known leader in his region. No, he had to totally depend on God. That's where you and I need to always be. 2. Shamgar did what he could not do with a stick he knew how to use. He used an ox goad. Shamgar turned his ordinary cattle prod into a powerful weapon. Don't think you have to be someone you're not to accomplish God's will. He will redeem your past experiences and abilities for building His Kingdom. Little is much in the hands of God. 3. He used Shamgar during a difficult time. We will read in Chapter 5, verse 6, that people did not travel the main highways. It was due to the reality that being a God-honoring person was not popular. (Sound familiar?) God always raises people up to help others during difficult times. Perhaps you're that person for now. Live by faith today...

DAILY READING:
Judges 4:1-5:31; Luke 22:35-53
Psalm 94:1-23; Proverbs 14:3-4
Focal Passage: Luke 22:47-51

LIVING BY FAITH

I THINK I WOULD HAVE WANTED TO CHOP HIS EAR OFF, TOO. The Gospel of John's account lets us know the master swordsman was none other than, Peter. He was something else, wasn't he? Do you see yourself in Simon Peter sometimes? I do. That can be good and bad. Depends on what passage you're reading about him. In today's passage, it's not good. Admirable? Perhaps. Would I have maybe done it? Probably. Emotions can be used for good and bad. Timing is everything! Peter chose the wrong time to demonstrate that he was a "black belt" in swinging a sword.

Really, why did he do this? Maybe it was because he was still waking up from a nap. Jesus had just called him and other disciples out for sleeping during a time they needed to be praying. Sometimes it takes me a while to wake up after taking a nap. Maybe it was because he was mad at Judas for betraying Jesus? I mean, aren't you upset when you discover a "Judas" in your circle of friends? There's a temptation for me to punch the person's lights out. Maybe it was because he thought he was doing the right thing? Or maybe it really was because he allowed his emotions to take over? He reacted instead of acting like Jesus would want him to act in such a moment. We can only conjecture about the "why." Let's stop here.

But we can learn what to do when Jesus is wronged. It may be a modern-day Judas. It may be someone uses His name in vain. It may be someone says something totally false about our Lord. It could be any number of things. What we can't do is "take a swing." As hard as it is, we just need to remember the words of Jesus in our text, *"No more of this!"* Now, Jesus can heal our missteps. I mean, He put the fella's ear back on his head. And He can provide appropriate healing to our overreactions or mishandling of critical situations while living the Christian life. But the more we can keep from making bad things worse, the better. Let's try to keep our sword in our sheath next time. It will keep us from having to clean up a mess. Live by faith today…

DAILY READING:

Judges 6:1-40; Luke 22:54-23:12
Psalm 95:1-96:13; Proverbs 14:5-6
Focal Passage: Judges 6:15-18

LIVING BY FAITH

IS IT OK TO ASK FOR A SIGN WHEN SEEKING TO UNDERSTAND GOD'S WILL? Gideon did. And he was a judge of Israel. Maybe he was like the man in the gospel of Mark who told Jesus, *"I do believe help my unbelief."* I don't really know for sure. He was obviously insecure about his family background. He said his clan was weak. God knew his family background. Check, not a problem with God! Sometimes we get in our own way because of putting too much emphasis on our family background. (That can go either way, my friend.) So, he wanted a sign. God gave him one. As a matter of fact, God continued to reassure him that He would be with him every step of the way. And He was.

I've certainly asked for a few signs in my life when making big decisions. God hasn't struck me down with a bolt of lightning yet. God is patient. Think about what we learned about Moses. He was apprehensive when God appeared to him in a burning bush. It's ok. Thank God we serve a very patient Lord! He loves us enough to give us time to "get it" or sometimes learn from our lack of understanding. That's who He is. That's who He will always be.

I believe the key to knowing God's will is walking closely with Him. Abide in Him and you will more likely understand God's will when making big decisions. He speaks primarily through prayer, the Bible, wise counsel, reflecting on experiences from our past, and occasionally even circumstances. None of us should try to determine what he wants us to do based solely on some kind of "test" we may come up with. This is dangerous. It omits faith. And faith is what salvation and our walk is based on. So be careful. Just know when you walk in an intimate relationship with Jesus, you can talk. He wants to hear your heart. He knows who you are and what your reservations may be. Just take a walk and talk. He loves that! And so, will you. Live by faith today...

APRIL 27

DAILY READING:
Judges 7:1-8:17; Luke 23:13-43
Psalm 97:1-98:9; Proverbs 14:7-8
Focal Passage: Judges 7:1-8

LIVING BY FAITH

SOMETIMES LESS IS MORE. Gideon was going to battle. We'd assume he was probably wishing he had more warriors to defeat the enemy, but not so. God told him to *reduce* the number. Isn't that just like God? His ways are just not our ways. We think one way. He thinks another. We can't imagine it being successful. He knows what success looks like. It's amazing being on God's team. So God continues to ask Gideon to reduce his numbers so he can be fully prepared for the battle before him. No glory should go to men. All glory should go to God. Reducing the number would certainly cause everyone to know—only God could have provided the victory!

The final test in discovering who would stay on the team was interesting. Those who lapped water from their hands demonstrated awareness, unlike those who just got on their knees and drank from the spring. Being aware, alert, and always ready to go to battle is an amazing sign of a true warrior. War is chaotic. People with character soar in the midst of chaos. That's who you want when fighting a battle. Especially fighting a battle against the enemy of God.

Maybe you think because your budget at work is less than most, you can't be as effective. Maybe your family is smaller than your neighbor's family, so, you can't make as big of a difference. Maybe you live in a small community, so, surely you will never measure up to those who live in the city. Do you see where I'm going with this? Sure you do. Less is more with God's people. Do not sell yourself short. God does not have the limitations we have. And our limitations are oftentimes what He uses to show us how awesome He is. Gideon is a great example of a leader who listened to God—even when it didn't make sense to him. Let's do the same. Live by faith today...

DAILY READING:
Judges 8:18-9:21; Luke 23:44-24:12
Psalm 99:1-9; Proverbs 14:9-10
Focal Passage: Judges 8:22-23

LIVING BY FAITH

STAY IN YOUR LANE OR YOU MAY GET RUN OVER. Gideon knew what God had called him to do. He had soared with his strengths and did not allow pride to take over. This is always a good thing. It is also not easy. He had experienced great success, so why wouldn't he want to be a king now? It was not his "lane." The road God had taken him down was the direction God wanted him to go. If he had listened to others, the road would not have been God's road. It would have caused a wreck. Have you ever looked up the definition of wreck? It is not good. It hurts. Gideon once again demonstrates how a leader must not allow victories to cause him to think he is something he is not. Once God clearly shows you what lane you are to be in, stay put.

One day you may be tempted to do something in your career that doesn't really fit you. Let me put it this way: it may fit, but it's not the best fit. In other words, it's not what God has called you to do. I believe there are some things I could do in my life, but it would not be in my best interest (or others) because it's not what God has called me to do. When I first went to college, I majored in PE. I wanted to be a coach. To this day, I think I could have done that. But I know God didn't call me to be a coach. A few times in my adult life I have had the opportunity to explore other professions in ministry besides being a Pastor. I actually did okay and enjoyed certain aspects of the jobs. But I was not in my lane and I knew it. If I had stayed in those positions for a long period of time it would have not only hurt me, it would have hurt others.

NFL Hall of Fame quarterback Peyton Manning has been asked about making a run for President of the United States one day. Numerous influential voices have encouraged him to do so. So far, he has declined a run for the Presidency. Just because he ran a great offense in football does not mean he could run a great country as President. Stay in your lane Peyton, unless the one voice that matters says differently. Be careful whom you listen to. The voice of God is **the one** to listen to above all others. Live by faith today...

DAILY READING:
Judges 9:22-10:18; Luke 24:13-53
Psalm 100:1-5; Proverbs 14:11-12
Focal Passage: Psalm 100

LIVING BY FAITH

MY SECOND GRADE TEACHER HAD US MEMORIZE THIS PASSAGE. Every time I read this portion of scripture, I not only think about the theme of praise, I think of my second-grade teacher, Mrs. Vashti Everett. She taught second graders in the Kosciusko, Mississippi public school system for decades. Her husband Ray was an elementary school principal. They never had any children of their own. We were their children and they loved us. Don't get me wrong, they were not pushovers. But I think we all knew they loved us and wanted what was best for us in the course of our lifetime. I certainly did. They were wonderful folks who impacted many, many lives, for not only educational purposes but Kingdom purposes. Hence why Mrs. Everett had us memorize this passage.

I wonder why she chose this passage. Out of the entire Bible, she selected this one Psalm for her little second graders to commit to memory. Some of us went to church. Some did not. She knew that. I'm thinking it may be because of the following reasons…

- Boys and girls, your attitude will impact your entire life. Well, it's true, isn't it? I've been around people who are glad and some who are sad. Now, I'm not talking about the reality of human nature. We have emotions and sometimes we are glad and sometimes we are sad. I'm talking about a pattern of life. Sad people who are mostly sad can make me sad. Glad people who have a posture of gladness rub off on me as well—in a good way.

- Boys and girls, accept that your one and only creator is good and loving. Can you imagine if from childhood we recognized that God made us, and He would never intentionally hurt us? Stuff happens because we live in a depraved world and are depraved. But don't ever, ever forget the core of who your creator is.

- Boys and girls, acknowledge that God's faithfulness will carry you, just as it has for generations before you, and will continue for those after you. You may be unfaithful, but He is not. He's not going away in your lifetime. Remember that—always.

Live by faith today…

DAILY READING:
Judges 11:1-12:15; John 1:1-28
Psalm 101:1-8; Proverbs 14:13-14
Focal Passage: John 1:27

LIVING BY FAITH

THE HIGHER YOU GO, THE LOWER YOU MUST STOOP. When I was playing ball growing up, I was taught to "stay low." I was told to stay low while running with the football. Don't stand straight up. While playing baseball, I was taught to stay low while fielding a grounder. And in basketball, you defend your opponent by bending your knees and keeping your hands up. Staying low obviously had a part in being victorious when playing ball. The same can be said spiritually.

John the Baptist was "the man." You read the entire chapter today, God sent him—no one else—to prepare the way for Jesus. Jesus was the Word. He was fully God and fully man. John was not God. John was man, sent by God. And he did a phenomenal job! Jesus said there was no one else like him born of a woman. Can you imagine? Can you imagine Jesus saying *you are the best man ever?* But the more John did for the Kingdom, the lower he went. Nothing seemed to go to his head. He did not allow pride to overtake him. We've read enough scripture to know that's not always the case with God's appointed leaders. We cannot miss the key to starting and finishing strong in our Christian life. Stay low!

Untying the sandals of someone in Jesus's day was the job of a slave. Think about it. The person had been walking on dusty, dirty, roads all day long. To have the job of untying his sandals was extremely menial. John the Baptist says even he doesn't qualify to untie the sandals of "the one who comes." He was talking about none other than Jesus. He was letting them know he was a mere man. He was letting them know they hadn't seen anything yet! He was letting them know he was simply the forerunner. He was letting them know The King was on the way and they needed to prepare themselves to bow the knee. Like John the Baptist, the more useful we are for Jesus, the more we stoop in being a slave to Him. It should never cause us to be prideful, but humbled. Therefore, we lay prostrate in total surrender that He would use us at all, thanking Him, not exalting self. Stay low, my friends. Live by faith today…

LIVING BY FAITH

SAMSON SHOWS HIS HAND FROM THE VERY BEGINNING OF HIS ADULT LIFE. Samson is a well-known judge of Israel. We know him to be physically strong. That does not mean he didn't have weaknesses. He did. I heard someone say years ago that he was a he-man with a she-weakness.

Yes, he was "set aside" from the start of his life. A Nazarite vow placed upon him from an angel of the Lord before birth meant he was set apart for God. His parents willingly accepted their role because they sought to please God. But he made choices that were costly. Even though the spirit of the Lord was upon him, he often allowed his weaknesses to rule his decisions. It cost him dearly as time went on.

Samson decided he wanted to marry a lady who was not a part of God's people. The Lord had warned His people not to intermarry with the surrounding nations because they didn't worship the one true God. A couple unequally yoked will run into multiple difficulties from the moment they say "I do." So Samson thought he knew what was best for him. Evidently, no one could tell him, what to do with his life. Maybe his power over man physically caused him to think he had power over man spiritually. I know this, if I had **told** my father what to do, it would not have turned out well. Perhaps Samson's parents raised him in the strict instructions of the vow, but for some reason omitted disciplining him as a child. It's fascinating, isn't it? It's sad, too.

Sure, he had a she-weakness. But it was deeper. He shows us he didn't respect authority. If we miss that lesson early on, it will hurt us from then on—meaning for our entire lives. Respect authority. You are set aside to live for God. Make choices which please Him. You will fulfill your purpose and finish strong. Live by faith today...

DAILY READING:

Judges 15:1-16:31; John 2:1-25
Psalm 103:1-22; Proverbs 14:17-19
Focal Passage: Judges 16:20

LIVING BY FAITH

THIS HAS TO BE ONE OF THE SADDEST VERSES IN THE BIBLE.
Samson had drifted so far from God that he allowed his relationship with Delilah
to be more important than his relationship with God. He let her take priority over
his commitments to the Lord. It cost him dearly! It cost others dearly! This is a
reminder that **no** human relationship is more important than your relationship with
the Lord. None. It doesn't matter how close you are to a person. No one
trumps God!

The phrase *"He did not know that the Lord had left him,"* is so sad. I mean, he had
drifted so far away from God that he missed the fact that God could no longer bless
him. He was resting on past victories. That's always a danger in spiritual leadership.
Just because God has blessed a ministry in the past doesn't necessarily mean He will
in the future. Sometimes the minister, for example, may drift from God. He begins
to think he was the reason it was successful. Yikes! Not good! It doesn't work that
way and God will have His say one day. Pride in accomplishments and allowing the
wrong people to get too close to us will bring disaster.

It is heartbreaking when someone you deeply love dies. You grieve and it's
normal. The thought of moving so far away from God, who loves us more than
anyone ever will, is also heartbreaking. We should grieve if we've allowed someone or
something to take precedence over our relationship with God. If so, turn from your
sin to Jesus. He never moved. He's been waiting for your return with open arms.
And if this is you, don't forget what it was like during the season you drifted away
from your close walk with Him. If not, you may not even realize it before it costs you
again. Live by faith today...

LIVING BY FAITH

THERE IS A REASON THIS IS LIKELY THE MOST WELL KNOWN BIBLE VERSE IN THE WORLD. It is the gospel of Jesus Christ in a nutshell. God is love. His love is not some type of sentimental love as if to say— *"Oh, you poor little people down there on earth."* Oh no, it's much more than that. His overwhelming love for us caused Him to take action. He gave His ONE AND ONLY SON to be our redeemer. Jesus was the one who willingly died for our sins. He was and is our substitute. It was our sin, not His. He was perfect in every way. It's faith. It's faith in Jesus alone. We must remember Jesus was explaining the way of salvation to a very good person—Nicodemus. It is not head knowledge. It is not good works. It is putting faith in the finished work of Jesus. Jesus was the perfect son of God. He willingly died on a cross for our sins. He rose again on the third day. If we believe by faith, He becomes our personal savior—our redeemer. He is our personal sin-bearer. He removes the divine judgment of our sin. He provides—freely—eternal life here and after death on earth. Yes, this verse is the foundation for being born again.

I learned this verse at a young age for a reason. My Sunday School teachers taught me this verse. My parents and family reinforced it. I've heard the great evangelist, Billy Graham, preach on this verse numerous times. I have studied this verse in seminary. I have preached on this verse and written about this verse before this moment. I've seen people hold up signs at athletic events with this verse referenced. Back years ago, a guy with a colorful afro wig would appear in random places all over the world with a sign that read—John 3:16. Tim Tebow used to use the reference as eye-black when he played college football for the Florida Gators. I'm telling you, it is the most well-known Bible verse in all the world and likely always will be until the Lord returns.

Do you have it memorized yet? If not, please do. It will serve you well throughout your entire Christian life. If you do have it memorized, thank God for the one who encouraged you to do so. And share it at every opportunity God gives you, for His glory. There's a reason it is used all over the world. Live by faith today...

LIVING BY FAITH

MERE TALK IS COSTLY. Have you ever heard the expression that God gave us two ears and one mouth for a reason? You probably have. If not, you have now. There's a lot of truth there. This verse backs it up. Actually, this verse (and others like it) was around long before the expression. I suspect the one that coined the expression was familiar with the Bible.

Proverbs is wisdom literature. God wants us to listen more than talk. Now, don't get me wrong, I know there is a time to speak. Ecclesiastes tells us this. Some people are even called to speak. It's the way they make their living, in essence. But wisdom says we should listen more than talk as a pattern of life.

Working hard pays off. When a person works hard at what they should be working at, God blesses. I'm not talking about staying busy. "Work smarter, not harder" has some validity to it. Work hard on the right things to accomplish the most every day. And mere talk will cost you every time. To talk about work, talk about current issues, talk about whatever, will not only cost you financially, it will cost your usefulness for Kingdom purposes. That, my friend, is serious. To waste any portion of our life because we talk more than produce shows a lack of integrity. Biblical ethics is valuable. This verse is an example. Numerous biblical characters demonstrated the value of hard work.

Talking has its place. Let's ask God to help us know when to talk and when to keep our mouth shut. Let's not be accused of being lazy. It doesn't work out well for anyone in the end. Live by faith today...

LIVING BY FAITH

THIS PASSAGE IS MORE THAN A SCRIPTURE READING FOR A MARRIAGE CEREMONY. That would be enough. And I have read it numerous times through the years while conducting weddings. It fits. Just read it slowly and think about the commitment that goes into a marriage and how these verses display the commitment that needs to go into the relationship long past the wedding day. But it's not typical to explain the entire background or go into more detail while reading it during a ceremony. So, let's dig a little deeper.

Our reading before these "wedding ceremony words" lets us know that Ruth was Naomi's daughter-in-law. After her son died, Naomi encouraged Ruth to go home so she could remarry. What Naomi was demonstrating was unselfishness. She was showing her true love and friendship. She was setting an example of loyalty. And though she didn't have to do so, Ruth was showing loyalty, too. She could have left her mother-in-law. She didn't. She remained with her and God greatly blessed the decision.

There is so much here in this passage. I want to focus on loyalty. We show true loyalty to Jesus when we live for Him day in and day out. When others may speak of Him casually, or as long as it doesn't make them look "foolish" in front of their peers, the loyal one doesn't hesitate to claim allegiance. Those disloyal to Christ may not claim to even know Jesus when the pressure is on in some way. (Think of the story of Peter denying Christ three times.) Loyalty to Jesus spills over in our relationships with others. It's natural. We should automatically be loyal to family and friends, for example. This does not mean we approve of a sinful lifestyle. As a matter of fact, if we're true friends, we'll be loving and appropriately confront friends about a lifestyle which will hurt them and their family in the long run. It also doesn't mean we always agree with them on various, insignificant matters. But it does mean we stand by them through celebrations and criticisms. I appreciate loyal friends and I want to be one. Don't you? Be a loyal friend. Don't be petty. Love Jesus and love people. Our world needs more people like Naomi and Ruth. The blessings long term may shock you in the long run. Live by faith today...

LIVING BY FAITH

DO NOT BE SURPRISED IF GOD REASSURES YOU THROUGH A MESSENGER. God reassures Ruth through Boaz. She just "happened" to run into him as she was doing life. Isn't it just like God to send a random person to reassure you that you are doing the right thing? That's exactly what happened here! This is called God's providence. Boaz reassured Ruth that she was reaping the blessings of kindness to her mother-in-law. Furthermore, she was informed that her decision to do what was right would bring blessing upon blessing. Those wings talked about are God's wings! God is our refuge and He protects us under His wings like a bird protecting her young.

Are you following God's path right now? Or are you compartmentalizing your relationship with God? Meaning you are basically saying, "God, you got parts of my life, but let me have this one?" You get what I'm saying? Jesus is Lord. He is King. He wants to take over our life, not just have a portion of our life. When we are sheltering under His wings, He's got us no matter what we have before us. It may look bad, based on your circumstances or what you've envisioned. Be careful! Faith doesn't operate like that. Trust Jesus with your obedience no matter what it looks like today. He will not leave you hanging! He won't! He is not like that!

Pay attention to who God brings to reassure you today, or tomorrow, or the next day. It may be someone you know. It may be a random person. For example, just yesterday I received a random FaceTime call. I usually don't answer. I did because I thought the area code was from my hometown. (A senior moment, I guess. Ha!) It was from a Godly older man who I greatly respect. God used him at just the right time. It was what some would call a "God wink." It was indeed. I got off the FaceTime call and thought, THANK YOU God! That was You, through him. So, when it happens, because it will if you are on God's path, don't be surprised. Just be thankful and don't forget to thank God. Live by faith today...

LIVING BY FAITH

WHY DO SOME PREACHER'S KIDS TURN OUT TO BE EVIL? Eli was a priest. His two sons, Hophni and Phinehas, were evil. They showed contempt for God's offerings. A priestly tribe doesn't automatically guarantee Godly behavior. Does this surprise you? Not if you've lived long enough. Not if you've been involved in church long enough. Not if you've heard enough jokes told around church folks about wild preacher's kids. They have a reputation and it's not necessarily good. Sometimes it's justified and sometimes it's not. In this passage, it's justified.

Some scholars believe that if you read the story in its entirety, Eli "winked" at his boys' behavior. You know, just sort of slapped their hands. Maybe so. Maybe some preacher's kids get away with more than they should because their parents feel sorry for them. Perhaps they think they receive such a hard time from friends and others that they give them great liberty at home. Regardless of why some preacher's kids turn out to be "bad eggs," there's no excuse for a pattern of evil behavior any more than there is for other children. Sure, it can be a challenge to grow up in a pastor's home. But the good far outweighs the bad in most scenarios. I know. I am a preacher's kid. So was my dad. And I had a few kids myself. Friend, it is a blessing beyond anything I could ever attempt to describe!

I know I sure wasn't the perfect preacher's kid. Neither were my kids. But some rebel and stay rebellious as adults. Eli's boys were adults in religious work too, but they still lived rebelliously. Preacher's kids grow up and have a choice. They can love God and live for Him, or they can hate God by living a consistent lifestyle of sin. If so, blaming it on being a preacher's kid is ridiculous. (If you know one who needs to read this, please share it with them.) Everybody has a hard time in life. I'm going to say something I often want to say to preacher's kids who seem to think they get a "pass" for certain privileges or misbehavior… stop it! You should be ashamed of yourself! You and I should be a lot better than we are with the multiple blessings of growing up in a pastor's home. And shame on me for not being a better person due to my Godly parents and church family who helped raise me. And if your dad was some sort of a fake because he was one guy in the pulpit and another at home, I'm very sorry. But not everyone in the church you grew up in was like that. And they often took care of you, taught you, and loved you unconditionally. So, move on. Live by faith today…

LIVING BY FAITH

I KNEW THE NAME ICHABOD WASN'T GOOD, BUT NEVER FULLY UNDERSTOOD WHY. As a young minister I would occasionally hear someone say something like, *"Yes, I'm afraid God has written 'ICHABOD' across that church."* Now, I knew they weren't saying the church was having a revival and God was blessing. Just the opposite. I knew they were saying that the church, for various negative reasons, was going to suffer consequences for disobedience. It was just one of those phrases you hear in ministry. I would usually just shrug my shoulders and move on. I've always tried to be careful about talking negatively about God's church. Every church is God's church. Some think it's the Pastor's church. NO! Some think it's the deacons' church. Not so much. Some think it's the founding fathers' church. Not at all. No, a true New Testament church is God's church. Hence, the problem at hand...

Ichabod means the glory of God had departed from Israel. The glory of God left the tabernacle with the ark because the Israelites had defamed God's glory. You read the scriptures leading up to our focal passage today. What had happened was a disgrace. And once again, we see God does not honor disregard for His great name. He can't! He won't! It's costly! It still is today. To pretend to be all religious and knowingly disobey God produces major negative consequences. It may not happen immediately. But it will happen in time.

So, if you hear that word from now on, you have a better understanding. We don't want that word associated with our church. We don't want that word associated with our name. We just don't want that name anywhere around us. At least, I don't. But understand this, more people are being named this today than ever before. Why? It may be because it's just more popular. It may be people don't know the biblical background on this Ichabod. It may be they haven't seen the movie that portrays the character Ichabod Crane in a negative way. It may be because fewer and fewer people fear God. Fear God. Love people—even those named Ichabod. And realize God can turn a mess into a message. Live by faith today...

LIVING BY FAITH

HURRY HURTS. Think about it. I have a tendency to be in a hurry. I move at a fast pace for some reason. It's not a good attribute. Hurry just seems to always have a negative result. I like to be prompt. I don't like to waste time in useless meetings. I want to maximize every day. But hurrying just hurts. It can hurt relationships, for example. Jesus never hurried. Yet, He touched so many lives in such a short period of time. This is proof we don't have to always hurry up… it hurts more than helps.

The Psalmist points out that Israel had sinned, just like in the past. God was faithful, once again, to provide. They would sing praises, then they'd hurry past His grace to live life on their own. They weren't patient. It's as if they'd quickly forget how good He was, and that life has challenges. When the challenges came, they'd often take things into their own hands and suffer the consequences. Ever done that? (Yeah, me too.) It always hurts to do things our way instead of seeking God and waiting to hear from Him. That does not mean you don't take the next logical step. Our passage today is saying in essence: don't forget what God has done in the past, and wait for Him to give you a word.

Don't hurry through your devotional time. Don't hurry through the crowd of friends and family. Don't hurry your time of raising your children. Don't hurry down the road and get a ticket. Don't hurry your workout. Don't hurry through your meal and table time with your family. Don't hurry your work and make it sloppy.

Got it? Good! Now, hurry and do it! Live by faith today…

LIVING BY FAITH

LOOKING FOR DONKEYS MAY LEAD TO A WORD FROM GOD.
Israel wanted a king like all the other nations. God acquiesced, with the people knowing exactly what that would entail. After being fully informed, the search began. Samuel was appointed by God to find the man. He found him. The man, Saul, was out looking for his father's lost donkeys. He was obeying his dad and while doing so, God spoke to him through his prophet. Samuel let him know what was in store for him. Saul was shocked but was willing to listen to the message.

Want to know God's specific will for your life? Just do what you know His will is for your life. God will speak to you along the way. Don't miss it! Saul was obeying his parents. We know from the Bible that it's God's will for children to obey their parents. So, while doing life, God provided His specific will for Saul's life. It was a major divine appointment!

Sometimes I think we make it too hard. We can get all uptight about what God's will is for our lives. Where do we go to school? Who do we marry? Should I take that job? Listen, all of these are major decisions. We should pray, read the Bible, seek Godly counsel, and do what we know is God's will all the while. If so, God will let us know in time His specific will for our individual lives. You may not look for donkeys today or tomorrow, but always be heads-up for a message from God. He speaks in and through the most unique ways. Yes, even in today's world! Live by faith today...

DAILY READING:
1 Samuel 10:1-11:15; John 6:43-71
Psalm 107:1-43; Proverbs 15:1-3
Focal Passage: Proverbs 15:1

LIVING BY FAITH

IT TAKES HUMILITY TO NOT RESPOND HARSHLY WHEN SOMEONE SPEAKS HARSHLY. Did you get that? Life brings hurt. It just does. We live in a sinful world. We are sinners in need of a savior. His name is Jesus. He alone helps us know how to live. He begins to do a work in the life of believers to help us be more like Him. Ultimately, only He can help us know how to not respond to hurtful words. A relationship with Christ brings about humility. We humble ourselves under the lordship of Christ and allow Him to rule. He keeps us from saying what we want to say in the flesh when hurt by the words of other people.

None of us like it when people speak harshly to us. Even if we may deserve it in some way, it's not enjoyable. There's a way to be confronted and led without being mean-spirited. I believe the writer here is talking about someone being rude or ugly with their words. It may be a family member. It may be a colleague at work. It can even be a friend. Regardless, the Bible clearly states that we are to be the bigger person. We are to take the high road. If not, the conversation will go south quickly. It will be worse than it already is. Humility is the key. We don't have to win the argument. We don't have to put the person in their place. Folks, this is hard for me. The natural me wants to respond when someone says something inappropriate or something I perceive as inappropriate. When I have, it has never turned out good. When I haven't, it is only due to the grace of God. He honors it whether I clearly see it or not. At times, I clearly see it. It's as if the person calms down. Their body language becomes more amicable. It's amazing. Well, actually, it's biblical, isn't it? God's Word never returns void.

The next time someone talks down to you, respond gently and see what happens. And sometimes you may even need to do what Saul did in your Bible reading today. When some troublemakers despised him, he kept silent. The Bible has a lot more to say about this. Don't hold your breath, but do hold your tongue. Live by faith today...

LIVING BY FAITH

IT TAKES HUMILITY TO SPEAK HONORABLY WHEN OTHERS SPEAK HORRIBLY. Today is the opposite of yesterday. Rick Warren in *The Purpose Driven Life: What on Earth Am I Here For?* says, "True humility is not thinking less of yourself; it is thinking of yourself less." That's what it takes to not respond harshly to others. It is also what it takes to speak honorably to others. The power of speaking words of encouragement to others never ceases to amaze me! But if we're not humble, we won't do it.

Our speech is a major theme in the book of Proverbs. Proverbs is wisdom literature. We are to pray for wisdom. A sign of wisdom is being an encourager with words. We have seen the dangers of an unbridled tongue. We must also realize the tongue can be used for good—much good. One version uses the word *wholesome* tongue. It is the Hebrew word for "healing, restoration, and cure." It can also mean "calmness." Those are positive words, aren't they? We can use our words to help someone heal from a deep wound received at some point in their lives. We can use our words to help restore broken relationships. We can use our words to bring calmness to a friend who just received word that a family member died suddenly. With so many people speaking horribly, it is very important that we do the opposite. Speak honorably to others. You will never, ever, regret it all the days of your life. And it can be a difference-maker in the lives of others, even though you may never know on this side of heaven.

Who will it be today? Maybe it's someone tomorrow. Look, you aren't living as a child of God to build yourself up. Let God and others do that along the way. You are still living to love others. True humility naturally, passionately, uses words to put life into others. It's life-changing for both parties. Target someone. Hit the bullseye. Watch their reaction. Live by faith today...

LIVING BY FAITH

WHEN DONE WRONG, TALK WITH GOD. This is what David did. He had been done wrong and he expressed his concerns to God. He's not always the first person we talk with, is he? Oftentimes, we talk with others first. That's not the order we should follow. We need to talk with God about others instead of talking about others before we talk with God about others. Did you get that? I'm not sure I did either. Anyway, WHEN someone hurts you, pray.

David did not seek vengeance here. He called for divine intervention. His enemies were falsely accusing him. We must always remember that ultimately, Satan is the accuser. Not people. Satan often uses people to accomplish his work. It's as if David was thinking about the love he had shown these people and now they were hurting him for loving them. Ever been there? Ever done this to others? If we have lived any length of time, we have. When we read Shakespeare's work (which I never enjoyed) in high school, we read about an incident that brought this to light. It's in *Julius Caesar* and had to do with a character named, Brutus. (Not the "Popeye" Brutus. Okay, I digress. For those of you who didn't do this assignment in school, you can go read it yourself. Just don't ask me about the story assuming I made a good grade on it. I was reminded of it while reading a commentary, but it's relatable.)

Let me be totally transparent with you here. As an adult, especially as a Senior Pastor, I have been "done wrong." I'm not saying I've not done others wrong. I am a sinner, too. But I can point to various incidents that have crushed my heart. If I think about them today, I hurt. If you're honest, you have been hurt by those you have shown love to, also. We forgive because Christ has forgiven us. There's no other option. But that does not erase the pain and give approval to what they did. So we pray just like David. We bring those guilty before the throne of God. We share our heart—all of it. We listen to Him. And we trust His timing and His ways. By God's grace, let's allow our hurts to keep us from hurting others. And let's talk with Jesus about our hurts before talking with anyone else, even though there may come a time for that. Jesus heals our broken hearts. He's been there! Live by faith today…

DAILY READING:
1 Samuel 15:1-16:23; John 8:1-20
Psalm 110:1-7; Proverbs 15:8-10
Focal Passage: John 8:7

LIVING BY FAITH

I KEEP SOME SMOOTH ROCKS IN MY OFFICE. Counseling is a part of the ministry of a pastor. I do some. And right beside one of the chairs that most of those who come in for counseling sit in, is a bowl with smooth rocks in it. They are not ugly rocks. They are nice rocks that have been polished. They are pretty, but that's not the primary reason they are there. The main reason I keep them is for those who feel they have committed a sin that can't be forgiven. It varies. Some think divorce is beyond the scope of God's forgiveness. Others think adultery, pornography, or homosexuality are sins that God can't forgive. The list goes on and on. When a brokenhearted person says to me that God can't forgive them for their sin, I ask them to grab a rock out of my bowl. I share our verse with them and remind them Jesus died for all sin. Even their sin, however bad it may be. Invariably they cry or a smile comes across their face.

I love this verse! Jesus is letting those who were trying to trick Him know He could have easily given them a smooth rock out of a bowl. Most scholars believe He was writing the sins of the woman's accusers in the sand. That's why they all seemed to be gradually walking away. His words were letting them know not one of them was qualified to judge. They knew the law commanded both parties had to be present. Where was the fellow? These religious hypocrites were busted! Don't you love Jesus? Me too. He defended the lady who had committed adultery and then asked that she sin no more. The one who *could* have thrown rocks never even thought about it. Jesus didn't endorse or promote her sin. He extended grace and mercy, then gave her direction for her future journey.

Do you need to find a rock? Maybe it's for you. Maybe it's for someone who can't forgive themselves. Maybe it's for those you encounter in the future who think their sin is too "big" for our BIG God to forgive. If so, put some in your office. Someone will be glad you did. And it won't be an interior designer, though they may think it's decorative. Live by faith today...

LIVING BY FAITH

KEEPING REMINDERS OF PAST VICTORIES WILL INSPIRE YOU AND OTHERS. The story of David and Goliath is universal. Most everyone has heard of this great feat. A young shepherd boy rescued the nation of Israel from a giant pagan. There is so much truth in this one story in the Bible. If you grew up in the church, you learned about these two from an early age. But have you ever considered our focal verse very much? I am convinced there is an important principle here for us.

I think David kept Goliath's armor in a prominent place so he could always remember the victory God gave him over the giant. It was significant. Sure, he had killed lions and bears that had threatened his sheep as a shepherd boy. But this giant was threatening the sheep of God! David would not and did not stand by and allow this pagan Philistine to continue taunting the children of Israel. In spite of those who did not believe in him, he stepped forward by faith. He knew the battle was the Lord's and not his own. He knew he would go in God's strength, being himself. He knew God was sovereign and regardless of the outcome, God would receive glory. And he knew others would see it and be inspired to live by faith. Everyone has heard of what took place that day.

We all need symbols, pictures, visuals, and recordings of past victories. As a believer, I have seen God accomplish amazing feats through the years. I keep numerous visuals in my study to inspire me. They help me press on despite whatever giant circumstances I may be facing. Do you? If not, start today. Think of ways God has used you or your family members in the past to bring Him glory. Create a way to be reminded through a picture or some other means. It will help motivate you for the rest of your days. And it will likely be a keepsake for family members who remain after you go to heaven. Live by faith today…

LIVING BY FAITH

JEALOUSY KNOWS NO BOUNDARIES. Jealousy is defined as *feeling resentment against someone because of that person's rivalry, success, or advantages (often followed by of).* That definition describes Saul at this point in his life. David had the courage to fight Goliath when King Saul should have stepped up. He didn't and everyone saw the result. David was successful and King Saul was pushed further into the background. And now this... the ladies fawned over David due to his amazing victories. They even made up a song! They sang it in front of God and everybody! Wow, this was the ultimate! David had been given more credit than Saul. King Saul had it "up to his eyeballs" and his life was never the same afterward. A jealous, prideful spirit automatically eliminates the blessings of God! It took over Saul because he thought David was going to seek the throne.

David never did anything to seek the position of King. He trusted God's Word and timing. He had nothing to try to work out himself. Trying to seek a position never works out in the end. David respected authority. Even more, he respected God's anointed. Why? He had a heart for God. A person who loves God with all his heart, soul, and mind, doesn't even think this way. Why? Because it's not natural. I'm not saying those close to God don't have temptations. We all know David had his weaknesses. But intentionally trying to be "the man" was not one of them. Thank God! This was the beginning of the end for King Saul. It can be the same for you and me if we allow jealousy to overtake us.

Search your heart. Are you jealous of someone? Confess it to God and think of all He's done for you. Think of how He's gifted you. Tell Jesus you are sorry, and remember to pray the next time jealousy surfaces. Commit a scripture to memory and say it when this occurs again. Trust God for what He says regarding humility. Besides, in heaven, we may be very surprised at the "rankings." You're OK. Be who God made you to be and don't waste any more time on this one. And rejoice in how God uses others. Live by faith today...

LIVING BY FAITH

NOT EVERY DIFFICULT SEASON IN LIFE IS DUE TO PERSONAL SIN. The ancient belief by many was that if a person had a serious illness it was due to a sin of some kind. It could be a personal sin or the sins of parents. Not so. We will be reminded of this reality when we read about Job. Now, this does not mean that some difficulty could not be the result of personal sin. It could be and that is why believers should always evaluate their spiritual walk while talking with Jesus in their personal prayer life. God does discipline those He loves. It's like a parent. A parent who loves his child will appropriately discipline him.

Difficulties can accomplish so much good. That does not mean it's easy for us. It's just that God uses tough times for various reasons. He can use a sickness to show people we trust in a sovereign God. He can use a person's platform for His glory when he gets knocked down for some unforeseen reason. He can use a failure for motivation to do better. God does some of His best work in His children when they go through a rough patch.

Are you experiencing an unexpected trial or sickness? Examine your heart. Confess your sin. If you sense it's not necessarily punishment for sin, embrace it for good. Ask God to give you the grace needed to be the soldier for Christ that you are. Demonstrate that you really believe in God, no matter the final result. You will have your difficult days. But use the trial as an opportunity to point people to **the light of the world**. He provides the ultimate example of how to walk through trials of various kinds. Live by faith today...

LIVING BY FAITH

WE ALL NEED A JONATHAN IN OUR LIFE. The best way to have a "Jonathan" is to be a "Jonathan." We've already learned this truth from our reading of wisdom literature. (Proverbs 11:25) That's not the reason we encourage others, which is exactly what Jonathan was doing here for David. God knows our motives. If our motives are selfish, we will not be blessed by God. That does not mean the other person will not be blessed by God. God uses various blemished spokespersons to accomplish His will. It's the message, not the messenger. Jonathan was a good messenger and true friend. A true friend backs up the talk when others are throwing spears.

When we sense others are experiencing a difficult season, we need to encourage them. Jonathan was sensitive to David and his needs. David needed Jonathan at this point and Jonathan knew it. How do we know when a brother or sister is at a low point? We are close enough to them that we can read them. We pay attention to how they are interacting with us and our family. We have to stay in touch enough to be able to do so. If we sense the person is down, we go see them, we text them, send them a video, we do whatever we can to help them know we have their back. That's what Jonathan did for David. It helped David continue his journey of faithfulness to God's call on his life.

Who is your David? Do you know? Have you paid attention to them lately? Maybe it's time. If you sense you are a David, remember to encourage yourself in the Lord along the way, as David did. God's encouragement never changes, and He is never absent.

Who is your Jonathan? Do you know? Do you have one? Maybe you need to be one for someone? God will honor you in time and in His way. You may be the key to a David type touching many lives for the Kingdom. Don't worry, the King will know who you are and what you did. The true Kingdom lasts forever. There'll be time to be recognized if indeed it's even necessary. Live by faith today...

LIVING BY FAITH

HOW CAN I REPAY GOD FOR ALLOWING ME TO RECEIVE A DOCTORATE? I graduated from Midwestern Baptist Theological Seminary on this day in May of 2001. I received the Doctor of Ministry degree, by the grace of God, after pursuing it for six years. Why was it such a huge accomplishment for me to receive an earned doctorate? Here are some of the reasons… My mom had been held back and she was determined to not do the same to me. It was not a good experience for her. They put me in another school, and I survived. I was in the slower reading class in elementary school. I had trouble doing homework growing up because I would rather be playing ball in the neighborhood. I failed two classes in high school. I started college on academic probation because I had a low ACT score. I failed a class my freshman year of college. (I'm running out of room here…) I had to take a basic English class my first semester of seminary due to a low score on an English proficiency entrance exam. So, to graduate from seminary with a B average was a God-thing. To finally be allowed to pursue my doctorate and graduate from a Southern Baptist seminary was a further God-thing. And I did so after moving during the middle of the process, having two small children, and pastoring a large church on the backside of earning my degree.

I told you! To God be the glory because it was all Him! I identify with what former President George W. Bush told a group of graduating seniors from Southern Methodist University: *"To those of you who received honors, awards, and distinctions, I say well done. And to the C students, I say, you too, can be President of the United States."* How in the world can I repay God for allowing me to do something that would have been laughable to me—and some others—during my growing-up years? The Psalmist mentions two things. 1. Continue to pursue an intimate relationship with the Lord. Why would I want to drift from the One who had delivered me all my life? 2. Continue to obey the call He has placed upon my life. I never stopped pursuing my doctorate because I believe God called me to it. I knew in spite of my limitations and various roadblocks along the way, somehow, some way, God was going to allow this to happen in time. I want to finish my race paying close attention to various calls He places on my life until the day I die. So can you. Live by faith today…

LIVING BY FAITH

JESUS HEARS YOUR PRAYERS, SO WAIT FOR THE ULTIMATE WIN. Do you ever feel like your prayers are hitting the ceiling? You pray, but God seems to not be hearing you. If you're being honest, you probably said yes. Do you ever feel like His timing is WAAAYYYY off? Me, too. Do you ever put a timeframe on a specific prayer, and He doesn't meet your deadline? Yeah, I've done that, too. Well friend, today's passage is for you and it's for me.

Jesus had a great relationship with this family. We know this from reading the scriptures. His love is identified in our text. He loved Martha, Mary, and Lazarus. So, you would think when His buddy Lazarus was very sick, he'd come running. Not so. He found out and hung out. He stayed where He was for two more days. What's up with Jesus? (Hadn't you asked that before? Yeah, me too. Don't pretend. Be honest.) Jesus wanted them to experience the ultimate win! His delay was an act of love. Look, if we're on God's team, we've won because of what Jesus has done for us on the cross. He died for our sins and rose three days later. If we put our faith and trust in Him, we are on the winning team no matter what happens down here. But we're still here to fulfill our purpose. And if we rush the process because of impatience, we won't experience the ultimate victories He desires for us in our lifetime.

Let's not assume God's "slow" timetable is punishment. There's always a purpose behind what may seem like an apparent contradiction to us. Our goal is His glory, not ours. We must trust His delays in life. He is not going to leave us hanging. Let Him do His work in us and allow His timing to work out the ideal situation for our future blessing. It will be the ultimate win! I've lived long enough now to know that doing a "rush job" is not the best job in the world. And I've also learned that waiting doesn't mean a waste of time, either. Lots can be accomplished while waiting. (I still don't really like it!) Love Jesus and realize His delay today is because of His love for you. The ultimate is coming! Live by faith today…

LIVING BY FAITH

WHEN YOUR TEAM MEMBERS TURN ON YOU THERE'S ONLY ONE THING TO DO. David's men obviously blamed him for the pain they all were experiencing. While they were away in battle, which David thought was the right decision, Ziklag was burned to the ground. The Amalekites had kidnapped the women and children. They were all grieving and in pain. David's troops were talking about stoning him. Bitterness was running rampant. What was David to do? He was hurting. He couldn't talk to his family. His men, the men he'd done battle with and who had stood by his side, were now talking about him and about to kill him. There was only one thing to do... *he found strength in the Lord*. It wasn't his strength; it was God's strength. David was strong, but he wasn't strong enough to survive this challenge. God helped him as he sought His will.

All through the Bible we find people turning on people. Today's reading showed us Judas lurking in the background with evil intent. We've already read about Joseph and Moses and those who turned on them. It happened then and it happens now. There has likely been a time in our lives when we have turned on a teammate (friend, family, church member, colleague, neighbor). Maybe we knew what we were doing. Maybe we didn't at the time. Maybe we still don't realize it. But I dare say we all remember when someone has turned on us. At least, we feel like they did. I've had family members, friends, staff, deacons, and even church members turn on me. Yes, it's true. We can hurt each other—even when following God's will. It's one of the hardest things to deal with in life. This issue has been around since the fall of man and will be until the end of time.

What do we do with it? Learn. Try not to turn on others. And when it happens to us, because it will, especially if you are a leader, seek God's face. He will rescue you. He will heal your wounds. He will take you to a deeper level, spiritually. It will change your perspective. Future victories will be won, as we'll see in tomorrow's reading. Live by faith today...

DAILY READING:
2 Samuel 1:1-2:11; John 12:20-50
Psalm 118:19-29; Proverbs 15:27-28
Focal Passage: 2 Samuel 1:25-26

LIVING BY FAITH

GRIEVING THE LOSS OF A CLOSE FRIEND IS HEART-WRENCHING AND HEARTWARMING. That statement seems contradictory, doesn't it? It's not. Let me explain. One of the greatest gifts in life is that of a close friend. We see it all throughout the Bible. And when the close friend is a believer, it goes to an entirely different level. I have grieved over these types of friendships and I will do so even more as the days go by. You see, deep friendships are like David and Jonathan's friendship. They were loyal to one another. They had had deep conversations about life. They had been in battles together and for one another. You see, when these things happen with a brother, the connection is intertwined. You can go months or years and still love each other. You see each other after a time and it's as if you were with the person the day before. Do you have someone like this? If so, give thanks to God. It's an incredible gift that doesn't come along with just anyone. This is why you are likely to do what David, a warrior, did when hearing the news that his friend had died. In this same chapter, it says he mourned, wept, and even fasted. Folks, that's what heart-wrenching means.

When your close friend dies, and it will happen if you live long enough, it can and likely will warm your heart. Yes, you hurt. Yes, you may cry, like Jesus did when Lazarus died. That's fine. God gave us our emotions. There is a natural grieving process. Let it run its course. You may hurt one day. Then your heart may be warmed the next... it's OK. Don't allow false guilt to do a number on you. But smile when you think of times you were "in the foxhole" together. Maybe you played on the same team. Maybe you served on staff during a difficult time. You may have been in the same youth group years before and battled peer pressure together. Those memories will be sources of continued blessings as the days go by, even though they may be tender at first.

David continued to live life after the death of his friend Jonathan. He did not allow the influence he had on his life to die. You can do the same. Let the Godly influence of a close friend live on through the rest of your days on earth. That way the legacy of your friendship has a ripple effect. Live by faith today...

LIVING BY FAITH

THERE IS SOMETHING INFECTIOUS ABOUT A JOYFUL LOOK.
Life can be hard. Believers experience difficulties just like everyone else. We just
have the ultimate "rescuer!" Jesus never leaves us nor forsakes us. Do you know
Him? If not, let Him rescue you from your sin and simply place your faith in Him.
Yes, life will still be hard, but your trials will never be the same. There's no smile
like the one of someone who has an intimate walk with Christ. He brings joy
unspeakable from the inside out.

Do you want to help people live their best life? Then consider your body
language. Do you relay positive vibes? If you don't know, ask someone close to
you who will speak the truth. I'm not saying we have to be fake. We all have our
moments. But what I am saying is that it's vital to have a pleasant disposition most
of the time. Not to bring you glory, but to glorify your Father in heaven. Pagans
smile. But their smile has no lasting substance behind it. A believer's smile has the
Christ-life behind it. That lasts… A beaming glance, glistening eyes, and a smile as
broad as one's face are impacting to all who see it. A smile is a universal language. I
go to other countries and often have no idea what they are saying. But if they smile
or I smile, we are having positive communication. It's amazing! Not only does Jesus
make us smile, I think He did quite often. Why else would children want to be
around Him? They don't naturally want to hang out with grouchy folks.

My parents smiled a lot. My sisters smile a lot. People who I admire most are
typically "grinners." It's a trademark worth desiring because it makes you feel better.
More importantly, it can make someone going through a difficult time (and you may
not even know about it or even know the person) be encouraged in an instant. Now,
that's something to smile about. Live by faith today…

LIVING BY FAITH

JUDGING HOW OTHERS WORSHIP THE LORD COULD BE COSTLY. I was raised in a more traditional Southern Baptist church. I am grateful. A lot more good than bad came out of the experience. The style of public worship was somewhat subdued. Perspective is everything. (I realize that for some, we were very expressive.) If someone had raised their hands during a song, most of us would have thought they were odd. I recall going to a less formal Southern Baptist church when I moved to Ft. Worth, Texas, for seminary. We visited a church where many raised their hands and were vocally expressive. I never went back because it sort of freaked me out. Here's what's ironic… Today I would fit fine in that church. My journey has taught me that as long as it's biblical, it's fine. David had danced before the Lord and many saw his expressions of worship. Michal, David's wife, and Saul's daughter, did not like it. She was not raised like that. He was supposed to be dignified. He was the King.

David let her know in no uncertain terms that he worshiped the King. And because God was his King, he'd go to an entirely different level of humility in worshipping Him if he felt so led. Michal was looking at it from an earthly perspective. Public worship should be viewed through a biblical perspective. Look, you can go to one Southern Baptist church and they may be extremely expressive. You can go to another and they may be a lot more non-expressive. Just don't judge, regardless of your denomination or non-denomination. God knows the heart of a person. We do not. And if your style of worship fits better in one church more than another, then keep that in mind. But we should never judge someone else for worshipping God differently than we do. This does not mean that everything goes. Church leadership should and likely will address anything that is unbiblical and has a pattern of distracting people while worshipping.

When we publicly worship, don't allow a person to keep you from expressing your love for God. Don't allow your past to keep you from enjoying your present. Worship freely and biblically. It can help others do the same. Live by faith today…

LIVING BY FAITH

I READ THIS PASSAGE AND THINK THE SAME THING ABOUT MY FAMILY. My grandfather on my dad's side, Atley Asher Kitchings, came from a poor, uneducated family, in a small community in Mississippi. He graduated from college and seminary, earned a PhD, and taught languages at Mississippi College for many years. He also pastored small churches on the weekends. My grandfather on my mother's side, Noah Webster Overstreet, came from a poor, uneducated family in a small community in Mississippi. He graduated from college, earned an architectural degree, and became famous in the south for honing his craft. One of his well-known buildings is First Baptist Church in Jackson, Mississippi, where he served as a deacon. My dad, Harold Tribble Kitchings, served as a pastor and denominational leader in Mississippi for many years. My mom, Ann Overstreet Kitchings, served by his side using her loving abilities to impact others for the Kingdom. I'm not finished, but do you see why I identify with the focal passage so much? I read it and think... *"God, I am not David and my family is not his, but THANK YOU for allowing me to be a part of the family you placed me in. I mean, who in the world am I? And to allow me to serve in vocational ministry in the places I've served, good gracious alive!*

David was praising God in a prayer for how good He had been to his family of origin. He was even given the privilege of knowing God was going to bless his family beyond his lifetime. We see David's heart here. He indeed was a man after God's own heart. David accepted his role and praised God for it. He was humble enough to know it was all God and he was just along for the ride. He didn't have to do so. He could have been prideful or squandered his good name.

I felt a responsibility to let my two children know where they came from. Trey and Halie knew their family wasn't perfect because they lived with me. But I tried to help them gain respect for their spiritual heritage even though they never personally knew any of my grandparents, nor my dad. Why was this important? Because of God's grace. He has been good to us and we need to know our history, as well as our incredible opportunities to carry the good work on into the future. They are both in ministry with their spouses and have children. May God use them for His glory and **always have a humble spirit of—who am I and what is my family that you have brought us this far?** Live by faith today...

DAILY READING:
2 Samuel 9:1-11:27; John 15:1-27
Psalm 119:49-64; Proverbs 16:1-3
Focal Passage: 2 Samuel 9:8

LIVING BY FAITH

GOD SPECIALIZES IN EXTENDING GRACE TO THOSE WHO FEEL LIKE DOGS. David never forgot his promise. He made a covenant and he wanted to honor it the best he could. He had respect for the former first King, Saul, and an unforgettable friendship with Saul's son Jonathan. What else could he do to honor his covenant? He found out. Ziba, the longtime servant of Saul's house, informed him of a little-known fact. There was this one guy who had been dropped years ago and made lame. He was crippled and not many even knew his name. His name was Mephibosheth – not a name you hear every day, but a name none of us want to forget. We're all like him. We may not be crippled physically, but we've all been crippled by sin. We need God to help us walk upright in all our ways.

Mephibosheth didn't know what was coming. He'd been in obscurity and now the King wanted to see him in person. Maybe he was going to be punished due to his grandfather? Saul's life didn't end with him and David being the best of friends. What happened is a picture of what Jesus has done for us. Grace. God's grace. David quickly helped Jonathan's son know he wasn't out to get him. Oh, no. He was out to bless him immensely. He would feast at the King's table for the rest of his life. His circumstances in life changed forever.

Do you feel like a "dead dog?" Maybe it's because of the way you look. Maybe it's because your family has a bad reputation. It may even be because of something you've done. Regardless, be encouraged today. No one is outside the reach of God's grace—no one. God invites you to eat at the King's table—King Jesus. And as you learned in your daily reading today, if you abide in King Jesus, the fruit comes naturally and never runs out. Live by faith today…

LIVING BY FAITH

THIS ONE VERSE HAS BROUGHT GREAT COMFORT TO THOSE WHO HAVE LOST A CHILD. I have had many people through the years ask if there is an age of accountability. I have answered yes, even though we don't know exactly what that number is. Is it twelve? Maybe. Where the Bible is silent, we had better be also. I do know for one to be born again they must realize they are a sinner in need of a savior. I have also had parents ask if their deceased child is in heaven. I have said yes, and usually point to our focal passage today. David had been praying and fasting for God to heal his child, who was very ill. When he discovered the child had died, he began to move on with his life, while worshipping God. It's when his servants didn't understand his sudden change that David gave us hope for deceased children. He didn't talk about reincarnation because that's not biblical. The baby wasn't going to be resurrected here. David simply said he'd go to where he was one day. We know that to be the house of the Lord.

You are reading through the Bible this year. You are seeing that God is gracious, just, redemptive, loving, and holy, just to name a few attributes that describe Him. An important part of proper interpretation is to keep the entire context of scripture in mind. I believe with great confidence that David was saying he'd see his child in heaven, and he'd somehow recognize him. Jesus loved children. In children, we see such innocent faith, which Jesus talked about. Yes, if you have a child die, you'll see him or her again if you have a relationship with Jesus. Maybe an important question here is, "Do you know for certain that if you were to die right now, you'd go to heaven?" You can be. Admit your sin and place your faith in Jesus for your salvation. If so, you will have life's most important question settled, and you will see babies too numerous to count when you get to heaven. Share this message with others. Use the scriptures to provide comfort for parents who may have a child die at a young age. And use the scriptures to share the gospel of Jesus Christ with those who don't know Him. HE is our only hope! Live by faith today…

LIVING BY FAITH

THIS IS THE ESSENCE OF THE CHRISTIAN LIFE. Knowing God is what it boils down to. This is how to know God. When we know God, we know how to live the life He has for us. That's really it in a nutshell. I recall memorizing this verse while being trained in personal evangelism years ago. This was one of the verses to memorize in order to share the gospel with lost people. I loved it! It explained what Jesus desires for all of us. When one receives eternal life, one enters into an intimate relationship with Jesus that never stops. That's right—never. It will grow throughout eternity. It is uninterrupted. It is a sense of a deeper knowledge of who God is. It is truly experiencing God. Folks, it is the reason we were created! This is it! And it's an amazing truth when we stop long enough to consider its impact on us and others we come in contact with.

Do you know Him? You may know about arithmetic, sports, music, politics, but do you know the one and only true God—Jesus Christ? I do. I'm still getting to know Him. I pray, read His Word, meditate, and journal as a part of doing so. As a matter of fact, the more I learn, the more I realize He has more for me to know. It's never ending and it's like no other relationship I've ever had or will ever have. It won't stop when I die. It won't stop ever. Jesus never changes. He changes me as I know Him. He will do the same for you. If He already is, stop and give thanks. Let's share Him with others. We don't have to go through weeks of training, though there is nothing wrong with that; we simply share this verse and our testimony. What a life! What an opportunity! Know Him. Live by faith today...

DAILY READING:
2 Samuel 14:1-15:22; John 18:1-24
Psalm 119:97-112; Proverbs 16:8-9
Focal Passage: Proverbs 16:9

LIVING BY FAITH

GOD'S PLANS FOR US ARE ALWAYS BETTER THAN OURS. There is nothing wrong with making plans. As a matter of fact, I encourage it. So do leadership gurus. At the end of every year, I get away and prayerfully consider the upcoming year. I ask God to direct my steps for my personal life, family life, and professional life. I leave my "retreat" with direction and share my plans with others. After receiving input, I calendar what's appropriate and execute the plans accordingly. There are times during the year when we tweak our plans. It may be due to unanticipated circumstances. It may be because God leads us in another direction.

Proverbs is wisdom literature. It is wise for us to pay attention. The writer makes it very clear that God is the boss. God is King over all creation. God knows what's best. God sees the big picture. We do not. We may think we do, but we don't. He is infinitely smarter than we are. He may take us in a different direction than we thought we were going. Let Him. He may take us ultimately to the same place we thought He wanted us to go, but by a different path. Let Him. He has ways to prepare us for our destination that cause us to be more like Him before our arrival. Trust Him. Pay attention to times He seems to be doing something different than what you understood to be the original plan. He is not the author of confusion. He just knows a better way to go. Keep talking with Him. Keep journaling your journey. Look back to when He's done this before. This invariably helps me to press forward. As the old spiritual song says, *He's never failed me yet*. His ways are always better than ours. Always. Live by faith today...

DAILY READING:
2 Samuel 15:23-16:23; John 18:25-19:22
Psalm 119:113-128; Proverbs 16:10-11
Focal Passage: Psalm 119:113

LIVING BY FAITH

THE FICTIONAL TV CHARACTER EDDIE HASKELL IS FROWNED UPON IN THE BIBLE. If someone calls you Eddie Haskell, it's not good. He was a "slick" character in the television series *Leave it to Beaver* years ago. He was the teenage friend who would woo your parents. Did you ever have that friend? Maybe you were that guy? Regardless, you get it. He was a fake. He'd act nice when he thought it best when in reality he was a conniver. He would stab you in the back in a heartbeat and not think twice about it. Yes, it's not who we want to be known as or called.

The psalmist's overwhelming love for truth continues in this verse. He points out the importance of not only knowing the Word but obeying the Word. Know what it says. Do what it says. Biblical knowledge is not just for information, it's for transformation. And we see this one principle throughout our entire daily reading today. Go back and read it if you need to do so. A son turning against his dad. Simon Peter denying Jesus. Being double-minded means one has different views at different times. It'd be similar to having a "double heart." The thought of two hearts trying to control a body would be disastrous. So it is with someone who is like an Eddie Haskell. Don't be that guy. He may dress nicely, groom his hair, and smile at the right time, but he will try to destroy you at every turn.

None of us are perfect. We are all in need of a savior. But we all probably know this type of person. If so, pray for them. Learn from them how not to live your life. But you better keep a safe distance. Don't hesitate to use church discipline, if this person is in your church fellowship. God honors truth. He will honor you standing for Him, no matter the cost. Live by faith today…

DAILY READING:
2 Samuel 17:1-29; John 19:23-42
Psalm 119:129-152; Proverbs 16:12-13
Focal Passage: John 19:38-40

LIVING BY FAITH

NEVER UNDERESTIMATE THE SEEDS OF THE GOSPEL YOU HAVE SHARED WITH OTHERS. Have you ever shared your testimony about the life-change Jesus brought to you? I'm speaking of your conversion experience. Let me put it another way—how you were born again. You know, the Word used by Jesus once to share the gospel of salvation with Nicodemus. You remember him, the Pharisee who came to Jesus at night earlier in our reading. He was curious. He knew there was something different about Jesus. He left, after hearing how to leave religion and enter into a relationship without our knowing the outcome of the conversation. I think it's safe to say seeds were planted by Christ and there came a time in the life of Nicodemus that he was indeed born-again.

God commands His followers to share the gospel of Jesus Christ. It's a privilege, not an obligation. (Angels can't. We can.) We are not responsible for saving anyone. We are successful when we testify. We leave the results up to God. At times, people immediately respond. Other times, they don't, and we may never know the final result of the conversation. If someone only listens and does not make a decision, that does not mean we shouldn't have shared our heart about Christ. It just means we trust God with the results—like we always should.

Please know that when you share any word about Christ or His Word, there may be those who do not seem to be listening. They may say nothing, or they may be verbal about their disbelief. Don't worry about it. Don't allow that to keep you from encouraging people through the scriptures in the future. They may just be like old Nicodemus. They need a little time and they come around. They may even do something radical like he did. Helping bury Jesus was a radical step of faith. What's God asking you to do that others might not do? Live by faith today...

DAILY READING:

2 Samuel 18:1-19:10; John 20:1-31
Psalm 119:153-176; Proverbs 16:14-15
Focal Passage: 2 Samuel 19:5-8a

LIVING BY FAITH

PROLONGED GRIEF CAN HINDER THE LIVES OF OTHERS. It is natural to grieve over a loss. Losing a child has to be the worst kind of loss anyone can experience. I have no idea but I have ministered to many parents who have lost a child to death. David was grieving over the loss of a son. Absalom wasn't a son to be proud of, but he was still his own flesh and blood. The entire story was tragic. His son rebelled and tried to take over the Kingdom. Many people who once followed David left to follow his son. And David's primary warrior-leader, Joab, ended up tossing spears into Absalom's chest. So I think we all understand the depth of David's grief to some level. The problem was that it was beginning to have a very negative effect on others.

Thousands of David's men had risked their lives to save David, David's family, and his throne. They needed to hear from David. He had grieved and now it was time to commend his mighty warriors for victory over the enemy. Joab helped the king know he was about to have a problem on his hands if he didn't pull himself together. He did and the men recognized his presence immediately.

Encouragement goes a long way, even when you are hurting. It even makes you feel better. Try it the next time you're not doing well. It's an amazing ministry our Lord has left for His church. The opposite is true, too... If you don't love on those you're responsible for due to not encouraging them, it will have a negative effect on everyone. I've witnessed parents losing a child and neglecting the other child or children God had blessed them with. It's not good. Go through the grief process when you experience any kind of loss, but please don't let it take over the rest of your days. People need you. Let God use your pain to minister to others. Live by faith today...

DAILY READING:
2 Samuel 19:11-20:13; John 21:1-25
Psalm 120:1-7; Proverbs 16:16-17
Focal Passage: John 21:20-22

LIVING BY FAITH

GOD'S SPECIFIC WILL FOR YOUR LIFE MAY BE DIFFERENT FOR YOUR FRIEND. Jesus told Peter what he was to do with his life. God has a general will for His church—His people. He has an individual will for His followers. So there's God's will corporately, and God's will individually. Simon Peter all of a sudden decided he needed to know what Jesus had in mind for John. Isn't that funny? Simon Peter seemed to have a way of being sort of random at times. Regardless, he didn't need to be concerned about what John's future held. Jesus had that covered and all he needed to do was follow Jesus's direction for his own life. It's often different than our friends.

We need to be careful not to judge others concerning the will of God. God may lead you to stay in one location and profession for your entire adult life. He may ask your buddy to move periodically and possibly change professions in his thirties. We are not to judge how others follow God's will for their lives based on how God has worked with us. It may be different. If we are following God's will, as we understand it, and not disregarding the truth of scripture, we need to go for it. If someone gossips in some way about how you have lived your life because it doesn't seem "normal" to them, they will have to answer for that.

Seek God and follow His will for your life. Encourage others to do the same. Don't be jealous or critical of your brothers and sisters in Christ. God made us all different. His plans for each of us are different. Live by faith today...

DAILY READING:
2 Samuel 20:14-22:20; Acts 1:1-26
Psalm 121:1-8; Proverbs 16:18
Focal Passage: 2 Samuel 21:20-21

LIVING BY FAITH

WHAT HAPPENS WHEN AN UNNAMED GIANT COMES YOUR WAY? Most people have read or heard about the iconic story of David and Goliath. If you are reading the Bible through with us, you know the story. Goliath was a Philistine warrior who taunted the Israelites. David whipped him! God used this young man in a mighty way and people have been inspired by the story for years. What people may not have thought about is the reality that other giants are mentioned in the Bible. There were other unusually tall warriors among the Philistines. Our giant today is unnamed. He had lots of fingers and toes. The only time this malformation, known as polydactylism, is mentioned in the Bible is in the description of this giant. Some scholars think he may have been Goliath's brother. We can only conjecture. Regardless, he was a seemingly ugly, nameless giant who was a threat.

Throughout life, we will face "giants" that are unfamiliar or "unnamed." They can be ugly. They can appear out of nowhere. Maybe we've never heard of them before, much less had to encounter them. You may have faced a giant problem you saw coming in the past. Perhaps it was earning a doctorate degree. You knew it would be hard, but to some degree you knew what you were up against. Some giant challenges we face in life are sudden. It could be a deadly virus or the sudden loss of a job. But it came your way. You see where we're going here? I'm sure you do. We all face them, and we need to be encouraged that God will take care of us. God used David's nephew to kill this giant. Another victory for God's people is due to warriors being faithful to their king. In the following chapter we read how David celebrated and gave God all the praise.

Be assured today when you leave this devotional reading that you know what's going to happen to that unnamed giant you may be facing... God's going to take care of it! He always does. You do your part and trust Him with His part. Live by faith today...

DAILY READING:
2 Samuel 22:21-23:23; Acts 2:1-47
Psalm 122:1-9; Proverbs 16:19-20
Focal Passage: 2 Samuel 23:13-17

LIVING BY FAITH

A TRUE FRIEND LISTENS CLOSELY AND RESPONDS SACRIFICIALLY. This is no doubt one of my favorite passages in the Bible. (We will read this account again when reading through 1 Chronicles.) I selected this text as the passage for the Florida Baptist Pastors' Conference years ago while serving as President. There is so much here, but I want to emphasize the role of a friend. Friendships are one of the greatest blessings of life. God made us for relationships.

David was in the stronghold with several of his mighty men. He was comfortable with them because he was just sharing his heart about where he grew up. Haven't you done that with people close to you? I have. These guys obviously listened and responded out of love and respect. They risked their lives to get water from David's hometown. We all know the power of our senses. When the men returned safely, David was so moved, he worshipped God. He expressed his deep appreciation for their sacrifices and then poured the water out as an offering. These mighty men evidently were fine with it. I'm not sure I would have been. I mean, risking your life for a cup of water and then pouring it on the ground? I know, I have a long way to go... What a precious passage!

When you want to bless someone, listen intently to their words. Maybe there's a way to bless them beyond what they could ever imagine. Sacrifice time, money, or whatever you may need to in order to encourage them. They may need it more than you realize. And they will never forget it. You won't either. Live by faith today...

DAILY READING:
2 Samuel 23:24-24:25; Acts 3:1-26
Psalm 123:1-4; Proverbs 16:21-23
Focal Passage: Acts 3:1-10

LIVING BY FAITH

MEETING JESUS HAS A GREATER IMPACT THAN GOING TO CHURCH OR ASKING FOR MONEY. I pastor a church located in the middle of several different types of neighborhoods. What does that mean? We have a very impoverished area on one side and a rather nice area on another side. It also means surrounding the church is a sort of in-between area. I guess what I'm trying to say is that we have all kinds of folks around us. We have people asking for money on a regular basis—more so than any other church I've pastored. We also have regular guests. Located near the beach, we have our share of visitors. These are not bad things. We have an incredible mission field right outside our door. But having people in and around the buildings of the church does not mean they know Jesus. Giving people money does not mean they know Jesus, though we certainly try to help those who ask in various ways. The only hope any of us have is meeting Jesus. And having someone take the time to introduce Him is a blessing.

The crippled man hung out at the "church" quite often. He asked for money and I'm sure he received a good bit through the years. Some people who ask for money today hang out at the church. Peter took the time to introduce the crippled man to the Great Physician—Jesus Christ. We have seen in Acts that God did amazing things to demonstrate His power through His church. This particular life change shows a guy getting pretty excited about the healing Christ brought and it impacted others. Jesus has a greater plan than ours. He will use us to influence others more than we can ever imagine. My daughter, Halie, was born on this day. Because she was born again years later and expresses her faith much like the man healed in our passage today, she has and continues to impact many others. It's amazing what God can do through one individual.

Hanging out at the church house for various reasons is fine. A building and some good folks who may give someone money only goes so far. Let's be sure we introduce people to the ultimate one who brings long-term hope for every area of life—JESUS. Live by faith today...

JUNE 6

DAILY READING:
1 Kings 1:1-53; Acts 4:1-37
Psalm 124:1-8; Proverbs 16:24
Focal Passage: Acts 4:13

LIVING BY FAITH

A DEGREE IS NO GUARANTEE OF A GENUINE LIFE WITH THEE. See what I did there? Ha! If you are using the King James Version of the Bible, you did. Or if you've ever read that translation, you get it. (Thee, thou, and thine are Early Modern English second person singular pronouns.) I'm referring here to God. The reality is you can earn all the theological degrees you want and not really know God personally. An intimate relationship with Jesus Christ is the most important aspect of Christianity. God works from the inside out. People see it. People recognize it. People know it. People realize there's something different. Why? Because they see Him more than they see you.

Peter and John were no dummies. They just had not been trained in the formal rabbinical training school of the day. (It would be our equivalent of seminary.) BUT they had received training from Jesus. During a three-year period, Christ taught these former fishermen what they knew. And it was impactful! Being a true disciple of Jesus has influence like none other. I'm a fan of formal education. It can be helpful in numerous ways. I will always be appreciative of professors who taught me and took a personal interest in my well-being. But I'm especially thankful for those who influenced me that never even visited seminaries I attended. During my younger years, many of them put up with some of my foolishness, because they wanted me to be a fool for Jesus.

You are being with Jesus today by spending time in His Word. With a steady diet of this, others will take note and you won't have to tell them you are spending time alone with God each day to somehow impress them. They will see it and hear about it because like verse 20 says, *"For we cannot help speaking about what we have seen and heard."* Live by faith today...

JUNE 7

DAILY READING:
1 Kings 2:1-3:3; Acts 5:1-42
Psalm 125:1-5; Proverbs 16:25
Focal Passage: Proverbs 16:25

LIVING BY FAITH

WHAT SEEMS TO BE THE RIGHT THING TO SAY OR DO MAY NOT BE. I used this verse years ago while speaking to a group of high school seniors. I was wearing a coat, a nice shirt, tie, dress shoes, and belt. It appeared I had on socks because my pants legs covered the top part of my shoes. I did not. When I showed the graduating seniors I was sockless, they were shocked. What seemed to be was not. This is the second time we've read this verse this year. (14:12) It must be important.

We live in a society that honors hard work. Usually, if someone is a hard worker, they are compensated. We live in a society that recognizes the benefit of athletes who practice hard. If a good athlete has a strong work ethic, he or she can become great. So, it would naturally seem that if a person is good, he will be "good" with God. God loves everyone. But not everyone is His child, even though everyone is His creation. You don't go to heaven because your good works outweigh your bad deeds. You go to heaven because you have admitted you can never be good enough and you have put your faith in Jesus. (Here's a verse we've read this year that supports this reality—John 14:6.) No matter how it may seem that God will allow you into heaven because of being good, it's not good.

Here is another example—racism. At the time of this writing, our country is experiencing another wave of racial tension due to the terrible death of a man named George Floyd. At present, I'm trying to listen and watch because what seems to be the right thing for me to say may not be. When and if I do speak or react in some other way, I need to have spent time prayerfully thinking through if it's really beneficial. What we seem to think is the right thing to say might be "deadly" in the long run. Be careful. Live by faith today...

DAILY READING:
1Kings 3:4-4:34; Acts 6:1-15
Psalm 126:1-6; Proverbs 16:26-27
Focal Passage: 1 Kings 3:9

LIVING BY FAITH

IF GOD ALLOWED YOU TO ASK FOR ANYTHING, WHAT WOULD YOU ASK FOR? Can you imagine? Me neither. I could only hope I would give the same answer as Solomon. David, his dad, had died. He was an incredible man. In spite of his flaws, he was a man after God's own heart. There was no one like him. Solomon had the responsibility of being his successor. Not an easy assignment for such a young man. God graciously asked Solomon in a dream how He could help him lead all these people. Solomon didn't ask for a nice horse with a leather saddle. He didn't even ask for a glowing crown from heaven. No, he asked for discernment. This indicated he was already wise beyond his years. He wanted what only God could give him—a heart for Him. He knew if he had a discerning heart from the Lord, he would know the difference between right and wrong. He would have a better idea daily what was God's will, not his own. That's valuable for anyone.

Most of the things we want and sometimes live for are of no eternal value. Knowing God's will helps us make a difference on earth. God wants us to know His purpose for our lives. He is not the author of confusion. You may not be a king, but you may be a child of the kingdom. If Jesus is your King, ask Him for discernment. Ask Him to show you how to live by faith and not feelings. Ask Him to help you recognize the difference. Remember that fear is not of God. Respect the Lord and seek Him for all things good. Evil is a part of our fallen world and the enemy wants to destroy your life. God has a better plan. Ask Him about it right now. Live by faith today...

DAILY READING:
1 Kings 5:1-6:38; Acts 7:1-29
Psalm 127:1-5; Proverbs 16:28-30
Focal Passage: Psalm 127:1

LIVING BY FAITH

YOU CANNOT BUILD A GODLY HOME WITHOUT HIS TOOLS.
Any attempt to build a Godly heritage must be done God's way. God's way is not through any secular means. Please do not allow the world's ways to dupe you. Our verse immediately points to God as our source for family life. You cannot do it on your own. No one can! God's covenant has not changed. The first institution ordained by God was and is the family. Trying to build a Godly heritage or maintain one will never, ever occur on an island without our Lord. He must be involved in the household. No matter how many books you read or radio programs or podcasts you listen to—which may be helpful—nothing replaces the daily inclusion of Jesus.

One of God's tools is prayer. When possible, eat together as a family. Dinner time can be a wonderful gathering spot for a family. If possible, the dad leads out in praying an honest prayer without it being extremely lengthy. Occasionally my dad, depending on the circumstances, would simply say—*Help us, Lord.* Another tool is family devotional time. We had ours on Saturday evenings. Our children knew at a young age this was a high priority. We made it age appropriate and they never balked. We were not legalistic with this life-changing appointment as a family. Great memories were formed, and spiritual disciplines were instilled. No regrets! One final tool as a parent is being sensitive to opportune moments during the day. God provides teaching times on a regular basis with our children. Pay attention and use them for loving instruction.

God's tools for building the family unit are the best. There are more than what I listed today. Know what they are and use them all to build a foundation in the home that lasts. Live by faith today...

JUNE 10

DAILY READING:
1Kings 7:1-51; Acts 7:30-50
Psalm 128:1-6; Proverbs 16:31-33
Focal Passage: Proverbs 16:31

LIVING BY FAITH

I DON'T LOOK AT GRAY HAIR LIKE I ONCE DID. My dad had what some call premature gray hair. That means one's hair turns gray at a young age. I actually thought, as a child, that the shaving cream they put on him at the barbershop to shave around his ears caused it. It did not. That's just where his graying started. He was fully grey by the time I was a teenager. Although I did not gray prematurely, I have more gray hair than blonde now. I once thought people with gray hair were old, regardless of their age. I don't think that now.

Adolescence causes us to do a lot of foolish things. (Some of us more than others.) Teenagers typically think older folks are out of touch. The reality is that older people who know the Lord can help us navigate life. And if an older person has walked with the Lord for many years—look out! That person is a treasure. When I think of my fully-gray-haired dad dying at the age I am now, it is surreal. I often think how much he could have helped me if he had lived. I was only twenty-six and not even close to being a senior pastor at the time.

No one will ever replace my dad, but God put a special someone in my life shortly after his death. His name is Dr. Jim Futral. He's the retired Executive Director of Mississippi Baptists. He doesn't have blonde hair. He doesn't have gray hair. He has no hair, but he is very wise. (I'm thinking that if he could grow hair, it would be gray.) I don't talk with him on a regular basis, but I know that I could. He's always been there for me, no matter where I lived. I always hear the truth from him. I usually listen. He loves me unconditionally. I am a better person because of an older man who has walked with the Lord for a long time. I want to be like that for others. I want to encourage you to do the same and be sure you have at least one gray-haired, God-fearing, person, in your life. If the person is bald, just make sure that if they could grow hair, it would be gray. Live by faith today...

DAILY READING:
1 Kings 8:1-66; Acts 7:51-8:13
Psalm 129:1-8; Proverbs 17:1
Focal Passage: Acts 8:2

LIVING BY FAITH

WHAT A MOVING PICTURE OF GODLY FRIENDSHIPS. I see it. I've seen it numerous times through the years. I'm reaching the age where I'll see it more and perhaps experience it personally. A group of pallbearers who carry the casket for a close friend in the Lord. Now you see it, don't you? All we have to do is close our eyes and visualize the scene. It's moving. As a pastor on the platform of a funeral service, I've seen it time and time again. There is something about a group of guys who love each other, especially the one who has gone home to be with the Lord, during a funeral. Watching them worship, shedding a tear, or perhaps a moment of laughter due to a story about their deceased friend, it's something to behold. And based on our passage today, it's been going on a long time.

Stephen was an incredible Godly soul. God had transformed his life and he was quick to share his testimony. It didn't make the religious folks happy and they killed him. Can you imagine that scene? "Good" people stoning a righteous man? And Saul, of all folks, approved it! Yes, and Stephen handled it like Jesus. No wonder the men who buried him are described as Godly. A man like Stephen had to hang out the majority of the time with like-minded believers. Iron sharpens iron. And his brothers in Christ mourned. The Bible says they mourned, deeply.

Is there someone who will mourn deeply at your funeral due to a Jesus connection? Will you mourn one day at a funeral because your Godly friend has transitioned to glory? Make time for Godly relationships. Be a Godly friend. You will weep when the person dies, but it will be what some call a "good" cry. I don't think I have to explain that. Believers don't grieve like those with no hope. Live by faith today...

DAILY READING:
1 Kings 9:1-10:29; Acts 8:14-40
Psalm 130:1-8; Proverbs 17:2-3
Focal Passage: Acts 8:34

LIVING BY FAITH

THE GOOD NEWS IS FOR THE UNEXPECTED TRAVELER. I will always be grateful for those who trained me to share my faith. I was taught to share how I met Jesus personally and the difference He is making. I can remember a season when I realized it was my privilege to share the gospel (Good News of Jesus) not only with those I knew but those I did not. Let me explain… Sometimes God prompts us to share Christ with those we meet along the way. It may be in a restaurant. It may be on a plane. We need to be prepared. How? Prayer. Pray that God will make you sensitive to opportunities—all of them, each and every day—to tell others about the transforming power of Jesus. **Everyone** needs to know. Even those who do not look like us.

It doesn't take a rocket scientist to realize what was happening here. Phillip and the Ethiopian were different. They were very different. It's vitally important to share the Good News with our family and friends. But do not forget those you come in contact with as you do life. Sometimes God leads us to share with those very different than us. I can't tell you how many times people will listen to me because of my accent. I have lived outside my native state for many years. God uses my southern drawl to get the attention of others. I try to use it to my advantage. Actually, for His advantage. Are you tracking with me, here? Do not assume your cultural background is only for "your" people. It is. But it's also for other people and God can use your distinctiveness to draw others to Him. Don't be ashamed of who you are. Don't be ashamed of your faith. Share Christ with that unexpected traveler like Phillip did. That one encounter may influence an entire country. Live by faith today…

DAILY READING:
1 Kings 11:1-12:19; Acts 9:1-25
Psalm 131:1-3; Proverbs 17:4-5
Focal Passage Acts 9:13-15

LIVING BY FAITH

NO ONE IS BEYOND THE GRACE OF GOD—NO ONE. Johnny Hunt said, "Christianity has never had a more dangerous enemy than Saul of Tarsus, or a more dedicated friend than Paul the Apostle; both are the same man." Those who knew the pre-converted Saul likely thought he would never, ever become a Christ follower. I would have, too. But not in God's eyes. He would never tell us someone is too bad or too religious to genuinely begin a relationship with Him. The Holy Spirit convicts man of sin. We are not omniscient. God is. We should never assume someone is beyond God's grace.

Phillip listened to the Spirit's prompting. He didn't make excuses or try to justify not taking the time to share the gospel with Saul. Aren't you thankful? We are blessed recipients of how God used Saul, who changed his name to Paul. Think about it. We will be reading many of his epistles soon. Is there a person you have in mind whom you assume would never want to hear about the transforming power of Jesus? I've thought of a few through the years. Forget about it! God is at work in ways we cannot see. He desires that everyone come to repentance. Let's never, ever scratch someone off our list. You or I may be the exact one that person needs to hear from.

Okay, you got your person? Me too. Pray for them regularly. Be prepared for an opportunity God may present. Tell them what Jesus has done for you and how the same can happen for them and leave the results to God. Live by faith today…

DAILY READING:
1 Kings 12:20-13:34; Acts 9:26-43
Psalm 132:1-18; Proverbs 17:6
Focal Passage: Acts 9:26-30

LIVING BY FAITH

RADICALLY SAVED PEOPLE NEED OUR SUPPORT, NOT OUR SNEERING. It's understandable, isn't it? The guy who was persecuting them all of a sudden wanted to join them. It's natural to be skeptical of a guy like that. Maybe he was a "spy" of some kind for the "other side." But he wasn't. History proves he was genuine. It also causes us to consider how important it is to embrace those who accept Christ. What if old Barnabas had led the charge of keeping him away instead of bringing him closer? Thank God we don't have to think about that long.

We need to be like Barnabas. His willingness to help others see that Saul was different allowed him to grow in his faith. He was maturing rapidly. Why? Because it was a genuine conversion experience and the disciples were pouring into him. We see from our passage that he was testifying about the grace of God in his life. He even debated with those trying to kill him. He was taught to be bold. He used his past for good. He even had some take him to his hometown—Tarsus. The dude was on fire! And it was partly because Barnabas supported him from the beginning.

Be open to wild folks who come to Christ. Maybe that person you went to high school with is born-again now. Don't sneer at him at your next reunion. Go talk to him. Be an encourager. We all need to be more like Barnabas. Live by faith today...

DAILY READING:
1 Kings 14:1-15:24; Acts 10:1-23a
Psalm 133:1-3; Proverbs 17:7-8
Focal Passage: Psalm 133:1-3

LIVING BY FAITH

GOD USES THE UNITY OF HIS PEOPLE TO REFRESH OTHERS.
Throughout the Bible we read about the value of unity. God blesses His children over, and over, and over when we are united. It makes sense, doesn't it? Hopefully, you have been a part of a church, team, small group, family, etc., that were united. That does not mean everyone agreed on everything. That never happens. We are all different. But the group was united around a common goal. For Christians, that goal is Jesus. Allowing His Word to be our textbook and His priorities to be our priorities. It is refreshing.

Our verses of focus use examples that were common. For example, there was moisture from Mount Herman that would transfer to the mountains of Zion. That moisture would bring refreshment and, therefore, productivity to the land. You see the symbolism? When believers are united, it frees God to bring blessings on them. Oh, the blessings are amazing. But when we are not united, the consequences are disastrous. It may take years to recover.

As we grow closer to the Lord, we realize the importance of uniting others. Do everything possible to help people come together in various ways. The enemy will be doing the opposite and he uses people. Don't allow him to use you. Be aware of his ways, but don't be fearful. Don't compromise but connect with others in love. Stand for the truth. Do so in the right way and at the right time. Make the tough call, if needed. It may be challenging for a while, but in the long run, you will be refreshed and so will others. Live by faith today...

DAILY READING:
1 Kings 15:25-17:24; Acts 10:23b-48
Psalm 134:1-3; Proverbs 17:9-11
Focal Passage: Acts 10:34-35

LIVING BY FAITH

I HAVE A COFFEE MUG WITH THE WORD *RACISM* **PRINTED ON IT.** I purchased it years ago while touring the National Civil Rights Museum in Memphis, Tennessee. I bought it and added it to my coffee mug collection. But I placed it where I can view it on a regular basis. Why? Because it reminds me of our passage today, as well as others in the Bible. NO ethnic or racial group is superior to another ethnic or racial group. God does not show favoritism. He does not show preferential treatment toward any particular race. So, as far as I'm concerned, the mug supports biblical theology.

Simon Peter eventually "got it." It took a while, but God is patient. THANK GOODNESS! Jesus died for all of us—Jews and Gentiles. He frees us up. He took care of what is clean and unclean. (I'm glad because July 4th is coming, and I eat lots of barbeque meats on that day.) The Christian life is the best life because it is truly abundant. Sure, racism exists, but God gives us the ultimate answer. We can come to our senses like Simon Peter and be intentional about including others. Who knows, someone who is not like you may be waiting for you to share what freedom in Christ looks like. Please don't miss the opportunity! Reach out to them. Maybe even buy them a cup of coffee.

Hey, please don't let your culture influence your convictions. Allow the Bible to guide you into all truth. Stand on it. Love it. Let others see Jesus in you. They may not agree, but I do think most will respect you for living out what you believe. And what better belief system than to believe in the one who made us. Live by faith today…

DAILY READING:
1 Kings 18:1-46; Acts 11:1-30
Psalm 135:1-21; Proverbs 17:12-13
Focal Passage: Proverbs 17:13

LIVING BY FAITH

HAVE YOU EVER BEEN HURT BY SOMEONE TO WHOM YOU GAVE A SECOND CHANCE? Before we dive into this, let's pause and ask ourselves that question. Have we ever hurt or disappointed someone who gave *us* a second chance? Maybe so. This should never happen! Think about it.

If this has happened to you, you know it's a deep hurt. How in the world could someone you believed in turn their back on you? And how in the world are you not supposed to react in the flesh? As hard as it may be, we are never given a "pass" as a believer to react in the flesh. We are to stand for truth, take appropriate action where necessary, but do so in a Christ-like manner.

Our focal passage today should provide amazing comfort if you have been wronged by someone you helped along the way. Again, God will take care of that person. IF the person truly paid back evil for the good you did for them, no worries. Move on and let God take care of it in His way and in His timing. He will. He alone is omniscient. Learn from it. Pray about it. And never, ever, intentionally hurt someone who has blessed you. It will cost you much more than it will them. Live by faith today...

JUNE 18

DAILY READING:
1 Kings 19:1-21; Acts 12:1-23
Psalm 136:1-26; Proverbs 17:14-15
Focal Passage: 1 Kings 19:1-9

LIVING BY FAITH

WATCH OUT FOR THE VOICE OF JEZEBEL AFTER A MOUNTAINTOP EXPERIENCE. Elijah had just had an incredible mountaintop experience. Literally, he did. You read where God used him to show that the God of Abraham, Isaac, and Israel was the one true God. The prophets of Baal were seized. Everyone was amazed! And Elijah was so pumped he outran Ahab's chariot. The Lord's supernatural anointing was on him. Then it happened...

Wicked Jezebel was told her god Baal had been mocked and her prophets killed. She threatened to do the same to Elijah—kill him. He ran. He probably didn't run as fast as he did earlier. He was fearful now. Fear is not from the Lord. He had listened to the wrong voice. The voice of this evil woman was used to take him to a dark place. Has that ever happened to you after a spiritual high? If so, you probably heard the voice of Jezebel. No, not literally, but a voice that caused you to be scared. The enemy has numerous "voices" to get us off track. Elijah got way off track, quickly. He was in the wilderness.

God sent an angel to get him back on his feet. He needed rest. He needed something to eat. He needed to listen to a voice from God. He needed some time to reflect and meditate in order to stop the "stinking thinking." He came out of the dark season. You can, too, if you are in one or ever go through one. Learn from Elijah and be aware of the voice of Jezebel. Not afraid, just alert. Keep your eyes on the Lord. Stay focused. Don't go anywhere unless He directs you. Always remember that nothing grows on the mountaintop, only in the valley. Live by faith today...

DAILY READING:
1 Kings 20:1-21:29; Acts 12:24-13:15
Psalm 137:1-9; Proverbs 17:16
Focal Passage: Acts 13:9-11

LIVING BY FAITH

HE WAS BLIND, BUT NOW HE COULD SEE. From this passage on, Saul would be called Paul. He was once *blind*. He could see clearly now who Jesus was and the impact a personal relationship with Him could have. It meant everything. It changed everything for him. Saul was a Hebrew name. Paul was a Roman name. The man who would become known as the apostle to the Gentiles is forever known as Paul. He was no longer blinded by religion. He was no longer blinded by prejudice. He saw Jesus and it changed how he saw others. And he became a bold witness for Christ. That's what Jesus does for true believers. We stand up for what is right no matter what.

Today is *Juneteenth*. This is an annual holiday observing the end of slavery in the U.S. and marks the day (June 19, 1865) when news of emancipation reached the people in the deepest parts of the former Confederacy in Galveston, Texas. This day has been called our country's second Independence Day. Today there will be numerous parades, concerts, cookouts, and other events across the country. I am reminded today of John Newton. He wrote the words of *Amazing Grace*. One stanza reads, *I once was blind, but now I see*. The song is a message of redemption and forgiveness. His relationship with Christ caused him to change his mind about slavery and he repented.

Stories like Saul, who became Paul, continue. John Newton is an example of a similar conversion experience. Jesus causes us to change. He helps us see things in a different light. He wants us to be bold. He desires that we stand up for Him and other believers—regardless of their background. On the flip-side, if you're hard-hearted and reject the truth of God, it can lead to terrible consequences. In our text today, Elymas had willingly embraced spiritual blindness to the truth; therefore, he literally became physically blind. When God gives us light, we need to respond to it. Don't allow prejudice to keep you from enjoying your freedom in Christ or missing out on people in your race—the human race. Celebrate with your brothers and sisters in Christ! Live by faith today...

DAILY READING:
1 Kings 22:1-53; Acts 13:16-41
Psalm 138:1-8; Proverbs 17:17-18
Focal Passage: Acts 13:36

LIVING BY FAITH

GOD HAS A SPECIFIC PURPOSE FOR EACH OF US TO ACCOMPLISH DURING OUR LIFETIME. I remember the first time this verse "jumped off the page." Has that ever happened to you? All of a sudden, a passage really connects with your heart. David lived long enough to fulfill his Kingdom purpose. He served his role by having a Godly influence on others. It has a ripple effect. Only in eternity will we truly understand God's timeline. From David's lineage came the Savior, Jesus.

Let me ask you something. Are you fulfilling God's purpose for your life? Be careful before you answer that question. Ponder your answer, please. This could be a turning point in your life. If you are, you will be motivated to finish stronger than ever knowing God chose you for this time in history. He is allowing you to have the opportunity to impact the next generation. Think about that. Your love, encouragement, and use of your gifts and abilities are causing others to be their best for the cause of Christ. Wow, what a life! When we know our purpose and fulfill it, our life counts! And even through the hard days, we know God is able to do more than we could ask or imagine.

If you are not fulfilling God's purpose for your generation, please talk to God. Tell Him you are sorry. Ask Him to forgive you and give you a clear direction. Pray that He will give you strength one day at a time to change the course of your life. Look for people who can assist you in your new journey. God won't hide them. And be teachable. It won't happen overnight. But you will experience joy like never before and those who follow you will be grateful. Eternity is worth it. You are worth it. Please don't waste your life. Live by faith today...

DAILY READING:
2 Kings 1:1-2:25; Acts 13:42-14:7
Psalm 139:1-24; Proverbs 17:19-21
Focal Passage: 2 Kings 2:9-11

LIVING BY FAITH

IF OUR FATHER WAS OUR SPIRITUAL FATHER, WE WERE DOUBLY BLESSED. Today happens to be Father's Day this year. What a blessing to have this passage in our reading. Elijah was Elisha's spiritual father. (Elisha was the son of Shaphat, a wealthy landowner of Abel-meholah.) Elisha became Elijah's attendant and disciple. A disciple is a learner. He was like a father to him. Elijah was about to "disappear" so he wanted to be sure he'd done everything in his power to bless his protégé. (I'd say it was a blessing just to see this type of journey into heaven, wouldn't you? Wow!) Elisha asked for a double portion of his spirit. He knew he needed an incredible amount of divine enablement for the tasks ahead. We all do. God gave it to him, and he didn't waste it. If you had or have this type of spiritual father, please don't waste the "stuff" they put into you. I pray I don't because my dad invested in me.

My daddy went to heaven well over thirty years ago now. He was sixty. I will be sixty in a few months. It's sort of surreal for me. But he left a spiritual legacy. Let me explain... Not only was he my earthly father, he was my spiritual father. (My daddy was actually a spiritual father to many, many, people. When I post something on Facebook about my dad, like I did this weekend due to it being Father's Day, hundreds respond due to his Godly influence on their lives.) Yes, he was in some ways like an Elijah. He fulfilled his call from God and by doing so, impacted others. That's why I want what Elisha wanted from his spiritual father. I want to take my daddy's Godly attributes and do even more. That's what Godly dads want. I want my two children to take their spiritual heritage and double, triple, or quadruple the impact for God's Kingdom purposes. That's what leaving a spiritual legacy is all about. Allow the focal passage today to catapult you to a new level of effectiveness for your heavenly Father.

I've been thinking a lot about my daddy this Father's Day weekend. I'm not sure why. I always do around this time of the year, but more so today than I have in many years. It's okay. It reminds me of my incredible opportunities to share his spirit for God until I'm "taken up" one day. I'm ready for whenever that day comes. Are you? Live by faith today...

DAILY READING:
2 Kings 3:1-4:17; Acts 14:8-28
Psalm 140:1-13; Proverbs 17:22
Focal Passage: 2 Kings 4:8-10

LIVING BY FAITH

GRANNY KITCHINGS HAD A FUNERAL, AND THIS WAS THE PREACHER'S TEXT. Beulah Mudd was her maiden name. She was originally from Kentucky. She was attending the women's school for missionary training when she met my grandfather, Atley Asher Kitchings. They fell in love and decided to join forces for the sake of the gospel. And boy, did they ever make a difference for many, many people. While Pop (that was his grandfather name, as Granny was Beulah's grandmother name) taught at Mississippi College and preached on the weekends, Granny faithfully raised five children, served as a pastor's wife, supported her local church, and greatly cared for many students going into the ministry. A scholarship was established in her name at Mississippi College, a Baptist institution, around the time of her death. She left a legacy not many people know about outside her family and those she influenced during a very critical time in their lives. College students make decisions that impact them for a lifetime. Here are just a few of those major decisions; choosing a career, deciding whom to possibly marry, and establishing values from peers, various adult influences, classes, and local churches.

Dr. Bill Baker preached at Granny's funeral service. I will never forget it. This passage was used and I'm not sure I'd ever really considered it before. It was so very appropriate for Granny. The Shunammite woman was prominent. People in her area knew who she was and that she was all about helping others. In our text today, we see she paid close attention to a "man of God." She provided a room with all the amenities needed to assist him in ministry. Granny did the same for numerous college students that Pop taught. She came alongside him and would encourage various students studying for the ministry. She knew what that was like and that they needed all the support they could get. She went the extra mile and so many never forgot her. Her faith lives on through people she supported and through the scholarship.

Thank you, Granny Kitchings, for being like the woman at Shunem. I will forever think of you when I read this passage. May we all think of those in ministry we can go the extra mile for as they fulfill their call. What might you do today to support someone preparing for ministry? Maybe it's a minister in your local church? Whatever you do will not go unnoticed. Live by faith today...

· ·

DAILY READING:
2 Kings 4:18-5:27; Acts 15:1-35
Psalm 141:1-10; Proverbs 17:23
Focal Passage: Psalm 141:5

LIVING BY FAITH

NEVER DISCOUNT A GODLY REBUKE. David was a man after God's own heart. So often we see this as we read the Psalms. Here he prays that God would give him faithful friends who were not afraid to tell him the truth. He envisions himself in the home of a Godly man who is not quick to flatter, but willing to share stinging reports. The truth can sting. This is not a bad thing; it can be a good thing. It can keep one from further hurt. A bee sting hurts for a little while. A jellyfish sting hurts longer. And a shark bite, well, you get where I'm going. God disciplines His children because He loves us. He will graciously provide wise counsel along the way. Case in point... The prophet, Nathan, would rebuke David for his sin with Bathsheba. This was a direct answer to his prayer. And he listened. When we pray for something, we need to recognize when God answers.

Using the analogy of the day, hospitable people would wash guests' feet and anoint guests' heads with oil. It was refreshing. As we travel through life, how refreshing it is to receive an honest rebuke from a Godly friend or person. I have been refreshed many times through the years by Godly counsel. I have also, at times, rejected some Godly counsel. (It wasn't the Godly thing to do.) Just recently, without getting into details, a mentor basically said, *stay in your lane*. He listened as I shared how I thought something was right for me to do. When I took a break, he said *"Oh, I hear what you are saying, but..."* And he continued with the truth about the matter. I could listen because I knew he had my best interest at heart, and he loved God with all his heart.

Let's be willing to give Godly counsel. Let's be willing to receive Godly counsel. How refreshing it will be! Live by faith today...

JUNE 24

DAILY READING:
2 Kings 6:1-7:20; Acts 15:36-16:15
Psalm 142:1-7; Proverbs 17:24-25
Focal Passage: Acts 15:36-40

LIVING BY FAITH

IF PAUL AND BARNABAS CAN DISAGREE, SO CAN WE. Why? Because we are depraved. Because we are at different points in our spiritual lives. Because we have different backgrounds. Because we have different temperaments. Because, because, because… It happens. And if it happens with these spiritual giants, it will happen with you and me. I have not found it the most enjoyable aspect of being a Christian. But I have found it to be profitable, just like these guys did.

John Mark had a difficult time on his missionary journey with these men. He left them to go home before it was over. Ministry is not for the faint of heart. Mission trips certainly aren't! I don't think we should be too hard on him; we don't know all the details. (And he made a great comeback!) But his departure caused some friction for a while between Paul and Barnabas. Both had a point, yet they couldn't reach a point to go on together. So they parted ways and God sovereignly doubled their Kingdom impact. God is like that, isn't He? He will take a mess and make a miracle! Perhaps you can testify…

When you disagree with a brother or sister in Christ, take it to the Lord in prayer. Ask for wisdom. Talk to the person in person, if at all possible. Determine if it's a conviction or a preference. Decide if you need a third party to assist you with your disagreement. Try to unify around what you do agree on. Let go of things that in the big picture mean little or nothing. Part ways if you must. Trust God with the long-term results. I have found this to be one of the most difficult parts of our journey. It certainly is for me as a pastor. But it also provides a way to draw near to the Lord and perhaps have an even closer relationship with the person you disagree with. Live by faith today…

DAILY READING:

2 Kings 8:1-9:13; Acts 16:16-40
Psalm 143:1-12; Proverbs 17:26
Focal Passage: Acts 16:25

LIVING BY FAITH

DEEP DIFFICULTIES BRING UNIMAGINABLE WITNESSING OPPORTUNITIES. Paul and Silas were in deep waters. They had been unjustly beaten, and thrown into prison for their faith. There they were with wounded hearts and bodies, praying and singing. Can you imagine? I wish I could say that I would have been praying but singing… but I don't think so. One, I am not a great singer. Two, I usually sing when things are going well. But, that's just it. Things were well in their hearts. So, they could sing praises to the King. Jesus was Lord of their lives and they knew He wasn't going to leave them alone. He did come through, as we saw from our reading the chapter in its entirety. And what else occurred? Others were influenced due to how they handled their difficulties. That can be one of the greatest blessings of all. The jailor, and in time his family, were impacted by their faithful witness. People need to hear the gospel message. People need to see the gospel message in our lives. It's one thing to live for Jesus when things are going well. It's another to live for Jesus when your life has been turned upside down.

I will never forget when a fellow Clinton High teammate, Philip Gunn, faced the reality that his mother, father, and only sister died at the same time in a car wreck. They had been visiting him and his young family one weekend while he was attending law school at Ole Miss. A drunk driver hit them, and the car exploded, killing them instantly. At the time I was the Student Minister of his church, Morrison Heights Baptist in Clinton, Mississippi. He handled it with such dignity and class. Many people were watching him during this difficult time. He faced unimaginable pain due to losing his family of origin all at once.

Because of his family's influence and his own, hundreds of people were involved in the funeral. And they saw him trust the Lord. The message by Dr. Ken Alford was powerful. Hymns were sung, and prayers were offered that inspired all. Anytime I think of someone demonstrating living in faith during difficulties, and the power of the comfort that comes from the Holy Spirit during such times, I think of Philip. He was much like Paul and Silas during a dark time. Only in eternity will any of us know the lives which were changed because of Jesus that day. It gives me courage. I hope it does for you, also. Live by faith today…

DAILY READING:
2 Kings 9:14-10:31; Acts 17:1-34
Psalm 144:1-15; Proverbs 17:27-28
Focal Passage: Acts 17:22-31

LIVING BY FAITH

THE APOSTLE PAUL STOOD UP IN A HOSTILE ENVIRONMENT AND PROCLAIMED THE TRUTH. Areopagus means "Mars Hill," and was typically where religious and philosophical debates took place. All kinds of people would gather there. Most were more interested in their own agenda than anything else. A relationship with Jesus Christ was furthest from their minds. Paul didn't care. He knew what God had put him on the planet to do—proclaim the truth regardless of the consequences. He knew his audience, he met them where they were, and sought to take them where they needed to be. He explained this "Unknown God" for what it was and what it could be pointing toward—the one true God. God has made every nationality. There is no special class of citizens. There is no room for racial superiority. And any idol or symbol worshipped leaves one empty. Idols can misrepresent and diminish the glory of the living and true God. Jesus does not dwell in temples or idols or symbols. As spectacular as some of those may be, HE is transcendent!

Philip Gunn, the man I mentioned yesterday, is the Speaker of the House for my native state of Mississippi. Yesterday, he and others spoke passionately about the need to change a symbol. The only state that has a flag representing the confederacy as a part of its design is Mississippi. Philip has been a proponent of change on this issue for years. He and several others who have spoken out are no longer alone. Some people worship idols. An idol can be a person, place, thing, or thought. The thoughts for some concerning this flag reek of idolatry. The thoughts of others concerning this flag are of hate. Not everyone sees the current flag as something that builds unity. It does the opposite. Because Philip took a bold stand on this matter, it's having a positive effect today that will impact others way beyond his lifetime.

Paul was willing to proclaim God's truth in a hostile environment. Philip has, and will do again in the future, I'm sure. Will you? Never underestimate your influence and opportunity. As Martin Luther King Jr. said, *"The time is always right to do what is right."* Live by faith today...

DAILY READING:
2 Kings 10:32-12:21; Acts 18:1-22
Psalm 145:1-21; Proverbs 18:1
Focal Passage: Acts 18:9-10

LIVING BY FAITH

IF GOD GIVES YOU A MESSAGE OF RECONCILIATION, KEEP ON SHARING. Paul was not a superhero, though he was a hero of the faith. God used him in miraculous, unbelievable ways. But he was not Jesus. He wasn't perfect. Here we see he struggled with fear at times. Maybe he sometimes thought about "shaking the dust" before he needed to, due to the complacency of his listeners. He decided to keep on building a bridge between the Jews and the Greeks with God's message of reconciliation. Why? God spoke to him and gave him the courage to fulfill his calling. Many others needed to hear God's Word about what life is all about. God speaks to us through His Word and prayer. The Holy Spirit confirms what we are to do in our journey. It is not easy. Nothing worthwhile is ever easy. Jesus died on a cross to pay the penalty for our sins.

I discovered that the official vote to change the state flag of Mississippi is **today**. The world is watching to see what the result will be. Regardless, God is still on His throne. The message of reconciliation, the gospel message, will continue. Only Jesus can change hearts. And many will "build bridges" in the days ahead without fear, though fear may creep in at times. I have always contended that the way to have lasting change with regard to racial reconciliation is to build bridges one relationship at a time. God works through relationships. Tony Evans recently said, *"While many of us are waiting on God to fix what's wrong, He is waiting on us to step up as men and women of faith and do what's right."* I pray those in leadership for my native state do what's right today. I pray that today is a turning point for the world to see the Mississippi of the past, is not the Mississippi of today. I pray the Mississippi of the future will be the result of many people coming to Christ and the world seeing the state model the reality that Jesus truly loves all the children of the world. Live by faith today…

DAILY READING:
2 Kings 13:1-14:29; Acts 18:23-19:12
Psalm 146:1-10; Proverbs 18:2-3
Focal Passage: Acts 18:24-28

LIVING BY FAITH

HELPING YOUNG BELIEVERS GROW IN THEIR UNDERSTANDING IS A TREMENDOUS BLESSING. Apollos was fired up about "the way." (Early name for Christ followers.) He was a Jewish man who had been introduced to the Messiah. It set him free! (Jesus does that to a person.) And because of his background, intellect, eloquent speech, and passion, people listened to him. Lots of people listened because we read that he spoke in the synagogue. We're talking more than a handful. The fact that Priscilla and Aquila listened is further proof of his listeners. As they listened, they realized he needed a little more understanding. They didn't embarrass him while speaking. It wasn't like he was sharing heresy or I'm sure they would have. They simply pulled him aside afterward and explained the teachings of Jesus more fully. That's what discipleship is all about. When we are disciples, we need to listen and change when appropriate. When we disciple, we need to do so at the right time with a Christ-like spirit.

It's critical that all of us continue to grow spiritually until the day we die. We have a responsibility to know what we believe and to share those truths with others. It may be that we disciple others in a group setting. It may be that we do so one on one. Sometimes it's as we go. Be prepared for those opportunities like Priscilla and Aquila were. They have the potential to impact a number of people beyond just the disciple. Such is the case with Apollos. You can tell he was a true disciple because he listened. The word "disciple" means learner. It does not mean you listen to the truth and then do it your way. We need to be careful about investing a lot of time in those who say they want to learn, but in reality only want to share their opinion over and over again. (See the Proverb passage for today.)

I thank God for those who have helped me accurately interpret scripture and taught me doctrinal truth. My prayer is that I can do the same. What about you? Live by faith today...

DAILY READING:
2 Kings 15:1-16:20; Acts 19:13-41
Psalm 147:1-20; Proverbs 18:4-5
Focal Passage: Psalm 147:3; Proverbs 18:5

LIVING BY FAITH

WOUNDS BEGIN TO HEAL WHEN JUSTICE IS SERVED. The Mississippi House and Senate voted yesterday to remove the Confederate symbol from the state flag. The governor is scheduled to sign the bill into law today. I do not want to miss this opportunity to focus on two separate passages today in order to tell the story of how God works.

1. The broken-heartedness of people. Psalm 147 is really all about the return of the exiles to Jerusalem. It recognizes God's power and strength in arranging their return. He provided and healed their wounds. Many of my black brothers and sisters have been hurt for decades over this flag issue. I have no idea how they feel! I just know from talking with them through the years and educating myself as an adult on racism, it's been hurtful. I know it's just a piece of cloth, but it represents evil for many folks. The change now provides a clearer path for healing. My heart is full today. God is the ultimate author of all things good. He uses people. That's exactly what has occurred the last few days. May the rejoicing and healing of all those who have been hurt continue in the days ahead. God heals wounds—all of them if we allow Him to.

2. The wickedness behind the flag issue has been brought to light through this process. Proverbs 18:5 supports this as a biblical truth. I have seen statements on social media that have shocked even me. Why? Because of some people I know who are active in church trying to justify their prejudice. That's all it was. I know because I did it in the past and by the grace of God will not "go there" again in the future. It's not good! Innocent people deserve justice.

When I think of children of my black friends growing up in the future in Mississippi, I rejoice they will not have to learn what the confederate symbol in their flag means. Why? Because it ain't going to be there! Hallelujah, what a day! Live by faith today…

JUNE 30

DAILY READING:
2 Kings 17:1-18:12; Acts 20:1-38
Psalm 148:1-14; Proverbs 18:6-7
Focal Passage: Acts 20:7-12

LIVING BY FAITH

IF YOU SNOOZE YOU LOSE. When I was a student at Mississippi College, the baseball team would usually sit on "the wall" in the quad area between classes. I know you probably think we were comparing notes from the class we were about to attend. Not necessarily. We were comparing notes concerning attractive ladies who were passing by. I know, you are disappointed. Well, I'm sure it was more them than me. So, why am I sharing this little tidbit with you? If a beauty walked by and one of the guys missed it, we would say, "If you snooze you lose." In other words, if you don't pay attention, you may miss something good.

Eutychus missed something good. But God used it for good. (He's like that.) I don't want to be too hard on the boy. Maybe he had been working the fields all day and was worn out. Maybe he selected a window seat so he could watch pretty girls who might be passing by. (I hear that happens with young adult males.) Maybe the fumes and the packed house caused the ideal setting for a nap. Regardless, he missed THE Apostle Paul's last sermon at the church he attended. The young fella fell asleep and fell out the window to his death. Just as Jesus had done numerous times while on earth, Peter and the Apostle Paul were given the power to raise the dead through the Holy Spirit. Here we have an example; Paul breathed life into the young man. It further confirmed his apostleship and the power of the one true God. The church members were pumped, and they went back upstairs so the preacher could continue his lengthy message. Not only is what happened with the boy amazing, the fact that they left happy after hearing the long-winded preacher was too. I'm sure they probably needed a nap! But their excitement about what God had done in their midst couldn't be contained. Fortunately, the church folks didn't miss the moment.

Please don't miss what God has in front of you. It may keep you from "falling." Perhaps it was something that took place on this day in the past. Maybe it happened today. It could be it's about to happen. If you snooze you lose. Live by faith today…

LIVING BY FAITH

A RELATIONSHIP WITH JESUS CHANGES OUR PERSPECTIVE ABOUT TRIALS. We all experience trials of various kinds. Sometimes they appear suddenly, sort of like rainstorms in Florida during the summer months. The locals call it the "rainy season." It's true. Most every afternoon, storms will appear out of nowhere. (There's a reason this area is called the "lightning capital of the world.") On the other hand, some storms are fairly predictable. The weatherman tells us they are coming. The dark clouds tell us they are coming. Usually, they do. The same can be true in the life of a believer. As we follow what we understand to be God's will, we know it's not if the storm *will* come, it's just a matter of *when*. But we do our best to follow His will anyway because we are children of God.

Paul knew his new destination was going to be difficult. Others knew it, too. People who loved him tried to persuade him not to go. A prophet even gave him details about the storm he would encounter. God's family had tears about his going, knowing he may not make it out alive. He went anyway. He explained that his life was not his own. He was a child of God. He was an ambassador for Jesus. If he died, so be it. He would transition to heaven and be with Jesus in glory. Bringing glory to God on earth brings glory to God in heaven. The life of a believer is all about the name of Jesus. His loved ones eventually commended him for doing God's will. That's what brothers and sisters in Christ do when someone is following God's will. At some point, they should bless those headed into a storm because they are following what they understand to be God's will, even if they don't "get it."

Have you ever done something for Jesus, knowing it would cause you pain? You probably have. I have. You know what happened? It was painful! But I wouldn't change a thing. God teaches us so much during difficulties. He has a reason for why He wants us to do things that don't always make sense. We must trust Him, even if it means we don't totally understand until we reach heaven. It's worth it because of the opportunities for spiritual growth. It's worth it for others because it usually has to do with others. It's worth it because it fulfills our purpose, not the purpose others may think we have. Always keep God's perspective in mind. Live by faith today…

LIVING BY FAITH

YOU KNOW WHAT THEY SAY ABOUT ASSUMING, DON'T YOU? Don't do it. (Well, did you answer the question right?) Our text today has caused me to ponder that question. Is it always wrong to assume? Not necessarily. For example, I have had the pleasure of working with some staff members who do a fantastic job with their ministry assignments. When I've had time to develop a relationship with them, observe their character, and witness their success, I tend to assume good things about them. I am currently serving alongside one now who seems to go overboard in explaining why she's doing what she's doing. I usually stop her early on because I trust her. I assume the best about her motives and reasoning for what she's doing. (Unfortunately, I've served with some staff members who have demonstrated over time that I should not assume the best about them.) So, assuming the best in certain individuals is not always bad. Assuming the worst in certain individuals can be understandable, at times.

What about our man, Paul? Well, some Jewish guys assumed he brought a Gentile man into the temple, which set them off. He obviously did not. They assumed wrong. They didn't like Paul because of his Christian beliefs and the influence he was having on others. It cost Paul deeply. He was mistreated physically and misrepresented to others by those wrong assumptions. God is sovereign, and ultimately this entire episode was used for good.

Hear me, folks. If you walk with Jesus, mature Christians who know you will usually assume the best about you. Unfortunately, there **will** be those who assume the worst about you. Some folks don't want to assume the best about you because you represent someone they don't know. Some people will assume the worst about you because they don't know you personally. Some people will assume the worst about you because they've been listening to the wrong folks concerning you. Do you get the picture? Please do not let wrong assumptions keep you from following Jesus every step of the way. Continue to be a warrior for Him, just like Paul. Justice will be served in time. And be careful about assuming, although it's not always bad. Live by faith today...

DAILY READING:

2 Kings 22:3-23:30; Acts 21:37-22:16
Psalm 1:1-6; Proverbs 18:11-12
Focal Passage: Psalm 1:1-3

LIVING BY FAITH

HOW TO BE HAPPY, HAPPY, HAPPY. Happy can be translated *blessed*. And to be blessed by God is to be happy. Very happy. Why? Because a consistent walk with the Lord is the key to living a blessed life. And the Psalmist provides three "happys" in these verses.

One happy: Don't seek advice from someone who does not know the Lord. If you want to live a helter-skelter, up-and-down life, ask a pagan what to do. He doesn't know God, so he is highly unlikely to share truth from God's Word. In other words, he doesn't have the Bible as his authority, so... There we go. Don't do it or you're setting yourself up for a roller coaster life of frustration.

Two happy: Don't hang out with those who don't know the Lord personally. It's important that we not live in a cave with just believers. No, no, no. We need to be salt and light. But we do not need to allow those who are "taking a walk on the wild side" to be our closest friends. If we do, they'll pull us down. Which is easiest, to pull someone up to you while standing on a chair or pull someone down from a chair while standing on the floor? There you have it.

Three happy: Don't sit out in the yard with a mocker "talking shop." A mocker has little regard for the things of God. This person makes light of Godliness. He will lead you to a worldly view in a heartbeat. Be careful. You may not want to spend a lot of time with a mocker tomorrow as you observe Independence Day. He will put a damper on the freedom you enjoy in Christ.

Be blessed by standing consistent. Now you know how. And have a happy 4th of July! Live by faith today...

DAILY READING:
2 Kings 23:31-25:30; Acts 22:17-23:10
Psalm 2:1-12; Proverbs 18:13
Focal Passage: Acts 23:1-3

LIVING BY FAITH

SOME PEOPLE WILL VISIT GRAVESITES TODAY TO PAY RESPECTS TO THE BRAVE MEN AND WOMEN WHO FOUGHT FOR OUR FREEDOM. When they do, most will recognize very bright, white tombstones. That's typically a priority for those providing upkeep for graveyards. Though having an appearance of cleanliness, it's actually dirty underneath. Furthermore, a graveyard represents death, regardless of how nice a particular gravesite may look on the outside. But this can be an excellent way to be reminded of why Independence Day in America is celebrated. As citizens of the United States of America, we live in a free country. I thank God for those who fought for the freedom of religion. And it is a reminder that some people have a dead religion like the Pharisees and the Sadducees did. There's an appearance of life, but it's a cover-up for death.

The Apostle Paul was a brave warrior. He had enlisted in God's army and was "all in." He didn't allow beatings, verbal criticisms, or imprisonments to deter him. He answered to his ultimate commander-in-chief, King Jesus. He had a past. He was all about religion once. He was trained by the best. That past was dead, and he was never going back. He knew what these religious leaders were doing. He had been there and done that. He had the t-shirt. And he wasn't putting it on again! Therefore, he had great confidence in who he was in Christ. He could be bold. He was liberated and was simply following his marching orders. What were they? To share his testimony of going from death to life. Boldly confronting those who looked like they had it together on the outside but were fake on the inside. Sharing the gospel with *everyone* in hopes they too would enjoy freedom in Christ.

This is the way to live. There's nothing wrong with celebrating your freedom today if you are an American. That's why our founding fathers recognized this day so long ago. But let this passage remind you of where our source of ultimate freedom comes from. It comes from a relationship with none other than Jesus Christ. He paid the ultimate sacrifice when He died for our sins. Live by faith today...

DAILY READING:
1 Chronicles 1:1-2:17; Acts 23:11-35
Psalm 3:1-8; Proverbs 18:14-15
Focal Passage: Acts 23:16-17

LIVING BY FAITH

THE UNKNOWN NEPHEW MADE A SACRIFICE THAT SHOULD NOT GO UNNOTICED. As a child, our vacations were built around the yearly Southern Baptist Conventions. Daddy would load us up and drive to the destination every summer, building in extra time before or after the three-day convention. The vacation portion of the trip was always fun. I wasn't real keen on attending the convention meetings as a child. They were boring. As a matter of fact, as an adult… Never mind! Anyway, one trip I'll never forget was when the convention was held in Philadelphia, Pennsylvania. I was about twelve years old and I recall it being especially enjoyable. One reason was because we saw the Tomb of the Unknown Soldier. Now, that was cool for a guy my age! After World War I, a group determined it was critical for America to remember unidentified soldiers who had died in battle while serving our country. Eventually, these patriotic citizens were successful with their cause. A single tomb that contains one unknown soldier serves as a symbol of all unknown soldiers who gave their lives for the United States of America. The guard posted at the tomb was really what got my attention back then. Today it's the meaning that gets my attention. Unknown soldiers who died are worth remembering.

Paul's nephew is worth remembering, too. He sacrificed his life for the cause of Christ. He could easily have been killed. He wasn't. He was at the right place at the right time to provide much-needed support for his Uncle Paul. Who knows what would have occurred if not for the unknown nephew? I'm glad we don't have to ponder it for long, just long enough to know that every soldier in God's army is important. Never underestimate your value. God's keeping the record books. Furthermore, never doubt that God will take care of you no matter what you're up against. Who knows, it may even be your nephew who God uses to take care of you. Live by faith today…

DAILY READING:
1 Chronicles 2:18-4:4; Acts 24:1-27
Psalm 4:1-8; Proverbs 18:16-18
Focal Passage Acts 24:24-26

LIVING BY FAITH

SOME PEOPLE DON'T MIND TALKING ABOUT GOD, AS LONG AS SIN DOESN'T COME UP. Have you ever noticed that? I have occasionally encountered skeptics who love discussing religious matters. They have lots of questions about Christianity. Usually, they have lots of answers, too. Every once in a while there are those who are genuinely seeking to understand the Bible. It just seems those are few and far between. But you can find lots of folks ready to talk "religion." I'm not sure if it makes them feel smart or perhaps causes them to think that their mere interest gets them to heaven. Only God knows. I do know there seems to be one common thread—sin makes them uncomfortable. It should. We all sin and there's only one answer—Jesus. They just don't always stick around long enough to discover what He has done for them. Or maybe they don't want to be accountable for their sins.

Felix was fine talking religion with Paul for a while. He likely felt good about his wife being a part of the conversation. Maybe he felt it would impress her? Who knows... but what we do know is there came a time he became fearful and put a stop to the conversation. Paul started talking about living righteously, exhibiting self-control, and even soon-coming judgment for all. Felix squirmed and basically said *don't call me, I'll call you*. Paul's Jesus didn't fit his agenda. Paul's Jesus wasn't going to automatically make him wealthy. Paul's Jesus was even going to mess up his sinful lifestyle. Accountability can cause anyone to be uncomfortable, to a point. But having a relationship with Christ means surrender. We admit our sins. We trust in Him alone by faith for forgiveness. He then totally transforms our lives. He makes all things new.

Do you know anybody like Felix? Pray for them and don't give up. Be sensitive to opportunities to share the truth, without compromising it. Keep loving them. Maybe you identify with Felix yourself? Listen, you can talk religion all day long, it'll never fill the void in your life. Give your heart to Jesus. Everything else fades in comparison to what He will do once you admit your sins and turn toward Him. Live by faith today...

DAILY READING:
1 Chronicles 4:5-5:17; Acts 25:1-27
Psalm 5:1-12; Proverbs 18:19
Focal Passage: 1 Chronicles 4:9-10

LIVING BY FAITH

THIS ONE PRAYER CAN CHANGE THE TRAJECTORY OF YOUR LIFE. Most of us know of the Lord's Prayer in the New Testament. Not everyone knows of the prayer of Jabez in the Old Testament. I knew very little about it before reading a book by Bruce Wilkinson years ago entitled *The Prayer of Jabez*. (The only time I remembered studying this passage was through a study by Chuck Swindoll, another Dallas Theological Seminary graduate.) Jabez is suddenly singled out on this genealogical list of the messianic line of David in the tribe of Judah, from which God's promised Savior would come. (It's a compact history of Israel. And you were wondering what in the world was going on! I understand.) Jabez literally means *pain*. Something happened during childbirth that caused his mom to give him this unique name. (How would you like to be a pain from the very beginning?) Well, he obviously got over his name. Perhaps it motivated him. The prayer was the main reason that he's focused on here.

I broke the prayer down into four parts, after reading more about it in the early 2000s. For years I prayed it regularly. I asked God to **Bless me**. It was with His blessing in mind, not mine. And to keep me from becoming selfish. I prayed God would **Broaden my territory**. Dream big for God's glory. Don't settle for the minimum. I want to influence the world for God's kingdom. May there be a ripple effect long after my years. I asked God to **Be with me**. I know He's in me because the Holy Spirit lives inside me as a believer. I'm asking every day to remember He's there to help me make the right decisions moment by moment and protect me from the enemy's plan to thwart God's good plan. **Banish temptation from me**. Much like the Lord's Prayer, it's praying that God would cause me to be alert to the devil's schemes. The more useful we are for God's purposes, the more the enemy comes to destroy. We need to be aware of how the devil works and pray about it regularly.

This prayer of faith worked for Jabez. This prayer works for me. This prayer will work for you. Pray it. Believe it. Live it. Obey it. And pass it on. Live by faith today…

JULY 8

DAILY READING:
1 Chronicles 5:18-6:81; Acts 26:1-32
Psalm 6:1-10; Proverbs 18:20-21
Focal Passage: Acts 26:28-29

LIVING BY FAITH

WE ARE RESPONSIBLE FOR TESTIFYING AND LEAVING THE RESULTS TO GOD. The Apostle Paul was bold, wasn't he? My goodness, I wish I was as courageous to share my faith. I have a ways to go. Think about it, Paul shared with those who didn't have much. Paul shared with those limited by their social status. Paul shared with the wealthy. Paul was willing to tell ladies about the gospel of Jesus. He shared with jailors, intellectuals, sick folks, and even government officials. This guy was willing to share his testimony of life-change with those he barely knew, as well as with those he did know. He set a wonderful example for you and me when it comes to sharing our faith with others.

King Agrippa sort of chided Paul concerning the thought that he might be persuaded to give his heart to Christ in such a short period of time. Paul did not deny that it could happen. We need to remember this. Sometimes we can be guilty of thinking someone cannot accept Christ in a short period of time. We may even talk ourselves out of sharing our testimony with strangers because we don't really know them or just met them. There have been times I have not shared my faith with those I just met. There have been times I have shared with those I did just meet. Once many years ago, I found myself seated by a minor league baseball player on a plane. His name is Martin Prado. (He went on to play in the majors.) He prayed to receive Christ that day. Was it real? I have no idea. I'm responsible for testifying, leaving the results up to God, and following up the best I can. I hope to find out one day. I just wish I had more stories like that to share with you. I don't. This passage has convicted me to be more open to sharing the gospel with anybody at any time. What about you? It's not either-or. We certainly need to share with those we have a long-term relationship with. No doubt about it! But let's not miss opportunities to share with people as we walk through our daily lives, no matter how much influence they may or may not have. Live by faith today…

DAILY READING:
1 Chronicles 7:1-8:40; Acts 27:1-20
Psalm 7:1-17; Proverbs 18:22
Focal Passage: Psalm 7:12-16

LIVING BY FAITH

SOME PEOPLE DIG A HOLE AND FALL INTO IT. Have you ever dug a hole? Probably at some point, we all have. People dig holes to put something into. It may be a post, or flag, or something else. But there's a reason. And the reason is not typically to fall into it yourself. In this Psalm, we discover some dig a hole and fall into it. Why? Because they are selfish. Because they don't have Godly intentions. Because they are hard-headed and have not learned a lesson. Because they are trying to get someone due to jealousy or some other ungodly reason. That is the case here. It appears Saul is at it again. He's pursuing David with evil motives. David trusts God to take care of payback. He expressed that God is fully loaded with an arsenal unlike his. Wicked schemes of man with ill intent never work. The ungodly will often get a taste of their own medicine, or worse. Let God take care of it and keep your nose clean.

There's an important truth here that we cannot miss. While we are praying to God about a person who seems to have done us wrong, we must ask God to reveal wrong in our own lives. Maybe, just maybe, God is wanting us to learn a lesson He's been trying to teach us for years. Ask God to reveal sin to confess and be made right. The sooner we repent of any wrongdoing, or at least open the door for it, the better. There is a reason for God's timing. I don't always enjoy it. But I'm learning to trust Him in the midst of it and be repentant myself. What about you?

Is someone after you? Talk with Jesus about it. If they have evil motives, the consequences of their actions are coming. And don't think it won't be fair or automatically in the afterlife. Breathe deeply. Allow David's experience to encourage you. Saul's life didn't end well. He dug a hole and fell in it. Live by faith today...

JULY 10

1 Chronicles 9:1-10:14; Acts 27:21-44
Psalm 8:1-9; Proverbs 18:23-24
Focal Passage: Psalm 8:1-9

LIVING BY FAITH

WHEN I CONSIDER THE WORDS OF THIS PSALM, I TEND TO GET WEEPY. This Psalm magnifies the greatness of God. David is expressing how minuscule he feels when considering how massive God is. When considering the night skies, the creatures of the earth, and the reality that God allows us as humans to rule on His behalf, it is mindboggling. It reminds me of how sinful I am. But God in His infinite wisdom allows me to be a small part of it. Who am I? What am I that God would allow me to be a small part of His Kingdom program? I am nothing without Him. He's been good to me.

This Psalm was set to music years ago by Tom Fettke. It is called *The Majesty and Glory of Your Name*. As a teenager, I used to hear Martha Bacon sing this song during worship at my home church. Mrs. Bacon is a pretty lady. She's also radiant because she loves Jesus. You combine that with her extraordinary talent as a soloist, and you have the making of a powerful instrument of God. So when my dad died, we asked Martha to sing this song. She agreed, but wanted her husband Bill to sing with her due to her tender heart toward my dad. He had supported Martha and Bill over the years. That was fine with the family because we loved them both. During the moving song, she broke down and cried. After regaining her composure, she and Bill completed the Psalm with its penetrating words of comfort. That was the most encouraging moment for me during the entire service. I'm so thankful! I'll never forget it!

Fast-forward decades later, and I was sitting on the platform as pastor of a large church in Tennessee. The choir sang *The Majesty and Glory of Your Name* right before I was to preach. I started weeping because of the words of the song and the history of the song for me personally. I thought to myself, *"God, you are so amazing. The thought of my being here, at this moment, is beyond my comprehension. Who am I?"* I also thought about Bill and Martha and how encouraging they would be to me at that moment even though they were not there in person. It helped me get up to preach and move forward with my life during a rather trying time of transition. I wonder if David was thinking about me when he wrote these words? I doubt it, but God was. He cares so much about you and me that He has a plan and it's a good one—always. Live by faith today...

DAILY READING:
1 Chronicles 11:1-12:18; Acts 28:1-31
Psalm 9:1-12; Proverbs 19:1-3
Focal Passage: Acts 28:11-16

LIVING BY FAITH

OTHER BELIEVERS HELP PUSH US ONWARD DURING OUR JOURNEY OF FAITH. *Onward Christian Soldiers* was my dad's favorite hymn. We have discovered through our journey in Acts that the Apostle Paul was certainly a soldier of the cross. What a guy! Just in our text today he's walking around in chains and was attacked by a snake. The brother had trial after trial and yet he journeyed onward. I believe one of the reasons he was able to do so was because of the encouragement from other believers he received along the way.

I was reminded of an incident that happened to me just yesterday in reading the portion that said, "*...at the sight of these men Paul thanked God and was encouraged.*" What I have gone through in life or am experiencing is nothing compared to what Paul experienced. But I do have my days, just like everyone else. Difficult days. I had no idea when I decided to write this devotional book this year that we would have a worldwide pandemic. COVID-19 has been challenging for all of us. We all have had to adjust and determine how to move forward. This is certainly true for pastors. I was a little down yesterday, but I heard from one of my interns from decades ago. John Cross worked with me as he attended Mississippi College and I was the Student Minister at Morrison Heights Baptist in Clinton, Mississippi. John left school before graduating and I lost touch with him. We reconnected through social media and talked on the phone yesterday after decades. It was as if I had just spoken with him recently. We did not miss a beat. I am so proud of him! His words blessed me! God is using him, and he has a wonderful family. We're going to stay in touch because we need each other.

When I got off the phone, I thanked God and was greatly encouraged. God knows when we need the encouragement of other brothers and sisters in Christ. God's family is vital in our journey. Stay connected and recognize the need to bless others. Give praise to God when He sends someone who's a part of the *Cross* family just when you need them most. Live by faith today...

DAILY READING:
1 Chronicles 12:19-14:17; Romans 1:1-17
Psalm 9:13-20; Proverbs 19:4-5
Focal Passage: Romans 1:16-17

LIVING BY FAITH

THE TERM "GOSPEL" MEANS GOOD NEWS. I've never met anyone who didn't like good news. Have you? I don't recall telling someone something positive and their responding, *"Look, Hal, don't you ever, ever tell me anything positive again."* As believers, we have the best good news to share, ever! I mean, ever! The gospel means the entirety of salvation, not just the sharing of it initially, which is so important. Here's the theological way of explaining it: Justification has to do with salvation past. (I have been saved.) Sanctification has to do with salvation present. (I am being saved.) Glorification has to do with salvation in the future. (I will be saved.) **Now that's good news!** It's a gamechanger, is it not? What a privilege we have to share it. There is no news better than the gospel.

Paul let it be known from the beginning of this rich book that he was a messenger of the gospel. He declares that he ain't scared! Why should he be? Why would he ever be ashamed of the good news that had and continued to change his life? It's powerful. It gives lost sinners hope. It provides saints the ability to live out the Christian life. It provides assurance for heaven one day. I mean, this is an incredible assignment! It's a message we will see clearly as we walk through the riches of Romans.

Make no mistake, being born again is not just about getting your "heaven papers." It's about the transformation of the trajectory of your life. It is your life, not just a part of it. Rejoice in the God of your salvation. Live by faith today...

DAILY READING:
1 Chronicles 15:1-16:36; Romans 1:18-32
Psalm 10:1-15; Proverbs 19:6-7
Focal Passage: Romans 1:18-20

LIVING BY FAITH

GOD REVEALS HIMSELF TO EVERYONE, SO THERE'S NO EXCUSE. When I was growing up, I'd often hear the question, and consider it myself, *"But what about the dude in Africa?"* In other words, what about the person in a foreign land who's never heard about Jesus? Will he go to hell if he's never had the opportunity to respond to the gospel? I have found that our focal passage today is my "go to" for this question. Paul makes it clear that when man suppresses the truth, it doesn't give him a pass. Suppress means "to hold down." As humans, we often don't want to deal with our sinfulness. That doesn't matter. Truth is truth and God doesn't give us the freedom to skip over what we need to deal with in our own lives. He loves us too much. God's revelation comes through His invisible attributes that are clearly seen. Take the wind, for example. We can't see it, but we know it exists.

Years ago, Dr. Adrian Rogers came to preach at a church where I was serving as the Student Pastor. He preached on this subject. The two things I remember most are this: 1. Creation shouts the glory of God. 2. When God provides light and we respond positively, He reveals more light. Either Jesus is the only way, or He is not. He is and there's no excuse. God is big enough to get His message to those who live in an area where there is not a church on every corner. He does so through missionaries. He does so through the internet. He does so through every way we can think of and then some. He is God. God is sovereign. His ways aren't ours.

When I have preached on this subject, I close with what could be an even more pertinent question. *"What about the dude who sits in an air-conditioned church building week after week and doesn't respond to the gospel after hearing it over and over again?"* Yes, that's probably a question we may not think about as much. Maybe it's because we likely know the answer. Live by faith today...

LIVING BY FAITH

SHOWING FAVORITISM REEKS OF A WEAKNESS. We need to really pause here and ruminate on this verse. Okay... Now, let's think about this. If we're not careful, we can show favoritism based on our cultural upbringing, family influence, or educational experiences. We may even allow the world's way of putting certain people on a pedestal to seep into our actions. The word favoritism here means *to receive a face*. Basically, this means to give special attention to a person due to their position, wealth, influence, popularity, or even appearance. We all deal with this proclivity, yet it's not God's way. He loves everyone! There is no prejudice. Paul was making it clear to his readers that salvation can come to the Jew and the Greek. We have all sinned. There is no elitism when it comes to the gospel.

An elitist attitude may cause someone to feel strong. That's so silly. In reality, it's a weakness. It is a sign of insecurity. A secure person loves everyone like Jesus does. I want to be more like Jesus, don't you? He's wonderful! And He would want us to notice the unnoticeable. None of us have it all together. Some of us have been so blessed by God to be where we are. We need to be aware of the person who has blown it recently. Maybe today you need to go eat out and pray for your waiter. Perhaps today is the day to go to a nursing home. There are numerous lonely folks in nursing homes who could use a visit from you. I don't know what God may be leading you to do soon, but I know you won't be sorry you listened. You might even come to realize you are a strong person. Not because of your power or position of influence, but because of your security in Christ and aptitude for loving the "invisible" people that exist everywhere. Live by faith today...

LIVING BY FAITH

A WISE PERSON IS PATIENT. It stings to type that. I have not always been known to be a patient person. All you have to do is ask my family and close friends. I like for things to have happened yesterday! Can I get a witness?

The Bible says it's important for us to pray for wisdom. (Praying for patience is an entirely different discussion for another day.) So for those of us who have been doing so, a good gauge is if we are becoming more patient. Furthermore, an even greater indication is if we are learning to hold our tongue. A person with great wisdom guards his tongue. If not, one brings pain upon oneself. Can I get another witness? If you've lived life long enough, you know exactly what the writer of Proverbs is stating. Wisdom comes from God. None of us can hold our tongue during certain conversations without almighty God's assistance. That's just the truth. That's an indication of whether or not we're wiser than we were a while back.

So, how are you doing? How am I doing? I can't answer for you, but I can answer for me. I'm doing better in this area, by God's grace. I have not yet arrived, but He'll continue to give me opportunities to grow in this area until I finally get it. Why? Because He loves me. I can't say I've totally passed the test, but by God's grace, my grade is no longer a D.

A wise person is, indeed, patient. Let's pray for wisdom. Let's give ourselves a spiritual check-up in this area. Let's patiently move forward. Live by faith today...

LIVING BY FAITH

I OCCASIONALLY USE MY WIFE'S MAKEUP MIRROR. I know what some of you are probably thinking right now. You guys are thinking, *"I don't believe I'd have admitted that."* Look, I'm a man. I'm not turning in my "man card" just because I need a closer look sometimes. Here's the deal… my wife wants me to look pretty. She encourages me to pluck my eyebrows. I want her to be happy and I want to look pretty, so I use the mirror. It's unbelievable what all I see. This makeup mirror reveals all kinds of things that need my attention. Who knows, one day I may go get some Botox to assist me with what's happening with my body as I age. We shall see. I'm still not turning in my "man card."

The mirror doesn't repair anything. It reveals. It shows me what eyebrow hairs are out of control. This is exactly what the law does. Paul tells us in this passage that the law is designed to reveal our sin. The verses prior showed our absolute sinfulness. We're all in trouble. We're all wretched. We are all depraved! We need help. And the law's purpose was always designed to show us our flaws.

Have you watched the news lately? If so, you know things are getting worse. Our world seems to be going nuts. Our reading today reminds us we are sinners and none of us measures up to God's standards. If you have ever wondered why God gave us the law, now you know. And we're also being reminded during this walk through the book of Romans that He solved our dilemma. All the law does is show us how gracious our God has been and continues to be. It's not a bad thing. It's a good thing. Thank Him. Shout hallelujah. And consider looking at yourself in a makeup mirror to remind you how "flawed" you really are. Let God fix you. He can and He will if you let Him. Live by faith today…

LIVING BY FAITH

HOW LONG MUST I WAIT, LORD, I FEEL LIKE I'M DYING DOWN HERE! Do you ever feel like that? Come on, it's just you and God right now. I do. There have been times I've sensed God was calling me to do something else and nothing happened. I mean, nothing! I'm talking, for what seemed like *years*. I've also had a few times through the years when it seemed like the "bad guys," were winning. Come on now, don't be super spiritual. It's just you and God here. Sometimes they were lay people in the church I was serving. Sometimes they were staff people I served alongside. Several I felt led to give an incredible opportunity. I know, you're surprised. Don't be. David was pursued by King Saul. That has to be the ultimate betrayal. Well, there is that guy in the New Testament named Judas. I guess *that's* the ultimate betrayal of friendship.

David wrote this Psalm. I love the way he openly communicates with God. That's the way it should be for all of us as children of God. He wants us to be authentic. Remember, it's just you and Him during your devotional time. David seems to be dying here. He felt God had abandoned him. Evil folks seemed to have the upper hand. As powerful as David was as a person and as a warrior, he realized where his strength came from. He kept going to the source—God. What's so neat is that he was determined to rejoice in spite of what seemed to be an unfair situation. He did not lose his joy. That's the sign of a true warrior of God. He knows it's not *if* God will come through, it's just a question of *when*. God is faithful!

If right now you feel like David did, be encouraged. Think about God's faithfulness in the past. Rely on the saints of old who endured as much or more than you are right now. If there's a delay, it just means it's going to be all the better in time. Live by faith today...

DAILY READING:

1 Chronicles 26:12-27:34; Romans 4:13-5:5
Psalm 14:1-7; Proverbs 19:17
Focal Passage: Romans 5:4-5

LIVING BY FAITH

I DON'T ALWAYS REJOICE DURING A TIME OF SUFFERING, DO YOU? We all understand the incredible blessing of having peace with God. Christians can rejoice in the hope we now have due to a relationship with Jesus. But to get all fired up about suffering? That's a little more challenging, is it not? Let's think about a few types of suffering... Headaches aren't enjoyable. Employees walking off the job with little warning isn't ideal. The death of a family member hurts, even if anticipated due to a long illness. Having to put your dog down is extremely difficult. You see what I mean? And we are supposed to get "pumped" about these types of hardships? Paul says YES! Why? Because of the end result. God is working in those afflictions for our good. He should know, he went through many. We read about them throughout the book of Acts. If he can have this view, there has to be something to it. There is!

Afflictions don't always arrive at ideal times in our lives. Quite often, it seems they come during less than ideal times. But God knows everything. He knows what's going on in our lives—all the time. He knows when to allow pain. Just as we trust Him with our lives for eternity by faith, we must trust Him for our daily lives by faith. Even when we feel like we're being punched in the stomach. I have no idea what you may be going through right now. But there's a good chance it might not be as difficult as some of Paul's trials. That's not to take away from your pain. Not at all! It's just to try to help you pause and gain a Godly perspective. What you will be as a result of your current pain can change the trajectory of your life—forever. God puts stuff in you as a result of challenges. Good stuff, if you allow Him to do so. You will be closer to Him, personally. You will be more sensitive to others going through difficulty. You will be a better family member and friend. I'll stop there. You may not have a cheering session during a heart surgery coming up, but you might after you get through it because of the end result. I'm not just talking about physically, but spiritually you will be more like Jesus. We can rejoice because we know after the painful season is over, it will be for good. Live by faith today...

DAILY READING:
1 Chronicles 28:1-29:30; Romans 5:6-21
Psalm 15:1-5; Proverbs 19:18-19
Focal Passage: 1 Chronicles 29:1-9

LIVING BY FAITH

WHEN DO YOU GIVE AN OFFERING TO SUPPORT GOD'S WORK? I believe in biblical tithing. I believe that at least ten percent of our total earnings should go to the local church. I really do. My parents taught me at a young age the principle of tithing. I had no idea how blessed I was that they made sure I understood we give our resources out of obedience and love toward God. He gave His all for us. I've never struggled with giving a tithe to where I belong or serve, by the grace of God, because I learned early on it's just what you do. There's no way to outgive God. So, what about this offering we speak of today?

I have learned over the years that it is appropriate to give an offering to support Kingdom causes. That's exactly what was happening in our text today. David was not called to literally build the temple for the glory of God. His son, Solomon, would be God's man for that overwhelming task. So, what did David do? 1. He laid out the vision. This "house of God" was for the glory of God. Any ministry in the name of Christ should be for His glory alone. It was no regular house. It was going to be Solomon's temple; it would ultimately be God's. 2. He explained what he had personally done to support this God-ordained project. He gathered resources for construction and personally invested in what was to come. In other words, he had skin in the game. Leaders always operate this way. 3. He challenged other leaders to step up. The tone was like...*who else is going to receive blessings for such a long-awaited God project?* 4. Those who felt led by God to participate gave willingly. It wasn't grudgingly, it was willingly. They gave wholeheartedly. And guess who was happy? King David. Wouldn't you be?

Assuming you give your tithe to your local church, do you give offerings from time to time or regularly to a Kingdom-based ministry? Maybe it's a project? Over the years my wife and I have felt led to give to building projects at the church where we serve. We have given offerings to young ministers. We have given offerings to church plants. We have given offerings to a Christian college we support. And we have given offerings to ministries of ministers we believe in. The reality is that I wish we could do more and hope to do so in the future. I gave you those examples so you might know what God wants you to do in the future. God provides so we can bless others. Live by faith today...

JULY 20

DAILY READING:
2 Chronicles 1:1-3:17; Romans 6:1-23
Psalm 16:1-11; Proverbs 19:20-21
Focal Passage: Romans 6:1-14

LIVING BY FAITH

WHY WOULD I WEAR MY OLD DIRTY RUNNING SHOES WHEN I HAVE A NEW PAIR OF WHITE ONES? I enjoy wearing white shoes. My daughter Halie makes fun of me. That's OK. I think it was the era I grew up in. When it came to baseball cleats, all my shoes were white (except for the year I had a coach who didn't allow it). I felt as if I could run faster with white shoes. Don't tell Halie, but I still do.

I just had my newer white running shoes washed. I could tell this morning; I think I broke my own personal record in a three-mile run. Now, I still have an old pair. They are cool, but they aren't white, and they are old. Why would I wear them? Just to not put wear and tear on my new ones, and because where I'm wearing them tends to not matter that much. You know, like helping someone move or something. Neither does it make sense to run the race of the Christian life, an analogy Paul used often, in the flesh. As believers, we have the Spirit of God living inside of us. It's foolish to live a life ruled by sin. God has us in THE race and we don't need anything to slow us down. We are no longer slaves to sin. If we continue in our sinful state or allow weaknesses to rule, we have forgotten our true identity. We live under grace and so we are motivated out of our love relationship with Jesus to live a life that reflects Him.

Living with one foot in the Word and one foot in the world is like wearing one new white tennis shoe and one old tennis shoe. You talk about an odd run! If we have truly been born again, our run to the finish line of life will always—always—feel odd, if we are living a double life. Christ died for our sins, let's run like it. Live by faith today...

DAILY READING:

2 Chronicles 4:1-6:11; Romans 7:1-13
Psalm 17:1-15; Proverbs 19:22-23
Focal Passage: Proverbs 19:23

LIVING BY FAITH

THIS IS BETTER THAN ANY SLEEPING AID AVAILABLE. Most of you young folks don't struggle to get to sleep. I didn't. Older folks tend to struggle in this area. I do. What do you do? Well, I don't prefer to take sleep aids. I do occasionally, but some of them made me crazy. (I need no help in this department!) Others work for a while and then they don't. It's odd. But it's never enjoyable to not get a good night's sleep. Some of you know what I mean.

So, does this mean those of us who struggle sleeping don't fear God? Not necessarily. It may just mean we're old. This verse speaks of fearing God. Biblical fear is an overarching theme of Proverbs. It means reverential awe of God or an overwhelming admiration of God. It is an ongoing state of mind that changes one's attitudes, will, feelings, deeds, and even goals. God naturally does this when we fear Him. It's a good fear, not a bad fear. And when we are living life out of biblical fear, we don't lay our head down at night convicted over ongoing deliberate disobedience. This does not mean we are perfect. It means we know what it's like to try to sleep as a child of God knowing we have disobeyed. I've been there, done that, and have the non-sleep shirt. That is the worst kind of night a child of God can have.

Know this—if you fear God, you have no reason to fear. When you lay your head down at night, HE IS WATCHING OVER YOU. Fear God. Sleep well. Be content. Live by faith today...

DAILY READING:

2 Chronicles 6:12-8:10; Romans 7:14-8:8
Psalm 18:1-15; Proverbs 19:24-25
Focal Passage: Romans 7:14-25

LIVING BY FAITH

SOMETIMES I WANT TO DO THE RIGHT THING, AND THEN I DON'T, AND THEN I SCREAM. Did you understand what you just read? Maybe not. At times, I don't understand how I can know what God would have me do, but I don't do it. When my children were little and would disobey, I often got so upset. It wasn't that they didn't need correction. Many times it was something they knew was wrong and they'd do it anyway. Hello! (Isn't that what we're dealing with here? I think so.) My body language and voice tone were sometimes too strong during those moments. Many times I'd have to tell them what they did was wrong, but the way I communicated their wrong was wrong. I'm sure they got tired of it. I got tired of it. I'd often think, *"How foolish! What a wretched man I am!"* Well, this doesn't excuse those moments, but I am in good company. Paul dealt with the same issue. He'd want to do right because he knew what was right, but he battled with the flesh. Sometimes he'd just go ahead and sin. And he'd feel miserable! Christians make lousy sinners! Why? Because the Holy Spirit convicts us of our sinfulness. He continually draws us to Himself.

Not once is Paul excusing sin in our passage today. He is just reminding us that evil doesn't define us. Jesus defines us by who we are in Him. When we are tempted, look upon Jesus. He really is the author and perfecter of our faith. So, there's this guy right now who is misbehaving. He's in my church. He knows better. God is using him daily, to cause me to pray aloud or silently at various moments, **"Dear God, please help me behave! PLEASE Jesus, cause me to react in the Spirit, and not in the flesh. Because God, I want to knock his block off right now—how dare he!"** Okay, pray for me. There you have it. Hopefully, I will behave due to your prayers. Oh wait, by the time you read this it will likely be in the distant past. Oh well, I hope by God's grace I handled it right. If so, it will only be due to depending on Jesus moment by moment. He is still working on me! He was still working on Paul at this point in his journey, as we read today. And if you are honest, Christian, you know He is still working on you. Let Him. And when there's a victory, may the words of Paul be expressed—*"Thanks be to God through Jesus Christ our Lord!"* Live by faith today...

DAILY READING:
2 Chronicles 8:11-10:19; Romans 8:9-21
Psalm 18:16-36; Proverbs 19:26
Focal Passage: 2 Chronicles 10:6-11

LIVING BY FAITH

BE CAREFUL TO WHOM YOU LISTEN. King Solomon had died. He surely had numerous sons, but only one is named in scripture. His name was Rehoboam. After being appointed as King, due to his father's death, he was faced with a big decision. (That comes with leadership positions. Sometimes you know what decisions you will need to make. Sometimes, you may have "surprise" decisions.) The people of Israel wanted relief from heavy taxation and overly difficult service. They enlisted Jeroboam, an influential leader, who had returned from Egypt after Solomon's death, to make the request. (He likely departed for a while due to Solomon's harsh leadership practices in the later part of his life.) Rehoboam took some time to seek counsel. This is vital in seeking to know God's will concerning a big decision. Just be careful whom you seek to advise you on important matters.

Wisely, seeking counsel from older experienced men was a good decision. They advised him to show kindness to demonstrate a good heart. He would earn the right to lead and they would love and serve him for years to come. He rejected their advice and sought the counsel of his buds. It appears he was looking for those who would tell him what he wanted to hear. This is always unwise. It's better to have a few trusted counselors who will lovingly tell you the truth. You want some folks who love you enough to do so, regardless of the outcome. Having "yes men" is a travesty. Having "no men" is, too. Balance! Again, balance is important in living out the Christian life.

Rehoboam made a foolish decision. He went in the opposite direction of what was suggested by the elders. Eventually, he reaped the consequences. If we choose to run off into a ditch, we will reap what we sow. We must not allow pride to get in the way of making good decisions. Seek God. Seek godly counsel. Be careful to whom you listen. Live by faith today...

DAILY READING:

2 Chronicles 11:1-13:22; Romans 8:22-39
Psalm 18:37-50; Proverbs 19:27:29
Focal Passage: Romans 8:26-27

LIVING BY FAITH

WHEN YOU DON'T KNOW WHAT TO PRAY, OR HOW TO PRAY, PRAY ANYWAY. Do you ever have times in your life when you just don't know how to pray anymore? Do you ever have times you don't *feel* like praying? Do you ever have times you feel like your prayers are hitting the ceiling? Do you ever have times you just think your words are not as eloquent as others that you've heard pray? And do you ever just sense you don't know the language of prayer? If you answer yes to one or more of these questions, you are in good company and about to be freed up in your prayer life.

God translates our prayers. When we are so overwhelmed with our circumstances that we just don't know what to say anymore, God intercedes for us. The word Paul uses here means "to appeal." The Spirit grabs that prayer and takes it to the will of God. If we are being real with God, He will be real with us. Heart prayers are the best. It's not about fancy words. It's not about using theological terms. It's about authenticity. Be real with God! If we are loving God and progressively being conformed to His image, our heartfelt prayers are powerful! So, if you are being too hard on yourself due to your prayer life, stop it! Pray. Focus on what this passage is saying. God will always work for our good when we seek to please Him. He knows our limitations. That's why He sent Jesus. Jesus came to set us free—even in our prayer life!

Prayer is not easy. Nothing worthwhile is easy. But it's worth it. Something happens when we pray real prayers consistently. Just keep praying and trusting God with the results. Live by faith today...

DAILY READING:

2 Chronicles 14:1-16:14; Romans 9:1-21
Psalm 19:1-14; Proverbs 20:1
Focal Passage: Proverbs 20:1

LIVING BY FAITH

CAN A DRINK CAUSE A STINK? Well, what does a careful examination of our verse lead us to believe? It certainly seems that way. I have an entire sermon that explores this question. I won't preach my sermon to you today, but I will pull some information from it.

I grew up in the deep South where most Baptists focused on the evils of alcohol. That's not necessarily bad, but there are a lot of evils. For example, racism is an evil. My grandfather Kitchings hated alcohol. The reason, from my understanding, was due to a family experience in his childhood. Someone evidently abused alcohol and the consequences weren't good. They never are when substance abuse is involved. So he didn't drink, and he didn't want his five kids to drink. My dad didn't drink. He hated alcohol because he was taught to do so, and it stuck with him. He taught me to hate it. I didn't drink, by God's grace, even though I was around alcohol growing up. I had friends who drank, and I loved them. (I still do.) Most of them respected me enough not to give me a hard time. I sometimes blamed it on my dad, and let them know he would "kill" me if I drank. And they'd usually smile and let it go. So, needless to say, I have a background with this subject. I just don't harp on it. I recall going out witnessing with my pastor, Dr. Byron Malone, when I was in my first full-time church. A guy drinking a beer asked Dr. Malone if he thought he was going to hell because of it. Dr. Malone said, "No, but it may make you think you've been there." I understand hangovers are awful.

Wine consumption is mentioned in the Old Testament and the New Testament. It was a common beverage. They didn't have water purification systems like we do today. I don't think they even had Diet Coke, either. Drunkenness is clearly and soundly condemned in Scripture. It's always been sinful. Think of consequences in our day due to drunkenness. Just ponder how it may have caused great pain in your own family or a friend. Is it worth it? If you never have the first drink, you'll never have too much to drink. It can't be wise to allow alcohol to be a source of happiness. If drinking becomes the place where one seeks to get their value or "relief" from troubles, it causes a stink. Be careful, my friend. Use good judgment. Someone is always watching our lifestyle. Allow the Holy Spirit to guide you in this matter. Live by faith today...

LIVING BY FAITH

IS THIS REALLY THE SINNER'S PRAYER? Yes and no. Hang with me. I grew up with an emphasis on "The Sinner's Prayer." Simply put, it's basically saying a prayer out loud to prove you believe you are a sinner and Jesus is now your Savior. That's good, right? Absolutely! I think this passage is what the prayer is based on. Paul is emphasizing that our righteousness is not based on our good works. It is based on the finished work of Christ. This is a way of assurance. Faith alone in Jesus is the answer to a relationship with Him. So, many of us have "prayed the prayer" to admit our sin, confess we believe in Jesus by faith alone, and we're not ashamed of Him. It has been a turning point for so many believers to have said this prayer, based on this passage. But there is no phrase in the Bible that says, *"You are about to say the Sinner's Prayer, and if you want to become a Christian this must be said so it can be recorded in heaven."* Not at all. There are thousands who say they pledge allegiance to the flag of the United States of America. Do all of them mean it? Only God knows.

To be overly critical of those who say "the prayer," is unnecessary to me. To be overly confident in the fact that one said "the prayer" is dangerous. For one to be assured of heaven just because at some point they "prayed the prayer" is poor theology. For example, if the person is not actively following Jesus, that person has little assurance. Great assurance accompanies the believer who is demonstrating genuine conversion by perseverance. Feelings are the caboose, not the engine. Being born again is the beginning, not the end. So don't neglect the one without the other. There is nothing wrong with saying "The Sinner's Prayer." There is something wrong in leading people to believe that's all there is to it; the belief that some magical words or some odd incantation will suffice for Christianity. Admitting our sin, repenting of our sin, believing in Christ alone, by faith alone, and knowing Jesus died for our sins and rose again works. It's not a work. It's His work. If we believe, it works. Does that work for you? I pray so. Have you said "The Sinner's Prayer?" If not, why not today? It can certainly provide great assurance and give you something to hang your hat on. But don't stop there or you're missing the point. Live by faith today...

DAILY READING:

2 Chronicles 19:1-20:37; Romans 10:14-11:12
Psalm 21:1-13; Proverbs 20:4-6
Focal Passage: Romans 11:2-5

LIVING BY FAITH

GOD ALWAYS HAS A REMNANT, WHETHER WE REALIZE IT OR NOT. As we've studied the nation of Israel, we have seen that some were faithful and some were not. Pause and think about that… Is that not the story of the church? Chances are you have even been a member of a particular fellowship where some were faithful and some were not. It's happened down through the ages. Paul reminds the believers of Elijah in the Old Testament. God had thousands ready to support Elijah, even though he thought he was alone. Sometimes we can be so overwhelmed by our circumstances, we don't see straight. We stop looking with the eyes of faith. Our minds are clouded with such worry and fear that we forget God has others living for Him, too. The Apostle Paul had a remnant, chosen by God's grace, who were also faithful believers. They were saved by the grace of God, not good works. He wanted his readers to know that God never leaves us alone, even though we may feel like it at times. He doesn't save us and then abandon us as we seek to serve Him. We are never alone.

I can remember feeling alone during various stages of life. Can you? As a child, I recall times I felt alone when I had to do something others didn't have to do because my dad was the pastor. I look back now and realize He always had a remnant. It had nothing to do with being a preacher's kid. It was doing what was right, regardless. There were other kids around who were doing what was right, I just chose not to see them. I remember similar incidents as a teenager. I remember playing baseball in college and feeling alone at times. I wasn't. I can name other strong believers who were on the team. As an adult, I've thought as a pastor I was alone sometimes. I wasn't. God always, always has a person or two or three. He is faithful not to leave you by yourself!

The next time you feel alone because you are living out your faith in the marketplace, please remember to see God's remnant. If you seem to not be able to see them, see them through His eyes. Remember the truth of this passage today. God is true to His Word. And certainly, remember that He is always with you! Live by faith today…

DAILY READING:
2 Chronicles 21:1-23:21; Romans 11:13-36
Psalm 22:1-18; Proverbs 20:7
Focal Passage: 2 Chronicles 21:18-20

LIVING BY FAITH

THIS KING DIED AND NO ONE CARED. Can you imagine? He died a terrible death and was not honored. That just doesn't happen when a King dies. Well, it did when King Jehoram died. He was buried and forgotten. He had ruled so ruthlessly that they couldn't wait for the moment of his demise. The sooner the better. There's always a cost for mistreating others. It may not be immediate, but it will happen eventually. It may not be seen, but God will see to it. He is a just God. We can't treat people with contempt and get away with it.

One day you will die. One day I will die. Will anyone care? Might people want to attend our funeral? What about this—might there be some who say or think "Good riddance!" I pray none of us have people who can't wait for our death. But we need to think about it. Maybe we need to do a better job of investing in others. Maybe we need to have that conversation with someone we're at odds with. Maybe we need to learn from this evil King.

Don't think just because you had a good dad that you will be one. King Jehoram's dad was King Jehoshaphat's son. Remember him? He was a Godly King. No, he wasn't perfect, but he sought the Lord, unlike his father. You see where I'm going. You can have a Godly dad and still turn out to be a reprobate. You can have an ungodly dad and turn out to be a man who seeks God whole-heartedly. We each are writing our own story. What will yours say? What will mine say? Let's seek God and follow Him with our whole heart. If so, others will care. How do I know? Because if you love God, you will love people. Live by faith today...

DAILY READING:
2 Chronicles 24:1-25:28; Romans 12:1-21
Psalm 22:19-31; Proverbs 20:8-10
Focal Passage: Romans 12:9

LIVING BY FAITH

DON'T WEAR A MASK UNLESS YOU HAVE TO. COVID-19 has changed our lives. Never before have we had a pandemic like the one experienced in 2020. What I most remember is that wearing a face mask became the new normal. I remember when this new method of doing life was introduced, I didn't take it seriously enough. I sort of laughed it off. Not after a while. I realized I needed to get on board and wear a mask at times. (I do think some of it was overkill.) When required, not wearing a mask is not an option. So, in a time when putting on a mask is what you do, the Bible says to take off your mask. Of course, Paul is speaking spiritually.

We are to love God and love people. Our verse commands us to love without hypocrisy. The original understanding of the term "hypocrisy" was used for actors. Actors wore masks. They were being someone they weren't. In life, there are some who are really hypocrites. Even in the church there are fakes. How often do we come together as the body of Christ and not really be ourselves? I'm afraid it's too often. Church should certainly be the one place we can come and take our masks off. I'm not talking now about social distancing. If social distancing is going on… put your mask on, while taking your invisible mask off. Be real. Be authentic. Be vulnerable. Be balanced. Now, I don't suggest you meet with your small group and dump a dump truck load of your "stuff" every time you meet. But don't be the other extreme either. If you can't be yourself and share your heart at times with your church family, where else do you share it? What group is safer? If it's safer outside the body of Christ, reevaluate where you go to church. But start with self-evaluation. What kind of mask, if any, are you wearing?

Church should be the kind of community where people can take their fake masks off. It should be a safe place. Maybe you need to be the one to help set an example? Maybe you're a part of a church that is real—authentic. If so, praise God! Don't wear a mask unless you have to. Live by faith today…

LIVING BY FAITH

A WALK ALONG THE BEACH MAY BE EXACTLY WHAT YOU NEED. I have always been a "beach person." Do you know what I mean? Some people like to go to the mountains. Some people like to go to the beach. Even though I have lived a big portion of my life in Florida, I still would rather go to the beach than the mountains. I discovered years ago that many people who live in Florida enjoy going to the mountains to watch the leaves in the fall. That's fine. But I watched enough leaves growing up. I'm good. And I do enjoy visiting the mountains occasionally. One of my favorite places to go is *The Cove* in North Carolina (the Billy Graham Training Center). But let me have the beach. I like everything about it. Besides, it's biblical.

Did you see it? No, really, did you see it? I saw it for the first time, all over again, yesterday. My wife Kellie and I had coffee with our longtime friend Billy Causey. It was our first time to sit down and chat since his wife, Mary Leigh, passed away due to cancer. (She was a precious person!) We talked about our recent journeys. He shared about taking time to walk along a beach in Florida for a time after her death. He repeated several times, "But most of the time, I walked along the beach and just stared at the water." And then all of a sudden, he shared this verse. It was a powerful moment for Kellie and me. We looked at each other and both said we would never look at that very familiar passage the same. He shared how God healed him through his time with Him at the beach. He went on to say it's vital for all of us to take time with God, especially when facing a major crisis or decision. (You may want to read our focal passage again right here.)

Take time to allow God to heal you. I love Florida! It's my adopted state. If you need to know of a few beaches to visit, give me a call. There are numerous beaches that God can use to lead you into your future. Live by faith today...

LIVING BY FAITH

SOME MATTERS ARE NOT WORTH EXPENDING A LOT OF ENERGY OVER. In the Bible, we have essentials and non-essentials. Meaning there are some things we need to lay down as our foundation, as believers. The virgin birth and the trinity, for example, are not open for discussion. Those are foundational beliefs. There are more. Then there's the issue in the passage about eating meat offered to idols. Jesus freed them up. They could eat meat. But if it caused a brother to stumble, eat an apple. Don't "wear him out." The mature Christian needs to be able to understand that some don't feel the same on certain issues. When it comes to disputable matters (where it is not crystal clear), be careful about judging someone.

Personally, I'm thankful that eating meat is not a huge deal where I live. I am a meat-eater. But there are other issues of the day. Some people don't celebrate Christmas or ever mention the "big fella." They believe all the commercialism takes away from the true reason for the season. Jesus was born of a virgin and it was a silent, profound night. I'm one who focuses on Jesus but I am okay about the "big fella." (Ask your neighbor who that is if you don't know.) The guy who thinks Christmas is too commercialized doesn't need to come down too hard on me. And I don't need to come down too hard on him. There's room for disagreement on some matters when it comes to our faith. Don't expend a lot of energy on these types of issues. Life is too short!

If you are thinking about boycotting a certain place, be careful and prayerful. Read this entire passage and pray over it. Is it really necessary? Is it owned by a secular company? Does it help or hinder your witness? What would a lost person think? Do you advertise it? These are all things to consider if you ever think about boycotting. Whatever you do, don't be self-righteous. Be like Jesus and represent Him best with your actions or non-actions. Live by faith today...

DAILY READING:

2 Chronicles 30:1-31:21; Romans 15:1-22
Psalm 25:1-15; Proverbs 20:13-15
Focal Passage: Psalm 25:15

LIVING BY FAITH

VACATIONS ARE REFRESHING, BUT NOT WHEN YOU TAKE ONE FROM THE LORD. I am on vacation right now. It has been refreshing. My wife Kellie and I have spent time with family and friends. We have enjoyed doing nothing. We have gone out to eat at some of our favorite restaurants. We have been swimming and boating. It's important to take vacations along the way. They can be so refreshing. God wants us to take time to rest and regroup. But it is never good to take a vacation from the Lord.

David is looking to the Lord for safety. He knows the enemy is pursuing him. He realizes that only God can save him from the enemy's traps. We too, have an enemy. It is the Devil. He sets traps and wants to ensnare us. And the world's system is used to tempt us with the desires of the flesh. Guess what, this will be reality until we get to heaven. The Devil never takes a vacation. But never forget, God doesn't either. And He is our victory!

So don't take a vacation from God. Stay connected. David is letting us know in this verse to keep our eyes on the Lord. Don't focus too much on the trap—if so, the enemy will use it to get you off track. It will be a snare. Sometimes it happens quickly. Sometimes it's a slow fade. Constantly stay focused on Jesus. Don't wait for Sunday morning, seek Him daily. He wants to be your constant friend. Yes, you fear God. But when done in a biblical sense of respect and awe, He's like no other friend you've ever had or ever will have. Take a vacation, but not from God. He's the ultimate refresher we all need every day of our lives. Live by faith today...

AUGUST 2

DAILY READING:
2 Chronicles 32:1-33:13; Romans 15:23-16:7
Psalm 25:16-22; Proverbs 20:16-18
Focal Passage: 2 Chronicles 33:10-13

LIVING BY FAITH

WE CANNOT HIDE OUR PRIDE FROM GOD. God never "winks" at our pride. Pride is a costly sin. God is holy. He does not tolerate a haughty attitude. If you want to receive an unbearable type of discipline, launch out on your own and take credit for it. It never, ever works well. Please refrain.

King Manasseh was an evil man. He did much to destroy the Kingdom of God and all that had been accomplished by his godly father, King Hezekiah. (Having a dad who loved God does not guarantee the son will do the same. We see this over and over as we read through the Bible.) God disciplined Manasseh. He was captured by the Assyrians and led away from Jerusalem like an animal. Is that not humbling! Finally, finally, he did humble himself and seek the Lord. Our gracious Lord was touched by his new broken attitude and answered his prayer. He was returned and finished strong in the Lord. There were still consequences to his years of disobedience. His reforms were limited because of the bad influence he had on so many.

God is gracious. God forgives. God redeems. Pride is awful! God knows when we are genuinely repentant. God hears our prayers. We all have influence— good and bad. God gives us a long rope, but enough is enough if we continue to be prideful. It is never too late to turn to God.

If you are struggling in your walk with God, turn to Him NOW. Please don't continue a rebellious journey. If you are doing fairly well in your walk, give Him all the credit and glory. It's Him, not you. And stay connected. Pride typically starts with a small step away from our Lord, thinking we've got it. We don't. He does. And He loves us. Live by faith today...

DAILY READING:
2 Chronicles 33:14-34:33; Romans 16:8-27
Psalm 26:1-12; Proverbs 20:19
Focal Passage: Romans 16:3-16

LIVING BY FAITH

A DIVERSE CHURCH UNIFIED IN CHRIST IS A POWERFUL TESTIMONY. As Paul closes his letter, he sends greetings to a number of people. A close examination reveals their diversity. There was ethnic diversity. There was a diversity of gender with the body of Christ. And there was even diversity of class. I love this picture! It's a picture of heaven on earth. Paul did not close this letter filled with rich truth without thanking people who were faithful. Faithful people help keep the church alive and moving forward. There were rich folks, poor folks, yellow folks, red folks, ladies in places of leadership, men singing, etc. Get the picture? Yes! We all do, and it should be a deep desire to diversify the church and be unified in Christ Jesus.

Are you a member of a church similar to the one described here? It takes a very secure leader, with a unified leadership team. It requires intentionality. It takes a group of leaders who know where the church is located and how to best point others to Jesus. It takes time. When failures occur, it requires prayerful warriors moving forward regardless. Educating the church on various cultures, abilities, and spiritual gifts is valuable. Engaging the community where the church is located is paramount. Humility is a hallmark of the people who are members. It means the Gospel is the top priority. It means new folks who join know their role and what the purpose of the church is. There is a constant challenge of intimacy with the Lord. The people of the church give glory to God alone and are grateful. Please don't miss that—grateful! And I'm not talking about just at Thanksgiving. Always.

Be the church. Don't major in non-essentials. Allow this list to encourage and challenge you. Live by faith today...

DAILY READING:
2 Chronicles 35:1-36:23; 1 Corinthians 1:1-17
Psalm 27:1-6; Proverbs 20:20-21
Focal Passage: 1 Corinthians 1:9

LIVING BY FAITH

THIS IS THE VERSE WE SAID AT THE END OF EVERY SUNDAY EVENING SERVICE. I served twice at Morrison Heights Baptist in Clinton, Mississippi. The first time, I was the Student Pastor for five years, serving alongside Dr. Ken Alford. The second time, I was the Senior Pastor for five and a half years. When I was Student Pastor, we sang *"All Day Long I've Been with Jesus"* at the end of the Sunday evening service. We would grab hands across the aisles and sing this together as our benediction. When I returned as pastor, I wasn't sure what they did at the end of the service with the pastor between Dr. Ken and myself. I decided we would share a verse together while holding hands across the aisles. Our verse today was the verse. So naturally, every time I read this passage, I think of its truth and my time at Morrison Heights as pastor.

Why this verse? Out of all the verses in the Bible, why would I pick this particular passage? Let me explain. Paul is writing to the church in Corinth that had lots of issues. He was letting them know from the outset that God is faithful. No matter what they were dealing with, God was victorious. He wanted them to remember it's a relationship. An ongoing relationship with Him. As a result of salvation, we have fellowship with the one and only true God. And we are called to live out our fellowship with other saints. This church was having trouble because there were prevalent sins in the church that were hindering their intimate relationship with the Savior. Paul was simply trying to be sure they went back to the basics. He was reminding them of who they are, in Christ.

Morrison Heights was not dealing with all the issues the church in Corinth was facing. But we did have some challenges and I was returning as pastor in my hometown. Serving where I had graduated from high school and college, and had served in a staff position before, was a tremendous honor. It was also overwhelming at first. I knew at the end of the day, I needed to be reminded of God's faithfulness. I knew at the end of the day, the church needed to be reminded of God's faithfulness. You know what, He was and is. He walked with us through 9/11 and relocating, just to name a couple of the challenges we faced. Whatever you are facing, remember this verse. It will never let you down because He will never let you down. Stay in fellowship with Him. He is faithful. Live by faith today...

AUGUST 5

DAILY READING:
Ezra 1:1-2:70; 1 Corinthians 1:18-2:5
Psalm 27:7-14; Proverbs 20:22-23
Focal Passage: 1 Corinthians 1:18

LIVING BY FAITH

STOP EXPECTING PEOPLE WHO DON'T KNOW CHRIST TO ACT LIKE HIM. Have you ever been guilty of such? I have. The culture of where I presently live is so different than other places where I've spent the majority of my life. (The one exception is that one time I lived in Las Vegas for a while. Have I told you about that? I digress...) In St. Petersburg, Florida, it's not uncommon to come across people who look and act lost. I can go to a restaurant and see someone with orange hair, tattoos everywhere, people I'm not sure are male or female, and they all seem very assured of themselves. And it's not just the outside, it's the inside. (We know God looks at the heart. You know the old saying, "Never judge a book by its cover.") These same folks cuss like a sailor, slander others, and have a philosophy that causes one to wonder if they are truly an American. Yes, I'm serious! And I've thought to myself, *"You have got to be kidding, I cannot believe that person."* Don't be super spiritual here. You've likely done the same thing or something similar. Here's the deal—if the person is lost, they will act lost. It's simple, but true. Lost people act lost. For example, when my terrible sense of direction takes me down a road I don't need to be going down, I don't pretend I'm not lost, like some. I get frustrated and people clearly see I am lost. Lost people act lost. Why do we pretend those spiritually lost should act like they aren't? They are, they don't know any better. Wouldn't you? Maybe you're lost now and that's what's wrong. Stop now, admit your sin, and put your faith in Christ alone for the forgiveness of your sins. God will start changing you to be like Him.

Paul is reminding the church that they are not to live like their former selves. Having been saved, they have been delivered from the power and effects of sin, so they need to live like it and stop allowing the flesh to take over. Their church was letting too much of the world creep in through the front door. This letter addresses a number of those issues.

Believers should not act like lost people. Believers should not expect lost people to act like saved people. Believers should pray for lost people and share the gospel so they may start the process of acting like believers. Let's stop expecting too much out of those who don't know any better. Let's start acting better because we do know better. Live by faith today...

DAILY READING:
Ezra 3:1-4:24; 1 Corinthians 2:6-3:4
Psalm 28:1-9; Proverbs 20:24-25
Focal Passage: Proverbs 20:25

LIVING BY FAITH

I MADE A VOW ON THIS DAY THIRTY-EIGHT YEARS AGO. I married my wife Kellie, on August 6, 1982. I know, we were young. She was nineteen and I was twenty-one. (We were just months away from being twenty and twenty-two, if it helps any.) My dad asked us both to repeat our wedding vows during the ceremony. We did. We entered into a covenant relationship. That's serious! It's not about us. It's about Him. Yes, we married, but He was a part of the contract. Marriage is a serious relationship. It is not to be taken lightly, no matter what the world says or does regarding marriage. I used to tell my youth that you do all you can to find the right mate, but once you say, "I do," he or she *is* the right mate. Don't look back. Look forward and realize God is capable of helping us fulfill our vows.

Our verse reminds us to be sure of what we're doing before we do it. We should seek God first. We should not jump into a serious decision lightly. For example, if I buy a pair of shoes that later I really wish I hadn't, it's OK. One day they will wear out. Not so with something like marriage; it should be permanent in our minds due to our relationship with Christ. Sure, there are "allowances" for divorce. But it's never, ever, God's desire for us to blow past even those biblical reasons for divorce without trying to work it out. I have a sermon entitled *Marriage Takes WORK*. It does. And when we allow Him to work with us, He works! It works!

Were we young when we married? Yes. Did we really know what we were doing? Not totally. Has it been smooth sailing? Are you kidding… no. If someone says their marriage has ALWAYS been fantastic, I'm pretty sure they are not speaking truthfully. Has God sustained us? No doubt. Has God kept His end of the deal? ABSOLUTELY! He is faithful! So, you may ask, how about right now, Hal? Are you at the best place you've been, overall, in your marriage today? Yes. We are doing better now than we ever have. Divorce has never been an option. By God's grace, our marriage will continue to grow stronger. I mean, we've got another thirty-eight years to go. I tell Kellie all the time that if I die before her, she will never find anyone like me. You know what she says? I know. (I'll leave that right there…) Live by faith today…

DAILY READING:
Ezra 5:1-6:22; 1 Corinthians 3:5-23
Psalm 29:1-11; Proverbs 20:26-27
Focal Passage: 1 Corinthians 3:18-23

LIVING BY FAITH

THOSE WHO THINK THEY KNOW ALL THE ANSWERS DON'T EVEN KNOW THE QUESTIONS. My dad used to say that to me every now and then. You know how some things your parents said just stick. This phrase, along with some others, stuck with me. Knowing my dad, I think I know why he kept saying it to me. 1. He was letting me know it was important to never think too highly of myself. He wanted me to have God-confidence, but not too much self-confidence. There's a difference. It's never OK to be cocky. 2. He was letting me know some people in life think they know all the answers. That's why he was saying those type folks really don't have a clue—they don't even know the questions. Sort of funny. 3. Don't allow any person to replace Jesus. Have heroes of the faith, but never allow them to replace THE HERO of the faith—JESUS!

Paul was letting the church in Corinth know that wisdom of the world is absolutely nothing compared to Godly wisdom. We will find in James that we are to pray for wisdom. It's a good thing. But what the world thinks is wise is usually contrary to biblical teachings. Be careful. Don't allow your favorite news program to become your primary source of truth. God's Word is where we get total truth. Did I say to be careful? Yes, be careful.

As wonderful as Paul, Apollos, and Cephas were, they weren't to be boasted about. They were not to allow these great men of the faith to be in competition somehow. Be thankful. Be supportive. Be aware that following a man can hurt the church. Christ is the head of the church. In Christ, we have enough to brag about. Everything and everyone else is futile, compared to our Savior. When I was growing up I learned another phrase from a variety of people that applies here too. *Don't get too big for your britches.* Live by faith today...

DAILY READING:
Ezra 7:1-8:20; 1 Corinthians 4:1-21
Psalm 30:1-12; Proverbs 20:28-30
Focal Passage: Proverbs 20:29

LIVING BY FAITH

I THOUGHT MY DAD'S GRAY HAIR WAS BECAUSE OF SHAVING CREAM. I never knew my dad without gray hair. Daddy had premature gray hair and I was the youngest child. Because he had dark hair, the gray showed early on in his life. When I was a kid, he'd take me to the barber shop with him. We'd head out on Saturday mornings to downtown Kosciusko, Mississippi, to get our hair cut. He'd go first. Mr. Nesbitt, a deacon in our church, would put white shaving cream around his ears before he got out of the chair. It was like providing the finishing touch to a good haircut. It especially removed unwanted hairs around the ears. I always thought it was so cool and looked forward to being old enough to have "the shave treatment." I never verbalized it that I know of, but I thought it was what was causing the graying around his ears, too. That's where he was especially graying at the time. He was fully gray by the time I was a teenager. Regardless, I didn't care. I loved him just the way he was.

Now my hair is gray. It's not fully gray because I have blonde hair. I don't mind that I'm graying. The Bible says none of us should mind, actually. It is a symbol of growing older. A person who has walked with the Lord for many years should have wisdom. Maturing in our faith requires that we have been through lots of trials and held onto Jesus. He has been faithful, and we have lived to tell about it. Our journey with the Lord takes on special meaning as we grow older. We reflect, meditate, and ask God to help us finish strong. We've come too far to quit now! God is faithful and will see you through to the end.

The primary principle being taught here is that we are to honor older folks out of fear of the Lord. That's huge. Respect. We should show respect for our elders. (By the way, if you thought you needed to stop coloring your hair, it's okay. You're not going to hell because of it.) Let's always be respectful to seasoned saints. They may not know the most up-to-date music, but their insights about life count. Guess what, one day you will have gray hair, too. And it won't be because of shaving cream. Live by faith today...

DAILY READING:
Ezra 8:21-9:15; 1 Corinthians 5:1-13
Psalm 31:1-8; Proverbs 21:1-2
Focal Passage: 1 Corinthians 5:1-13

LIVING BY FAITH

CHURCH DISCIPLINE HURTS SO GOOD. I recall times my dad would tell me, while sitting in a big rocking chair, that the discipline I was about to receive was going to hurt him more than me. I understand now but didn't really get it then. He disciplined me because he loved me. God will use the church to discipline members for a good purpose. The ultimate purpose is for the sinner to repent and be reconciled to God and the church. Allowing a member to continue in their sinful lifestyle will have a negative influence on the church fellowship. For example, we cannot "wink" at the deacon having an adulterous affair. It's costly. Church discipline is not easy. It's one of the hardest things I do as a pastor.

Paul is letting the church at Corinth know they needed to clean house. The church simply cannot make people comfortable in their sinful ways. If your church has a system for dealing with the wayward sinner, it's vital to use it. If your church has a more loosely knit way of dealing with the church member who is in blatant sin, use it also. Just know that to let it fester is to allow a spiritual infection to run amok.

The church is a hospital for sinners, not a country club for saints. I love that saying! I say that all the time. Lost people need Jesus and His church. But His church is to help people who don't know Him have a relationship with Him. Part of that is to help them mature spiritually. We love sinners so much that we not only take them in, we "turn them loose," if absolutely necessary. There are steps to lovingly and prayerfully take. Did I say it's hard? Yes, I think I did. No one is perfect and nowhere does this passage say that the ones leading the discipline process are going to be perfect. But it certainly means they need to do a spiritual inventory. To have no method of church discipline is not good. To have an obsession with church discipline is not good either. Just do it and allow Jesus to guide you. It's His church and His people anyway. He died for the church. Live by faith today...

DAILY READING:
Ezra 10:1-44; 1 Corinthians 6:1-20
Psalm 31:9-18; Proverbs 21:3
Focal Passage: Ezra 10:1-6

LIVING BY FAITH

WHAT DOES IT TAKE FOR A CHURCH TO BE HEALTHY? I realize there are many books, posts, articles, and experts that regularly address this subject. Whatever you read from them or me should be taken to the Lord in prayer. We should always be sure that what we read lines up with scripture. I am not an expert on this subject. I do know there are some truths here concerning God's people that I don't recall noticing before. Isn't that neat? We can read the Bible over and over again and still know God will reveal things we've never really noticed before. That's because the Bible is active. That's because we are in a different place spiritually. There are other reasons. So, keep reading the Bible through in a year, my friends. You are over halfway there!

I've heard it said that everything rises and falls on leadership. Ezra was being authentic before God and his people. He was broken over sin. He didn't hide it. People saw it. Pastors need to be real. Now, there's a time and place for everything. But you can usually tell when your leader is authentic. Pastors need to be vulnerable, with great discernment. If so, most parishioners will do what these did. They wept, too. They realized they had sinned and wanted God's forgiveness, mercy, and blessing. They took ownership of their spiritually depleted circumstances. Then they had a leader speak up and suggest that they trust God and support Ezra. It gave Ezra courage and he rose up and faithfully moved forward.

Come in close for a moment. Can we talk? As a pastor, it's not easy to be vulnerable in front of your folks. Why? Because some misunderstand you. Some misrepresent you. It's true. But I do have a responsibility to be real. And people know if their pastor is real, by and large. I never want to be accused of being fake, although I have done this long enough to know some will. Provide an environment in your church or with some leaders in which the pastor can bare his soul. Then join him in taking ownership. Surround him with love, prayer, and real support. It will strengthen his resolve, just like it did Ezra. If so, the church is likely to thrive and not just survive. Live by faith today...

DAILY READING:
Nehemiah 1:1-3:14; 1 Corinthians 7:1-24
Psalm 31:19-24; Proverbs 21:4
Focal Passage: 1 Corinthians 7:1

LIVING BY FAITH

ENGAGING IN SEXUAL ACTIVITY IS FOR MARRIAGE, REGARDLESS OF WHAT THE CULTURE SAYS. Folks, misuse of sex has been going on for a long time. You are seeing this as you are reading the Bible through. Here we find Paul providing clarification for a church that is in the midst of moral corruption. The Corinthian culture tolerated fornication, homosexuality, and adultery, just to name a few. Sound familiar? The literal rendering of the Greek is that it is not good for a man to touch a woman. Abstinence is God's plan until marriage. God created sex and He knows when it's best—marriage.

Singleness is elevated here. Don't allow the culture to cause you to think or promote that everyone is to be married. Some are not and that can be a good thing according to scripture. One can be more devoted to serving Christ with fewer "distractions." This is for those with the gift of celibacy. For those whom don't have that gift, marry. But don't marry just anyone. Marry a believer who God has led you to marry, by faith. If you are married, don't divorce to be single. That is not what this passage is saying. Not at all! Marriage is a covenant bond. Neither the one who is single nor the one who is married, is more spiritual.

Let me tell you a secret about this verse. Numerous times I've had couples come in for marriage counseling and I immediately read them this verse and ask why they are in my office. I wish you could see their faces. It's a great place to start in discussing if it is God's will for them to marry. If you are single, don't rush into marriage just because of your culture. Ask God to guide you to the one you are to marry if it is His will. And don't allow sexual sins to creep into your life, whether married or unmarried. It's costly. Live by faith today...

DAILY READING:
Nehemiah 3:15-5:13; 1 Corinthians 7:25-40
Psalm 32:1-11; Proverbs 21:5-7
Focal Passage: Nehemiah 4:6-9

LIVING BY FAITH

HERE IS A BIBLICAL WAY TO RESPOND TO CRITICISM. When God leads you to do something monumental for the Kingdom, you will receive criticism. Expect it. Don't be afraid of it. Just know it's coming. It's not if, but when. And it may be from those you least expect. Listen, living for Jesus is not for wimps. It is for warriors. And if you've never received criticism as you are living out the Jesus life, you had better pause right here and hold a spiritual evaluation. There are always "walls to be rebuilt."

We were introduced to Nehemiah yesterday. God put a burden on his heart to rebuild the broken-down wall of Jerusalem. We're now seeing that God used him and others to do so. And we're seeing three main fellas who were not pleased. What did they do? They did what many people do today—stirred up trouble. What did Nehemiah do? He led the people to pray and prepare. It's always important to expect the best but prepare for the worst.

If you are in the midst of obeying God and it's difficult, pray. Keep on praying. Don't stop praying. Enlist prayer partners. Did I mention prayer? Yes. Pray, pray, pray. Trust, trust, and trust some more. And just in case you have some buzzards hovering around, have people posted to protect you. Let them help you with your God-sized project. Let Godly folks defend and support you. God's church is an army. The best around. This does not mean you don't have faith. Nehemiah and his people had great faith. It just means you aren't a dummy. (Calm down, I'm a dummy quite often.) God gave us a mind to use. Use it with Godly discernment and plan accordingly. He'll let you know what to do. Don't be afraid of those who try to derail the plan God has given you. Live by faith today...

DAILY READING:
Nehemiah 5:14-7:60; 1 Corinthians 8:1-13
Psalm 33:1-11; Proverbs 21:8-10
Focal Passage: Nehemiah 6:1-4

LIVING BY FAITH

SOMETIMES YOU HAVE TO SAY NO TO ONO. Geshy, Toby, and Sandy just would not leave Nehemiah alone. (Those are nicknames I came up with for these fellas years ago.) Satan was using these guys to hinder God's work. The enemy will especially attack the leader. And he holds nothing back. At times, it's the same bunch. Nehemiah had refused multiple times to meet with these "representatives." This time they wanted to meet in the village of Ono, on the Judah-Samaria border. Nehemiah had the discernment to know their intent was evil. He had no intention of wasting time over a meeting he knew was not going to be productive. So he said no. If their desire was for peace, they would have had a better track record. He lived with a sense of urgency to fulfill God's will. Furthermore, he didn't want to risk deeper consequences over having met with these schemers. Sometimes you have to say no.

Be careful. When you take on leading a God-ordained project or ministry, there will be distractions and distractors. A distractor is not your enemy. Always keep in mind that the enemy is the enemy. Usually there's one vocal distractor who has some type of following. If you sense it would not be in your best interest for your sake and the sake of others to meet, don't meet. It's not easy. They will misrepresent you to others for not doing so. Allow their reputation and your reputation to stand on their own. And pray, like Nehemiah continually did. Staying in constant communication with God gives you wisdom and peace. Stay so connected with God that you can say with great confidence—no, to Ono.

Are you going through something like this right now? Be encouraged to do the right thing. Have you never been through anything like this? Ask yourself why. Just saying... Being a peacekeeper is not being a peacemaker. God blesses the peacemaker. One more thing, don't use this passage as an excuse not to have a Godly meeting that may be necessary. There's a balance between when to say no and when to say yes to meetings over various issues. Let God guide you. Nehemiah's example will help. Live by faith today...

DAILY READING:
Nehemiah 7:61-9:21; 1 Corinthians 9:1-18
Psalm 33:12-22; Proverbs 21:11-12
Focal Passage: Nehemiah 8:8

LIVING BY FAITH

WHEN YOU READ THE BIBLE, IT'S VITAL TO KNOW WHAT IT MEANS. Translating and giving the meaning of Bible verses is what's called *exposition*. It is not enough to hear scripture if you don't know what it means. It's not enough to read scripture if you don't know what it means. The people in our passage were not just receiving a reading of God's Word for the first time, they were being told what it meant. We see their excitement as we read on.

Studying and reading God's Word is not just for information. Many people consider themselves deep when they know a lot of information about the Bible. God bless their hearts. It won't change their lives. When a believer approaches the reading of God's Word with great humility, asking God to reveal the truth and how to apply it, something will occur. Why? Because the Holy Spirit inside the believer reveals the truth. And as we discover how to apply the truth to our everyday lives, God begins to transform our lives into His image. That's why we are here: to know God. There's no other relationship like it. And there's an anticipation to times of reading His Word. There's a type of expectation that He will speak to us individually.

One of the biggest blessings that has come out of writing this devotional book is the way God speaks. Every day He speaks through His Word. I can't wait to see what passage I sense He's leading me to apply and write about. He is so faithful! I trust you have a Bible you can understand and a study Bible or commentary to assist. And I trust you make notes on what God is teaching you as you spend time reading the Bible through this year. If not, please start today. You will have no regrets. God's Word applies to everyday life! I don't care what you are going through, He's got the truth for you. He desires to help you, just like He helped God's people after hearing it for the first time, as Ezra and those teachers with the odd names taught. They taught to help the listeners, not to impress them. There's a difference. Live by faith today...

LIVING BY FAITH

GOD WILL GIVE YOU A WAY OUT OF YOUR GREATEST TEMPTATION. At the moment of someone's conversion, he is sealed with the Holy Spirit. The Holy Spirit resides inside the believer from that moment on. Therefore, no temptation will be overpowering because Christians are no longer slaves to sin. The Helper is with you. The Helper is in you. God gives us the freedom to choose what is good. What does this mean? He will provide a way out. He will give you the strength at the right moment to say no. Sinful enticements do not have to overtake you day, after day, after day. The Holy Spirit gives us what we need, when we need it, to withstand temptations.

We are not talking about trials here. We have trials we cannot handle without the grace of God. We become desperate and cry out to God for help. We are talking about temptations here. Jesus was tempted just like we are, but He did not sin. A temptation is not a sin. It's when we fall to temptations that we are guilty of sin. Paul is reminding the church in Corinth that God is with them. He has not abandoned them while they live the Christian life in a wicked city. He has not left them when they face temptations, even while dealing with church folks. God will provide a way out somehow, someway, every time temptation comes. All they have to do is believe it, look for it, and follow it, instead of what they're being tempted by. He is faithful!

We will face temptations all the days of our lives. They will not go away because we live in a depraved world. They can actually be used to our advantage. Every time we resist, we become stronger in our faith. Our roots grow deeper. That's a good thing. Don't succumb to temptations. Please don't blame God or someone else. Live by faith today…

DAILY READING:
Nehemiah 11:1-12:26; 1 Corinthians 10:14-11:2
Psalm 34:11-22; Proverbs 21:14-16
Focal Passage: Psalm 34:18

LIVING BY FAITH

I REACHED FOR THE PEW BIBLE AND READ THIS VERSE. I was living in the Memphis area. Kellie and I heard Robert J. Morgan was going to preach in a nearby church. We were introduced to him years prior and enjoy his teachings. So we invited our friends Tom and Donna Stovall to go with us to hear him. As we were waiting for the service to begin that night, I reached for a pew Bible. I can't tell you why. I can only speculate. I'm pretty sure I had brought my own Bible. Maybe not? Maybe I was going to look on with Kellie. Maybe I was using the Bible app on my cell phone. Maybe I forgot it? More than likely, I was being hyper and just reached for the Bible instead of the hymnal to read. Regardless, I read this verse. As often occurs as we read the Bible, the passage jumped off the page. Wow, God is close to me when I've been broken. That's exactly what I needed to hear that night. I have to admit, I don't recall what Rob preached about, but I do recall the moment I read our focal passage. Brokenness certainly means being broken over our sin. David was broken over his sin after he was confronted by the prophet Nathan. It's Godly sorrow over sin that leads to repentance. All we think about is Him and His grace. He is the one who rescues us from the depths of our depravity. True brokenness is a tool God uses to bring His wandering sheep back into His loving arms and His fold. It hurts so good.

Brokenness can also mean coming to the end of ourselves. You see, that's where I was when this passage spoke to me. I had chosen to resign from Germantown Baptist because I had come to "the end." I couldn't fix it. For the first time, I felt I was not successful in bringing long-term revitalization to a church I pastored. For the first time, I felt like many people didn't like me. I was not accustomed to that. Now, I was accustomed to people not liking me due to my decision to lead in a certain direction as a pastor, but not like this. I had always been able to relate to folks; I really felt for the first time in my life most folks didn't care for me. (I learned later that was really not reality, but at the time...) I was a broken man. I was at the mercy of God. And I never felt closer to God. I discovered who I really am, in Christ. I am His. He is mine. Brokenness is a good thing, even though there is pain involved. Live by faith today...

DAILY READING:
Nehemiah 12:27-13:31; 1 Corinthians 11:3-16
Psalm 35:1-16; Proverbs 21:17-18
Focal Passage: Nehemiah 13:4-8

LIVING BY FAITH

PLEASE DON'T ALLOW A FAMILY MEMBER TO CAUSE YOU TO MAKE A SPIRITUALLY FOOLISH DECISION. This passage is about allowing family relations to come before Godly decisions. Eliashib was a relative of Tobiah. (You remember Toby, don't you?) Tobiah was an enemy of God and the Kingdom work done through Nehemiah and others. (Read Nehemiah 2:20, if you need a reminder.) So, here we have a priest allowing a family member to hang out in the temple. Eliashib should have been setting an example of loving God before others—even family. (That's what Jesus said to followers. Luke 14:26) The priest let a family member rent a room. I'm not talking about just anywhere. I'm talking about a room in the temple house! His actions are a reminder that we must be careful not to allow those in our family to influence us to act foolishly. Family members do not get a pass when it comes to following God's will.

It's tough, isn't it? Absolutely! It's one of the hardest choices we make as believers. To please God, not man. And if that man is a blood relative, it can be even more difficult. Sometimes we have to take up our "sword." (That's what Jesus said to followers in Mark 10:34.) God's warriors face very difficult decisions. But as we study the Gospel accounts, we should not be surprised. Jesus is our ultimate example. He made hard choices and He fought Kingdom battles. He did it all for you. He did it all for me. Let's please Him even when family members don't understand. If not, it can weaken our witness and influence. That's what Eliashib was doing by allowing a family member in where he did not belong.

Nehemiah stepped in and took care of the family issue. He loved enough to make hard decisions for the sake of everyone. Is there something going on in your family right now that needs to be addressed? Maybe you're "winking" at disobedience in your own household. Nehemiah continues to show us how to lead. It means making tough decisions for the good of everyone. Kingdom causes are worth it. Even if the family doesn't get it. Live by faith today...

DAILY READING:
Esther 1:1-3:15; 1 Corinthians 11:17-34
Psalm 35:17-28; Proverbs 21:19-20
Focal Passage: Proverbs 21:19

LIVING BY FAITH

SOME HUSBANDS THINK LIVING IN THE DESERT IS BETTER THAN LIVING WITH THEIR WIFE. Why? Because of this verse. It's straightforward. As a matter of fact, the writer of Proverbs provides two ways to absolutely drive your husband nuts. (Another way of saying *driving him into the wilderness*.) 1. Be quarrelsome. This woman tends to get in fights. I'm not talking fist fights, necessarily. The person is moody or overly sensitive. Other people usually don't like to be around them much. 2. Be ill-tempered. It's not totally unlike the first word. It means being grumpy or grouchy. (Let me tell you a secret. I've come across a few of these women in churches I've pastored. Usually they seem to have the nicest husbands and I've thought to myself, "Brother, what were you thinking!" Remember now, this is our secret. I'm just being honest with you.)

So, let me try to help a brother out here. 1. Only God can change a woman like this Proverb is describing. (By the way, other Proverbs are similar.) So, pray. Pray and fast. Enlist a few Godly, trustworthy men to pray with you in confidence. 2. Be the spiritual leader in the home. Have a regular devotional time. Lead devotionals with your wife. Get plugged into a local church. Make sure you find an older couple in your church you can do life with. Allow them to be your marriage mentors. (Needless to say, be sure the woman is the opposite of your spouse in her Christ-like attitude. Sweet. Yeah, be sure she's a sweetie.) 3. Remember we are growing in Christ-likeness. Allow your marriage to help you grow spiritually. When we are dependent on God for every moment of every day, it's a good thing. Actually, a lot of good came out of wilderness experiences in the Bible, even though they weren't always necessarily fun. May God bless you and keep you, men. This too shall pass. It may be in heaven, but it will pass. Live by faith today...

DAILY READING:
Esther 4:1-7:10; 1 Corinthians 12:1-26
Psalm 36:1-12; Proverbs 21:21-22
Focal Passage: Esther 4:13-14

LIVING BY FAITH

NEVER UNDERESTIMATE THE OPPORTUNITY GOD WANTS TO GIVE YOU. Esther is some kind of woman, isn't she? God blessed her with good looks. Her beauty on the outside was used to get her on the inside. She wasn't supposed to be in this influential position. But it seems she needed a little reminder from Uncle Mordecai. Remember, he was Esther's adoptive father. But he served as her mentor, confidant, cheerleader, and fellow leader to stand up for the Jewish community. Basically, he was "the man." And as we've read—he ain't scared! So he challenged Esther by reminding her that only God could place her in such a position—a position to save the Jewish people from wicked Haman's plan to kill the Jews.

Esther had a choice. God is sovereign. He doesn't have to use us. He graciously allows us to be used. And if we balk at the opportunity, He will accomplish his will through someone else. He's a gentleman. He doesn't force His way. He puts us in various positions to ultimately accomplish our purpose as believers. We have a choice, just like Esther did. She was challenged with a phrase we probably have heard before... *"For such a time as this."* Mordecai reminded her that for all she knew the main reason she was in her current position was for future freedom. It was not just about her. It never is. It's about others. It's about God's glory. It's about God's Kingdom purposes.

What about you? Have you underestimated why God has you where you are right now? Please don't miss it. Maybe you're supposed to be somewhere else, but you don't think your current position can make it without you. Really? Examine where you are headed. What is God saying to you? Live by faith today...

DAILY READING:
Esther 8:1-10:3; 1 Corinthians 12:27-13:13
Psalm 37:1-11; Proverbs 21:23-24
Focal Passage: 1 Corinthians 13:8-13

LIVING BY FAITH

PERHAPS THIS PASSAGE SHOULD BE READ AT FUNERALS, TOO. For obvious reasons, this chapter is well known because it's read so often during wedding ceremonies. I've used it over and over, and will continue to do so. Married couples always need to remember what love really means. The world's definition of love is no comparison. But our focal passage speaks of eternity. When believers enter God's presence, spiritual gifts will end. There will be no need for them.

Paul made it clear that one could be gifted, but useless, if love was not exhibited. Love is the hallmark of Christ followers. And love lives on into eternity. Faith ceases in glory because we will have sight. Hope is no longer needed because all expectations will have been met and exceeded. God is love. It continues because we will have our eternal relationship with Him. Yes, love never fails! Love never ends. Love God. Love people.

I received word last night that Jon Harper, a classmate of mine, died of a massive heart attack. Jon and I played baseball together at Clinton High School. He was a wonderful teammate. He leaves behind a wife and three young adult daughters. If I were to preach his funeral, I would read this passage. He was extremely gifted and talented. Jon exhibited faith, hope, and love. BUT he loved deeply. He was a people person. I believe with all my heart it was because he genuinely loved God. Loving others was a natural overflow from his relationship with Jesus. Today, he's in His presence. But the greatest of these is love. Live by faith today…

DAILY READING:
Job 1:1-3:26; 1 Corinthians 14:1-17
Psalm 37:12-29; Proverbs 21:25-26
Focal Passage: Job 2:11-13

LIVING BY FAITH

WHEN A LOVED ONE IS GRIEVING, SHOW UP AND SHUT UP. I know, "shut up" is a little strong. But I want to make a point here. Through the years I've heard some goofy statements made to people who were hurting due to the death of a loved one. When someone has a broken heart, the last thing we need to do is make it worse. Now, I think most people don't intend to make awkward or hurtful statements during the "visitation line." I think most just don't know what to say, so they say whatever comes to mind. Folks, that's not always good. Say as little as possible. A basic "I'm sorry," or "I'm praying," or "I love you," is fine. I speak from experience; being present speaks loudly to the grieving person. Words may come later.

Job's buddies showed up. That was good. We can show up, too. Sometimes it's literally. Sometimes it's through another person representing us. Sometimes it's through a flower arrangement. Sometimes it's through social media. There are various ways to "show up." The best way, when possible, is to literally be there. Just be careful to follow Job's friends' example: grieve with them as genuinely as you can and don't say anything. Listen.

Maybe you should start a Presence Ministry at your church? You train people in how to grieve with those who grieve. Seriously, maybe you've had experience with this, and God can use you here. Sometimes the best comfort you can provide is a quiet **presence**. One of the greatest blessings of a church family is to be there when someone has a hurting heart. Live by faith today...

DAILY READING:
Job 4:1-7:21; 1 Corinthians 14:18-40
Psalm 37:30-40; Proverbs 21:27
Focal Passages: 1 Corinthians 14:33, 40

LIVING BY FAITH

CRAZINESS IN THE CHURCH IS CRAZY. The Apostle Paul makes it clear that spiritual gifts are for edification. Gifts from God to His people are to uplift, and to provide moral improvement and guidance. God gives them at salvation. There is no "second blessing." The Holy Spirit is sealed in the believer and you can't shake Him. You can grieve Him, but you can't get away from Him if you've genuinely trusted Christ by faith alone. So make no mistake, His gifting is not about you. It's not about me. It's about others. We use our gifts to build up the church. Gifts help provide unity in the church when used biblically. The church in Corinth had some craziness going on due to misuse and misunderstandings concerning spiritual gifts. Clarification is provided here, and our verses clearly let us know that *craziness in the church is crazy.* It is not of God.

God is a God of order. If you are in a worship service, for example, and folks are running around and all types of hollering is going on, you run out the door. There is no way that can be edifying. Someone has missed the boat. And more than likely, the church is sinking in some way. A church operating with a level of order (pastors should always be open to the moving of the Holy Spirit), with members using their spiritual gifts for others, has peace. Peace comes from God. The lack thereof means the enemy has deceived some folks. If you are in a church that allows tongues, there better be an interpreter ready to interpret. And if the interpretation is not scriptural, you gots a problem. By the way, I've never understood why we need another word when we have the Word. I think the entire tongues gifting was for the Apostolic age. But I'll say that God is God and I am not. If He wants to "kick it in" He has the prerogative. One more thing before we leave this subject... if you have some type of private prayer language, keep it that way. No one should even know. If so, you are out of bounds. Personally, I have no idea why it would be beneficial. But I don't have it and am not seeking it. The enemy looks for opportunities to deceive us, folks. Be careful. Study and apply the Bible. Use your spiritual gift to build the church. Live by faith today...

DAILY READING:

Job 8:1-11:20; 1 Corinthians 15:1-28
Psalm 38:1-22; Proverbs 21:28-29
Focal Passage: 1 Corinthians 15:1-4

LIVING BY FAITH

HERE IS THE GOSPEL IN A NUTSHELL. If you have been looking for a passage to memorize or refer to in order to clearly share your faith, I suggest this one. Paul shares the need to be saved. It's not just believing in the mind. (The demons believed and trembled.) It means deliverance from the power of sin. It is an admission of one's sin and placing faith in Christ alone for salvation. There is a starting point to the wonderful faith journey with Jesus. Then we see that Paul makes clear what we are believing in to be born again. Jesus was fully God and fully man. There had to be a sacrifice for our sins. This is even made clear in Old Testament prophecies. Christ was our substitution because He was perfect, and we are not. He died and was buried. Then Paul emphasizes the three days. He was raised from the dead on the third day. This is the gospel in a nutshell. This is the wonderful message of Easter.

We saw this clear and steady testimony of the early church in Acts. The resurrection is continually emphasized. It should be because God accepted the payment Jesus made for all of our sins. Your sins. My sins. Yes, Jesus paid it all. And here, within a few verses, we have a way to share our faith with others. While doing so, we testify to the grace of God in our own lives. We look for an open door to share what our life was before being saved. We share what our life has been like after being saved. There should be a change. When we abide in Him, He does His work in us from the inside out. We are not what we used to be, and by God's grace, we won't be tomorrow what we are today. People need to know our faith journey is our life. The gospel is changing our life and can change others. Once we share these truths, we simply ask the person we may be sharing with this one question: *Has anything like this ever happened to you?* Then God will help us know what to say based on their answer. Let's ask God to give us opportunities to share the gospel in a nutshell. He will. Live by faith today...

AUGUST 24

DAILY READING:
Job 12:1-15:35; 1 Corinthians 15:29-58
Psalm 39:1-13; Proverbs 21:30-31
Focal Passage: 1 Corinthians 15:33

LIVING BY FAITH

THIS ONE DECISION WILL BRING YOU DOWN. I have a little exercise I want you to do or imagine doing. Stand in a chair. Now, let a person pull you down with one hand. It was probably easy to be pulled down. Now, stand in the same chair. Take one hand and try to pull the same person up to you. It's not as easy, is it? The Corinthian believers were allowing those who were not believers to pull them down. There were those promoting false doctrine, denying the resurrection of Jesus Christ, and living wildly with no regard for Christ. Paul was helping the Christ followers know that if you make unbelievers your constant companions, you will not escape the negative consequences. It happens every time. If you cozy up to lifestyles far away from Jesus, you will end up far away from Jesus. And fellowship with Christ is the greatest joy one can have on this earth.

This does not mean you should not be salt and light. We are commanded to be in the world, but not of the world. We are not to go huddle up in our "holy huddles," all the time. We are to love people—all people. We are just not to allow those who don't know Christ to be our best buddies. That's it. Spend some time with lost folks. Love them to death. Be ready to share the love of Jesus, and be Jesus to them when they hurt. But make sure your closest friends are those who have an intimate relationship with Christ. Allow them to be the ones you confide in and spend the majority of time with. They help keep you accountable. These Godly relationships will help you finish strong. And we want Jesus to say in the end *"Well done, good and faithful servant."*

This is a verse I would share with my youth groups when I was a Youth Pastor. But let me be sure to remind you that peer pressure is not just a teenage challenge. Adults deal with peer pressure, too. PLEASE don't skip over this verse, no matter what age you are right now. Ponder it and evaluate your relationships. It could make the difference in the rest of your days, both here and in eternity. Live by faith today...

DAILY READING:

Job 16:1-19:29; 1 Corinthians 16:1-24
Psalm 40:1-10; Proverbs 22:1
Focal Passage: 1 Corinthians 16:13-14

LIVING BY FAITH

HERE'S WHAT TO DO AND HOW TO DO IT. As Paul comes to the close of his letter to the church in Corinth, he gives them a quick exhortation. He has a little more to say, but what a power-packed few verses. The church had been gripped with self-centeredness, prideful attitudes, and multiple divisions. (Not good, is it?) We know he had said a lot leading up to this point. There was a lot that needed to be said. But it's almost as if he gives them a quick formula for Godly success. Let's look at it closely…

Be alert. The devil wants to destroy us. We don't need to be afraid. We live by faith. But just be aware that He will never leave us alone on this side of heaven. Stand firm. We stand on a rock-solid foundation in Christ. Stay grounded every day. Did you get that? Daily. Read the Bible and pray. When? Every day. Stay connected to your church family for strength. Be courageous. Living the Christian life is not easy. You and I must be warriors. Find warriors in the Bible and study their lives. How did they do it? Follow their examples and those you see being bold in their faith around you. You be you, but allow them to help you be the courageous leader God wants you to be. Be strong. We gain strength from the trials we experience. And we *will* have trials along the way. Allow them to strengthen your spiritual muscles. Lifting weights can make one physically stronger. It's the same principle. Realize what you go through in this journey we call life is meant to grow your spiritual roots deeper. Do it all in love. Remember chapter 13 of this book? Yes, he's repeating what's most important in our walk. Faith, hope, and love, but the greatest of these is love. As we fall in love with God, we naturally should fall in love with people. We don't have to work at it. It should be the natural overflow from our walk with God. And in the end, we would want others to describe us as a person who loved others deeply.

He's helping move the church to a more God-centered mentality. Let's do the same. And let's never, ever forget the love part. Love conquers all! Live by faith today…

DAILY READING:
Job 20:1-22:30; 2 Corinthians 1:1-11
Psalm 40:11-17; Proverbs 22:2-4
Focal Passage: 2 Corinthians 1:3-4

LIVING BY FAITH

SOME OF THE HARDEST THINGS I'VE BEEN THROUGH HAVE HELPED ME THE MOST. I've lived long enough to experience various trials in life. Some of them have been especially difficult. You've likely been through some stuff, too. If we live long enough, we all have. No one avoids pain in this life, regardless of education, status, or skills. So Paul launches into this new letter to the church at Corinth making sure they know how beneficial it is that they are going through so much difficulty. They needed a Godly perspective. Don't you? We all do, because sometimes we forget in the midst of our pain how it will help others. God wants to use it. He wants to use us, just like He wanted to use this church so long ago.

The Apostle Paul knew what it was like to go through trials of various kinds. He had been there. As a matter of fact, most of us will never, ever go through all that he did during his Christian life. He speaks from experience. Don't you like to hear from someone who has been there? I do. They cannot only sympathize, they can *empathize* with us. Grief is a natural process for all of us to go through. But don't waste your pain. At some point, God wants to use what you and I have been through to help others who may go through the very same thing.

Let me close with just one example from my own life. My dad died when I was twenty-six. We were close and I had just graduated from seminary. All of a sudden, he was diagnosed with cancer and he died shortly after. God gave me peace. I grieved, and I still have my moments. I miss him. God was my primary source of comfort. I went to a whole new level in my personal relationship with Him. And it has given me the desire and, by God's grace, the ability to comfort others who may lose their dad at a young age. Remember the devotional a few days ago about my buddy Jon Harper dying and what I would have shared at his funeral? Well, I was honored to be asked to speak and I did share that passage. At the graveside service, I was able to look at his three young adult daughters (Haley, Sarah Powell, and Lindsey) and suggest how to move forward. I did so with great confidence because I have been there. With God's help, they will move forward and do the same for others during their lifetimes. Some of the hardest moments in life can help you the most in your personal walk and witness to others. Live by faith today...

DAILY READING:
Job 23:1-27:23; 2 Corinthians 1:12-2:11
Psalm 41:1-13; Proverbs 22:5-6
Focal Passage: 2 Corinthians 2:1-5

LIVING BY FAITH

HAS YOUR PASTOR EVER WRITTEN YOUR CONGREGATION A TEARFUL LETTER? Maybe. But most likely not. Most pastors write letters of encouragement or instruction to parishioners. Sometimes it's a written form of communication about an upcoming event or new ministry. Challenging members via an email or post is not uncommon either. But it's not often you will receive a letter, like Paul had evidently written, to the church concerning his hurting heart. Someone had deeply hurt him and the cause of Christ. He let the church know that the person needed to be dealt with and why. Church discipline is critically important. If left undone, it hurts the entire congregation. From all indications, as we read on, the person received some type of discipline. They listened to Paul and didn't allow the one in the wrong to continue sowing seeds of discord. Leaders took action and were not guilty of just hoping the issue would somehow go away.

Please know there are those who will deeply hurt your pastor from time to time. It may be because they've wandered from the truth of God's Word. It may be because of some blatant sin. It may be because they are criticizing him or someone in his family. Regardless, it happens. And more than likely in today's church culture, you will not receive a letter from him in the mail pouring out his heart. I didn't say he might not want to, but that he likely won't. You see, many churches have no system in place to deal with discipline issues. What happens? The pastor is typically the one having to navigate the troubled waters. And if a person is targeting him for some unjustified reason, it's tough. I could have written a few tearful letters through the years. Most pastors could. So please pray for your pastor. And please protect him. If you know of someone hurting your pastor or a key spiritual leader in your church, stop it immediately. Address it in a biblical way. But stop it. For heaven's sake, stop it. Too many pastors burn out or get deeply hurt because some churches just think that's the way it's always been. Not according to this passage. Do the right thing. Live by faith today...

DAILY READING:
Job 28:1-30:31; 2 Corinthians 2:12-17
Psalm 42:1-11; Proverbs 22:7
Focal Passage: Psalm 42:3-5

LIVING BY FAITH

WHAT DO YOU DO WHEN YOU DON'T KNOW WHAT TO DO?
Does that ever happen to you? You just don't know exactly what to do next? When I decided to write this devotional book at the end of 2019, I had no idea what 2020 was going to be like. COVID-19, Hurricane Laura, multiple protests for racial justice, and supposedly, Murder Hornets. Who knew? Then, we all have personal challenges of various kinds. Occasionally you think, "Hey God, I'm down here. Are we okay?" (You know it's okay to have honest conversations with God, right?) Yes, it's been a crazy year so far and it's not over. So what do you do, when you don't know what to do, because of what's happening, and what may be coming next?

The Psalmist helps us out. There are two things we can do. 1. Ponder God's faithfulness in the past. That's why journaling is so important. We can look back over our life and see how God was faithful during times of discouragement. The writer recalls times when he celebrated with the people of God. God has been faithful in the past when we didn't know what to do. Be encouraged because God has come through before. He is faithful. He will do it again and again. How quickly we forget. 2. The Psalmist draws near to God with the truth. He realizes God is the ultimate source of hope during dark times. So he puts his hope in God even when he can't see Him working. It's called perseverance. It's called contentment. Keep pressing into God. He is an on-time God. He will be faithful like He was that one time. (Actually, He's been faithful many times.)

Even though you may be taking a last-minute vacation during this time of the year, it doesn't mean God is going to do the same. He needs no vacation. He is God. No worries. He hasn't left you and He hasn't left me. He is up to something good. Don't miss it. Remember His faithfulness from the past and keep pursuing Him. Live by faith today...

DAILY READING:
Job 31:1-33:33; 2 Corinthians 3:1-18
Psalm 43:1-5; Proverbs 22:8-9
Focal Passage: Job 31:1

LIVING BY FAITH

EVERY MAN'S VERSE. Years ago, I heard someone say that John 3:16 is everybody's verse. It makes sense. "For God so loved the world that He gave His one and only Son, that whoever believes in Him shall not perish but have eternal life." (NIV) That's all of us! It's good news! Jesus accepts us no matter what we've done or who we are. I like it—everybody's verse. But today we're going to discover every *man's* verse.

There was a book written several years back entitled *Every Man's Battle.* It dealt with stories of those who had escaped the trap of sexual immorality and detailed a plan for any male who desired sexual purity. In today's world, sensuality is everywhere! I went to the gym this morning and guess what was in the same room? A scantily dressed woman working out. And for all I know, when I enter the sanctuary to preach this coming Sunday, the same thing may be awaiting me—a scantily dressed woman sitting on the front row. Folks, this verse is every man's verse.

Job decided way ahead of time to exercise the willpower necessary to not think lustful thoughts about young maidens. He determined that, by the grace of God, he'd discipline himself not to take the second look that leads to lust. The word used in the verse is not to "glance briefly," but to "gaze, stare or look intently." There is a difference. If a man considers "diligently" the looks of a woman, it spells trouble. The spelling is rendered in various ways, but it ultimately spells T-R-O-U-B-L-E. As Job is in this discourse proclaiming his innocence to his misguided friends, he explains another step he took as a holy man of God. And to make this type of covenant is holy.

Guys, the temptation of lust is not going away on this side of heaven. It's just not. So, we have a choice. We can accept it and develop a strategy to have victory over it, or we can allow it to overtake us. The latter is not a choice if we are going to fulfill God's ultimate purpose for our lives. A glance is unavoidable. A gaze is avoidable. I memorized this verse years ago. If you haven't, I suggest you do so immediately. We need all the help we can get. This, my brother, is **every man's verse.** Live by faith today…

DAILY READING:
Job 34:1-36:33; 2 Corinthians 4:1-12
Psalm 44:1-8; Proverbs 22:10-12
Focal Passage: 2 Corinthians 4:7-11

LIVING BY FAITH

YOU MAY BE KNOCKED DOWN, BUT YOU ARE NOT KNOCKED OUT. In this letter, Paul is trying to encourage the church to persevere more than anything. Here he lets them know that yes, they are fragile. Have you ever held a clay jar? They are weak and have little stability. They are dirt put together in some type of shape. Paul says here that believers need to remember how fragile we really are. We are weak and have no value in and of ourselves. Christ makes us worthwhile! He gives us meaning when we are connected to Him. When we are knocked down again, and again, and again, we are not knocked out. Why? Because that's when Jesus does His best work in and through us. We come to the end of ourselves and rely totally on Him. That's a good place to be. Not a fun place, but a good place.

Paul is also letting them know here that hard times do not always mean they are doing wrong. Sometimes it may mean that they're doing right but God wants them to go even deeper with Him. The divine life of Jesus shines through even clearer when we stay reliant on Him through our deepest hurts. Jesus is on display for all the world to see. I have seen this in the lives of people who have gone through unimaginable pain. When this occurs, I realize how far I still have to go in my walk with Christ. And it often makes me want to duck in shame over whatever I may be going through. Quite frankly, it's usually nothing compared to the trials of others. I'm inspired. I'm motivated to keep on going.

Keep getting up, my friend. You may need to get off the bench. Take another turn at bat. Next pitch. Maybe, just maybe, you've felt you have been knocked out and just can't get back up. Not so. Realize you have the power of Christ in you as a believer. Rely on Him and you will realize you were not knocked out. You were just knocked down to get back up stronger. Live by faith today...

DAILY READING:
Job 37:1-39:30; 2 Corinthians 4:13-5:10
Psalm 44:9-26; Proverbs 22:13
Focal Passage: 2 Corinthians 4:16-18

LIVING BY FAITH

HOW CAN WE GROW OLDER AND YOUNGER AT THE SAME TIME? Paul tells us how in these verses. Physically, we grow older. I'm experiencing a little of this at my age. If you haven't, it's coming. Trust me, I'm doing all I can to keep it at bay by exercising and eating right. (Well, I sort of eat right occasionally.) Anyway, my time in the mile is not good. No, I'm not telling you what my time is. You're going to have to trust me on this and the other. As we age, our bodies grow older and decay. (I'm even looking into some Botox. Not convinced it's for me right now, although it must be for some of my old buddies.) Now, for getting younger. As we grow older, we should be growing stronger spiritually. Think about it. The years spent with the Lord provide such an advantage. We go through all kinds of trials and victories and He's been with us the entire time. He's carried us when we couldn't take another step. Wow! What a deal. Our inner person should continually be growing stronger. We are, by God's grace, growing spiritually younger.

If we have the same perspective as Paul, we will do much better through the seasons of life. Our difficulties will end one day. In the meantime, they are working for our good. They help us know Jesus at a much deeper level. And heaven is going to be that much sweeter. We see that in the verse where our afflictions are producing absolutely incomparable eternal good. We must, like Paul, see life with the eyes of faith. This way our perspective is different than looking at life through whatever vision we may come up with. Any view of life other than God's view, is a clouded view.

If you are growing older physically, like me, let's do what we can to take care of our temples. I believe in exercising and eating somewhat healthy. (I have no intention of eating bark off of trees, though.) But let's never allow these things to take priority over growing spiritually. Our time in prayer, Bible study, service, and the church are immeasurably more important. The good that comes out of growing spiritually healthier as we age brings blessings here and in eternity. Live by faith today…

DAILY READING:

Job 40:1-42:17; 2 Corinthians 5:11-21
Psalm 45:1-17; Proverbs 22:14
Focal Passage: Job 42:7

LIVING BY FAITH

   YOUR FRIENDS DON'T ALWAYS SPEAK TRUTH DURING DIFFICULT DAYS. We just walked this journey with Job. He went through a lot. Actually, he went through a lot more than most of us will ever experience. You may recall when his three friends first arrived on the scene, they were model friends. They showed up and listened. They even cried with him. But as we read on, we saw where they drifted away from God's will. They began to prejudge Job. They even did some of that with God. Never good to do that! It's one thing to think you understand what a buddy is going through and speak a bunch of garbage, but to speak as if you know the mind of God, too? Yikes! Yet once again, we see a God who is gracious toward these guys. We actually see God being gracious toward Job too, don't we? Wow! Just, wow!

   I have likely said things to friends during their difficult days, that I shouldn't have said. You know, stupid things because you feel like you need to say something. Or maybe words that I thought were accurate that proved to be inaccurate in time. We have all been there. We don't need to be too hard on these guys, but we can sure learn from them. 1. Learn to listen more than talk when a friend is grieving. 2. If you're doing the grieving, don't listen to everything your friends may be saying to you. Sure, sometimes what they say is comforting. Praise the Lord! But at times, they have no idea what you are going through. Please don't allow their words to hurt your heart for long. Take it to Jesus and allow Him to help you sift through it. If not, you'll lose lots of sleep. You may even get depressed. Remember, God knows the truth. He understands the big picture. Trust Him. He will take care of you. And He will even take care of them, in His own time, and in His own way. Be careful who you listen to. Always listen to God. He is your source of total truth. Live by faith today...

DAILY READING:
Ecclesiastes 1:1-3:22; 2 Corinthians 6:1-13
Psalm 46:1-11; Proverbs 22:15
Focal Passage: Ecclesiastes 3:11

LIVING BY FAITH

THIS IS A VERSE THAT MUST NOT BE OVERLOOKED. It's understandable if we do, but we don't need to. I mean, what a fantastic book in the Bible! This is the powerful book of Ecclesiastes, written by Solomon, the wisest man who ever lived. This is considered wisdom literature, like Proverbs. These books help us grapple with practical and philosophical issues of the day. Solomon went through a ton of stuff during his lifetime. It wasn't all good. He discusses the pleasures of life and how they leave one empty. He speaks from experience. And he lets the readers know that nothing, absolutely nothing, will give meaning to anyone without God. Only God as a part of one's life, makes life make sense. Make sense? Sure it does. Either we know personally, or we know someone who has tried to make life about things like money, position, or even sex. There's a God shaped void that cannot be filled with any of those things, or other things not mentioned. Only God can fill the void in and through a relationship with Jesus Christ.

Do you see why this verse should not be overlooked? Read it again. Now, go back and read the last part of the verse once again. See it? There it is, folks! Solomon had just finished a discourse about time. There's a time for everything under the sun. There certainly is! These verses are so practical, as well as powerful. The first part of the verse even says God has given us enough to be involved in during our lifetime to occupy our time here on earth. But He put eternity in our heart, too. Meaning nothing here on earth will fill the void God put in us, but God.

Why am I making such a big deal about this verse? 1. It may be that you just realized why you are so empty. Maybe you've been trying to find the ultimate meaning in life through "stuff." Maybe it's been through a person? Maybe even religion? Take it from this wise man, none of that will bring ultimate peace to your heart. Give your heart to Jesus today. Life will start making more sense. 2. It may be that you've been allowing other things to crowd out your walk with Christ. In other words, your relationship with Jesus is not your top priority. Remember, He doesn't want to be a part of your life, He wants to *be* your life. I have found He does a much better job at being boss than I do. Some of the things mentioned in these first chapters are not bad in and of themselves. They just can't be first or expected to fill the void only Christ can fill. Live by faith today…

DAILY READING:

Ecclesiastes 4:1-6:12; 2 Corinthians 6:14-7:7
Psalm 47:1-9; Proverbs 22:16
Focal Passage: 2 Corinthians 6:14

LIVING BY FAITH

HERE'S THE "DO NOT MARRY AN UNBELIEVER" VERSE. As a Youth Pastor, I would often be asked by one of my youth if it was okay to marry a non-believer. I would take them to this verse. Not only would I share this verse, but I'd often say *your date can be your mate*. It's true. I encouraged them not to even date unbelievers. I've witnessed too many couples who decided to be married who should have never said "I do." Why? Because one of them was an unbeliever. Unfortunately, often the couple ends up divorcing or just surviving from day to day. It's sad. And I wish I didn't have to communicate this, but it is an absolute reality in today's world. Furthermore, it's a terrible witness and can scar children who may be involved.

If you are single, please memorize this verse. Please do not compromise truth for any reason. If you are married to a non-believer, take it to Jesus and be His light in your home. God is able to do more than you can ever hope or imagine.

Guess what? This is not just about marrying unbelievers. One can have close partnerships in business or friendships. Please don't do it. The potential compromise and negativity may affect your relationship with God. Their practices, values, and beliefs will contradict your biblical convictions in time. Say no, before you ever say yes. That way you won't have to say no after you've said yes, and the damage is already done. The whole idea of being "unequally yoked," comes from an Old Testament teaching. The Israelites were told not to have an ox and a donkey plow together. Can you imagine? Not a good team. Form good partnerships with Godly folks. You are on God's team and He wants your closest team members to be suited up in the same way you are. If not, it'll be like trying to make a donkey and ox go in the same direction. It will not happen. Ask God who your most intimate relationships should be with. He'll tell you and you will be much better off in the long run. Live by faith today...

SEPTEMBER 4

DAILY READING:
Ecclesiastes 7:1-9:18; 2 Corinthians 7:8-16
Psalm 48:1-14; Proverbs 22:17-19
Focal Passage: Ecclesiastes 9:9

LIVING BY FAITH

ENJOY LIFE WITH YOUR WIFE ON HER BIRTHDAY AND EVERY OTHER DAY. Today is my wife's birthday. Kellie Diane Vaughn Kitchings is fifty-eight years as of the day of this writing. (Among other things, it means I am only one year older than she is. Well, for a little over a month.) I am going to do what our focal passage says to do today. I am going to enjoy her birthday. We will eat ice cream. (Because she loves ice cream, and I don't want her to eat ice cream by herself. Yes, I am that kind of husband.) And I am hoping we will have birthday cake under the ice cream because I love cake. We enjoy eating together. We will especially enjoy desserts today and other activities of the day to recognize this meaningful day in our lives. Kellie is a gift to me and many, many other people. She loves deeply, and those who have experienced it understand and love her for it.

The Bible says I should enjoy her every day of the year. The writer of Ecclesiastes once again provides great wisdom for us. Basically, he is saying that life is short and has challenges. Don't always wait for the perfect season in your life to enjoy what you have now. You know, what we think or say sometimes, *"Well, when I finally graduate from seminary, we will..." "Well, when we are empty-nesters, we will..." "Well, when I get to retire, we will..."* You see where I am going here? Of course, you do, if you are married. We are all guilty of this from time to time. We can MISS THE MOMENT if we are not careful. Marriage is meant to be enjoyed. Marriage is not something a couple just survives. Our marriages should thrive. They can if we recognize how important it is and put in the effort.

I know one day I may not be able to celebrate Kellie's birthday because I have passed away or she has. I need to make the most of today AND every other day of this year with her. We never know when our life will come to an end. As a matter of fact, we need to heed what this verse is suggesting—life is short, live every moment as if it's your last. One day it will be. Let's enjoy what God has blessed us with while we have breath. Live by faith today...

DAILY READING:

Ecclesiastes 10:1-12:14; 2 Corinthians 8:1-15
Psalm 49:1-20; Proverbs 22:20-21
Focal Passage: 2 Corinthians 8:1-5

LIVING BY FAITH

THEY DIDN'T HAVE MUCH, BUT THEY GAVE ANYWAY. The Apostle Paul was encouraging the church in Corinth to be generous. He had experienced rich generosity and he wanted the believers there to understand the concept of grace giving. Jesus gave His life so we might have life. As Christians, giving should be a natural overflow from our lives. That's not always the case. So he used the example of another group of believers. He highlighted the churches in Macedonia. (See Acts 16:6-17:15) These folks had experienced an incredibly severe trial, yet this did not keep them from expressing generosity. As a matter of fact, because they had been recipients of generosity, it caused them to give freely. Let's put it this way, they did not give out of guilt. They did not have some worldly view of thinking they were getting some type of deal by giving. God doesn't operate with worldly views. They gave out of their love for God. They understood grace giving. They were excited about the opportunities before them. They raised the bar on what giving is all about. The church in Corinth benefited by their example.

Yesterday, my wife Kellie and I delivered resources for hurricane victims in Louisiana on behalf of our church, Fifth Avenue Baptist. Pastor Rick Julian, a friend, is pastoring Bethel Church in Jennings, Louisiana. He and his wife Rachel, received our gifts with open arms as we arrived with blessings from Fifth folks. We were able to make the delivery on behalf of people who have been there. Floridians understand hurricanes and have been blessed by people from all over the country through disaster relief efforts over the years. When this opportunity presented itself, we were able to exercise grace giving. Our church is not a wealthy church, but we understand what it means to help others in a time of need. I also have a much deeper appreciation for hurricane help after having such a hands-on encounter yesterday. I'll never forget the expressions of gratitude for the small part we played in assisting those who had been without electricity for weeks and whose houses had sustained major damage. It is amazing what God can do through believers working together to bless others. All it does is make you want to be even more generous than you were before. Who might need *your* generosity? Live by faith today…

LIVING BY FAITH

YOU LIKELY DO NOT WANT TO TELL HER SHE HAS HAIR LIKE A FLOCK OF GOATS BUT DO COMPLIMENT HER. Cultural context is important. When Solomon wrote this book, he did so with the language of the day. Most Palestinian goats have long wavy black hair. So when a flock of these particular goats moved down a hill, it appeared the entire hillside was alive. Can you visualize it in your mind right now? If not, it's okay. I'm struggling here a little bit, too. Here's the deal—the husband is complimenting his new bride. That's the main takeaway. This is a lover's song. Most scholars believe it is a story about God's love applied to human relationships. God allows Solomon to bring in poetic, sometimes sensual, language in describing this married couple's journey. This unique book in the Bible not only assists us in knowing how to relate to God, but how to relate to one another within the bounds of marriage. God created sex for marriage, and it's meant to be celebrated. It is a good thing. The world has used and abused sex for years and that's not a good thing. (Please allow your journey through the Song of Solomon to give you a fresh, healthy, view of biblical romance, within the context of a married relationship.)

My dad would often compliment my mom in front of us. He would just randomly talk about how pretty she was. Many times we were the audience and heard those appropriate, sweet expressions of love. You could just see my mom's face glow with appreciation. I have tried to do the same with my wife, Kellie. I probably haven't done as good of a job with this aspect of marriage as my dad did, but I've tried to follow his example here. The verse talks about eyes. My Kellie has pretty brown eyes with a spot in one of them. How cool is that! And she has thick, black hair. I often tell her that and how mine is totally opposite. She has never, ever stopped me from complimenting her on the beautiful features God blessed her with. Guys, don't stop complimenting your wife after your honeymoon. It will enhance your long-term marriage relationship. And please don't try the "goat hair" phrase on her, unless it fits your cultural context. Live by faith today...

LIVING BY FAITH

THIS IS THE NEXT BEST THING. When I am counseling engaged couples, the first session is focused primarily on two things. 1. I want to know if they are both believers. In a recent devotional, I addressed what the Bible says about being unequally yoked. If a couple is unsaved or one has not accepted Christ as his or her personal savior, I present the gospel and provide the opportunity. A couple must be born again to have a biblically sound, Christian marriage. 2. I listen to them discuss their relationship. I will often ask questions to prompt more insight into their journey together. The word I'm hoping to hear is *friend*. I want to know that they are friends. What a blessing it is to hear one or both at some point say *he is my best friend* or *she is my best friend*. The good news is that I often do hear those words. When a couple has a relationship with Jesus and are besties, they have a good chance of having a marriage that will last.

In our text today, the bridegroom seems to be a "looker." They are intimate with each other. But what we cannot miss is the phrase *and this is my friend*. Outside of knowing a relationship has its foundation on Jesus, this is the next best thing.

A couple may be drawn to each other because they met at church. They may have chemistry due to their personalities, or likes and dislikes. They may even have a physical attraction toward one another. But in the end, if they decide to marry and they are not great friends, they will not have a great marriage. When my wife Kellie and I have had significant disagreements, it's the reality that we are great friends that often helps us set aside our differences. I cannot imagine life without her and vice versa. God establishes our home. He is our sure foundation. And He likes it when we really like each other. Love your significant other and be sure you like them, too. Live by faith today...

DAILY READING:
Isaiah 1:1-2:22; 2 Corinthians 10:1-18
Psalm 52:1-9; Proverbs 22:26-27
Focal Passage: 2 Corinthians 10:3-5

LIVING BY FAITH

HERE IT IS—THE KEY TO BREAKING A STRONGHOLD. Do you have a sin that just seems to not go away? You know, that besetting sin that so easily entangles you. The one that keeps popping up after you've been up several hours each day. Maybe it's drunkenness? Maybe it's adultery? Maybe it's anger that does not please the Lord? I dare say that all of us have a weakness or two. Most describe it as an addictive behavior. Everyone is different, but we all have certain sins that seem to tempt us more than others. If we're not careful we will excuse it away. Sometimes we blame it on our upbringing. Maybe we even justify it in some way. Regardless, if the Bible defines a stronghold as a sin, it is a sin. As believers, Jesus has set us free from sin. He does not want us to continually give up on resisting some sin because we may find it difficult. He died for that sin and has set us free. Please don't keep going into that ditch. It's muddy in there and hard to get the dirt off of you. The more you go there, the worse it gets.

This passage has the key to breaking strongholds. Please do not be held captive or held hostage any longer. When your personal knowledge of the living Word and the written Word meet, you can overcome your stronghold. Strongholds are demolished by a knowledge of biblical truths. An addictive behavior is just the fruit of sinful behavior. As you grow in your personal walk with Christ, He will show you your weaknesses. (He continually shows me mine.) When the Bible speaks to those areas, take captive the verse or verses. Memorize them. Familiarize yourself with them. When the temptation arrives, because it will, start talking to Jesus and saying the verse. Or start focusing on the verse in some way and talking with Jesus about it. Keep doing this and watch what God does from the inside out. Sure, it may take some time. Patterns don't become patterns overnight. Remember, we are saved by faith and we are to live by faith. Like the line in the old hymn, *"Faith is the victory that overcomes the world."* Live by faith today...

DAILY READING:
Isaiah 3:1-5:30; 2 Corinthians 11:1-15
Psalm 53:1-6; Proverbs 22:28-29
Focal Passage: 2 Corinthians 11:4

LIVING BY FAITH

THE JESUS OF SOME IS NOT THE JESUS OF THE BIBLE. False teachers had promoted themselves. The Apostle Paul was not insecure. He was confident in who he was in Christ Jesus. God had saved and called him to a great work. Here Paul makes sure the church in Corinth was made aware that some of the teachers were false. They had deceived many and even made them think Paul's teaching was less than adequate. Do you see how Satan deceives? Never be afraid but do be aware of his schemes. If the enemy can cause some to believe Paul was a weak, misguided teacher, just imagine what can occur with you and me. Satan hates the true gospel of Jesus Christ and biblical doctrine. He is relentless in trying to get people off track. When you hear or read something that doesn't sound right, pause. Pray. Study scriptures. Seek Godly counsel. Stand for the truth that has stood the test of time.

Some teach a different Jesus than the one of the Bible. False teachers do this with skilled deceitful ways. For example, if you are engaged in a conversation, and the person is trying to get you to understand their religion, be careful. I have found that cults will try to make you think they believe the same about Jesus. They do not. Their Jesus sounds like the real Jesus, but he is not. Jesus may just be a great teacher to them, but He is more. Jesus may be one of many ways to God to them, but He is not one of many. He is the only way. Jesus plus anything is heresy. Jesus is the one and only Son of God. He lived a perfect life, died on a cross for our sins, and rose three days later. He is our Redeemer. If you dig a little with those who do not believe in the same Jesus, you will usually uncover their deceitfulness in time. Jesus is a "sticking point." I have even found some false religions don't even want to pause and pray *to* Him, concerning the conversation *about* Him. That's always a red flag! Don't let them intimidate you. Allow the Holy Spirit to guide you in how far to go at the time. Arguing never gets you anywhere positive.

Be careful, but don't be afraid. Be trained, but don't be tacky. Be prayerful, but don't be prideful. Be bold, but don't be bombastic. And for heaven's sake, be like the Jesus of the Bible when engaging in conversations about Him. Live by faith today...

DAILY READING:
Isaiah 6:1-7:25; 2 Corinthians 11:16-33
Psalm 54:1-7; Proverbs 23:1-3
Focal Passage: Isaiah 6:1

LIVING BY FAITH

THE ABSENCE OF A GODLY FIGURE MAY BE EXACTLY WHAT GOD USES TO GET YOUR ATTENTION. King Uzziah died. He had been an overall good king for Judah. Isaiah, the great prophet, appears on the scene to help the people realize how vital it was for them to repent. They had been drifting for years and Uzziah's death needed to be used as a wake-up call. Even in their grief, they needed to call on God for comfort and direction. God was still on His throne! The King was still alive and well. He always is, my friend!

God can use tragedies of all sorts to get our attention. I know that's the way it's worked with me. Whether it was being told I had a heart condition and couldn't play competitive football; moving as a teenager; my dad dying at a relatively young age; pastoring a church that was having a difficult season; or dealing with what seemed like loss after loss for a while, God is faithful. And He always used these to take me to another level spiritually. It is not easy, but the reality is that I am still on this earth for God's purposes, not my own. His ways are not mine. Just like Isaiah was reminding God's people that there was still hope, we need to be reminded there is still hope. You and I must keep allowing the loss of a Godly person or loss of a "whatever" to cause us to cry out to God. He longs to hear from us. So, the worse it gets, the more we should be driven to the Lord.

My dad died and God used it to drive me to Him. I miss my father. But I know my heavenly Father intimately now due to my dad's early departure from this earth, as well as so many other challenges that have come. I'm pretty sure there are more to come because I am still alive. God loves me too much to leave me where I am. The same goes for you too. Let's give our full attention to the Lord. Look up. Live by faith today...

SEPTEMBER 11

DAILY READING:

Isaiah 8:1-9:21; 2 Corinthians 12:1-10
Psalm 55:1-23; Proverbs 23:4-5
Focal Passage: 2 Corinthians 12:7-10

LIVING BY FAITH

I RECALL WHERE I WAS THEN, BUT I'M TRYING TO FOCUS ON WHERE I AM NOW. I recall where I was when I received the news about the planes crashing into the Twin Towers in New York City. Many of us who were alive and old enough on that terrible day think about that first. You know, the old *"I'll never forget where I was when I received the news."* It's common. Some people do the same with the death of Elvis. Although I go through the same thoughts and emotions on this date every year, I believe today there is something I should focus on more. *Where am I now?* I'm not referring to my physical location. I'm referring more to my spiritual condition. Am I ready for the next tragedy that strikes out of nowhere? Are you? I mean, who would have thought, as I write this in 2020, that we would have been quarantined earlier in the year? Tragedy can strike nationally, internationally, or individually.

Our focal passage today can be helpful. Paul had a thorn in his flesh. Theologians have debated for centuries what his particular thorn was. I'm certainly not going to attempt to solve the debate today. What I believe is most important to understand is that it was painful. Obviously, being a strong Christian does not mean we won't experience pain. God uses our pain. It is some type of irritant that consistently troubles us on a continual basis. Satan delivers the pain, God allows the pain, and we can use the pain for our good. That is if we allow God to take over. These "thorns" keep us humble, do they not? Self-sufficiency goes out the door. We cry out to our all-sufficient God over and over again. We totally depend on Him. Who else are we going to depend on? An aspirin isn't going to help in times of sudden crisis or an ongoing painful situation. We are better off to experience God's grace and His amazing power.

Tragedies come with little warning. Be prepared ahead of time by staying close to God now. Tragedies come with lots of opportunities. Be focused on what God wants to teach you and how He wants to use you. He can handle our "whys," we just don't need to stay there. So, back to our focal point—where are you now? By focusing more on this today, we'll be ready for our tomorrows. Live by faith today...

LIVING BY FAITH

ALWAYS REMEMBER THAT GOD IS BIGGER THAN YOUR BIGGEST FEARS. Every year when September 11 rolls around, multiple films are shown depicting what happened that day in 2001. Many show the fears people experienced in our country. An attack on New York City was significant. At the time, no one knew for certain what would happen next or who might be killed in the line of duty. And the devastation at what came to be known as *Ground Zero* was astronomical. Fear was common for most people in the United States due to this giant catastrophe.

Shortly after 9/11 my family and I heard music put to this particular Psalm. A minister, David Nassar, had it produced. We purchased the CD and played it over and over again. The reason I have verse 23 memorized is because we played it so often. Usually, we would go to sleep playing the music put to scripture. Every time I read this Psalm I think about that season in our lives and how God used His Word to provide comfort. It still works.

The heading of Psalm 56 connects the psalm with David. Studying the life of David, we know he had battles with the Philistines. He learned how to overcome fear. Saying this simple yet profound prayer served him well. When thinking about the size of his enemies, they were small compared to God. God is trustworthy. When reflecting on David's warrior life, I'd say this worked. Wouldn't you? This perspective serves all of us well. God is bigger than your biggest fears. He is bigger than my biggest fears. No man or giant situation is too much for our God. The next time you or I possibly find ourselves gripped by fear, recall this passage and realize *"What can mere man do to us?"* Trust Him. Live by faith today...

LIVING BY FAITH

THERE ARE SOME PEOPLE YOU DO NOT TRY TO ADVISE.
Proverbs is wisdom literature. Proverbs is so practical for daily living. I really like Proverbs. You likely like Proverbs. It is just so down to earth. Many people read a chapter a day. It's a great practice, for there is a chapter for every day of the month. Please keep this in mind if you sense you just want to hear something extremely practical for living out your faith journey every day. And if you did not grow up in a Christian home or a Christ-honoring church, I would highly suggest you practice spending time in this book on a regular basis.

Here we find something extremely practical for daily living. The writer basically says there are some people we should not waste our breath on. I know, it seems harsh, doesn't it? (We need to first look in the mirror and see if perhaps we are "that guy." I pray not.) Think with me for a moment about people who seem to have all the answers. The person who wants to talk most of the time. The one who, when you do speak, seems to not even realize you said anything. You with me? Sure you are. I dare say we all know folks like this. THANK GOD there are not tons of them, but they exist inside the church house and outside the church house. I believe this passage deals with those people. They despise wisdom. They hate knowledge and correction. They will likely heap abuse of some kind on the one who dares to rebuke them in some way. Again, are you with me? Again I dare say, you probably are and have been wondering what to do.

Pray for the person. (Let's be sure we also pray we are not like the person the writer is speaking of in our focal passage.) When you find yourself in their presence, listen with very little, if any, response. Watch out for body language that relays approval to their words and do not feel like you have to try to straighten them out every time you are around them. Some people need a miracle from God to not be "this guy." This is another type of verse that supports the *"Don't cast your pearls before swine"* passage. There are some folks whom we realize in time we can't advise. Life is short. Please don't waste words over and over again on this individual. Others are teachable. Find them and help them. Live by faith today...

DAILY READING:

Isaiah 15:1-18:7; Galatians 1:1-24
Psalm 58:1-11; Proverbs 23:12
Focal Passage: Galatians 1:23

LIVING BY FAITH

GOD CAN CHANGE A REALLY GOOD PERSON TOO. Paul was a really good person. He was sort of like the older brother in the story of the prodigal son. He was very religious and counted on his righteousness to make him right with God. That all changed. Once he met Jesus personally, people were amazed at the change that took place in his life. This guy who criticized followers of Christ even to the point of approving of their deaths was now preaching the gospel. Wow! If that can happen to Paul, it can happen to anyone. Has it happened to you? It can. And it can happen to the most religious person you know, too.

Religion doesn't save you. Our righteousness cannot get us to heaven. This letter is primarily about Paul being sure to confront the Judaizers. These guys were telling Gentile believers they had to be circumcised to be right with Christ. They were undermining the pure gospel that saves. The Galatians were confused, and many were still living with the burden of works that Jesus had taken away. In other words, they were carrying a load that was unnecessary now. The load of sin had been paid for by Jesus's death on the cross. They were not enjoying the liberty found in a relationship with Jesus. Paul got that and he was sent to set them free. Makes sense, doesn't it? God redeemed Paul's past. God will do the same for us, if we let Him.

All too often we focus on the reality that Jesus can change a really bad person. He certainly can. The story of the prodigal son had another son... the prodigal. He was a wild man until he met Jesus. God can save a "wild man." He can also save a "good man." Which camp are you in? The best camp to be in is team Jesus. Be sure you have joined His camp. Let others know about Him—even the really good folks. Live by faith today...

DAILY READING:
Isaiah 19:1-21:17; Galatians 2:1-16
Psalm 59:1-17; Proverbs 23:13-14
Focal Passage: Galatians 2:11-13

LIVING BY FAITH

WE MUST NOT ALLOW OUR OLD BUDDIES TO KEEP US FROM ACCEPTING OUR NEW BUDDIES. Peter was fine eating and hanging out with his new Christian friends. They were Gentiles. But when his old Jewish buddies came around, somewhat skeptical about his dining with non-Jews, he backed off. In other words, his cultural practices from old hindered his new practices in Christ. (He was raised an orthodox Jew.) So much so that Paul confronted him in front of those at the scene. And rightfully so because this sin was happening in front of them, so it needed to be corrected in front of them. Paul was bold. Peter was weak. Even my man Barnabas, who was such a blessing to others, fell short on this issue.

There is freedom in Christ. All are equal before our God. The gospel of Jesus breaks down all barriers. We must not preach one gospel and live another. The Gentiles' food was not unclean. Neither were they. Before we get too down on Peter, let's examine our own life. Do we act one way around those raised like us and then another for some unbiblical reason around those not like us? This passage is about more than legalism. This text deals with race issues. We must accept all, all the time. We should not abandon our cultural upbringing, as long as it doesn't hinder our witness. I've never tried to intentionally change my southern accent to fit in. I don't try to dress in a way that is totally contrary to me in order to fit various cultures. Now, I want to be in style, and I don't want to talk like a hick, but I have got to be me. You need to be you. We are to be who we are in Christ and love everyone. If not, we can lead others astray.

Are we going to be like Paul when we see blatant racial injustice? I hope so. We certainly need it in our day. Ultimately, Jesus is the only answer to racial issues. And He counts on us to be His hands, feet, and voice for racial equality. Even if it means losing some old buddies. We never give up something based on our convictions without God replacing it with something better. Live by faith today...

LIVING BY FAITH

IT'S HIM, NOT ME. You got it? It is HIM and not me. Let's say it together now... *"It is Him and not me!"* Sometimes I need to say this out loud. There are days I need to say it out loud over and over again. What about you? What a powerful verse! If you have not memorized it or put it where you can see it on a regular basis, today is the day. It will help you in your journey with Jesus all the days of your life.

As believers, our identity is in Christ. Paul was reminding the Galatians of this vital reality as a follower of Jesus. Some of them had been misled. Leaders had been confused about what makes one right with God. It is not religion. It is not one's ethnicity. It is not one's good works. It is Jesus! It is HIM, not them! Let's do this again—"It is Him and not me." Our identity, just like the identity of the Galatian believers, is wrapped up in Jesus Christ. Jesus came and gave His perfect life so we wouldn't have to live our own life on our own. Make sense? Sure it does. Trying to live my life apart from Jesus messes it up. What about you? All together now... **"It is HIM and not me!"**

Here's the deal... If we are seeking to do God's will as we abide IN HIM, HE will see us through WHATEVER we face. I know, sometimes it's hard to see. That's the issue, faith is not seeing. It is believing. In whom? HIM! Keep doing what's right. Allow your identity to be wrapped up in Jesus. One day at a time He will work things out for your good and His glory! Live by faith today...

LIVING BY FAITH

DON'T ENVY THE BAD GUY. Do you ever wonder why a person who seems so mean seems so blessed? You know, like the guy down the street who has a boat, a nice car, and family seems to never have an issue. But he is wicked. He curses like a sailor and never goes to church. You with me? Okay, here's another example: the beautiful family that goes to your church and has it all together. But they are super religious. They certainly do the right things but seem fake. Hopefully, you get the picture. Some folks seem to not have problems, even though they are far away from Christ. This verse helps on this issue that sometimes may surface in your life.

We shouldn't envy evil people who seem to prosper in this world. 1. We don't know what's really going on in their home. Maybe their lives are not going so hot. Everyone has problems. Our world is depraved. And they have no one to turn to who can ultimately give them peace because they are operating outside a relationship with Jesus. 2. Fearing God is the better path. Why? Because it means we have a friend like no other. God never changes. God is everywhere. God knows everything. God is just. God is merciful. God is the one we can always respect (fear) because He is God alone. No one demands the respect He does. He is perfect in every way. He will take care of His own. If we have a personal relationship with Him, we're in the best spot ever. Even if at times our "spot" is difficult. He will use our challenges for good. We have someone to go to who has the answers, not just suggestions.

Let's not envy the "bad guy" (the person who doesn't know Christ and is living as a lost person because he's, well, lost). His day is coming. Our day is coming. But I'd rather have my day with God than without Him no matter how things look down here on earth. Instead of envying the "bad guy," pray for him. Live by faith today...

DAILY READING:
Isaiah 28:14-30:11; Galatians 3:23-4:31
Psalm 62:1-12; Proverbs 23:19-21
Focal Passage: Proverbs 23:19-21

LIVING BY FAITH

HERE ARE TWO WAYS TO DESTROY YOUR LIFE. The company we keep can make us or break us. I cannot emphasize this enough. I have written about it before today and I'm sure I'll write about it after today before the year ends. As we've read, *Bad company corrupts good character.* All we have to do is allow the wrong type of people to take the wrong place in our lives and we are sure to go down a path of destruction. As our text tells us, use wisdom and keep your heart pure. Be careful whom you hang out with for long periods of time. This is not just for teenagers. This is for adults, too. Think about your relationships today. Evaluate them in light of the passage.

Now, for the two ways to destroy your life. Here they are: 1. Drink too much alcohol. 2. Eat too much. I grew up in a church that addressed the former and rarely mentioned the latter. Drunkenness is clearly forbidden in the Bible. It can cause one to not think properly. It can lead to doing things one would not normally do that can even lead to jail time. There are those who have dealt with alcoholism for years and continue to battle this stronghold in their lives. It's awful. I've witnessed those who were once financially stable end up poor due to drunkenness in their life. The best way to be sure you don't have to fight this battle is to drink iced tea or some other non-alcoholic drink. It's just not worth the risk.

Eating way too much is equally destructive. Gluttony is one of the seven deadly sins that can inspire further sin. (This alone should tell us something.) It causes laziness or slothfulness. (Slothfulness is another one of the seven deadly sins.) Each day should be our best day yet. How can we passionately fulfill our mission if we're eating too much? We can't take this lightly. Listen, I enjoy eating. There are times I eat way too much. I know me. I know my upbringing and those who have gone before me in my family tree who liked to eat. This is one I struggle with and I personally know this verse to be true. It can hinder my purpose. It can hinder your purpose. Balance is key and putting boundaries in our lives is vital.

So we don't want to destroy our lives. Let's pay attention to our focal passage and be wise. Keep your heart on the right path. Live by faith today...

DAILY READING:
Isaiah 30:12-33:12; Galatians 5:1-12
Psalm 63:1-11; Proverbs 23:22
Focal Passage: Galatians 5:7-10

LIVING BY FAITH

ALL IT TAKES IS ONE BAD EGG. I usually make eggs for breakfast on Saturday mornings. My children never seemed to appreciate my occasional egg-making before they went to school. They indicated mine were not as "nice" as their mom's scrambled or fried eggs. I know, I'm surprised too. Nevertheless, we are empty-nesters now and so I make them on Saturdays. Now, I'm the only one who eats them, but that's ok. I learned years ago that if I allow one bad egg to join the other good eggs then my scrambled eggs taste awful; otherwise, they're good. (Even if I have to say so myself.) The same can apply to church life. One person who misrepresents the grace of God can mess up a lot of good.

The teachers in the Galatian church were overall very good. But some taught destructive doctrine. The Judaizers continued to bring works in as a part of salvation. Paul believed the Galatian teachers would adopt God's view of salvation. Justification and sanctification by God's grace would prevail in the end. The false teachers would pay one day. And Paul was certainly building a case for the leaders to confront the troublemakers. Satan works through those with ill intent.

Are you a "bad egg" in your church? Please repent and do otherwise. If not, your day will come. Do you know a "bad egg?" Pray for the person and be willing to confront the evil. If not, your church will pay the price. It can even lead to a dead church. You need to trust me on this one. More than that, you need to trust the Bible. This focal passage today is extremely significant for the local church. Think about it for a while. Do what's right. All it takes is one bad egg. Live by faith today...

SEPTEMBER 20

DAILY READING:
Isaiah 33:13-36:22; Galatians 5:13-26
Psalm 64:1-10; Proverbs 23:23
Focal Passage: Galatians 5:22-24

LIVING BY FAITH

A ROOTIN' FRUITIN' CHRISTIAN. I preached a sermon series once on the fruit of the Spirit. I took each fruit listed in our focal passage today and preached an entire message on its meaning. For example, you may have heard the saying that you are fine as long as you don't drink, smoke, or chew, or go with girls who do. That's not in the Bible. Here's how you and I know if we are reflecting the life of a Jesus follower: love, joy, peace, patience, kindness, goodness, faithfulness, gentleness, and self-control.

The verses leading up to this passage let us know what the works of the flesh are. They reveal in no uncertain terms how we can know if we are still living opposite of what Christ desires for His children. Now, if you are not in a relationship with Christ, you cannot overcome those fleshly desires on your own. You must be born again. Admit your sin and put your faith in Jesus. You see, only when the Holy Spirit resides in a person can one exhibit the fruit as a regular part of their life. You can't work these things up on your own. It's God working in and then through you.

The fruit of the Spirit benefits others. It provides refreshment for those who need it. It proves to others that you have been changed. You may not walk in cowboy boots and be referred to as a *rootin' tootin' cowboy*. But you can walk in the Spirit and be a *rootin' fruitin' Christian*. Live by faith today...

DAILY READING:
Isaiah 37:1-38:22; Galatians 6:1-18
Psalm 65:1-13; Proverbs 23:24
Focal Passage: Galatians 6:1

LIVING BY FAITH

RESTORE FELLOW BELIEVERS VERY GENTLY OR IT WILL DO MORE DAMAGE THAN GOOD. I did what this passage says not to do, and it did lots of damage. In anger, I confronted a close friend about a sinful act. What he was doing was wrong and causing much damage to his family and witness. But I had no right to talk with him about it with an angry spirit. Yes, I was hurt and disappointed. I mean, the guy knew better! He was my close buddy. He was representing Jesus. Others knew we were tight. Regardless, my role was to talk with him with a spirit of love. Now, he didn't deny his wrongdoing. He just didn't receive it well. I wouldn't have either. So, his pattern of drifting from the Lord continued. And when I came to my senses and apologized, he used it as an excuse to continue his sinful ways. There is a reason this verse is here for Jesus followers.

What did I learn? A lot. I must be very careful and prayerful before confronting a fellow believer with sin. I need to know the facts. In my own prayer time, I must confess my own sinfulness and see if there is anything going on in my own life that would keep me from being the one to address the sin of another. And most of all, I need to have a loving spirit regardless of how I feel about it. Yes, sometimes we can be shocked to know someone who knows better would do such a thing. All we need to do is look in the mirror and ask, *"Am I capable of doing the same or worse?"*

I thank God for those who have come to me through the years when I have strayed. Those who did it right showed me how to confront. I also know there have been those who have come at me in the wrong way. Those have shown me how not to confront. So, let's be loving enough to our brothers and sisters to confront them when their sins warrant it. Let's do so gently. And let's be careful not to allow the enemy to trip us up. We would have regrets, but the enemy would have no regrets. None. None whatsoever. It would further promote his cause. Live by faith today...

DAILY READING:

Isaiah 39:1-41:16; Ephesians 1:1-23
Psalm 66:1-20; Proverbs 23:25-28
Focal Passage: Isaiah 40:30-31

LIVING BY FAITH

THIS PASSAGE WAS USED IN MY FAVORITE MOVIE OF ALL TIME. *Remember the Titans* is my favorite movie. There are many reasons why. It is based on a true story. A newly appointed black coach to a football team in the South is torn up with racism in the early 1970s. The players went through a lot together and at one point were at a breaking point. A team meeting was called, and our focal passage became a focal point in the scene. In the face of all the adversity, one player, Lastik, shared this verse that his fellow player "Rev" was always talking about. He quotes (and sort of sings, along with Rev at one point) the verse and tries to encourage the team to stay strong. It was a rallying point for them. It can be the same for us.

God asked the Jewish people to do the impossible. They were looking only at the long road ahead of them. They felt they just didn't have the strength to move forward. Isaiah assures them that if they trust in themselves, they will fail. If they trust in the Lord, they will soar. An eagle soars and has incredible vision. We must look with the eyes of faith. We must rely on God's strength for our journey. Let's meditate on the character of Christ. Read and apply God's Word. Pray. Glorify God alone. To renew means "to exchange." Like taking off an old pair of socks and putting on a new fresh pair. We exchange our great limitations for His great glorification by allowing Him to be the ultimate source of our strength.

Perspective is everything. Does yours need changing? God can do it. Maybe you need to Google my favorite movie and watch this one scene? Maybe you just need to allow God to show you a different scene than what you've been seeing in your own strength? Regardless, soar with your strengths and win at the game of life God has so graciously given you. Live by faith today...

DAILY READING:
Isaiah 41:17-43:13; Ephesians 2:1-22
Psalm 67:1-7; Proverbs 23:29-35
Focal Passage: Ephesians 2:10

LIVING BY FAITH

DO YOU HAVE A FAITH THAT WORKS? Now you've been with me long enough this year to know I do not believe in a works salvation. Ephesians was written primarily to let the church in Ephesus know that Jews and Gentiles are brought together in Christ. Those who trust in Jesus by faith alone are one family. No more divide. We are to live in harmony, growing in our faith in Christ. The result? We will do good works.

Immediately following the verses that are often used to explain the truth of the gospel—we are saved by faith and not works—is a verse that might be overlooked due to the emphasis on the preceding verses. Yes, they are incredibly important! But we must not forget God has a work for us to do as His children. That's why we remain on earth. We glorify Him and His kingdom by fulfilling our purpose. I think there are Christians who are unfulfilled and miserable inside because they are not doing God's work. I think deep down they know this to be true. Are you one? Please stop it. Allow God to change the trajectory of your life so you will be fulfilled, and the dash between your birth date and your death date won't just be a mark on a tombstone. It will represent the work God had for you due to your faith in Him.

No one else on the planet will be able to do the work that God has designed specifically and especially for you. Oh, He will accomplish His will with or without us. But you are not still down here to just sit on your hands or sit in a pew on Sundays. No, not at all. God has lives to touch through you. God has something to build through you. God has family members to be taught and inspired by you. Do not waste your life! It's short. Make it count. Live by faith today…

DAILY READING:

Isaiah 43:14-45:10; Ephesians 3:1-21
Psalm 68:1-18; Proverbs 24:1-2
Focal Passage: Isaiah 43:18-19

LIVING BY FAITH

DON'T LET THE GOOD OLD MESS UP THE GOOD NEW. God is always up to something good. It is His character. He takes bad stuff in our lives and the world all the time and uses it for good. When He does, we celebrate. We rejoice. We thank Him. We remember what He did when we go through difficult seasons in order to be encouraged. But we must not camp there. If so, we miss all the new things God wants to do in our lives. Just as we enjoy various seasons—fall, winter, spring, summer—we enjoy all God desires to have us experience in every season of life.

I'm sure the promise in our passage today was a reminder for Isaiah's readers. It was about the exodus from Egypt when God saved their forefathers from bondage and led them through the wilderness. But the exodus from Babylon that was coming soon would even be better! It would restore the Jews to their homeland from which they had been expelled because of their sinfulness. Can you imagine? Wow, the future was going to be good, so they need not just relish in the "good old." If so, they would mess up the "good new."

Guilty! I am guilty of doing this in my own life. Are you? God allowed me to be a part of some amazing experiences as a younger minister. I will be forever grateful. But my life is not over. By God's grace I must not, I *cannot* allow my "good old" to mess up the "good new" that my God has for me. My life is not over. Your life is not over. Look ahead by faith. God has something new for you to do. He wants you to touch lives like no one else. If you know what it is, go for it! If you are not sure, pray for it! Once it registers in your heart and mind, go ahead because He is making a way for it to happen. Live by faith today...

DAILY READING:
Isaiah 45:11-48:11; Ephesians 4:1-16
Psalm 68:19-35; Proverbs 24:3-4
Focal Passage: Ephesians 4:3

LIVING BY FAITH

KEEPING UNITY TAKES EFFORT. Paul doesn't just urge, he *commands* the church to keep unity. Folks, that's serious. God calls His children to protect what He has already established. God holds us together when we are operating under the leadership of the Holy Spirit and not the flesh. It's His church. When we go with our human point of view, we get off track. It causes disunity every time. Peace comes from God alone and offers harmony where there was once conflict. It's like a rope that holds us together. The few verses before our text tell us how to live. So yes, it's possible. But I cannot emphasize it enough—it takes effort. That effort must come from every member of the body of Christ.

Some churches are passive when it comes to keeping unity within the church fellowship. It is a travesty. Why? Because so often there are good people who attend. So often there are lost people in the area where the church is located who need to be reached. Many times, their doctrine is solid. It's just that they let those who cause disunity slide. What does that mean? They pretend they are invisible. (By the way, it may just be one primary person causing conflict. It only takes one bad egg to mess up an omelet.) They decide in their mind that it's not their battle. They may even leave it to the preacher. Now let me be clear, the pastor, staff, and leaders have a responsibility to help keep the peace. But it's everyone's responsibility to do their part to keep unity. If you know someone who is causing disunity in the fellowship, pray about it. If you are led to do so, talk with the person and help them see the damage they are causing. Perhaps they don't see the error of their ways. If that doesn't work, don't stop. It takes effort to keep unity. Whatever you do, please don't turn the other way as if it is not your battle because you tried. It's everyone's battle. Take the next step.

God may be calling you to confront someone who is causing dissension in your church right now. Walk in the Spirit. Allow the Spirit to lead you. Make the effort. God is the God of peace. May His peace be with you going forward. Live by faith today...

SEPTEMBER 26

DAILY READING:
Isaiah 48:12-50:11; Ephesians 4:17-32
Psalm 69:1-18; Proverbs 24:5-6
Focal Passage: Ephesians 4:29

LIVING BY FAITH

OUR WORDS CAN AFFECT THE TRAJECTORY OF SOMEONE'S LIFE. Do you believe that? I do. I can recall moments when people spoke words of life into me. It was usually during a season I needed a certain someone to encourage me. No, I didn't always know who that certain someone was at the time. But I look back and know those certain someones at certain times were instruments of God. You and I can do the same. God can and will use us to help people get back on track after a difficult day or time in life.

Paul believed it. He had been the recipient of encouragement from Barnabas during his early days of Christianity. In fact, we may not have been blessed like we are by his writings if Barnabas had not done so. The church in Ephesus needed to be sure to use their words for good, not bad. It was not easy being a part of the early church. They certainly didn't need to make it any harder by tearing each other up with negativity. The body of Christ should focus on helping each other be all that God intends for them to be. Speaking words of life accomplishes this as much as anything else. As a matter of fact, it can help a dying church move forward in a positive direction after getting off course. I've seen it done. And it can certainly help individuals. I've seen Godly deacons pull aside church members who were discouraged for various reasons and speak words of life into them. There was an instant change because they had believed some sort of lie from the enemy and a person of integrity took the time to help.

We all needed this reminder. Our words need to be calculated. They can be used to hurt someone deeply or build someone up mightily. May our words be beneficial to others for the rest of our days. Live by faith today...

DAILY READING:

Isaiah 51:1-53:12; Ephesians 5:1-33
Psalm 69:19-36; Proverbs 24:7
Focal Passage: Ephesians 5:15-18

LIVING BY FAITH

THE CLOCK IS TICKING—DO WHAT GOD MADE YOU TO DO WHILE YOU STILL HAVE TIME. It is never too late to be who God made you to be. If you are still alive, and I trust that you are if you are reading this, God has a purpose for you to fulfill. He's sovereign. Don't talk yourself out of it because you are 105 years old. No. Please don't do that. God will meet you where you are and take you where you need to be before you breathe your last breath.

Paul encourages the church here to be consistent in their walk of faith. He's stressing the reality that we are to make the most of every moment of every day. Evil exists in our world. It is not easy to be a light, but it is possible. It takes intentionality. Every day we are to make wise choices. We do not want to come to the end of our journey (the "fourth quarter" of life) and have lots of foolishness in our life because we were influenced to make stupid choices. No. Let's be wise and make Godly choices one day at a time, one moment at a time. They add up. God has won the victory for us already through Jesus. If you are a believer, you are on the winning team already. Live like it.

I see people quite often live below their potential. It makes me sick. Don't be that person. Start today. Pray for wisdom. Trust God to turn unwise choices you've made in the past into something good. Don't be afraid of the enemy but be aware of his ways and how he uses some people. Plan each day. Don't go overboard, but intentionally build time alone with the Lord. That is a wise use of time. God will honor it and you'll be forever grateful. Live by faith today...

SEPTEMBER 28

DAILY READING:
Isaiah 54:1-57:13; Ephesians 6:1-24
Psalm 70:1-5; Proverbs 24:8
Focal Passage: Isaiah 55:8-9

LIVING BY FAITH

GOD DOESN'T ALWAYS DO THINGS LIKE YOU AND ME. That is because He is holy. We are not holy. When we have an intimate relationship with Him, we are more likely to be in step with Him. We are reminded in our focal passage that God is on a much higher plane than us. The reality is that we are sinners. God sent His only Son, Jesus, to die for our sins. Needless to say, God's ways are not our ways.

Reflect on your thoughts. Are all your thoughts wholesome, good, Godly? I'm not thinking you answered that question in the affirmative. Me neither. Sometimes the enemy gives us those fiery darts out of nowhere. We can't blame those on God. He had nothing to do with them. So all of our thoughts are not His.

Think about your ways. You know, the way you want to do something at work or with your family. Do they always line up with God's Word? No. Me neither. Sometimes our way of doing something at home is out of selfishness. It may even be an old habit we picked up from our parents. What about work? Do you always go to work with great anticipation, zeal, passion, and an incredibly positive attitude? No. Me neither. Maybe we had a late night eating pizza and didn't sleep well? Regardless, our ways at work aren't always holy or positive. God has ways of doing things that don't line up with our flesh. This is why we need to know Him intimately. His Word helps us here.

What's going on with you right now? Maybe you are abiding in Him and regularly praying. Perhaps you even see in His Word that the direction you are going certainly seems to line up with who you are in Christ and the truth of the Bible. But things just don't seem right. Maybe God is taking His time to put the finishing touches on what seems to be His plan and yours. Go look at the heavens and marvel at His creation. It may put things in perspective. Trust the God of creation who created you for good and Godly purposes. Live by faith today...

DAILY READING:
Isaiah 57:14-59:21; Philippians 1:1-26
Psalm 71:1-24; Proverbs 24:9-10
Focal Passage: Psalm 71:18

LIVING BY FAITH

THE NEXT GENERATION IS COUNTING ON YOU, YOU OLD GRAY-HAIRED MAN. I know, you can't believe I wrote this. Me neither. But when you are older and gray-headed, you become more of who you are. This can be good, or this can be bad. I've always been a little "outside the box," so I am likely to be even more so in the days ahead. Also, I can do so because I have gray hair now and I did not say, *you old gray-headed woman.* (Although I believe it applies to older ladies, too.)

The Psalmist is sharing about his faith from when he was much younger. God had been good to him through the years. He's praying God would continue to bless him so he can continue to praise Him all the days of his life. He had a deep desire for the Lord to allow him to invest in the younger folks. He wanted them to know God personally. He wanted them to learn from his mistakes and his good decisions. He got it. There comes a time we become less, and the next generation becomes more.

About a week from the day of this writing, I turn sixty. My dad died at sixty. I don't have the advantage of being able to watch how he aged after my age. I still know how to do it. I know how by the Bible. I know how by other Godly men I've watched transition. This I know—investing in younger men who are open and teachable is going to be a priority. This verse says it should be. This text says that as long as I'm in good health, I have a wonderful privilege to do so until the day I die. They need to know of the mighty power of my awesome Jesus. "The greatest use of a life is to spend it on something that will outlast it." (William James) Okay, all you gray-haired folks like myself, let's invest in others so we can have a ripple effect. Our influence for Christ can and will go on long after we are dead and gone from this world. Live by faith today...

DAILY READING:
Isaiah 60:1-62:5; Philippians 1:27-2:18
Psalm 72:1-20; Proverbs 24:11-12
Focal Passage: Philippians 2:14-16

LIVING BY FAITH

HERE ARE TWO WAYS TO RUIN YOUR LIFE AND MAYBE THOSE AROUND YOU. Grumble and argue. That's it. If you want to have a no good, very bad, awful life, grumble a lot and argue with people every time you have the opportunity to do so. I pray I am not "that guy." Lord, please forgive me if I am. Lord, please change me and anyone who reads this if we are like the character in the Winnie-the-Pooh books, Eeyore. When I think about these two characteristics, I think of him. (Or her.)

This passage, of course, really explains how to have a great life. Don't spend it grumbling all the time and arguing every chance you get. Sure, we all have our days, but there are some who have a pattern of being a grumbler and just looking for a fight. That is not the way to reflect the Lord Jesus as a Christ follower. Grumblers find something they don't like and respond with negative emotions. A true grumbler does this most every day. It does not win friends or influence people in a good way. And arguing is just being one that likes to fuss. If there's nothing to fuss about, this person will make up something. Our perverted world does not need this type of argumentation, they get enough of that through pagans.

The Apostle Paul points out that when we don't constantly complain or argue in life, we have a better afterlife. Why? Because of our Godly influence and making the most of every day. Our race down here as a believer is not easy. It is not lengthy in light of eternity. So, let's not ruin it or make others miserable. Let's indeed have the same attitude of Christ. Look back over the verses preceding our focal passage and we will see how. Live by faith today...

DAILY READING:
Isaiah 62:6-65:25; Philippians 2:19-3:4a
Psalm 73:1-28; Proverbs 24:13-14
Focal Passage: Isaiah 64:4

LIVING BY FAITH

IF YOU WAIT, YOU WILL BE REWARDED. That's easy to say and read, but it is not so easy to live by. I know there are exceptions to the rule. Most of us have difficulty waiting. Waiting in line at Chick-Fil-A is not easy, although it's worth it. Waiting in line at a wedding reception is not easy. Waiting for your hair to grow out after your barber scalped you is not easy. Waiting in line for tickets is not easy. I'm telling you, waiting is not an easy thing to do for most people. Even when it comes to things of God, it is not easy. Our passage indicates that waiting will be rewarded. How so?

Let's start by thinking about what happens when we don't wait. Stop and consider what can take place. I have met with couples who "ran ahead" of God and are struggling because of it. We have all been guilty of "running ahead," and we paid a price. Some of you reading this right now may still be recovering financially due to a decision you made years ago out of impatience. It is costly in numerous ways to not be patient. This has been an ongoing struggle for me. This passage got my attention.

God acts on behalf of those who wait. Go back and read that again. I did. How incredible! That does not mean we sit on our hands and do absolutely nothing every day. It means to trust in God's agenda and not our own. We pray and wait on Him to answer in His own time and way. We allow Him to tweak what we thought He was doing, knowing it will be best. We allow Him to mold and shape us in the meantime. We trust that whatever it is we are waiting on is going to be worth the wait. We must keep believing that He has our best interest at heart. His heart is perfect in every way. If you wait, He will bless. Read the verse again if you need extra reassurance. Live by faith today...

OCTOBER 2

DAILY READING:
Isaiah 66:1-24; Philippians 3:4-21
Psalm 74:1-23; Proverbs 24:15-16
Focal Passage: Philippians 3:10

LIVING BY FAITH

IT ALL COMES DOWN TO THIS. The Apostle Paul figured it out. Knowing Jesus Christ intimately was the ultimate purpose of life. He learned it wasn't good works. He was a really, really good person as far as being a rule keeper. God clearly showed him there was a better way during his Damascus Road experience. He learned it wasn't putting his trust in God's people; they let him down time after time. He had some close friends who were Christlike, but even they were not perfect. Neither was he perfect. God showed him that believers go through trials. Many trials. He was in prison while penning this letter to the church in Philippi. God taught him to use his journey through the fires of life for good. He determined that difficulties were opportunities. He used them to get to know Jesus better. My friends, it all comes down to this—**know Him.**

Have you had a tough life? Are you going through trial, after trial, after trial? Maybe you are being tested in an area to see if you will "pass." Instead of complaining or asking way too many questions, maybe you should consider it a badge of honor? Perhaps, God wants to use you in a mighty way during your lifetime, just like He did Paul. You think that's funny? If so, go ahead and laugh. The devil is laughing with you. The one who seeks to destroy will seek to distract you from fulfilling your Kingdom purpose. Please do not allow your life to go to waste. Intimacy is the all-important part of living the Christian life.

Know Him. Pray constantly about everything. Find a verse and stick with it. Read devotionally each and every day. Stop dwelling on the past—the good and the bad. Encourage others. Journal how you are getting to know Christ. You have a purpose, or you wouldn't still be on earth. Live by faith today...

DAILY READING:
Jeremiah 1:1-2:30; Philippians 4:1-23
Psalm 75:1-10; Proverbs 24:17-20
Focal Passage: Philippians 4:10-13

LIVING BY FAITH

LIFE WILL BE MUCH MORE ENJOYABLE IF WE WILL LEARN TO BE CONTENT. Paul closes his joy-filled letter to the church at Philippi with the key to having a joy-filled life: contentment. It is not natural for me. It is not natural for you, either. But we can learn how to be content. If not, we will struggle with worry. We will lose our joy when a sudden trial comes. We will do "stinkin thinkin," which is why in this same chapter he mentions what to think about. Yes, I say this because I am a fellow struggler. Do you ever feel as if you're being piled on? Me too. I've been fighting those thoughts the last few days. It's hard not to at times. Maybe like me, you say, *"Okay God, you have my attention. What is it?"* Don't you love God? He wants us to be authentic with Him. And when I'm going through what seems like challenge after challenge, I'm talking about it in my car, in my prayer closet, at my desk, while I'm jogging, and before I go to bed. I mean, what's up?

Contentment means being satisfied and at peace when life piles on. Regardless of what's going on, you trust God and keep smiling. (Even if it's on the inside.) Folks, it is not natural or the first thing we do in the flesh. It must be learned over time. And God teaches us through the good times and the difficult times during our journey. He wants us to learn to lean on Him and trust Him **no matter what**. When we are content, He can supernaturally enable us not to lose this joy Paul talks about throughout this letter. So, I'm learning to just smile and talk with God no matter what happens next. What about you?

We all go through trials. We likely will never go through all that Paul went through. He said he does it through Christ. WE can do all things through Him who gives us strength as well. Maybe, just maybe we need to approach life with the thought of… *"OK, bring it, God's in me and He's got me. All this trial is doing, by God's grace, is making me an even stronger warrior for the Kingdom."* Live by faith today…

OCTOBER 4

DAILY READING:
Jeremiah 2:31-4:18; Colossians 1:1-20
Psalm 76:1-12; Proverbs 24:21-22
Focal Passage: Colossians 1:17

LIVING BY FAITH

THERE HAS NEVER BEEN A TIME WHEN JESUS WAS NOT. Now, stop and let that sink in. One of the primary reasons Paul wrote this letter to the church in Colossae was to deal with a number of heresies that had crept into the church. (I hate when that happens!) A primary theological falsehood that was making its way through the early church was about Jesus. Some were teaching He was not really that unique. Mainly—the deity of Christ was being questioned. Paul presents powerful evidence for the reality that Jesus is both God and man. He represents God, the Father. Our focal passage is outstanding! Read it again. Wow! Jesus has always existed. The planets are held together because He put them there. He who holds them together can hold you together.

I had rather trust in the One who put the world together and created man in the first place than anyone else. Hadn't you? I mean, who would that be? No one! There are idols and false gods and the enemy. Look at history. That has not worked out in the end for anyone that has allowed them to be in control of their lives. I'm going to go with Jesus. I want to encourage you to go with Jesus.

He is the One who will not abandon you. I have no idea what you may be going through. But I can assure you Jesus knows and He knows exactly where you are. (Remember, He made the world.) Think of it this way. He had His eye on you before the trial you are going through or about to go through. He will have His eye on you after, too. So don't believe for a second that He will ever take His eye off you. That's not who He is. He can't be. He is Jesus. He loves you and wants what is best, even when life hurts. Live by faith today...

DAILY READING:
Jeremiah 4:19-6:14; Colossians 1:21-2:7
Psalm 77:1-20; Proverbs 24:23-25
Focal Passage: Colossians 2:4

LIVING BY FAITH

JUST BECAUSE SOMETHING SOUNDS RIGHT DOES NOT MEAN IT IS RIGHT. I grew up watching the *Andy Griffith Show*. Ol' Barney was the Deputy Sheriff for Andy, who was the Sheriff. One of his well-known sayings was, "Nip it in the bud." Nipping something in the bud means that you're putting an end to it before it has a chance to grow or start. Some people use the phrase, "Nip it in the butt." It is not the same, even though it sounds like it. Nipping something in the butt means you're biting its behind. Friend, that is not the same and may get you in trouble one day if you've been saying it.

As we've already learned about the Colossians, Paul was concerned that they would go to false teachers who were acting like they had a great understanding of the things of God. Secret spiritual "understandings" may sound reasonable, but that does not mean they are. Lies can even sound reasonable sometimes. They are still falsehoods. Paul continued to emphasize that they had an absolute full understanding of Christ. He would keep the church from being deceived by persuasive arguments.

Jesus is our truth. He sets us free from heresy. Always remember that when we abide in Him, He will give us a nudge in our Spirit when someone comes along with a false doctrine or twisted scripture. This is why we should know what we believe and why. Stay close to Jesus and His Word. Be careful who you listen to on the radio, TV, or podcasts. Stay on the solid foundation of Christ and don't go down a slippery slope. It can be challenging to get back on the right path. Live by faith today...

DAILY READING:
Jeremiah 6:15-8:7; Colossians 2:8-23
Psalm 78:1-31; Proverbs 24:26
Focal Passage: Colossians 2:8

LIVING BY FAITH

PLEASE DON'T ALLOW THESE TO DECEIVE YOU. Satan will do whatever he can to get you off track. He will often use the same methods he's used for ages. The most serious error of the false teachers at Colossae was that they went about their spiritual lives with human light. That was it. They would never go to God to learn from the true Light of the world, even though the light of Christ was available for them. Here Paul described the worldly ways of philosophical views. He points out that they were human, elementary, and non-Christian. Without going into great depth, most of us have a basic understanding of what these mean and the damage they can cause. Worldly ways leave one empty. They do not, and will not, fill the God-shaped void in all of us.

Maybe you went to college and took a philosophy class. Perhaps you can trace your confusion concerning these matters back to that. If so, I suggest you stop for a while and study this passage. Spend some extra time to clearly see what's being addressed here. I'm not saying it's not good to study philosophy. I had several philosophy classes in seminary. What I'm saying is that at times, people get off track in their daily walk with Christ due to things of this world that may sound deep, only to be left empty or confused. Pray, pause, and ponder what Jesus really means to you. It's not worth going another day without clearing this up, if needed.

Maybe you are allowing some human tradition to keep you from moving forward. This could be in your home, workplace, or even church. Please be careful. There can be some okay human traditions that became not okay because some have made them like scripture. This is so dangerous. I've seen many homes and churches split over traditions. Pick your battles and be sure they are truly worth it in light of Christ and His Word. Live by faith today...

DAILY READING:
Jeremiah 8:8-9:26; Colossians 3:1-17
Psalm 78:32-55; Proverbs 24:27
Focal Passage: Colossians 3:15

LIVING BY FAITH

I HAVE PEACE AND AM THANKFUL ON MY BIRTHDAY. At the time of this writing, I am celebrating my 60th birthday! My dad passed away when he was my age. It is surreal. I will never, ever forget the peace God gave me when daddy graduated to heaven. All I can say is, God did it and I knew it. And it's happened numerous times since then. Why? Because during those times, by God's grace, I have set my mind on Him. (Like the verses previously mentioned.) When that happens, I know that regardless of how things may be, God is faithful. The times I do not do so, it's awful! I have no peace and I worry. Worry is a sin. It's basically calling God a liar. That's never good! And it means we're out of alignment. Sort of like a car gets out of alignment sometimes. When we allow Jesus to be Lord (Boss) He makes life so enjoyable. God's peace makes us thankful. How can we be anything but that—THANKFUL.

I have a pastor friend who uses the phrase *struggle bus*. Have you ever been on it? Sure, you have. Me, too. I've actually felt like I've been in the front seat recently. Well, today I have a peace about reaching another landmark birthday. It's a blessing. I know God is not going to leave me hanging now. He's brought me way too far. He's done the same with you. We need to get off that struggle bus and on the peace train. (Is that a song from the past? Remember, I'm 60!)

I am so thankful. God has bombarded me with encouragement today from family and friends. Folks, life boils down to relationships. That is why Jesus said to love God and love people. It's so important to do so every day of our lives. It gives us peace, regardless of our circumstances, and overwhelms us with gratitude. Live by faith today...

OCTOBER 8

DAILY READING:
Jeremiah 10:1-11:23; Colossians 3:18-4:18
Psalm 78:56-72; Proverbs 24:28-29
Focal Passage: Colossians 3:21

LIVING BY FAITH

FATHERS SHOULD ENCOURAGE THEIR CHILDREN, NOT EXASPERATE THEM. Jesus should be the centerpiece of every Christian home. Paul stresses the role of each member of a family leading up to our focal verse. Our passage deals with the way dads relate to their kids. Fathers have a biblical responsibility to discipline. Many dads today miss the mark when it comes to loving their children enough to teach them the difference between right and wrong. Maybe they don't know how because they didn't have an example growing up. Maybe they're too lazy. Maybe they think it's better to buy them things. There are numerous reasons. None are right. We should love our children enough that we will take the time to intentionally teach them the difference between right and wrong. If not, the price is great in the long run.

A parent does not have to provoke the child to anger in order to discipline. Lovingly correct. Explain in the right way and at the right time what the child did wrong. Always capitalize on pointing out when the child does something right or good. Encourage them every opportunity you get. A dad and mom should be the biggest cheerleaders when it comes to their children. We must not place demands on them they cannot meet. If so, the child will feel defeated. Please don't do that. And when you parent wrong in some way, it's okay to tell the child you are sorry. Remember, rules without a relationship will often lead to rebellion. It's always easier to correct and instruct when your child knows you love them. Spending time intentionally and regularly will enhance your relationship. There's really no substitute.

I was blessed with a dad who balanced discipline and encouragement. I tried to do the same. If you are a dad, please apply this verse. If you struggle with it, get some help. It will be well worth your time. Children are worth it. They are gifts from God for a season that you never get back. Love them. Love them real good. Live by faith today...

DAILY READING:

Jeremiah 12:1-14:10; 1 Thessalonians 1:1-2:9
Psalm 79:1-13; Proverbs 24:30-34
Focal Passage: 1 Thessalonians 1:6-8

LIVING BY FAITH

YOUR HARD TIME MAY BE EXACTLY WHAT SOMEONE NEEDS TO SEE. Paul wrote this letter to the believers in Thessalonica during a time when they were suffering due to their commitment to Christ. So one of the primary reasons he wrote to them was to encourage them to remain faithful. He stressed in the letter that Jesus could return at any moment. The thought that Jesus might return today helps us keep the right perspective. We are more likely to live in a way that pleases God—even if we are experiencing trials of various kinds.

Paul commends the believers because they were setting a good example among unbelievers. What a compliment! They were putting action to their words and it brought glory to God. When our lost friends see us continue in our faith during a difficult season, they are convinced we really do believe. It can be the single most important moment for them in regard to helping them turn to Jesus in faith. Don't miss the moment or waste your pain!

Are you going through a hard time right now? I pray this passage helps you today. It doesn't mean you are not hurting or that you don't want the hard time to end. We are human! It hurts, and it's okay to admit it and talk with Jesus about it. Please do. But never underestimate that this may be what God uses in your life to speak to your community. It may be what finally reaches that lost person you've been praying for all these years. Your faith can be an example for your faith community, and the community in which you live. That is exactly what was happening in this passage. It can happen now, and you may be the instrument. Live by faith today…

OCTOBER 10

LIVING BY FAITH

TECHNOLOGY IS A WONDERFUL TOOL BUT IT MUST NOT REPLACE SOMEONE'S TOUCH. If not for technology, I would not have had the opportunity to communicate with my church family during the COVID-19 pandemic we are experiencing at the time of this writing. I am thankful. I was able to preach through the time we were quarantined, and people still listened. Meetings took place via the internet in various formats. No doubt, technology is a wonderful tool and it continues to be used to spread the gospel and to minister to others. I believe it will actually enhance ways the church can minister in the years to come. But here's what I know—nothing can replace a person's touch. People need people.

Paul needed Timothy, but he needed to encourage other believers more. We see his heart here. He recognized that the church folks in Thessalonica were hurting due to various trials. They needed a seasoned saint to encourage them. Paul sent Timothy. They knew trouble was always around them, even as believers, but they didn't recognize just how much. Timothy, being a seasoned pastor, was able to be a blessing at just the right time. They needed his touch. When we hurt, we need to be able to look at people in person. Talk with them. Pray with them. Listen to them. Have eye contact with them. Share a meal with them. ENCOURAGE them by spending some time with them. Real intimacy comes through these authentic touches the church can provide in person. Please don't allow technology to replace God's people in your life.

I visited one of our senior adults recently who couldn't see anyone for months. He told me that it was worse than World War II. He loves God and loves His people. We must not take the church for granted. God made us for relationships—especially as believers. The church is His idea. Live by faith today...

DAILY READING:
Jeremiah 16:16-18:23; 1 Thessalonians 4:1-5:3
Psalm 81:1-16; Proverbs 25:6-7
Focal Passage: Jeremiah 18:1-6

LIVING BY FAITH

TRUST GOD'S HEART AND HIS HANDS. We often hear the phrase, "Always trust God's heart." And we should. But we see in our passage today that we should trust His hands. I cannot think of a better illustration of this than when the Bible uses the potter and the clay as an example. As clay yields itself to the potter, so the Christian must submit to the authority of the Father. When clay is first brought in, it's unusable. It is refined through a process in order to be used. The same is true of the Christian. As God molds and shapes us, we must not forget that part of the process is going through the fire.

I took Pottery 1 and 2 in college. No, I'm not kidding. This was the only type of art I resonated with. I needed to raise my GPA after a difficult freshman year academically. (I had a great time socially!) Someone suggested I take pottery. It was probably my sister Kathy, who majored in art at the same college and knew the professor. Regardless, it was a good decision. I excelled in this particular class. It had a lot to do with the professor, because I loved him. And it had everything to do with using your hands to mold and shape the clay pot. I enjoyed the process. But the true test of how the pot would turn out was after it had been through the fire. You've heard the phrase "Trial by fire." Yes, this is what happens when the pot is placed in a kiln. A kiln has been around for a long time and is a type of oven used to turn clay objects into pottery. I was always happy after this process was completed—especially when the pot turned out better than I had imagined it would.

We are in God's sovereign hands. They are big. The molding and shaping can be painful. The fires we go through can result in a beautiful work of God. Let's keep this in mind as we go through our journey of faith. Trust His heart and His hands. Live by faith today...

DAILY READING:

Jeremiah 19:1-21:14; 1 Thessalonians 5:4-28
Psalm 82:1-8; Proverbs 25:8-10
Focal Passage: 1 Thessalonians 5:24

LIVING BY FAITH

THIS IS MY SIGNATURE VERSE. Every verse in the Bible is equally important. If not, God would not have put it in there. They all have various meanings and it's important to put them in context. But some just seem to be especially suited for us. Don't you think? Maybe it's because of our background or because we have had additional teachings on certain passages. Regardless, it is so meaningful when one or more verses seem to especially resonate. This one does for me.

Paul is closing out his letter to the Thessalonian Christians with various exhortations and blessings. He emphasizes that God doesn't start a project and leave it unfinished. No, no. He will complete it. That's what sanctification is all about. He is transforming us from the inside out, from conversion until the day we die. You are not a piece of trash. You are a child of God if you have put your faith and trust in Him. He will never, ever toss you aside. You are way too valuable for that or for that mindset. The worse your circumstances become, the greater glory that can be brought to Jesus when you realize this truth.

Now, this verse can also apply to the call. He calls us as believers to certain professions or projects or various other things in life. When I finally surrendered to be a Senior Pastor, I kept this verse very close. It reminds me even today that I did not decide to be a Senior Pastor. He did. I just said okay. Knowing He is doing it through me takes tremendous pressure off of me. I still have responsibilities. Absolutely. But it's comforting to know I am not on my own. Additionally, when I sense He's calling me to do various things in ministry, it helps. It helped in relocating a church. It helped in moving to broken churches. It helped in completing my doctorate. It helped in writing my first book. It helps in knowing I am in my sixties. You see? Yes, this is my signature verse. (I even write the reference under my name when I have the opportunity.) Maybe it can be yours. God's Word helps us do what we are here for. Live by faith today...

OCTOBER 13

DAILY READING:
Jeremiah 22:1-23:20; 2 Thessalonians 1:1-12
Psalm 83:1-18; Proverbs 25:11-14
Focal Passage: Proverbs 25:11

LIVING BY FAITH

DR. BYRON MALONE PREACHED MY ORDINATION SERMON, BUT THAT IS NOT WHAT I REMEMBER MOST. For many years, Dr. Malone pastored Daniel Memorial Baptist Church in Jackson, Mississippi. I was his Youth Pastor after I graduated from seminary. He preached my ordination sermon during the time I served with him. I loved him and thank God for his continued influence on my life. I wish I could say I remembered specific words from the message he preached at my ordination. I do remember it being comforting and a huge blessing. My dad was in the audience, but very ill with cancer. (He died several months later.) What I remember most, as far as specific words, came years later.

I had been a Senior Pastor for a few years when Dr. Malone invited me back to Daniel Memorial to preach for revival services. I remember one night before a service while putting my microphone on in the privacy of his office, what he said in response to a statement someone else in the room made to me. A person in our presence made a nice comment about my preaching. Dr. Malone said, "Yes, and he is only going to get better." It encouraged me greatly. I have always tried to get better and hope to until the day I die. Why wouldn't I? God wants us to always do our best and be teachable. And Dr. Malone told me I would only improve as the years passed. He had always spoken the truth before. I believed him. Encouraging words that stick are often given on the spur of the moment.

This verse was referring to expensive jewelry. Pointing to the rarity of the golden apples and the appropriateness of their setting, Solomon was intentionally pointing to the rarity of a fitting word being spoken at an appropriate time. Who do you need to give a golden apple to? Do not underestimate the timing of an encouraging word. Golden apples don't rot. Live by faith today...

OCTOBER 14

LIVING BY FAITH

WHEN YOU WALK WITH THE LORD, IT'S A GOOD THING. As believers, we are not perfect. We are forgiven by the perfect Son of God. That is a good thing. Why? Because we have the opportunity to fulfill our purpose and bring glory to Him. We are given opportunities to grow in our faith in order to be more like Him. And we see in our passage today that He will never, ever withhold any good thing from us if we walk with Him by faith. You may think otherwise at times, but that is not true based on this passage.

Sun and shield in the passage depict God's overall provision and protection. Isn't that good to know during these days in which we live? You see, if we walk by faith, then whatever begins with God's grace will eventually end in God's glory. Now, God does not give me everything I want. I'm pretty certain He does not give you everything you want, either. Am I right? Yes. But He does provide, bestow, and even give us all that is good for us. He gives us all that we need. (Need is a key word, here. Please don't miss it.)

Most of us who walk with the Lord, don't usually have a problem believing in the goodness of God. All we have to do is look back over our lives and we are reminded of how good He has been to us. What we may be challenging is timing. Or maybe how God is going to rescue us during our dark times. That's where this verse comes into play for us. Remember, He is our protector and our light. He will give us good things, per His definition of good, when we walk daily with Him in His righteousness. Live by faith today...

OCTOBER 15

Jeremiah 26:1-27:22; 2 Thessalonians 3:1-18
Psalm 85:1-13; Proverbs 25:16
Focal Passage: 2 Thessalonians 3:14-15

LIVING BY FAITH

FELLOW BELIEVERS NEED TO KNOW WHEN THEY ARE GOING DOWN THE WRONG PATH. The family I grew up in felt a responsibility for each other. We celebrated victories and lamented defeats of various kinds. We provided support for one another. My wife grew up the same way. We took the same approach with our children and now our grandchildren. It's what families do. It is a sign there is love for one another. According to this closing chapter, Paul is basically saying the same for God's family. He emphasizes in these verses our role in addressing fellow believers who are not following God's instructions.

We should never assume that we should not make people in the family of God feel ashamed. Now, we shouldn't do so in a haughty way. But we have a great responsibility when they are going down the wrong path. Just as we should accept a fellow believer confronting us when we are wrong, we should do the same out of love. But rest assured that Christians who refuse to take personal responsibility and obey God's directives need to experience legitimate guilt. We warn them in the right way and at the right time. If they ignore or refuse to repent, it could very well be time to break fellowship with them. Sometimes even those close to us within the family of God need a lesson. It does not mean being hateful, it just means asking God to help you know how to let them know the seriousness of their decision. Distancing oneself is hard, but sometimes absolutely necessary. Don't beat yourself up over it. Just do what you sense God is leading you to do. Make sure it's Him.

We are often known by the company we keep. Who are your closest Christian friends? Are they going down the right path? Are you? Maybe today is a good day to do an inventory. It's helpful for all of us. Live by faith today...

DAILY READING:

Jeremiah 28:1-29:32; 1 Timothy 1:1-20
Psalm 86:1-17; Proverbs 25:17
Focal Passage: Jeremiah 29:11-14

LIVING BY FAITH

THIS MIGHT BE ONE OF THE MOST FAMILIAR, YET MISUNDERSTOOD, VERSES IN THE BIBLE. I love this passage. Jeremiah is not one of the easiest books to read for daily living. The story of what many call "the weeping prophet" due to his sorrow caused by the disobedience of God's people can be hard to read day after day. Yet this prophet had the privilege of reminding everyone of God's righteousness. The good news he presented overall was that despite sin, God offers restoration when repentance occurs.

Our focal passage could very well be the most familiar scripture in this entire Old Testament book. I don't want to disappoint you, but it is not a "name it and claim it" verse. We need to understand the context of scripture when we read it. God was promising His people that He would do His will even in the midst of a pagan culture. He would communicate and even reverse circumstances if they would give Him their hearts 24/7. This passage was never meant to be a phrase used as a means of protecting one no matter how the person lives from day to day. If a person "lives like the devil," the consequences will be anything but hopeful and good. The future will be unspeakably bad.

The New Testament parallel to this passage is usually said to be found in Romans 8:28—another familiar passage that can be misunderstood. It speaks of a believer knowing all things work together for good. And the emphasis, like our passage today, is for those who trust Him. In other words, sometimes the greatest victories in our lives come as a result of living fully and freely within the context of our trials. He does His best work in and through us when we stay strong *in* the difficulties of life. Jesus would not have come to this world to offer us abundant life here and then deliberately destroy us. Think about it. It doesn't make sense, does it? His life of hope and a wonderful future are available to live, not to claim with some odd phrase with no thought given to daily living. Live by faith today...

DAILY READING:
Jeremiah 30:1-31:26; 1 Timothy 2:1-15
Psalm 87:1-7; Proverbs 25:18-19
Focal Passage: 1 Timothy 2:1-2

LIVING BY FAITH

REGARDLESS OF YOUR POLITICAL PREFERENCE, THIS IS WHAT YOU ARE TO DO. Pray. Paul provides some instructions on prayer for young Timothy. It works for us, too. And it was very important for the early church to understand their political climate. If you study history, you will find that politics has always caused tension. But God expects us to submit to Him in spite of the political environments in which we live. If you live in a culture that allows religious freedom, you can be more of a public witness and share your faith. If not, the oppressive regime causes one to live in a totally different way. Praying for those in authority works either way.

I am amazed at how some believers allow politics to hinder their witness. I was taught to pray for those in authority, vote my convictions, and stand on truths in the Bible, regardless of what political party I may be affiliated with. King Jesus is always on His throne no matter how difficult things in our world may be. We must not allow politics to come before people. Not everyone views life like we do because they may not believe like we do. So we must not risk losing our opportunity to witness because we vehemently disagree with one's view on various candidates or their political values. Please be careful. It's not easy, but attainable. You may win an argument on politics, but you may lose an opportunity to lead someone to Christ.

I am blessed to live in a free country right now. I have found it helpful to create a prayer acrostic for whoever is President. I take each letter of their last name and make a word out of it as a matter of prayer. For example, if the President has an M in his/her name, I may pray for his marriage. It helps. Do whatever you need to do to remember to pray for those in authority. It matters, no matter whom you vote for or where you live. Live by faith today…

OCTOBER 18

DAILY READING:
Jeremiah 31:27-32:44; 1 Timothy 3:1-16
Psalm 88:1-18; Proverbs 25:20-22
Focal Passage: Jeremiah 32:27

LIVING BY FAITH

I REMEMBER WHERE I WAS WHEN THIS VERSE JUMPED OFF THE PAGE AND INTO MY HEART. I'm sure I had read our focal passage before. Since my dad was a pastor, I grew up going to church. And I had already graduated from a Christian college and seminary. But on a Sunday evening, when a supply preacher was preaching for our pastor, this verse became real for me. You see, I was a student pastor in my early thirties waiting for God to open a door for me to move into a senior pastorate. I didn't know how, when, or where. I just knew I sensed God calling me to transition. The preacher that Sunday evening preached this verse, and all I really remember is this verse. I don't remember anything else he said. No illustrations. No biblical background. No word meanings. I just remember the power of this verse on my life. I knew God had given it to me for "such a time as that." It's happened at other times. And I'm sure it's likely happened to many of you reading this devotional right now. That is the power of God's Word.

This is a rhetorical question because we all know nothing is too hard for God. Jeremiah knew it, too. God was about to tell Jeremiah that after Judah's punishment was complete, He would do something impossible. You see, God disciplines His people for a purpose. It's not just to show us how little we are. It's to show us how big He is and how much He loves us. He was going to bring the nation back to its land and the people would enjoy prosperity again, after a season of difficulties. The same God still lives and continues to work wonders in the lives of His children.

Nothing was too hard. He put me in my first senior pastorate role, and others, through a series of amazing events. Events only He could make happen. No man could orchestrate how gracious He's been to me through the years. I've learned much through good times (and not so good times). And I'm still hanging on to that verse that jumped off the page on a seemingly random Sunday night many years ago. What is this verse saying to you? Live by faith today...

OCTOBER 19

DAILY READING:
Jeremiah 33:1-34:22 ;1 Timothy 4:1-16
Psalm 89:1-13; Proverbs 25:23-24
Focal Passage: 1 Timothy 4:12

LIVING BY FAITH

THE GODLY EXAMPLE OF A YOUNG PERSON HAS GREAT INFLUENCE. When I was Student Pastor at Morrison Heights Baptist in Clinton, Mississippi, this scripture was the theme verse. When I wrote an article, this verse accompanied the writing. If I sent out a publicity piece on an event, this verse was close by for the student to read. Students needed to be reminded of their importance. So many youth think that Jesus is not really for them, though He's OK. They think that He's more for old folks. Not so! Paul was letting young Timothy know the value of Godly living. Timothy could teach. But there was more. He needed to be sure he demonstrated by his lifestyle that he truly believed what he taught. Paul laid it out for him—conduct, love, faith, and purity. You put all those together, and you have one powerful witness for the Kingdom! This is true for any age, but for young folks, it reaches an entirely different level. Why? Because so many people in the world think that youthfulness is an excuse for ungodliness. It's not. It provides an incredible opportunity for youth to impact the world and the local church.

Adolescence is the phase of growth between childhood and adulthood. Basically, this is a person between the ages of 10 and 19. Timothy was a little older at the time of this writing, though influenced by Paul prior to this point. PLEASE don't neglect young people. Be sure they understand the ways of Christ and the difference He can make NOW. It will influence them for the present and will go with them in the future. It could very well be that though you may not see much fruit from your investment in teenagers now, one day it will be what causes them to wake up. Pray for them. Love them. Discipline them. Laugh with them. Be there for them. Their worth is invaluable. Look at history. Most revivals were sparked by the younger generation. Live by faith today...

DAILY READING:
Jeremiah 35:1-36:32; 1 Timothy 5:1-25
Psalm 89:14-37; Proverbs 25:25-27
Focal Passage: 1 Timothy 5:19

LIVING BY FAITH

SUPPORT YOUR PREACHER AND PROTECT HIM FROM THE RIFFRAFF. It feels so good to type those words. Why? Because as the pastor of a local church, it's not like I'm going to lead the way in doing this. Sure, I'm willing to preach this verse. But think about it… it would be much better if someone else preaches it, teaches it, and more than anything applies it in the local church. It is biblical to support your pastor. I'm not talking about financially here. That's already been addressed in this devotional and rightfully so. Those that want to starve the preacher are clueless about what the Bible says. I'm talking here about not allowing people to slam the guy. Far too much of that is allowed in local churches. It's time to STOP IT!

It should not be the norm for a disgruntled church member to falsely accuse the pastor. If so, this verse explains what should be done. And it should indeed be done. But some of the time the Pastor is talked about behind his back and leaders will often just let it go. It hurts the cause of Christ! It hurts the Pastor and his family! Godly men and women should speak to the riffraff at the right time and in the right way to stop the hurt. Most of the time it concerns preferences and not convictions. If an elder does something immoral, illegal, or unbiblical, by all means, address it appropriately, like the verse says. But please do not be scared to confront those who cause disunity in the fellowship over petty matters. I could point out other verses, but those are for another day.

Maybe God is speaking to you right now? Perhaps He is calling you to protect your Pastor? God will honor your new ministry, the church will be blessed, and the Pastor will never, ever forget you. It is a "behind the scenes" ministry. You will likely not be recognized publicly. But remember, our ultimate recognition is in heaven. Heaven knows how you will be recognized one day for your willingness to go to battle for your leadership. Live by faith today…

DAILY READING:
Jeremiah 37:1-38:28; 1 Timothy 6:1-21
Psalm 89:38-52; Proverbs 25:28
Focal Passage: 1 Timothy 6:6

LIVING BY FAITH

IF WE GET THIS, WE GET WHAT THE CHRISTIAN LIFE IS MEANT TO BE. I'm convinced this is a major factor in enjoying the life Jesus wants for His children. Contentment. Have you really thought about that word before? I think it means to abide in Jesus, work hard, and relax. Is it possible to do those things at the same time? Yes! That is exactly what Paul is sharing with young Timothy as he's reaching the conclusion of this powerful letter to his protégé. Timothy needed to be sure to display contentment. Not only was he a spokesman for God, he represented what it looked like to live the Christ life. If he and others were complaining much of the time, he was displaying the opposite—discontentment. Contented people know that God is working on their behalf, regardless of what things look like. You trust Jesus day by day. You thank him regularly. You are at ease with whatever you have or don't have. You put feet to your prayers. You let go of what you cannot control. Remember, you can't control what others do. But you and I can control how we respond to life. Contentment is a powerful witness and gives great freedom to be who you are in Christ.

We are to learn to be content. I am still learning. Here's what I can tell you... **it is liberating!** There was a time I really struggled with worry. It still raises its ugly head at times. It's awful. Worry is a sin. Contentment destroys worry. I mean, it blows it out of the water. Maybe you struggle with worry? If so, here's your answer. Do some more study on contentment. Memorize this verse or others that deal with this great word for Christians. If we allow this to be a regular part of our lives, no matter what our circumstances are, we will be blessed and be a blessing. Gain ground—be content. Life is short. Live by faith today...

DAILY READING:
Jeremiah 39:1-41:18; 2 Timothy 1:1-18
Psalm 90:1-91:16; Proverbs 26:1-2
Focal Passage: 2 Timothy 1:5

LIVING BY FAITH

I THANK GOD FOR THE GODLY WOMEN HE PUT IN MY LIFE. This is Paul's final letter. He knew he was approaching the end of his life and he wanted to encourage Timothy. Timothy had been through a lot at this point in his ministry. He begins by letting him know that he has noticed how the influence of his grandmother and mother has impacted his faith. That had to greatly inspire Timothy. Paul knew how to speak to the heart. Timothy undoubtedly loved them both and caught what they had—a genuine love for Jesus. The influence of godly ladies upon a boy is immeasurable.

I was blessed to have the same. My grandmother Kitchings (Beulah Mudd, from Kentucky) was training to be a missionary when she met my grandfather. My grandfather, Atley Kitchings, was attending seminary in Louisville, Kentucky. They married and formed a mighty team for the Lord. I knew her better than my other grandparents because I was able to spend more time with her during my growing up years and she lived to be ninety-two. She prayed for a rich spiritual heritage to come from their offspring. She was an example of what it meant to take prayer seriously. My mother, Ann Overstreet Kitchings, demonstrated love. She just loved people. Why? Because she truly loved God. Sure, she was a wonderful pastor's wife and enjoyed teaching the Bible to young people. But she embodied what it meant to love people. And the smile on her face was a permanent fixture. I was blessed, just like Timothy. If you can identify, you were too. May we never, ever stop thanking God for the godly women He puts in our lives. Even if you can't identify, you likely can point to other godly ladies who have influenced your life. Thank God!

Are you a female? If so, let this verse sink deep within your soul. Be a Lois or a Eunice to your family of origin or to someone in the family of God. Your deposit in their lives could reach a level of influence for Christ that you may never know about. Leave the results to God. But don't waste any opportunity the Lord may give you in the days ahead. Live by faith today...

DAILY READING:
Jeremiah 42:1-44:23; 2 Timothy 2:1-21
Psalm 92:1-93:5; Proverbs 26:3-5
Focal Passage: 2 Timothy 2:16

LIVING BY FAITH

BE CAREFUL NOT TO SPEND TOO MUCH TIME TALKING ABOUT NOTHING. Paul is letting Timothy know that those who preach and lead need to be approved. In other words, they need to use their words carefully. If not, it will have a negative influence on others. Believers need to avoid unbiblical teachings at all costs. One must know the Word in order to know counterfeits. Furthermore, believers should avoid using words that are disrespectful. Not only that, stay away from talking too much about what really doesn't matter in the grand scheme of things.

Let me share a few examples that come to mind. These topics all have their place in life, but some allow them to be their only place. It's as if it's all they can think about so it's what they always seem to talk about. We must ALL be careful here... 1. Favorite team. I have several sports teams I support. I talk about them. You, if you are into sports, talk about yours. It's okay. But some take it to an extreme. That's all they talk about. They even argue about aspects of their team. It is hurtful and in light of eternity, it means nothing. 2. Politics. It is important to vote. Some are even called to enter the political field as believers. But I know some folks who will talk about their political persuasions to an extreme. I have them in my church. When I speak with them, I know at some point the subject will come up. 3. A pet doctrine. Doctrine is critically important for the life of believers. But some people like to engage you in their "pet" doctrine for various reasons I will not get into. It may be eschatology. It could be the doctrine of election. It may even be speaking in tongues. Know your doctrine. But be careful about camping out on any one. Allow Jesus to consume you. He helps provide balance. If a believer or, especially, a non-believer sees you coming and knows you are "that guy," he will likely avoid you. I would. I do, oftentimes. It can hurt the Kingdom causes more than help.

We don't want our words to produce more godlessness. This doesn't always mean cussing or immoral speech. Sometimes it means talking about good things too much. Let's be careful not to talk too much about nothing. Live by faith today...

DAILY READING:

Jeremiah 44:24-47:7; 2 Timothy 2:22-3:17
Psalm 94:1-23; Proverbs 26:6-8
Focal Passage: 2 Timothy 3:12

LIVING BY FAITH

LIVING A LIFE FOR CHRIST HURTS SO GOOD. It just does. Christianity is not just about getting your "heaven papers." Paul is letting Timothy know that he needs to teach followers of Christ that living for Him is not for wimps. It's tough! I'm sure you read the verses surrounding our focal passage today. There is a universal message in our verse for the day. Jesus followers will experience pain. Now, not everyone will suffer in the same way. We have no idea what pain we will experience in our lifetime. At least I don't. Think about it. Do you? But to seek Jesus and serve Him faithfully means we are inviting trouble. The world doesn't like it. Jesus reminded the disciples of this in John 15:20: *"If they persecuted me, they will also persecute you."* That goes for us too. When are we going to learn? Life on earth will never be perfect. It's a battle, but you are preparing for battle by reading God's Word. That's good.

It's all good. Here's why. The more pain, the more likely we are to draw closer to Jesus. The more intimate our relationship is with Him, the more joy, peace, and other fruit of the Spirit we will have. There's no other way to get those things as a believer. And others will be inspired and encouraged by our witness. What a life! Not only that, we will have rewards in heaven. Although I don't fully understand what that means, I believe King Jesus will present them, and it will be good. I'm about to take off running while writing this. There's no greater life than the life of a Jesus follower. Furthermore, think about all the people He allows us to know. Good grief! The incredible godly influences in our lives are immeasurable.

Here's the deal. You can go through life on your own and experience pain due to a depraved world and end up empty. Or you can go through life with Jesus and be rich! I'll take the riches of Jesus over the riches of this world any day. They don't last. What's done for Christ does. C. T. Studd once said "Only one life 'twill soon be past. Only what's done for Christ will last." Remember this as you walk through hurts in this life. For a Christian, it hurts so good because it's for good. Live by faith today...

DAILY READING:
Jeremiah 48:1-49:22; 2 Timothy 4:1-22
Psalm 95:1-96:13; Proverbs 26:9-12
Focal Passage: 2 Timothy 4:5

LIVING BY FAITH

KEEP YOUR HEAD IN ALL SITUATIONS. As Paul closes out his instructions to Timothy, I believe this phrase (*keep your head*) may be the most important phrase for lasting in ministry over the long haul. Now, I am not underestimating everything else in the final chapter of this book. Not at all! I'm just saying this is what struck a nerve for me. Every believer needs to heed the instructions in this verse, but certainly, we recognize this was especially for Timothy. He needed to endure hardships because they would come. He needed to personally share the gospel because people wanted to know he was practicing what he preached. And he certainly needed to fulfill all areas of his ministry calling to the best of his ability, trusting God with things outside his control.

The New International Version says *"Keep your head in all situations."* I wish I could say at this point that I have kept my head in all situations. I do think I have learned from times I did not. It's painful. Did you know that sometimes preachers are stubborn? Did you know sometimes we lose our cool? Did you know... I could go on and on. God's grace has helped me through the years. God's people have helped me through the years. Learning from experiences has helped me through the years. I pray all of this continues as I'm faced with times when I might mishandle ministry situations. God is faithful. I am thankful.

Hey Preacher... Keep your head when someone criticizes you right before you preach. Keep your head when someone asks you an insignificant question immediately after you preach your heart out. Keep your head when someone you thought was supportive proves otherwise. Keep your head in volatile church business meetings. Keep your head when you experience "upward delegation." I'll stop here with examples. But do you understand? You do if you have pastored long enough. So *keep your head* because it is worth it! God called you and me to this. What an honor! If He didn't think we were capable of *keeping our head*, He wouldn't have given us this wonderful opportunity. Live by faith today...

DAILY READING:
Jeremiah 49:23-50:46; Titus 1:1-16
Psalm 97:1-98:9; Proverbs 26:13-16
Focal Passage: Titus 1:9

LIVING BY FAITH

THEOLOGICAL TRAINING IS EXTREMELY IMPORTANT. Titus was one of Paul's sons in the ministry who was given a specific assignment. Paul sent him to an island called Crete. This little letter was given to him to help him know what to do and why. It is a very important book! It packs a punch! He begins by giving him a charge to find and train leaders. The emphasis is on character. Character counts! Finding those who are qualified to spiritually lead the church of Jesus is critically important for the church to function properly. If a pastor does not take this charge seriously, all kinds of problems will occur. It's better to have fewer people in places of leadership than to have more who are just not ready.

Elders are supposed to have sound doctrine. Just because I am a huge proponent of biblical application does not mean that I think less of theological education. I was fortunate enough to have others invest in my theological training. It was not easy, but it was worth it. I encourage younger ministers to invest in their education, regardless of their situation. Find a way sooner than later. It won't get any easier. And in today's world, online and virtual classes seem to be the norm. Just don't miss out on spending time with classmates in person every time you have the opportunity. They may end up being some of your closest friends. You will need them as you go through the ups and downs of ministry.

New believers must also take doctrine seriously. Get in a small group. Find someone to disciple you, if possible. Take online courses, when available. Journal what you learn. Be balanced in your theological understandings. Ask questions and pray through what you believe God is teaching in the scriptures. Doctrine was important for Titus and it's important for you and me. Live by faith today...

DAILY READING:
Jeremiah 51:1-53; Titus 2:1-15
Psalm 99:1-9; Proverbs 26:17
Focal Passage: Proverbs 26:17

LIVING BY FAITH

MY TWO BASSET HOUNDS DID NOT LIKE THEIR EARS TO BE MESSED WITH. Big ears are synonymous with Bassets. If you think of a Basset Hound, you likely think of big ears. And there's something about them that can cause you to want to touch them, pull them, or take a tape measure and see just how long they are. I can speak from experience; they don't like anyone messing with their ears. In college, I had a female basset hound named Walter. (My crazy friend's idea… long story.) Years later, I mentioned Walter in a sermon and shortly after that, a church member gave me my second basset hound. (No kidding. Kellie wasn't happy. The kids and I were thrilled.) Her name was Missy, short for Mississippi. Okay, now back to the ears. It is just not right to pull any dog's ears, no matter how tempting it may be. You don't have to have a Basset to know this. No dog likes to have their ears pulled. They just don't like it, and someone might get hurt. Even if the dog is yours!

The same is true for being a busybody. Our passage today compares that person to someone who likes to find a dog and pull its ears. It makes no sense. We should not stick our noses in someone else's business. It is none of our business. Look, we all have enough challenges in our own lives; no need to make others' issues worse. This does not mean we don't help reconcile others, when appropriate. It does mean that we don't go looking to stir up stuff with people who don't need our help. Stay out of it! Let's be a help to people, not a hindrance.

The next time you may be tempted to be a busybody, go find a basset hound and get busy petting it. He/she will be happy, and you will too. And no one gets hurt. Live by faith today…

OCTOBER 28

DAILY READING:
Jeremiah 51:54-52:34; Titus 3:1-15
Psalm 100:1-5; Proverbs 26:18-19
Focal Passage: Psalm 100

LIVING BY FAITH

THIS PSALM OF THANKSGIVING MAKES ME THANKFUL FOR MY SECOND-GRADE TEACHER. One of my favorite teachers of all time was Mrs. Vashti Everett. She was a loving disciplinarian who cared about every student. I went to public schools when I was growing up, and back then it was not abnormal to talk about God or even pray occasionally in the classroom. But I do not recall having another teacher who had us memorize scripture. Mrs. Everett had us memorize Psalm 100. I do not recall if we received a grade on our memorization work. I just remember the class saying it out loud, over and over and over. It makes me thankful for my second-grade teacher and for the experience. And I do not think it's an accident that this Psalm of David was a very worshipful expression of thanksgiving and praise. Some believe it was sung when the last of those coming to the temple for worship entered. Worshipers would recite, sing, or chant this psalm as part of their praise.

I wonder why Mrs. Everett chose this psalm. Why not Psalm 23 or some other familiar psalm? I do not know, but I have an idea or two. Jesus said that in order to be great, one must be a servant. Serving the Lord with joyful gratitude is paramount to a wonderful life. There are a lot of gods in the world, but only one true God. Why not let this truth register in the minds of six or seven year olds? His truth is absolute. He alone is always good. His love is unconditional and unfathomable. And He has been faithful for generations and will be for future generations. I think these may be just some of the reasons my second-grade teacher chose this particular psalm.

You probably didn't have Mrs. Everett. But you do have this psalm that can help shape your thought life. Let it. Live by faith today...

DAILY READING:
Lamentations 1:1-2:19; Philemon 1:1-25
Psalm 101:1-8; Proverbs 26:20
Focal Passage: Philemon 1:10-11

LIVING BY FAITH

WHEN A REPROBATE IS TRANSFORMED BY CHRIST, HELP PAVE THE WAY FOR THEIR FUTURE. This little book of Philemon is power-packed! I'm focusing in on what I believe could be the focal passage of the entire letter. Paul is writing to his fellow servant Philemon, on behalf of his brother in Christ, Onesimus. He ran into Paul, and anyone who did so heard about Jesus. Onesimus changed once he put his faith in Christ alone. Paul discipled him and discovered he had some matters he needed to tend to from his past life. One of those was to go to Philemon and make things right with him. So Paul paved the way by helping him grow in Christ, sending him back because it was the right thing to do, and providing this letter of support. He did not have to do so. Paul wanted to be sure that Philemon remembered what life was like before Jesus and that he did for Onesimus what Paul had done for him in the past. He invested in him so he could be all that God wanted him to be. It worked. The same could happen for a former employer who was now a brother. Philemon needed to forgive him and celebrate Onesimus' newfound freedom in Christ Jesus. He was changed. He would be useful. And he needed to give him a second chance.

Do you know what's interesting about this story? We don't know how it ended. Did Philemon forgive him? Did Onesimus stay for the long haul? Did Paul ever make it back, like he indicated he would in the latter portion of the letter? It is obviously not what's most important or God would have let us know. We can trust Him with all things. What is most important is that we do everything we can to support a lost person who meets Jesus personally. Believe in them. Help them in their newfound freedom in Christ. Instruct and love. And do everything you can to get others to give them a break. Don't hold things over their head unnecessarily, as long as it depends on you. And certainly, don't keep bringing up their past behavior to the point of embarrassment. Jesus can change anyone. Has He changed you? Live by faith today…

DAILY READING:
Lamentations 2:20-3:66; Hebrews 1:1-14
Psalm 102:1-28; Proverbs 26:21-22
Focal Passage: Lamentations 3:22-23

LIVING BY FAITH

I AM CONVINCED THE MORNING IS THE IDEAL TIME FOR RENEWING OUR FAITH IN GOD. There is great freedom in Christ! I do not want to come across as legalistic here with my statement. I just believe it's important to be reminded every day of God's faithfulness. It is the key to enjoying one's relationship with Jesus. Even Jesus would spend time with the Father early in the mornings. We saw that time and time again as we studied the gospels together. He is our ultimate example. Now I admit, I am a morning person. So if you believe you just can't do it early in the morning, okay. But that does not give you an excuse to not spend personal time with the Lord. He longs for you to know Him and remind you daily of His faithfulness.

Lamentations is a book about pain and suffering—but with great hope. The Babylonians had attacked Jerusalem and brought an end to the southern kingdom of Judah. Many of the people had been taken into captivity, while many others had fled. Although this is a book of poetic expressions of pain and sin's consequences, we see the author, Jeremiah, highlight the faithfulness of God. God is always, *always* ready to show mercy when people repent and return to Him alone. That is just who He is and will always be!

Thomas Obadiah Chisholm wrote the old hymn *"Great is thy Faithfulness"* based on reading these verses. He suffered ill health most of his adult life. God led him to write the words of the song that has inspired many people through the years. He sought God's mercy, just like the prophet. Pain is not denied. God is merciful through it all. Maybe you are suffering right now with some type of pain. Friend, His mercies never end. They are still going on. We need to be reminded every morning—*GREAT IS THY FAITHFULNESS*. Live by faith today...

OCTOBER 31

DAILY READING:
Lamentations 4:1-5:22; Hebrews 2:1-18
Psalm 103:1-22; Proverbs 26:23
Focal Passage: Hebrews 2:14-15

LIVING BY FAITH

THERE IS NO NEED TO FEAR BECAUSE JESUS IS NEAR. Have you been spooked yet? Chances are before the day is over, you will be. It doesn't have to be Halloween for me to be spooked. I think it's in the Kitchings' genes. (My dad and my grandmother, his mom, were the same way.) I'm just jumpy. There's nothing wrong with having a little fun at someone else's expense, as long as it's good clean fun. Being spooked is one kind of fear. But there is another kind of fear that is not fun at all. Actually, it's unhealthy. It can cause one to wake up every day with a sense of dread. Some are even overly terrified of death because of fear. None of us have to experience this kind of fear.

Have no fear, Jesus is near! Our passage reminds us that Jesus has destroyed the enemy. He lived a perfect life, died on the cross, and rose again so that we might have no fear. The enemy, the devil, is a defeated foe! Don't let him trick you. Remember, he is the father of lies. He majors in deception. Death has been defeated by Jesus forever and ever. If you truly know Him, you know this to be true. Sometimes we just need to be reminded.

We're in an election year at the time of this writing. Next week a new President of the United States will be elected. Regardless of who wins, he will not take office until next year. This is sort of what is going on with the devil right now. Jesus won, but Satan and his demons have been given some time before His Kingdom is established. God is using this time to ultimately show the devil what can happen when we are dependent on Him. Glory can be brought to God through His children. Satan hates this reality! So if you are on Team Jesus, don't be intimidated. Listen to the right voice. Focus on Christ.

Stay close to Jesus today. Have fun. Eat candy, if you want. Just don't allow anyone or anything to cause you to experience an unhealthy fear. Jesus is forever near to those who love and know Him. It's a promise. Live by faith today...

DAILY READING:

Ezekiel 1:1-3:15; Hebrews 3:1-19
Psalm 104:1-23; Proverbs 26:24-26
Focal Passage: Hebrews 3:12-14

LIVING BY FAITH

THIS ONE THING WILL HELP YOU MAKE IT TO THE END.
Encouragement. Surprised? You shouldn't be. Why? Well, primarily because
you just read it in the Bible. This is God's Holy Word and this ministry of His is
mentioned numerous times in the Old Testament and the New Testament. It is not
easy living for Jesus day in and day out. And it will become even more difficult in
the days ahead. The writer of Hebrews is reminding the believers that it is vital to
encourage others until Jesus returns or until they go to their heavenly home. That
means there should not be a day that goes by that you and I don't encourage someone
in some way. It can be a note, a text, a letter, a phone call, an appropriate hug, a
financial blessing. It can be as simple as saying to someone in your church family a
timely, Christ-honoring, "I love you."

Some believers grow "cold" through the years. I get it. It can happen to any of
us. What do we do? Well, besides making it a practice to encourage others, we stay
plugged into a church family. Let's say you had a godly grandmother like I shared
about a while back. She's gone to heaven. No one will replace her. But let me share
something with you—there are other godly grandmother types in the church. It's
true. I can name some right now in the church I pastor. And I'm 60! There will
always be, no matter how old we become, a grandmother type in a church family. So
what am I trying to say? I'm saying God knows that our ultimate family is the family
of God. The church isn't perfect, but it's God's idea. We will spend eternity with
them, albeit a better version. We will all be like Jesus. Let's get used to each other
now. Let's encourage one another so our brothers' and sisters' hearts won't grow hard.
It can happen. It may be that you sense your heart has become hard. Share your
heart with someone in your church family whom God leads you to. And if you don't
have a church family and your heart seems hard—you just got the answer to your
problem. Find another "grandma."

I shudder to think where I would be without my church families through the
years. Be an encourager and let your church family be the same for you. They can't if
you're not there in body and spirit. Live by faith today...

DAILY READING:
Ezekiel 3:16-6:14; Hebrews 4:1-16
Psalm 104:24-35; Proverbs 26:27
Focal Passage: Hebrews 4:14-16

LIVING BY FAITH

SINCE JESUS UNDERSTANDS WHAT YOU ARE GOING THROUGH, TALK WITH HIM ABOUT IT. Jesus was like us in that He faced temptation. He went through heartache. He suffered unbelievable physical pain. Yet He never sinned. Hallelujah! What a Savior! So He is the perfect high priest who can sympathize with our struggles down here on earth. We don't serve a God that can't help. He can help. He wants to help. He gets it. Let that sink in…

Do you ever talk with Jesus about your life? Do you thank Him for all He's done? I mean, even the little things. And do you talk with Him about your struggles? I mean, the big things. Nothing is hidden and He desires that we cry out to Him. I'm going to tell you a secret. There are times in my quiet time with the Lord that are not quiet at all. I cry out. Yes, sometimes I literally cry, but that's not what I'm talking about here. It's more like a shout. I say things like "God, I do not understand, and I need your help NOW!" You ever do that? It's okay. This passage says we are to be bold. This passage says approaching Him is approaching the throne of grace. This passage says we can receive mercy when we are in need. So I'm telling you, I cry out to Him when I feel like I do not know what He's doing. You know what, I actually think He likes it. Realistically, I think He REALLY likes it. He longs to have a deep, intimate, relationship with us. What better way than to put me in a situation that I can't handle anymore.

Be reminded today, Jesus understands your life's journey. He gets it. Talk with Him about it. I mean have a gut-wrenching, loud, conversation. And if you need to relocate to another room from your usual place of Bible study and prayer, do it. Do it for heaven's sake! Live by faith today…

LIVING BY FAITH

AN IDEAL PASSAGE FOR THE ELECT ON ELECTION DAY.
Christians are often called "the elect" throughout scripture. And Christians should vote when an election comes along. At the time of this writing, a new President of the United States of America is about to be voted on. I have no idea who will win. Regardless, these verses are absolutely ideal. Why? Because the Psalmist reminds us that we are to seek the face of God always, election day or not. God is God and we are not. He is the maker of all things. Considering the wonders of the world is comforting. Go look at pictures of mountains or oceans if you need to. Furthermore, consider His miracles. Those recorded in the Bible and those that you may have been a part of. Salvation is a miracle! Just think about it. Only God can change the heart of man into a new creation for His glory. And what about the judgments? We have seen in our readings that God does some of His greatest works in the lives of believers when they are under the authority of evil rulers. Yep, we're good no matter who wins elections. That does not mean we should not be salt and light and vote our convictions. This is just a reminder to relax if you are all uptight when elections come around.

Can you imagine what non-believers experience on election day? They probably think they will live or die based on who is elected. What a terrible thought. To base one's ideals and values on a person—any person—is horrifying! I ain't doing it. And if you are a Christian, you shouldn't either. And if you are not a Christian, surrender to King Jesus. He accepts you just as you are. You may "ride" a donkey, an elephant, or some other animal. Just vote—Jesus! He is the winner of all winners!

Maybe you need to share this passage with someone on an election day? Maybe you need to keep it in front of you? Live by faith today...

LIVING BY FAITH

A VISUAL ANCHOR FOR YOU TO SEE ON A REGULAR BASIS MAY BE A GOOD IDEA. I have always liked visuals. I am a visual learner. Many people are. I once had a large, official anchor placed in the foyer of Morrison Heights Baptist, in Clinton, Mississippi. I was pastor at the time, and I was leading the church to relocate. I found an anchor from the state of Florida, where I had pastored prior, to place where everyone could see it. (Many of us are visual learners.) This verse we're focused on today was our focal passage for a portion of the relocation process. Why? Because Jesus goes with us wherever we go. It's like the writer of Hebrews says, *"He alone is our hope."* And no matter where we are, He is there with us. He is not limited to a piece of property. He is not limited to our hometown. He is not limited by anything or anyone. When He is anchored in our soul, there is absolutely nothing that can cause Him to move. So the physical anchor in the foyer of the old sanctuary was something the people saw on a regular basis as a reminder that Jesus would go with us to the new property and buildings one day.

So do you need some type of visual of an anchor? I'm not suggesting you purchase a real one and put it in your home. That would not be practical if you had one the size that we had. Maybe a picture of an anchor? Maybe a small version of an anchor? Whatever it takes as you walk through life to remind you that once you trust Jesus, He is with you. He is with you if you move. He is with you no matter who is President. He is with you if your kids go off to college. He is with you if you lose your job. He is with you even if your child dies. Have you ever tried to lift a gigantic anchor? It's not an easy task. They are designed to stay put. Jesus stays put. The Holy Spirit seals us upon conversion and does not move. You may move, He does not. He's going with you every step of the way. Trust Him. Allow Him to take the lead. Follow Him as ultimately, He is your only hope. Live by faith today...

DAILY READING:
Ezekiel 12:1-14:11; Hebrews 7:1-17
Psalm 105:37-45; Proverbs 27:3
Focal Passage: Ezekiel 12:17-20

LIVING BY FAITH

REBELLION AGAINST GOD HAS A TERM LIMIT. Rebellion will not go on forever. It may be our rebellion or someone else's. But mark my words, it *will* end. Ultimate rebellion is rejecting Jesus and what He has done for us. The result is living on earth without Him, as well as throughout eternity when death occurs. The result for a nation that has turned its back on God is discipline. The believer that drifts from God will not be left alone. Divine discipline will occur and will continue to occur until the end. Yes, rebellion against a holy God has a term limit.

Ezekiel began prophesying when he was thirty years old. His messages were primarily for the Jewish exiles. The dude's prophetic ministry lasted twenty-two years or longer. The people of the southern kingdom of Judah were incarcerated because of their rebellion against God. Zeke wanted them to know that as bad as things were, God would rescue them if they would repent. God's people are to exercise faith in the worst of circumstances. In this particular passage, God stripped the land bare and destroyed cities because of the inhabitants' violence. This finally got the deaf rebels' attention. God's glory and His renown are worth it. He keeps His covenant promises and restores those who drift, no matter how far.

So how goes it? Are you living in a country that is experiencing the results of leaving God out? Pray for genuine revival and hold on to Jesus. Be the salt and light you are commanded to be. Maybe you are experiencing some pain right now. Is it a result of disobedience? Do a spiritual survey and ask Him to show you. Just know this, rebellion cannot go on forever. Whether it is yours or someone else's. God is Holy. His glory cannot tolerate it. He is gracious. We must listen while we can. One day, there will be no opportunity to "turn back the clock." Live by faith today...

NOVEMBER 6

DAILY READING:
Ezekiel 14:12-16:42; Hebrews 7:18-28
Psalm 106:1-12; Proverbs 27:4-6
Focal Passage: Proverbs 27:6

LIVING BY FAITH

A TRUE FRIEND WILL NOT ENCOURAGE YOU TO EAT A DOZEN DONUTS IF YOU WEIGH THREE HUNDRED POUNDS. A true friend will not allow you to hurt yourself without attempting to help. Speaking of eating too much, I have a friend who has and will hold me accountable when I start gaining too much weight. I never asked him to do so. We just have that kind of relationship. I want him to because I have the potential of eating a dozen donuts in one sitting. I have another friend who has and will hold me accountable for my mental health. My family struggles with depression and there was a time I ignored it. Once I aged and went through a very difficult pastorate, I needed help. This friend knew it and lovingly confronted me about it. These two guys are the types of friends the verse is speaking of.

Judas betrayed Jesus with a kiss. Just because someone is especially nice to us doesn't mean they have our backs. As a matter of fact, I can think of one friend from my past who was, unfortunately, similar to a Judas type of person. It's scary. Actually, I am scared for him. May God be gracious to people who pretend to be nice, while at the same time not caring about your total well-being. The wounds of a true friend keep us from having deeper wounds. They see us digging a hole of some kind, and they rush to take the shovel before it's too late. I thank God for these types of friends. I pray God gives me the discernment to distance myself from the ones who are toxic and to not be "that guy."

It is not easy to talk to a friend about a problem they are having. Sometimes, they actually don't like it and may not like you. Do it anyway. It can save the friend from "falling in the ditch" and hurting himself and others. Even if he gets upset, he may come around in time. If not, pray for the person and trust God. He is faithful. When we do or say something out of what we understand to be obedience to the Lord, we just can't go wrong, regardless of the results. Just make sure it's what God leads you to do and not what you want to do. Live by faith today...

DAILY READING:
Ezekiel 16:43-17:24; Hebrews 8:1-13
Psalm 106:13-31; Proverbs 27:7-9
Focal Passage: Proverbs 27:8

LIVING BY FAITH

REJECT THE TEMPTATION TO WANDER FROM YOUR RESPONSIBILITIES. This verse is a warning to those who may be tempted to wander away from home or from responsibilities. Think about the bird that leaves the nest. It doesn't make sense, does it? We all know that female birds protect their young, and male birds go to find food in addition to providing protection. So the writer gets our attention just by mentioning a wandering bird.

A wandering man is not out for exercise. He is wandering from responsibilities God has given him and could end up in trouble. Deep trouble. I can think of a wandering man in the Old Testament who just took a stroll outside that ultimately cost himself and others great harm. If it can happen to David, a man after God's own heart, it can happen to me. It can even happen to you. Can you think of other wanderers in the Bible who got away from their responsibilities? Sure you can. The principle we need to learn here is to be careful about idle time. Don't take your commitment to your family lightly. If married, recall what you were saying when you spoke those vows during your wedding. A covenant relationship includes God.

This is more than just a cute little "bird in a nest" passage. This is a picture of destruction. All it takes is a few steps away from God-given responsibilities to destroy multiple lives. Play it out in your mind to help keep you far away from taking steps in the wrong direction. Time spent away in disobedience is time wasted. We only have so much time. Listen to the truth of this passage. Think of others who have wandered and where they ended up. Don't go there. Live by faith today...

DAILY READING:
Ezekiel 18:1-19:14; Hebrews 9:1-10
Psalm 106:32-48; Proverbs 27:10
Focal Passage: Hebrews 9:9-10

LIVING BY FAITH

THE OLD SACRIFICIAL SYSTEM IS DEAD, SO LET IT GO. Hebrews is not an easy book to understand for the casual reader. The writer is very dependent on Old Testament writings especially to help the Jewish Christians facing hard times. They had a tendency to go back to the sacrificial system of old. Judaism was familiar for them and so they naturally would drift back to what made them comfortable. The writer of Hebrews continued to urge them to go on in Christ. To allow Jesus to help them mature beyond reverting back during challenges. In other words, Jesus is better than any system you have because He is a person you can draw near to.

The sacrifices referred to here would not and could not perfect the worshipper's conscience. No system can change a heart. External actions from the past dealt temporarily with sin until the new order would come. What was the new order? JESUS. No food or drink, or numerous washings, would come close to what Jesus does to wash away our sins. There is great freedom in knowing Him and Him alone for all things. The writer will go further in the days ahead as you read from this significant book.

Now, what do you and I do that is comfortable when we suffer? Do we revert back to drinking something that doesn't help? Do we start eating more than we should? Do we drift back to old friends we know aren't good for us? Do you see how this relates to us today? We must be careful to remember that Jesus is the ultimate answer, not our old life. Let's allow difficulties that come along – because they will – to be used to help us mature in our faith. That's what God desires for you and for me. Jesus is alive. Sacrificial systems or anything in our day that may be remotely similar are dead. Live by faith today...

NOVEMBER 9

DAILY READING:
Ezekiel 20:1-49; Hebrews 9:11-28
Psalm 107:1-43; Proverbs 27:11
Focal Passage: Psalm 107:8

LIVING BY FAITH

MAYBE THIS SHOULD BE A KEY VERSE FOR THE MONTH OF NOVEMBER? Why? Well, here in the United States of America we celebrate Thanksgiving on the fourth Thursday of this month. This verse is about giving thanks to the Lord for His unfailing love and wonderful deeds for men. More about this in a minute. Thanksgiving has been celebrated nationally on and off since 1789. In 1863, President Lincoln proclaimed a national day of "Thanksgiving and Praise to our beneficent and Father who dwelleth in the Heavens." Thanksgiving, by an act of Congress signed into law by President Franklin D. Roosevelt, received a permanent observation date. So those of us living in the US have been eating a lot, spending time with family, and watching football games and parades on that day for years. Numerous Christian families will take time to give thanks for all that God has done. Personally, an American and as a believer in Jesus, I have always enjoyed this holiday.

This psalm exhorts God's people to give thanks to Him for redeeming them from Babylonian exile and giving them their land back. He reminds them of the captivity and hard labor they suffered as a result of their rebellion. We continue to see how God is gracious to a point. And if we turn our backs, He allows difficulties to go to a new level so we might repent. This happens over and over and over throughout biblical history. Take note. This same focal passage occurs four times in this chapter. It is listed not only in verse eight, but verses fifteen, twenty-one, and thirty-one. No matter how difficult your life may be, God is gracious. Focus on what you are thankful for right now, not what troubles you are experiencing. Go ahead. Take a moment to list what you are thankful for as you consider what He has done for all humanity.

It's not so bad anymore is it? Christians should be thankful every month of the year. We should probably make it a practice to do this exercise on a regular basis. We are a blessed people. Those who live in other countries would tell us how blessed we are. But as believers all over the world, we should be thankful for what Jesus has done. The life He has brought us is indescribable. The future He has promised is beyond comprehension. Enjoy the month. Enjoy this passage. Enjoy your life. It could be much worse. Live by faith today...

DAILY READING:

Ezekiel 21:1-22:31; Hebrews 10:1-17
Psalm 108:1-13; Proverbs 27:12
Focal Passage: Ezekiel 22:30-31

LIVING BY FAITH

MAYBE GOD HAS YOU IN A DIFFICULT PLACE TO PROTECT OTHERS? Have you ever been in a difficult place? For example, you may be in a difficult church. They are out there, you know. No church is perfect. But there are some that have a reputation of being a little more difficult than others. So maybe you have wanted to leave a particular church, but God has not released you. It happens. I have spoken with many a godly layman who asked God to let them leave and He never gave them the freedom to do so. Maybe, just maybe, it was because God was using them to influence His people for good. It could be with their presence; judgment was being withheld. God uses intermediaries whose righteousness can be credited in order to benefit the less righteous. But when those types are absent, and the people just will not repent, judgment occurs. Please never leave a church of Jesus Christ before He truly releases you. You could be the church's last hope before its death. Some churches have the name of Jesus, without Him. It's sad. Don't assume you're not where you are in order to protect others. Remember, it's not about you or me.

God spoke through Ezekiel to proclaim the truth. The people could listen to or reject his proclamations. Just because a prophet spoke did not mean the people would listen and obey. We've seen this over and over throughout our reading of the scriptures. The same is true today. Just because God may have spoken to you just now about a matter doesn't mean you will listen and obey. Has He spoken? Will you obey? Don't answer that too quickly. Just be sure.

Listen, God may be calling you to stand in the gap for your family. You may be what's holding the family unit together. He can and will keep you there for things not to get worse. God's wrath is awful. Please don't abandon your family outside of the will of God. The family was the first institution He ordained. It was even before the church. We need godly homes today. Yours may be impacting others. That doesn't mean it's not difficult. Who knows, others may see that and yet they see you standing in the gap. God bless you. Live by faith today…

DAILY READING:

Ezekiel 23:1-49; Hebrews 10:18-39

Psalm 109:1-31; Proverbs 27:13

Focal Passage: Hebrews 10:25

LIVING BY FAITH

WE DECIDED TO BEGIN WORSHIP AT 10:25AM BASED ON THIS VERSE. Once upon a time I was a church planter. I have no regrets. I had thought for years that it may be a good fit for me. I learned so much during those two and a half years. I certainly learned that I was just the one to get it off the ground. But one of the early decisions we made was to start Sunday morning worship at 10:25am based on this verse. We were located in a very challenging area of Memphis, Tennessee. The people, as well as those of us seeking to plant the church, needed encouragement. It was one of the hardest ministry assignments I have ever had. If not for the encouragement of the Lord and others, I would not have made it to the launch service.

Some of those who were reading this letter had been neglecting gatherings with other believers. Church is God's idea. He knew we needed each other. It is God's primary means of helping us live out the Christ life. So the writer of Hebrews made sure they clearly understood how important it was for them to make it a priority. The "day approaching" is referring to the return of Christ. In other words, don't stop your church life until you die or until Christ returns. It is clear to me. Now, I understand some are not physically able due to their health or various other legitimate reasons. (Even then, those who have been active in their local church through the years usually find ways to connect.) Most of us have no excuse. We cannot miss being an active part of God's family.

Encouragement is God's way of using people to pound courage into us. If we are alive, we need it. Life happens. Our world is depraved. Go to church and worship the Lord. Go serve Him with the gifts and abilities He gave you. Go because you may be the person someone needs to keep them from ending their life prematurely. Go to experience the power of prayer and authenticity. Need I go on? We need this verse as much as those it was first written for. You may need it more right now. If you are not involved in a local fellowship, please do so as soon as possible. It doesn't have to meet on Sundays at 10:25am. It just has to meet so you can meet with people that need you. And you need them. Live by faith today...

DAILY READING:

Ezekiel 24:1-26:21; Hebrews 11:1-16
Psalm 110:1-7; Proverbs 27:14
Focal Passage: Hebrews 11:13

LIVING BY FAITH

THE PILGRIMS WE OFTEN THINK OF THIS TIME OF THE YEAR WERE NOT THE ONLY PILGRIMS. When I think of Thanksgiving, I think of eating, family, and watching parades and football. But I also think of those folks with the funny-looking outfits back in the day. You know, the ones so many of us drew pictures of during grade school. Yes, those pilgrims. A pilgrim is defined as an original settler in a region, a traveler, or a person on a journey. The people mentioned in Hebrews 11, often referred to as *The Hall of Faith*, were really the first pilgrims before the first pilgrims. They were on a journey. They were just traveling through.

The Pilgrims we sometimes think of this time of the year were definitely people of faith. (Hebrews 11:1,6) But the people in Hebrews 11 were great men and women of faith. Think about it. They were looking forward to the Messiah who would come. They were anticipating a heavenly city, though they didn't understand it all. They accomplished great feats because of their trust in God. What an amazing group of people!

They died in faith even though they had not received all they were having faith about. Now that, my friend, is faith. I have to be honest, I'm hoping to see some things I'm trusting God for before I die. I'm not talking about salvation here. I'm talking about some things I'm praying to Him about and trusting that they will occur because I have faith in Him. But what if they don't? Maybe He has a better plan than mine. If I knew now that they weren't going to happen as I see them, would I still keep going like our passage mentions? I pray so. I hope so. I believe by God's grace I've come too far and seen Jesus do too much to stop living by faith now. I desire to finish like those mentioned in this great chapter of the Bible—die living by faith. Pray for me.

What about you? How surrendered are you to live by faith every day? Please don't give up. Read this passage again and be encouraged in your journey, pilgrim. If need be, draw a picture of one of the original pilgrims and put your name on it to celebrate what's to come here and in eternity. Live by faith today...

DAILY READING:

Ezekiel 27:1-28:26; Hebrews 11:17-31
Psalm 111:1-10; Proverbs 27:15-16
Focal Passage: Hebrews 11:27

LIVING BY FAITH

THERE ARE CLEARLY TWO CHARACTERISTICS OF THE
FAITHFUL. When Moses died the scripture says there was no one else like him.
Although there are a number of faithful servants in this chapter, I want to focus
on Moses. He is certainly worthy of our attention. This verse points to the two
characteristics of his faithfulness and I believe, the faithfulness of others. 1. Moses
did not fear people. Here we see he did not blink at going against the King. Most
people aren't like that. Man often is afraid of his own family or close friends, much
less someone in charge of everyone in an area, like a king. 2. Moses kept pressing
forward throughout his journey. The Bible says that he persevered because he saw the
invisible God. Friend, that is faith, in a nutshell. (Hebrews 11:1) And we cannot
fulfill our purpose or enjoy the journey without this kind of daily living.
(Hebrews 11:6)

Does this describe you? Are you overly concerned about what people think of
you? If so, you will be miserable as a believer. Fearing God means respecting Him
so much that you can't imagine not obeying Him more than a person. Any person.
Develop such a love of Christ that you long to stand up for Him. Just be sure it's
Him, and you do it in a way He would want you to do it. Next, are you quick to give
up? Let me put it another way, are you impatient? Yikes! I struggle more with this
one than the other one. I like for things to happen quickly. If not, I become anxious.
I tend to think I'm done with whatever I'm working on and it's time to move on. *Not
so fast*, God is teaching me. The word *persevered* is key to fulfilling God's will. This
means as long as God has not released us from a project, a place, a job, a whatever—
we take one day at a time. We seek Him and trust Him. We do our part and leave
the part we cannot control to His great work. Just think back on our study of Moses'
life. The guy went through so much during his journey. And remember, he didn't
start out like he finished. Completing the race strong is the goal for all of us. This
verse teaches us how. Live by faith today...

DAILY READING:
Ezekiel 29:1-30:26; Hebrews 11:32-12:13
Psalm 112:1-10; Proverbs 27:17
Focal Passage: Hebrews 12:7-11

LIVING BY FAITH

IT WAS NOT ALWAYS EASY TO CONNECT THE DOTS WITH THE SWITCH USED TO DISCIPLINE ME. As most of you know by now, I am a preacher's kid. Once a preacher's kid, always a preacher's kid. (Ask an adult preacher's kid, if you don't understand.) I was raised in a pastorium. When I did something wrong, I would sometimes get a switching. Depending on the level of punishment due to the wrong I had done, I sometimes had to go select the switch to be used on my backside. (Are you tracking with me here?) You might think it was better because you could find one that wouldn't hurt as badly. That's not so. It was my experience that regardless of the size, they still provide adequate pain. Yikes! I am having a flashback right now. So I was a child growing up with a preacher dad, in a Baptist church's parsonage, who was providing the tree from which I was getting a whipping. I couldn't really connect the dots then, but I do now. My dad loved me deeply. One way of demonstrating it was disciplining me when I did wrong. And he used the property of a church that also loved me to administer the punishment. What a deal! Was I blessed, or what? Yes! I see it as a blessing now.

The writer of Hebrews reminds us that God's true children receive discipline at times. If not, one better go back and check their "heaven papers." The person may find they are illegitimate. True believers that desire the blessings of God must submit to our heavenly Father's divine discipline. Doing so means increased strength and righteousness here on earth. And who knows what kind of rewards in heaven!

My dad did not always discipline me correctly. At times, the punishment did not fit the crime. I did the same thing with my children. I loved them enough to discipline them but because I am imperfect, it was not perfect. God is perfect. His discipline **always** fits the crime. Therefore, we should be encouraged that our perfect heavenly Father loves us enough to discipline us for correction, perfection, or maybe redirection. Maybe you should go take a look at a little bush right now and ponder our passage today. I am looking at one right now as I complete this devotional thought. Live by faith today...

DAILY READING:
Ezekiel 31:1-32:32; Hebrews 12:14-29
Psalm 113:1-114:8; Proverbs 27:18-20
Focal Passage: Hebrews 12:14-15

LIVING BY FAITH

IF AT ALL POSSIBLE, BE AT PEACE WITH OTHERS, OR ELSE THERE MAY BE A BIGGER PROBLEM. The writer of Hebrews takes the opportunity toward the end of the book to remind the believers not to reject God's grace. For example, we cannot trample over people—certainly not our brothers and sisters in Christ. We are to pursue peace. Jesus said that we would have troubles in this world. If we aren't careful, we make our troubles worse. How? By not letting some things go. Let's say you are driving and someone cuts in front of you. What do you do? I know, it's difficult. But we should let it go. What if a fellow church member shares a confidential prayer request with others? What do you do? You go to them and try your best to work it out instead of ignoring it, slamming them with others, or taking revenge. Again, I know, it's difficult. But the Bible makes it clear that we are to try to make peace, or not cause a sense of unrest, with everyone.

A root of bitterness compounds our problems. If we don't learn to intentionally do everything we can to pursue peace with everyone, we provide the possibility of a bitter root. A bitter root causes problems for you and others. I know. I've experienced this before. I have a natural tendency to want to confront people when I am wronged or when I perceive something as wrong. Now to be clear, this is not always a bad trait. It can be good. But I've learned through the years that there are some things I just need to let go. They are not a "hill to die on." Or maybe I'm being oversensitive. Do you ever do that? We must be very careful here or what could have not even been an issue becomes an issue. Or what could have been a very small skirmish will become a big problem.

A bitter root is hard to get rid of. Ask God to help you discern how to lovingly relate to others. And take an inventory right now. Do you wish ill will on someone you know? Pray for God to do surgery on your heart no matter what it takes. One step at a time is best. If you jump to thinking you have to go on vacation with the person, you will likely live with a bitter root for a long time. Please don't die with bitterness in your heart. God's grace will help you. Be at peace with everyone. Live by faith today...

DAILY READING:

Ezekiel 33:1-34:31; Hebrews 13:1-25
Psalm 115:1-18; Proverbs 27:21-22
Focal Passage: Hebrews 13:17

LIVING BY FAITH

THIS ONE VERSE WILL HELP CHURCHES THRIVE. I have never preached an entire sermon on this passage. Maybe I should. But I have no hesitation to write a devotional about it. To stand up as a pastor of a church and preach this message could certainly cause the parishioners to be skeptical. Think about it. So there is a place for it, and I have mentioned the verse in a message or two, but never focused on it like I am about to for rather obvious reasons.

The writer of Hebrews is providing some final exhortations for the church of Jesus Christ. And he includes this one verse that can make all the difference in the world between a church thriving or just surviving. A pastor is called by God to preach, lead, and shepherd the flock. If he is not called, he's a fruitcake and should run away. It is not an easy job. There is far more good than bad. But I can testify that the congregations that were more apt to follow me were more enjoyable. They refreshed my soul week after week. This does not mean they blindly accepted everything I said or did. No, not at all. It means there were appropriate checks and balances and they prayed for me. They didn't automatically question me. They served and came alongside of me. They took the time to encourage me along the journey. They realized I had great limitations and could not do everything. They protected me and my family. They will never be forgotten by me. The Lord knows who they are.

Pastors will be held accountable. (Go back and read that again.) God will judge them more strictly. (We are about to see this in James, the next book of our New Testament reading.) Never think your pastor is somehow getting by with something unscriptural. There will be a reckoning day. So pray for him, please. Don't focus on insignificant preferences. God made each one of us different. Don't force him into a mold. Allow him the freedom to be who God made him to be. If there is something illegal, immoral, or unethical, address it biblically. More times than not, this is not the case with most churches. A pastor should not be a dictator nor a puppet. He is a shepherd. Let him be. Love him. Pray for him. He has limitations. He is simply trying to obey the call of God. Live by faith today...

DAILY READING:
Ezekiel 35:1-36:38; James 1:1-18
Psalm 116:1-19; Proverbs 27:23-27
Focal Passage: James 1:2-4

LIVING BY FAITH

"TRUST THE PROCESS" IS MORE THAN A SPORTS PHRASE.
Legendary Alabama football coach Nick Saban is known for saying, "Trust the process." He has put systems in place that have produced winning football teams. So all he does is win because he walks everyone in the organization through a particular process that works. Numerous other teams have a similar philosophy.

James jumps right into it. He says that believers will have trials. They are a part of the process of becoming mature. James basically says we should be fired up, pumped, excited, thrilled, and even overjoyed that we have trials of various kinds. These divinely appointed opportunities help us conform to the image of Christ. That's why we are still down here on earth. We should be more like Jesus from the time of our conversion to the time of our departure to our heavenly home. We should be very careful not to dismiss opportunities for spiritual growth because we're going through a difficult time. We need to trust the process.

No matter what trial you may be experiencing, keep doing what you know to be God's will. Pray regularly and authentically. You can't fool God. Be honest with Him. Read His Word devotionally. Don't neglect hearing the total truth! Get in the Bible daily in a way that helps you keep taking a step forward. Talk with a few trusted Christian friends. Share with them, but don't dominate the conversation. They have needs, too. Serve. Fulfill God's call. In other words, do what you know is God's will and He will see you through whatever difficulty you have. Do these things every day to the best of your ability, and trust that God will give you discernment in making wise choices. God knows where you are and what is going on. Don't get caught up in trying to figure out why your life is so different than others. No two lives are ever the same. Trust the spiritual process—the one God has for you. Live by faith today...

LIVING BY FAITH

WHEN YOU GO THROUGH A DRY SEASON, ALLOW GOD TO BRING LIFE AGAIN. Have you experienced a dry season, spiritually? I have. If you are honest, you probably have too. You may be going through one right now. If we stayed on a mountaintop, we wouldn't know what it was like to be in the valley. There are different reasons we go through a dry spell. Usually, it's caused by a drift away from the things of God. It may be not spending time reading the Bible. It may be a drift from a close church family. It can even be that you started spending a lot more time with someone who doesn't have the same core values you developed as a Christian. But it happens. We find in this scripture passage that no one is beyond experiencing revival. Anyone can be revived by the Spirit of God!

God gave the prophet Ezekiel a vision to provide understanding. In this vision, he found himself in a valley of dry bones. As he was walking amongst a huge valley of dead folks, he was asked by God if he thought they could live again. Ezekiel correctly responded that only God knew the answer. (Good answer, Zeke!) God commanded him to prophesy over them in order to bring them back to life. He did. Then God breathed life back into this vast army. The house of Israel had been denied their land and many died due to not obeying God. Yet one day, they would be restored, and prosper due to turning their hearts back to God. Their spiritual dry season would be over and life with God would be better than ever.

This picturesque vision has spiritual application for you and me. No one is beyond revival. It doesn't matter how we might arrive at a dry spell. We just have to admit to Him that we need revival. Confess sin. Cry out to Him to do something fresh and new. Make things right with people the best you can. Stay connected to Christ through prayer and daily reading of the Bible. Go on a retreat. Do something different! But don't stay where you are or believe the lie of the devil that you cannot come out of a dry season. You can. Why? Because the Holy Spirit lives inside of believers. Listen to the voice of God through this Old Testament prophet. Live by faith today...

LIVING BY FAITH

THIS HAS BEEN CALLED THE WORLD'S DEADLIEST WEAPON.
As I enter the pulpit, I bring a bag and my Bible. I place them on the podium and say, *"In this bag is the world's deadliest weapon."* Immediately, I have the attention of the audience. Then I proceed to name various weapons that it might be. Eventually, I reach into the bag and pull out a cow's tongue. Some laugh. Some are shocked that I would do such a thing. Some are even offended. I immediately show them the visual and talk about how I know there are some so upset I would actually bring a literal cow's tongue into the sanctuary of a church that they can't even listen. I then share how there are tongues that enter the sanctuary every time the church gathers that do more damage. The passage explains. Yes, a tongue is a small part of the body, but it can destroy relationships, tear up families, ruin best friends, and even hurt the fellowship of a church.

James illustrates the power of the tongue when comparing it to a bit in the mouth of a horse, a rudder guiding a ship, and a small fire destroying an entire forest. The tongue is a small part of the body, but it can do much damage or much good. It depends on what direction we are going with our words. The scripture says it sets the course of life on fire if we use our words in a negative way. That's not good. It's not good for the person, nor the people they come in contact with.

The use of the tongue for believers is mentioned throughout scripture. Proverbs has numerous verses on the power of our spoken words. Many reference the heart. What's in our hearts often comes out of our mouths. We must allow the Lord to continually give us a clean heart by reading and applying His Word. Be careful who you emulate. Listen to the words of the music you listen to. Do they lift up or tear down? Here's an idea, practice saying something positive and encouraging to three people a week. (That's the way I conclude my sermon, by the way. And for those wondering, I only had one person ask for the tongue after the service. Yes, I gave it to her because she said she eats cow tongue. That's all I'm going to say about that because the timing on saying something negative would not be good.) Okay seriously, if you struggle with negativity, start intentionally saying positive words. God will bless you. Others will be blessed. And no one can accuse you of having a tongue used as a deadly weapon. Live by faith today...

LIVING BY FAITH

THIS IS ONE OF THE CLEAREST VERSES IN THE BIBLE. James was explaining making the most of our days. Our days are numbered, and we should desire to follow God's will the best we can. But we must be open to God's direction. Sometimes His ways aren't ours. Believers should never be boastful. This especially applies to knowing God's will for our lives. We should pray for wisdom, direction, discernment, and to follow God's will every day. And when we know what God wants us to do, do it. Sometimes we get so focused on what might be God's will for our lives that we omit what *is* God's will for our lives.

Let me explain. Do you pray? Do you give generously? Do you use your spiritual gift for building up your local church? Do you encourage others? Here's the point: There are some matters God makes clear in His Word. They are His desire for every believer. And some believers don't do it. You know what that is called? Sin. It can be the sin of omission. We just chose not to obey God's Word.

Are you in trouble? Yes. I am, too. We are sinners! What good is God calling you to do? This is your opportunity to not sin. What a gracious God we serve. Plan and pray for God to give you direction in matters that are important. Follow them the best you can, being open to His tweaks along the way. And do the things you know He has been clear about. This is the way to live life. James again shows his practicality in how he views faith. Faith has teeth to it—meaning, it works. Live by faith today...

LIVING BY FAITH

BE CAREFUL AROUND A PERSON THAT ALWAYS SAYS *I PROMISE*. The book of James has always been one of my favorite books of the Bible. Why? Because it's very practical. Biblical application is something I believe in with my entire being. We read the Bible for more than information. We read it for transformation. Biblical Application is a core value of the church I pastor. We want people who attend worship or a small group to know what the Bible says in order to live what the Bible teaches. It's that simple. And the book of James is extremely clear in its presentation on practical Christianity. Today's verse is a wonderful example.

Once upon a time I had this friend. (You probably did too, if you've lived long enough.) I noticed he had a pattern of using the expression *I promise*. You know, the one we used as kids. It's a lighter version of *I swear*, which is what the verse literally says. If someone has to say either of those phrases, certainly as an adult believer in Jesus Christ, they are letting others know they are likely not trustworthy. It's true. There's a reliability problem.

As Christians, we represent Christ. If we have a pattern of not being trustworthy, what are we doing to the reputation of Jesus? We represent Him down here on earth. Jesus is The Truth! He embodies everything there is about trustworthiness. My friend, shame on us if we don't let our "yes" mean "yes" and our "no" mean "no." James has made a point to talk about the tongue. What we say is critical in fulfilling our Kingdom purpose. So before he ends his letter to the Jewish Christians of his day, he takes another shot at it. BE CAREFUL ABOUT WHAT COMES OUT OF YOUR MOUTH! *Don't lie. Tell the truth, no matter what. You may fool some down here on earth, but you won't fool everyone, and you certainly don't fool God.* Live by faith today…

LIVING BY FAITH

THE TRIALS THAT YOU FACE MAY RESULT IN BRINGING GLORY TO GOD. Peter wrote to Christians in multiple regions of Asia Minor. This is the region we know as modern-day Turkey. He likely wrote the letter from Rome. He was encouraging churches to persevere in spite of their personal sufferings, trials, and deliberate persecutions. It was a message of hope—the overall theme of the book. He certainly understood suffering because he had been through a lot as a disciple of Christ. He allowed God to use it for His glory.

How did Peter reach this point? He was a leader by nature. So as he exercised leadership, God continued to show him how to lead. Strong leadership is learned through various trials. There is no greater teacher than Jesus and the trials He allows us to experience. Trials prove if we really believe, or if we are just pretending. If pretending, it will show up quickly when going through the fire. Trials develop our faith. I can look back, just like many of you, and see how my faith was developed through crisis times. I didn't enjoy them but wouldn't take anything in exchange for them. Why? Because by God's grace, these difficult seasons in life brought glory to God. Brokenness brings about humility. I mean, when we are absolutely going through something that is beyond our capability to fix, we are broken before the Lord. We cry out to Him alone.

Have you been there before? Are you there now? Rejoice because He is developing character. He is doing something in you that is more valuable than gold. If none of this is making any sense to you, maybe you need to be sure your hope is in the Lord. He is the only one who will make sense of the pain you experience in life. There is a purpose. Live by faith today...

DAILY READING:
Ezekiel 45:13-46:24; 1 Peter 1:13-2:10
Psalm 119:33-48; Proverbs 28:11
Focal Passage: 1 Peter 1:22-23

LIVING BY FAITH

THE LOVE WE HAVE FOR EACH OTHER IS SUPERNATURAL.
Are you always easy to love? I'm not. (If that shocks you, ask those closest to me. Actually, never mind…) None of us are always easy to love because we battle with the flesh. But when we abide in Christ, He helps us love deeply from the heart. Jesus said others will know we are His by our love. He summarized the commandments in this way—love God and love people. So it's something that moves within us that is beyond us.

Peter is helping the believers understand that they are to love differently, now that they see things differently. If you have walked with Jesus for a while, you can look back and point to occasions where you loved people in spite of what they did that may have hurt. You can look back at how others have loved you deeply, even though you hurt them at some point. Can you not? If not, pause and contemplate that troublesome thought. God moves deeply within the depths of our souls causing us to love in a way we really can't even describe. It's deep! And it's risky because love is risky, but we can't help it because of experiencing God's deep love personally. It's a beautiful thing. It makes life worth pursuing.

When God has given you this kind of love for someone, pay attention to it. Every opportunity you can, make sure they know of your godly love for them. There's a reason for it. You may not see it on this side of heaven. Do it anyway. And if you are clueless as to what this passage is really talking about, ask God to show you in an undeniable way how to love deeply from the heart so you will maximize your Kingdom living. Live by faith today…

DAILY READING:
Ezekiel 47:1-48:35; 1 Peter 2:11-3:7
Psalm 119:49-64; Proverbs 28:12-13
Focal Passage: 1 Peter 2:11-12

LIVING BY FAITH

HERE IS THE BEST WAY FOR PEOPLE TO KNOW YOU ARE NOT BERNARDO IGOR SAMUEL. I woke up today to a friend letting me know someone had stolen my identity on Facebook. My initial thoughts were as follows: 1. Why would I ever not want my given name? I'm pretty sure no one else in the world has the name Harold Tribble Kitchings, Junior. 2. Why would someone from Spain, where they said I was from, be wearing an Ole Miss mask in their profile picture? Anyway, I didn't let it destroy my day. I reported it and moved on. Why? Because I hope people who know me know I'm not pretending to be someone else to pull some sort of shenanigans. As a believer, we are not perfect, but we are to be different. We are to live in such a way that others don't automatically believe false reports that are shared about us from time to time. And if we live for Jesus, false reports of various types will be shared occasionally. Jesus told us we would be persecuted because we are His followers. We should not be surprised unless there's never any bad news about us. If no one ever reports negatively on us, we probably aren't living for Jesus.

The Christian's job here on earth before going home to heaven is to make a difference for God in the world. We are to abstain from sinful desires. We are to conduct ourselves differently, so people know there's something different about us. Not because we are trying to be some sort of weirdo, but because a Jesus follower lives and loves uniquely. Our neighbors, colleagues, classmates, and others just know we're different because of our daily lives. Such a life brings glory to God. And when we live the way Peter encourages the early church to live, our reputation precedes ourselves. When the slander comes, people think twice before automatically believing it. Hence why I am not concerned about being called Bernardo. I'm Harold and I'm not perfect. But I am forgiven, and Jesus continues to help me be different. Live by faith today...

LIVING BY FAITH

ALWAYS BE READY TO SHARE WITH PEOPLE WHY YOU HAVE HOPE. There is no way to know all there is to know about all there is to know. But as a believer in Jesus, we can know some things. For example, we certainly should be able to share our personal testimony. 1. What was life like before I came to know Christ personally? 2. How did I meet Him as Savior and Lord? 3. What difference is He making in my daily life? No one can argue with our personal story because it's just that—our story. And it is amazing how God can take our mess and make it a message. A message that can impact others. Be ready to share it because you never know when you may have the opportunity to do so. Who knows, it may be around the Thanksgiving table as you gather with family?

Peter continues with the theme of hope. When Christ is Lord, He's boss. We allow Him to rule and call the shots. Others will take note. They will often ask questions about why we live differently. WHEN they do, because they will, we need to be ready to share why. Don't panic. This does not mean you have to have a theological degree or have been a Christian for decades. It just means you need to steadily grow in your faith through prayer and Bible study. It means you need to journal how God works in your life from day to day. It means you are open to taking courses and reading books about why you believe what you believe. And if someone asks a question you don't know the answer to, you tell them you don't know. Then you go find out and get back to them.

What another great verse! People need hope. We have it. God gives us opportunities to share it. Live by faith today...

LIVING BY FAITH

BUT IF NOT, DO IT ANYWAY. If you grew up attending a local church, you likely learned this well-known story in the Old Testament. King Nebuchadnezzar of Babylon besieged Judah. Daniel's book is designed to teach how God's people are to live while undergoing divine discipline. This book includes a lot of spiritual nuggets to digest, but make no mistake, it mainly shows how God in heaven is in control when the earth below seems out of control. And this passage demonstrates this reality. The King wanted his golden statue to be worshipped. These three Jewish boys only worshipped the one true God and refused to bow down. They were promptly thrown into the fiery furnace and didn't seem to mind. The phrase **but if not** is powerful! They were assured God would rescue them, *but if not*, they were going to do God's will. They had rather die than be unfaithful. God showed up and it ended up being a blessing.

One of the very first sermons I ever preached was on this text in the Bible. I remember where I was and some of the people in the audience. I especially recall believing that I wanted to be like these guys, and I encouraged others to follow their example as well. Nothing has changed. I want to obey God even when He is not on my time schedule. And it's important to do what's right even when everyone else seems to be doing what's wrong. It's easier to follow the crowd. There's not as much pressure to obey your King as to disobey. We might not have a king like these Hebrew boys, but we can allow some type of leader to lead us astray if we're not careful. Do not, allow someone to rule your life in a way that is directly against God. Deal with the consequences. God will take care of you—always.

Are you afraid to follow God's will because you may lose your job, lose a friend, or even possibly lose a family member you love? Your hesitation may be compounded because you are not sure how God's going to replace what you're losing. God will show up. If He doesn't immediately or in a way that you can literally see, do it anyway. Trust me. More than anything, trust God. He is God. I am not. You are not. Live by faith today…

DAILY READING:

Daniel 4:1-37; 2 Peter 1:1-21
Psalm 119:97-112; Proverbs 28:17-18
Focal Passage: 2 Peter 1:20-21

LIVING BY FAITH

THE BIBLE IS GOD'S WORD AND CAN BE TRUSTED. Peter probably wrote this toward the end of his journey in life. The recipients were Christians who were being confronted with false teachers. He reminds them of what true doctrine looks like so they can recognize counterfeits. In this first chapter, he explains how to add to their faith in order to mature spiritually. And he makes absolutely sure they know that scripture from God is from His hand. God graciously used human authors to record His word. The Bible has no error, just like Jesus had no sin. Jesus came to earth as Emanuel—God with us. God's Word helps us know the Word that the Gospel of John talks about in saying the Word became flesh and dwelt among us. When you read it, trust the Bible as from the very hand of God. It is.

When I was growing up, I never even thought about the Bible not being God's Word. My parents believed it to be and the adults who taught me believed it to be. Evangelist Billy Graham believed it was God's Word. While I was in seminary years later, there was a controversy in my denomination surrounding the inerrancy of the Bible. Most days were filled with talking about if the Bible contained God's Word or was God's Word. Today's passage was often quoted because it supports the reality that the Bible is God's Word. It is without human error. When the Holy Spirit is involved, we know its truth. Why? Because the Holy Spirit is God—the third person of the Trinity. The Bible wasn't just randomly put together. The canon of scripture is regarded as authoritative. The word canon means "measuring stick." It meets certain criteria. I believe this is important today, just as in Peter's day, so any form of doubt is eliminated. Please don't allow a barrier about the inerrancy of scripture keep you from God's Word and His will for your life. Unfortunately, some people have, and it was costly. The enemy creates doubt. The Holy Spirit does not. If need be today, settle this once and for all and move on.

Keep reading the next verse in your Bible. Keep living out its truth. Fulfill your Kingdom purpose. Live by faith today…

DAILY READING:
Daniel 5:1-31; 2 Peter 2:1-22
Psalm 119:113-128; Proverbs 28:19-20
Focal Passage: Daniel 5:5-6

LIVING BY FAITH

WHEN YOU SEE THE HANDWRITING ON THE WALL, PAY CLOSE ATTENTION. Belshazzar paid no attention to the consequences of his predecessor. The man's ancestors had pride and God hates pride. The results were catastrophic! Yet, he ignored them and continued on in his pride. Then it happened... the handwriting on the wall. We literally hear this phrase today, yet here we find its origin. The Lord writes about the upcoming doom of Belshazzar on a wall, with His hand. The king lost control—serious control—of his bowels. (I'll leave that there.) He brought in his "wise" men and they proved themselves to be the foolish men that they were. Daniel was brought forth and interpreted the dream, not concerned with rewards from the King, and it proved true. The King reaped the terrible consequences due to pride.

It is not too late for you to change. Do you see the "handwriting on the wall?" Are you headed down the wrong path? Make a course correction. Not tomorrow. Not when you think it would be a more ideal time for you and those around you. Today. We learned in the study of James that God punishes pride and gives grace to the humble. Humble yourself today, if you know that you're headed toward destruction. Please do not allow pride to keep you from obeying God. If you see His hand at work in your life, repent. Turn from your sin and self to Him alone. Cry out to Him and take one step at a time in a newfound direction. A direction He is leading you toward. You will come out much better and save yourself, and others, from pain. There is a reason the phrase *"He can see the handwriting on the wall"* has stood the test of time. Let's not let it be used of us, but only by us. There's a difference and the difference can be a matter of life and death. Live by faith today...

DAILY READING:
Daniel 6:1-28; 2 Peter 3:1-18
Psalm 119:129-152; Proverbs 28:21-22
Focal Passage: 2 Peter 3:8-9

LIVING BY FAITH

GOD DESIRES THAT ALL COME TO KNOW HIM. God's measurement of time is not like ours. We see life with a starting point and an ending point. We are finite. God is not. He's always been, so His ways are just not like ours. For example, some don't understand why God delays returning. Maybe it's so you or someone you know will come to know Christ personally? This passage says as much. Maybe it's for people far away who you and I have never met? The text clearly identifies our God as one that wants **everyone** to come to know Him. He is not a God who desires for certain ones to be lost without Him. Please don't ever believe that lie!

You know that person you've been praying for who doesn't know Jesus personally? Keep praying for them and be hopeful. God wants them to be born again more than you do. You know that person who lives in your community who has a reputation of being evil? Yes, that guy or gal. God wants them to be saved too. Maybe you need to start looking at them a little differently? You know that religious family member who hasn't come to know Christ yet? Yes, the one who seems so perfect in their religiosity. God wants them to know Him too. Folks, no one is beyond the grace of God. Never doubt it.

Be cautious of those who talk a lot about some people not being able to know Christ. Whatever their theological bent or misdirected belief, please do not allow them to be used by the deceiver. And for heaven's sake, don't regularly get caught up in heated conversations about the matter. People are dying and going to hell. Life is short. Fulfill God's purpose. Be a witness for Him as much as possible. Don't give up on the one your heart is broken over because they don't believe. Keep believing. Live by faith today...

DAILY READING:
Daniel 7:1-28; 1 John 1:1-10
Psalm 119:153-176; Proverbs 28:23-24
Focal Passage: 1 John 1:8-10

LIVING BY FAITH

I HAD A NEIGHBOR WHO SAID HE NEVER SINNED. I can only recall one adult conversation where a neighbor years ago in central Florida told me he was not a sinner. He stands out to me because in all my years I had met no one who had the audacity to lie so blatantly. Think about it. He was an adult male about fifty-five years of age or so. What was he thinking? He wasn't. He was lying through his teeth! Maybe he was trying to impress me? Maybe he forgot the gravity of sin. There are the sins of omission, you know. Maybe he was working his way to heaven and thought he was on a roll? Regardless, he was not telling the truth, and he was calling God a liar.

John had a passion for intimacy. This is the same apostle who wrote about the vine and the branches in John 15. Here in this little book, he speaks to believers about having fellowship with God. He knew of its importance because he literally walked very closely with Jesus while Christ walked the earth. Many people who were doubting their salvation have found great peace by reading this book for a period of sixty days. Meaning, if you read this book once a day for two months, you should know if you know Jesus personally. And if you don't realize you are lost, you cannot be saved. This is why our passage today is so critical.

If you've never admitted your sinfulness, please do so today. That is the starting point to a relationship with Jesus. It is not trying to be a good person. It is not starting to go to church. It is not "turning over a new leaf." It is admitting you are a wretched, sinful human being lost without Christ. Once this truth is exclaimed, your life has really just begun. God made us for a relationship with Him. And we can't have it begin if we call Him a liar like my neighbor did years ago. By the way, at the time he never admitted his sin. Hopefully the seed was planted, and he has since done so and entered into a relationship with Christ. Who knows, maybe he'll greet me in heaven, cleansed by the blood of the lamb. Live by faith today...

DECEMBER 3

DAILY READING:
Daniel 11:2-35; 1 John 3:7-24
Psalm 122:1-9; Proverbs 29:1
Focal Passage: 1 John 3:16-18

LIVING BY FAITH

A CHRISTMAS PASSAGE? Sure, why not? This is the season for giving. Yes, it's the season for celebrating the birth of Christ with your church family. Yes, it's the season to enjoy all the sights and sounds of the most wonderful time of the year. Yes, I think it's okay to watch our favorite movies of the holiday season. I mean, it's a wonderful life that we're living as God's children. Let's celebrate! But let's not miss opportunities to put love into action. Meeting the needs of our brothers and sisters in Christ is paramount. Those needs may be physical, emotional, or even financial. This would be a practical demonstration of what Christmas is all about – expressing the love of Jesus and making Christmas real. Jesus was the greatest gift of all! Emmanuel means "God with us." A baby changes everything! And when we truly know Him, He changes our perspective on this time of the year.

There are so many ways to apply this passage all year long. Let me share just one to consider for this month. The Christmas season can be a lonely time for some. I have found that some of the loneliest people are in nursing homes. A tradition we had with our children was scheduling a night to visit several nursing homes in the area to take cookies and sing carols. (Yes, I sang, too. As a matter of fact, I led. No one ever complained.) We didn't always let the homes know we were coming. It's best to do so, though, if possible. I would make a brief announcement in the hallway or in a gathering spot and we'd sing carols. That's it. We would typically leave the cookies with those in charge to pass out at their discretion. Our kids loved it. My wife and I loved it. The other family whom we usually invited to participate every year loved it. Most of all, the residents loved it. We unashamedly represented the Christ of Christmas. Enjoy the weeks ahead and be intentional about demonstrating love. Live by faith today...

DECEMBER 4

DAILY READING:
Daniel 11:36-12:13; 1 John 4:1-21
Psalm 123:1-4; Proverbs 29:2-4
Focal Passage: 1 John 4:4

LIVING BY FAITH

DON'T FORGET WHO IS IN YOU. At the moment of conversion, the Holy Spirit comes to reside in you. John was reminding the believers that they could live the everyday Christian life because it is not dependant on them. It is dependant on the One inside of them. The Holy Spirit is God. Jesus ascended into heaven so He could come—the Spirit. The Bible says that the Holy Spirit is the seal that never leaves a true believer after conversion. That provided great comfort for the early Christians in their day-to-day dealings. They confronted heresies and hierarchies. They had multiple problems within their own families and in the world they lived in. Sound familiar?

I have no idea what or who you may be facing. I do know that if you are not careful, fear will grip you. Please do not allow it to do so. You are not on your own. If you have a relationship with Christ, the Holy Spirit lives inside of you. Don't forget this important truth. It will help you face tomorrow. And the next day. Prepare for your God-given assignments in life, but just remember that it's not all you. Let me explain it this way, this coming Sunday I am leading the music portion of our worship service due to our Worship Pastor being on vacation. (I basically know how to turn on the radio. I am not musically inclined.) There's a major reason I am not uptight. I am not going to be on my own. There is going to be a recorded professional singer singing, with all the instrumentalists pre-recorded as well. All I have to do is sing along the best I can, and I will survive. Guess what? You will survive whatever you are going through because God almighty is going to help you with whatever assignment you have. Reread the verse and rejoice. Live by faith today...

DAILY READING:

Hosea 1:1-3:5; 1 John 5:1-21
Psalm 124:1-8; Proverbs 29:5-8
Focal Passage: 1 John 5:16-17

LIVING BY FAITH

GOD WILL BRING US HOME EARLY IF HE NEEDS TO. I believe it. John closes his first epistle with a strong warning. 1. If we have a brother or sister in Christ who is struggling, we need to intercede for them. They may be in such a bad way that they don't feel as if they have the energy to pray anymore. Pray for them. Minister to them in every way possible since you are the stronger one at the time. Let them piggyback off of your strength in the Lord. The one struggling will appreciate it and the one helping will be all the better for it. This is why the church is so vital to the Christian faith. We need each other. 2. If a believer gets off track badly enough, God will bring the person to heaven early. This is why it's important not to overlook an erring fellow believer. Don't let them drown in the ditch! Save them. Listen, some believers can get so out of fellowship with God that they wreak havoc on a church. God will take them home early if they are unrepentant and committing gross sin against the body of Christ. Severe discipline will come from our Holy Father. And as heavy as this may be, it's an act of love in the end. He keeps the person from further crippling his witness and hurting the body of Christ.

As a youth pastor years ago, I had to send one of my precious teenagers home early from youth camp. Why? Because the student would not change, and it had begun to have a negative influence on others. I didn't hate the student or the other youth at camp. I loved them and was left with no option. God may be left with no other option but to call someone home before their time. Let's not be that person, but let's be the person to help someone turn from their sinful ways so they can stay their allotted time to fulfill their purpose. Live by faith today…

DAILY READING:
Hosea 4:1-5:15; 2 John 1:1-13
Psalm 125:1-5; Proverbs 29:9-11
Focal Passage: 2 John 1:7-11

LIVING BY FAITH

DON'T LOSE WHAT YOU'VE GAINED BECAUSE OF A GOOF. John goes a little bit further in his second epistle to explain why it's so important to stay close to the truth. Here he warns of staying away from a goof. According to one source, the noun form of this word describes a person who is foolish. Deceivers are foolish when it comes to the truth regarding Jesus. They can try to make Him out to be less than God. How foolish! We must be careful—very careful—not to allow them exposure. That does not mean we should not share the truth of the gospel of Jesus Christ based on the Bible with them. It just means that if they preach or teach a different Jesus than the Bible, **do not** give them exposure. In other words, do not give them an audience. It will be detrimental in every way.

The verb form of this word has another meaning. It means we can make a goof in using poor judgment. It can even mean we make an error or waste time. Hence the other clear teaching here for believers. You and I can commit a goof if we drift from the truth of God's Word and all that we have learned and applied to our Christian life. There will be rewards in heaven. If we get too far off track, we can lose ground and our heavenly rewards. God has much in store for His children in heaven. We certainly don't want to miss out on every good and perfect gift. Those gifts will be greater than any Christmas gift we have ever or will ever receive here on earth.

Stay close to Jesus. Stay far away from those who have a non-biblical Jesus. Stay in the race by taking one step at a time. Using American football terminology, keep moving the ball down the field. Live by faith today...

DECEMBER 7

DAILY READING:
Hosea 6:1-9:17; 3 John 1:1-14
Psalm 126:1-6; Proverbs 29:12-14
Focal Passage: 3 John 1:13-14

LIVING BY FAITH

NOTHING BEATS FACE TO FACE. John closes his third epistle like he did his second one. He stresses the value of meeting face to face. He's not discounting the blessing of being able to communicate in writing. Thank the Lord for the good that comes through communicating via pen and ink. Additionally, thank the Lord for the blessing of being able to communicate virtually today. But make no mistake—*nothing beats face to face!* John could have continued his writings. He did not because of his anticipated personal visit. He wanted to see them and let words of encouragement and instruction flow from his mouth to their hearts. There's no better way to accomplish that than eyeball to eyeball.

Do you do church online? That's fine. Please don't allow it to be long-term or your only form of connecting with your church family. Do you need to talk to someone right now? You know, I mean really talk? Wait until you can do so face to face, if at all possible. It will be worth it. Maybe you have someone on your mind whom you could see, if you make the effort, during the holidays? This could be a family member or old friend from way back when. Regardless, make the effort to see them in person and share whatever it is that God may have placed on your heart. It could be the greatest gift of all this year. For you or perhaps for them. Yes, no amount of texting, emailing, etc. beats face to face. Pay attention to what God is saying to you. Live by faith today...

DECEMBER 8

DAILY READING:
Hosea 10:1-14:9; Jude 1:1-25
Psalm 127:1-5; Proverbs 29:15-17
Focal Passage: Hosea 14:1-2

LIVING BY FAITH

RETURN TO THE LORD, FOR HE IS GRACIOUS. That sounds super spiritual, doesn't it? Don't let the familiarity of the phrase cause you to miss the truth of this book and passage. Hosea is set against the backdrop of a covenantal marriage. (Marriage is a covenant with God, never to be taken lightly.) Hosea's marriage with his wife Gomer, is used to illustrate God's amazing grace. She was extremely unfaithful to him, and yet he took her back. Israel too, was unfaithful to God in her sacred covenant with a Holy God. The people committed spiritual adultery with false gods. Yet, God was willing to take them back upon their repentance. Although His heart was broken time and time again, He was gracious to receive them over and over. Hosea did the same with his wife, following in obedience to God's instructions to do so in this prophetic book. And this particular passage in the final chapter is another reminder that He will forgive all of their iniquity and honor their praise as they move forward.

I took a drama class my last year in college. (I needed to raise my GPA and thought this might be a way to accomplish this great need.) The main emphasis of the class was acting out the story of Hosea. I remember who had the main part. It was not me. Actually, I am not certain what my role was, I just remember the story. Sure, I had read about Hosea, since I had grown up in the church and had Bible classes in college. But the grace this prophet of God had for his wife was absolutely mind-boggling. I finally got it. God used Hosea to help His people understand His graciousness. I needed that message at that time in my life. As a matter of fact, I still need this reminder. What about you? Do you think you've hurt God's heart too much over the years? Perhaps you think He's run out of grace because you continue to fall back into a stronghold? Hosea says—not so! God never runs out of grace for those who repent and turn to Him. You can even move forward in praise and adoration for His grace and how He will redeem whatever lost time you may have had. Live by faith today...

DECEMBER 9

DAILY READING:
Joel 1:1-3:21; Revelation 1:1-20
Psalm 128:1-6; Proverbs 29:18
Focal Passage: Revelation 1:9-11

LIVING BY FAITH

JESUS CARES ABOUT WHAT GOES ON IN HIS CHURCHES. The apostle John wrote what Jesus revealed to him while exiled on the isle of Patmos. This profound spiritual experience was none other than Jesus speaking to him on a Lord's Day—Sunday. John had not heard His voice since Christ returned to heaven over sixty years prior. He was commissioned to write this letter to seven individual churches in Asia Minor. Many of the directives for the churches would also be applicable to God's churches, for all time until the Lord's return. And speaking of the Lord's return, much of the remainder of the letter primarily deals with Christ's return—God's prophetic program.

A church is a light to a dark world. God cares about what goes on and about what does not go on. Why? Because church was His idea, not mine or any other pastors in the past. (We learned this earlier this year while reading through the book of Acts.) Jesus is Lord—boss—of the church. A pastor is an under-shepherd or, as we will see in this letter, the *angel-messenger* of the church. The role is vital, but never more important than Jesus. He is and <u>always will be</u> the Head of the church. The sooner we allow Him to be, the more light we will illuminate in our communities.

Are you a part of a church in your community? If so, do you serve? Do people in the community know you love Jesus and His church? Does the Spirit speak to you concerning your local fellowship through Holy writ? Let this be a reminder that you are the church and Jesus cares. Live by faith today…

DECEMBER 10

DAILY READING:
Amos 1:1-3:15; Revelation 2:1-17
Psalm 129:1-8; Proverbs 29:19-20
Focal Passage: Proverbs 29:20

LIVING BY FAITH

YOU MAY OR MAY NOT COUNT TO TEN, BUT YOU BETTER
THINK BEFORE YOU SPEAK. Proverbs covers speech, among other topics.
Does it not? Over and over this wisdom literature covers the power of the tongue.
Our words can be used for good. Our words can be used for bad. And if we spout
off too soon, yikes! I'm talking a BIG yikes! We've all likely heard the expression
of counting to ten if you're upset. That may or may not be ideal. But the principle
of not venting anger or saying something you might regret is true. All of us have
probably had a moment of regret because of not thinking before speaking. God is
gracious. He does expect us to learn from our mistakes and grow in our
spiritual maturity.

The best way to keep this from happening is to spend time alone with Jesus in
Bible study and prayer. Abiding in Christ produces the fruit of the Spirit. Also, if
you realize you are prone to speak before you think, that's a good thing. You realize
you have a weakness. Pray about it. Memorize verses that address the issue, like the
one today. (There are multiple possibilities in Proverbs.) It's never a good look to
look foolish. We represent Jesus to our family, friends, and a lost world.

Never talk just to be talking. Have you ever heard the expression *"Silence is
golden?"* It really can be. It's okay at times just to be quiet. Especially if you are
tempted to say anything that you may regret. Do you have a reputation of talking
before thinking? I hope not. I hope I don't. Maybe we need to ask someone close
to us? Just be sure to let them know you're asking them to talk. Just be sure you're
ready to hear what they may have to say. Live by faith today...

DECEMBER 11

DAILY READING:
Amos 4:1-6:14; Revelation 2:18-3:6
Psalm 130:1-8; Proverbs 29:21-22
Focal Passage: Revelation 3:1-2

LIVING BY FAITH

PLAYING CHURCH IS FINE AS A CHILD BUT NOT AS AN ADULT.
Did you ever play church as a child? I did. It was probably normal for a preacher's kid to do so. As a matter of fact, I remember pretending to be a preacher for a short period of time. I did a funeral for one of my favorite pet turtles that died. Yes, my first funeral was for a turtle. None of his family members attended and I think I was the only one present. Yes, playing church is fine as a child. Many of you probably did the same if you grew up attending church on a regular basis.

Playing church as an adult is not good. The church in Sardis had a reputation of being a good place to worship the Lord. Many in the community felt it was the place to be to serve God and learn how to mature in Christ. Maybe it was the fantastic music program with all the bells and whistles some churches have. You know, one with a spectacular orchestra, band, soloist, and tech team, not to mention the magnificent choir. Or maybe the preacher was a wonderful pulpiteer? Perhaps it was the building? Some churches have incredible facilities that can leave one in awe of their beauty. Lastly, some churches are filled with people who have been trained on how to do church due to cultural Christianity. Some or all of these examples help us see why God was communicating that this church in Sardis was **dead**. Jesus can't be fooled. He knows what's really going on in our churches.

Don't waste your life playing church. Work to improve the church where you find yourself. Pray. Don't complain. Follow authority. The church in Sardis had hope. More than likely, so does yours. If you must, go somewhere else if you truly sense you need to because you are in a dead church. Only do so if you are released by the Holy Spirit. Live by faith today...

DECEMBER 12

DAILY READING:
Amos 7:1-9:15; Revelation 3:7-22
Psalm 131:1-3; Proverbs 29:23
Focal Passage: Revelation 3:14-16

LIVING BY FAITH

TEPID TEA IS NOT FOR ME. I grew up in the deep south. We like our tea sweet and cold. I just don't prefer having a nice glass of tea that is lukewarm whether I'm in the deep south or in an igloo in Alaska. As a matter of fact, as much as I enjoy coffee, I don't even like lukewarm coffee! In the spiritual realm of life, God finds tepidness nauseating. When believers are lukewarm, it makes God want to vomit. That's what's up with the upchuck in this final message to one of the seven influential churches in Asia Minor. He saved His strongest words for last—to make God sick is sick—extremely sick!

When we consider the historical context, we have an even better understanding. In the city of Laodicea to the north were healthy hot springs and to the south were cold springs. Both had terrific advantages. But Laodicea had ongoing water problems. They often lacked water supply and the water was tepid—lukewarm. It would often make people sick. Our Lord knew those reading this message would understand His words. The lukewarm Laodicean church had been influenced by the ways of the Roman Empire—the rich and famous. So many had embraced the lifestyle of the elite and stopped drinking from the Living Water. When believers allow the world to influence them to a point of making the church a type of country club, it stops accomplishing its kingdom mission. Compromising God's values occurs when believers fall out of fellowship with God. Lack of intimacy with Jesus leads to God being on the outside knocking and waiting to get in.

Is He knocking on the door of your heart? What about the church you belong to? It wasn't too late for the church at Laodicea at the time. Please don't let it be too late for you if you believe God has convicted you of being lukewarm. Open the door and let Him in. Live by faith today...

DAILY READING:

Obadiah 1:1-21; Revelation 4:1-11
Psalm 132:1-18; Proverbs 29:24-25
Focal Passage: Proverbs 29:25

LIVING BY FAITH

IF YOU ARE SCARED OF MAN, YOUR IMPACT WILL BE SCARCE.
Our church had an outdoor Christmas event this year. There were games for
children, snacks, music, a petting zoo, and an ugly Christmas sweater competition. (I
did not own a sweater, so I wore my Christmas shirt that some in my family think
is pretty ugly.) There were three judges for the ugly Christmas sweater competition.
They each wore fake reindeer antlers with the word JUDGE printed across the top.
I even had my picture taken with them because they stood out in the crowd. It was
fun and there was a winner and it was not me.

There will be no human judges in heaven. We need to be reminded of this
fact occasionally, so we won't live a life here on earth pleasing man. We live for no
man. Do we respect man? Yes. Can others have a godly influence on us at times?
Certainly. But only Jesus is Lord. Lordship means boss. He calls the shots! All of
them, even those that some close to us do not like. The Bible says if we are afraid of
man we can be trapped. We can be deceived into thinking we are better off by being
a peacekeeper. Not at all. As a matter of fact, we move away from the protection of
God. If we ultimately trust God as our boss, then we can be certain He has got our
backs. Don't try to figure out how, just trust Him. If we trust Jesus with our eternal
life, we can certainly trust Him with our daily life. We have but one life to live and
we do not want to have little Kingdom influence. Live by faith today...

DECEMBER 14

DAILY READING:
Jonah 1:1-4:11; Revelation 5:1-14
Psalm 133:1-3; Proverbs 29:26-27
Focal Passage: Jonah 1:17

LIVING BY FAITH

GOD PROVIDES IN SPITE OF OURSELVES. Most people have heard about the story of Jonah. Assuming you have, what stands out in your mind? More than likely, it's that a runaway preacher type (prophet) of his day got eaten by a whale. That's sort of right. Jonah was God's spokesman, much like the other minor prophets we're reading about, to tell the wicked city of Nineveh to repent. He didn't like the people he was preaching to and didn't like the message God had given him to share. Besides that, he probably hadn't been to seminary school. But the whale was more of a blessing than a spanking. God disciplines those He loves. No doubt about it. Let's just not be too quick to see his time in the belly of this giant fish as a negative. God rescued Jonah from drowning and it's obvious that when he came out, he was a different man. He was ready to obey, even though we continue to see why he's so often referred to as "the reluctant prophet." Newsflash—it's the message, not the messenger, that's most important! People are simply instruments in the hands of God. He can use any of us if He chooses. Even if we have an attitude problem and don't get what He is doing. He's God.

God's grace really is amazing. Is it not? Not only did He provide for a prophet with a stinking attitude, He provided for people who were wicked. Jonah's hesitancy was that these Ninevites were the worst of the worst. I mean they were bad folks. And God wanted to save them! What about the good folks? What about the Jews at the time? Though Israel's sins put them in the same category as the Ninevites, God was showing that God's love is for all who repent. He provides for **everyone**.

Are you running from God? Please allow this message to speak to you about your disobedience. Are you afraid to speak for God? Please allow this message to remind you that you are simply a tool in the hands of God. Are you struggling with prejudice? This story of what God can do with those you dislike can be your story. Live by faith today...

DAILY READING:

Micah 1:1-4:13; Revelation 6:1-17
Psalm 134:1-3; Proverbs 30:1-4
Focal Passage: Psalm 134:2

LIVING BY FAITH

THERE IS A BIBLICAL REASON TRUE WORSHIPPERS LIFT THEIR HANDS DURING WORSHIP. This brief Psalm deals with a subject that could contain volumes upon volumes. The worship of a Holy God is vast. Our verse reminds us of why it is biblical to raise holy hands during worship. Worshipers are lifting their hands to the heavens. Jesus is the source of all good things there are and ever will be. We praise Him for His mercy and grace. It can be a sign of surrender. We allow ourselves to be caught up in the moment of praise indicating we are all His. True worshipers even lift clean hands because of the redeemer Jesus and have a pure heart only because of a Holy God. We are getting practice for what will occupy a lot of time in heaven. Some pray to God while lifting hands in worship. It's biblical.

I didn't grow up in a hand raising church. That's okay. Some churches do and some don't. Only God knows the heart, and some don't realize the true biblical purpose. To be honest, I used to think that people did it to draw attention to themselves. Maybe some do. Who am I to judge? We are to worship Jesus in spirit and in truth as we gather with fellow worshippers. We please the audience of One— Jesus. We worship Him like the shepherds did in the plains of Judea. They kneeled in a posture of surrender to the King.

Worship biblically and regularly both privately and corporately. Jesus is worthy of our worship. And don't be concerned about those around you as you worship with others. God knows our hearts. Live by faith today...

DAILY READING:
Micah 5:1-7:20; Revelation 7:1-17
Psalm 135:1-21; Proverbs 30:5-6
Focal Passage: Micah 6:8

LIVING BY FAITH

MIGHT THESE BE YOUR GOALS FOR THE NEW YEAR? Actually, we should apply these obvious, practical truths today and every day. In the prophet Micah's day, the kingdoms of Judah and Israel were experiencing fantastic economic changes. Many benefited financially and fell into a lifestyle of the rich and famous. There was sin and moral decline everywhere. Micah's message was that God was greatly displeased with their misuse of blessings. Personal holiness was absent in many, and there were a number of people being mistreated. Our belief in God should affect our daily lives, and when it doesn't, God is displeased. There's a better way.

The first time I truly recall this verse being taught was from a man named Paul Nunnery. He was the Director of the Mississippi Baptist Children's Village for many years. I was the student minister at the time he talked about these three principles. They are: act justly, love mercy, walk humbly. He lived these before my eyes as a young man. (And I wasn't the only one who noticed his walk with God!) So when I read these words I automatically think of him. That's not a bad thing. It's good because it is a reminder that he was a man just like me. These three truths are attainable, by God's grace and with His help.

To act justly simply means to do what's right even when it hurts. To love mercy means to excitedly extend mercy at every corner. To walk humbly means you have no interest in getting credit because you know it's God working in your life and others. What a way to live! What an impact one can make during a lifetime. Let's do this. Live by faith today...

DAILY READING:
Nahum 1:1-3:19; Revelation 8:1-13
Psalm 136:1-26; Proverbs 30:7-9
Focal Passage: Nahum 1:7

LIVING BY FAITH

A GOOD VERSE FOR A TROUBLED TIME. We all have times of trouble. Sometimes it's just a bad day. Sometimes it's a series of bad days. Occasionally, we just think trouble is everywhere! This verse brings comfort for a troubled soul. I don't have as much scripture memorized as I should, but I learned this one years ago. I cannot tell you how often God has brought it to mind during a weary season. The prophet reminds us that the Lord truly is good—no matter what's going on. He's our refuge—our hiding place. Here's my paraphrase: *Hunker down with your Bible; journal; and pray to your faithful God who's about to take you to an entirely new level in your spiritual walk due to difficulties, as you abide in Him.* He cares. Trust Him. And don't forget the phrase you may have heard your southern friend use, "God is good all the time and all the time God is good."

Keep in mind that there's no contradiction here with God's righteousness being just. God punishes sin. This verse does not serve as a pass to do whatever you want, sinful or not. Since God is good, He must address evil. That's what this is about. God is announcing judgment on the kingdom of Assyria, especially on its capital city, Nineveh. Nahum's name literally means "to console" or "consultation." So the prophet Nahum was letting people know that God will punish sin. He will bring judgment. He will not ignore evil. But none of this cancels out His undying love. God is loving and at the same time, He is always and forever just in all His ways. Nahum mixed in just enough consolation to give them eternal hope.

Ask God to show you any stronghold that may be hindering your walk. Repent and trust God daily for victory. He's a good God. He's not out to get you. He wants to use troubled times to give us the opportunity to watch Him at work like never before. Live by faith today...

DECEMBER 18

LIVING BY FAITH

IF WE KNEW WHAT GOD KNOWS ABOUT OUR FUTURE, WE WOULDN'T BE ABLE TO HANDLE IT. I had just turned thirty and was attending a Youth Ministry retreat at Lake Tiak-O'Khata in central Mississippi. God had spoken to me before as a teenager at this beautiful camp with the most incredible food you will ever find. He did it again! And it was through the book of Habakkuk and this particular verse. The prophet Habakkuk was crying out to God for help. Though most prophets spoke to the people on behalf of God, this was the opposite. Habakkuk spoke to God on behalf of the people. He was struggling to understand the ways of God. You ever done that? God had used an evil group of people to judge righteous people. It didn't seem fair. God tells him in this verse that he wouldn't believe it if he knew what was coming down the pike. Using a phrase from an old movie, *he couldn't handle the truth!* But he sure finally accepted the truth of trusting God. God is sovereign. God wants us to cry out to Him. God wants us to live by His faith.

I am at a stage in life that causes me to almost laugh at what happened that day. You see, I had gone to my room awaiting the next session, frustrated. Not frustrated at anybody in particular; the speakers were great, and I enjoyed seeing my fellow youth minister buds. I had sensed God calling me to be a senior pastor and even though I had FINALLY surrendered, nothing happened. My pastor knew and he was helping me walk through the next steps, but I guess I thought I'd go somewhere immediately. So just as Habakkuk didn't understand why God waits when we are trying to do what's right, I didn't understand either. God used this entire book, and especially this verse, to give me peace. God has done many things over the past thirty years I would never have believed, most of them good, and the bad He has used for good. One more neat part about the story. The church where I was serving as a student pastor ended up being my second senior pastorate. If I had known that then, I would have laughed and been a bit overwhelmed. TRUST GOD even when it doesn't make sense. *Especially* when it doesn't make sense! Live by faith today...

DECEMBER 19

DAILY READING:
Zephaniah 1:1-3:20; Revelation 10:1-11
Psalm 138:1-8; Proverbs 30:11-14
Focal Passage: Psalm 138:8

LIVING BY FAITH

BE HONEST WITH GOD WHEN YOU TALK WITH HIM. I enjoy reading the Psalms for many reasons. One reason is because they demonstrate how to pray. They also demonstrate that David was human like you and me. He would often pour out his heart to God. He praised Him. He expressed disappointment. He cried out. He just let himself be vulnerable. Maybe that's why he was described as a "man after God's own heart?" God wants us to be authentic. He can handle our ups and downs of life. Our willingness to talk with Him about anything and everything demonstrates we believe and know who to go to for answers, comfort, and direction. We can be brutally honest with our heavenly Father. Maybe some couldn't with their earthly Father, but not so with God.

We see that it's okay to ask God to not let you down. David is saying to God to please allow him to fulfill his purpose here on earth. Even during seasons of great difficulty, talk to God about your situation. What if you pray something like this? *"Dear God, I am yours. We have come way too far for you to leave me hanging. Please don't. And I have come way too far to leave you. You've got too much invested in me and I've got too much invested in you. Jesus, I am struggling some right now. Please show yourself faithful to me once again. I wish I was stronger, but I am not. God, make me stronger during this time, please. You are faithful and loving regardless. I know that even when I don't feel it or am able to see it. I believe by faith. Just please allow me to fulfill your plan, not mine, for the rest of my days. Like the old spiritual says, you never failed me yet."* Yeah, maybe pray like that. It's sort of the modern-day David style. Live by faith today...

DAILY READING:
Haggai 1:1-2:23; Revelation 11:1-19
Psalm 139:1-24; Proverbs 30:15-16
Focal Passage: Psalm 139:5

LIVING BY FAITH

GOD HAS YOU HEMMED IN, SO YOU MIGHT AS WELL REST IN HIM. I like the way this verse is translated. The phrase "hem in" was fairly common where I am from. (Another translation uses the word "encircled.") When someone is hemmed in, they are prevented from moving or changing because they are surrounded by something or someone. It may be people or obstacles. Regardless, the person cannot go anywhere. It's like an army in a battle when they give up due to being surrounded by the enemy.

David is reflecting on the overwhelming omniscience of God. He knows everything about everything. He knows it all. Nothing escapes Him. Nothing. He knows all there is to know about all there is to know. And He knows everything about you and me. He always has and always will. I know it's mind-boggling, but it's true. Don't allow that to get you thinking sideways. Trust God and not any sort of disjointed thinking from the enemy. Listen, when we ponder what God can do when we find ourselves in an incomprehensible set of circumstances, we get relief. Why wouldn't we? He knows who we are and where we've been. He knows what's ahead and what we are facing. He knows why we are where we are and if it's due to our sin or living in a depraved world. It may be because of someone else. Who knows? God does. He knows it all and the sooner we trust that he's all around, the better off we will be to move forward. Friend, He has you hemmed in. Praise God today for this incredible truth and rest in Him. Live by faith today...

DAILY READING:
Zechariah 1:1-21; Revelation 12:1-13:1a
Psalm 140:1-13; Proverbs 30:17
Focal Passage: Revelation 12:5

LIVING BY FAITH

A CHRISTMAS PASSAGE IN THE BOOK OF REVELATION?
Absolutely! There is a plethora of symbolism in the book of Revelation. Here we find the writer clearly using symbolism to share truth concerning things to come. Most scholars believe the twelve stars in this chapter represent the twelve tribes of Israel. The woman mentioned is a representation of Israel. The pregnancy symbolizes the reality that Jesus Christ, the Messiah of the world, came through Israel. Jesus, we know, was born of Mary, a Jewish woman. So this text is pregnant with biblical truth that certainly can be tied to this time of the year.

Jesus is coming again. He will not come as a baby; He will come as a Warrior. Everyone who desires to be His must put their faith and trust in Him alone. It won't matter that you are a Jew, Catholic, Baptist, or any other religion or denomination. What will matter is that you have repented of your sin and put your faith in Jesus alone for your salvation. I don't know about you, but I want to be on His team when He returns. Allow this passage to cause you to reflect on the fact that Jesus was born and what that means to you personally. It should mean everything to you and to me. The Messiah was born that we might be redeemed. We see Him throughout the scriptures—both Old and New Testaments. Here is just one more clear example. Rejoice, Jesus has come! And be certain you are ready for when He comes again. Live by faith today...

DAILY READING:
Zechariah 2:1-3:10; Revelation 13:1b-18
Psalm 141:1-10; Proverbs 30:18-20
Focal Passage: Zechariah 2:3-4

LIVING BY FAITH

ANGELS NOT NAMED CLARENCE. Angels are mentioned throughout the Bible. The ones in our passage are not named Clarence, even though he may be on your mind during this time of the year. One of the most watched Christmas movies ever is *It's A Wonderful Life.* Many of us make an effort to watch it every year. If you're familiar with the characters in the movie, then you know about Clarence the angel. (He's probably one of my favorites—not angels, but characters.) Even though he's fictional, his role is fairly accurate according to the Bible. He was a messenger. A very important one who was used to help the main character, George Bailey, turn his life around.

The prophet Zechariah called on God's people to continue building the temple, in spite of being discouraged. Angels were used to accomplish God's will. We see them here as messengers with specific roles. At times, we can become tired and lifeless, due to the weariness that comes with fulfilling God's will. Living for Jesus is not for sissies! This prophetic book is filled with visions and symbols. Also, the plan to bring about His kingdom through the Messiah is foretold. Furthermore, Zechariah literally means "the Lord remembers." He is telling God's people that the Lord remembers His promises no matter how challenging accomplishing God's will can be. God is faithful! He will do whatever it takes to accomplish His will—even if it means using His created angelic beings. They can be used to help turn a life around.

There were times in the movie when Clarence told George he was limited in what he could do. Angels do indeed have limitations. God does not. We are never to worship angels. We are to worship Jesus, just like the angels did at His birth. And never forget that God never abandons His truth. He is worthy of our praise. Live by faith today...

DAILY READING:
Zechariah 4:1-5:11; Revelation 14:1-20
Psalm 142:1-7; Proverbs 30:21-23
Focal Passage: Proverbs 30:21-23

LIVING BY FAITH

ONE OF THE BEST GIFTS WE CAN GIVE PEOPLE IS TO BE A BLESSING. The Christmas season will soon come to an end for another year. Maybe you are trying to determine what to give that special person in your life. Perhaps you are considering what you can do for someone not expecting a gift from you. I understand. But I think we see from our verses today that being a blessing to others can be a gift like none other. Many people get depressed during the holiday season. Others are lonely for various reasons. (Of course, these issues are not limited to the end of the year.) The last thing we want to do is make things worse for people. Jesus even said that the most important commandments are to love God and love people.

These verses are a part of an entire chapter that deals with various aspects of leadership. The verses we're focusing on describe people whom no one wants to encounter. Let's focus on the third person listed: *an unloved woman who is married.* This depicts a woman who is despised due to her disgusting ways. The word "contemptible" is the Hebrew word used most often for "hated." This woman is a not-too-friendly person, to say the least. So the observation is that the guy who marries her will not experience a "picnic." It won't be easy. It will be hard—very, very, hard. Marriage takes work even in the best of circumstances and it's worth it. But take note that this kind of lady, in this kind of marriage, does not make for a kind couple. Perhaps you have just been reminded of someone in your neighborhood? There you go, bless them with an act of kindness. Someone in the house needs it. Probably everyone in the household does.

There are people and couples like this in our world. We need to be sure we are not them. If so, God is still in the miracle-working business. And we can all be encouraging to others, especially difficult people, all year long as God leads. Before we end today, ponder who may need a special blessing from you right now. It doesn't have to be expensive. It can be as simple as a kind text, note, or call to someone. Let's be a blessing. Live by faith today...

DAILY READING:
Zechariah 6:1-7:14; Revelation 15:1-8
Psalm 143:1-12; Proverbs 30:24-28
Focal Passage: Proverbs 30:24-28

LIVING BY FAITH

HAVE AN ANT FOR CHRISTMAS. Perhaps you've heard of the expression, *"Dynamite comes in small packages."* This passage suggests it's an accurate statement. God can use small things to accomplish amazing feats. Four are listed as examples. Let's focus on the ant today. The ant is able to store provisions for the future. Ants are also great providers. They work together to accomplish much good. Isn't that amazing? If you haven't taken the time to watch them at work, you may want to consider doing so to allow the truth of the Bible to sink in. I know, you're probably like me, I'm pretty quick to step on them with my foot because they can bite and eat leftovers. (I don't want ants eating my leftovers—especially this time of the year.)

Christmas is centered around a baby boy. He too was small at the time. But not too small to make a difference! He changed everything! Jesus came to provide salvation for all. Jesus's birth meant the future would be different. He was now **with us.** Please do not allow this Christmas to slip by you without contemplating the incredible magnificence of something small. Just be sure Jesus is the priority.

Before we end our time together this Christmas Eve, let me challenge you. Do something small today for someone else. Be intentional. It could make a big difference. Live by faith today...

DAILY READING:
Zechariah 8:1-23; Revelation 16:1-21
Psalm 144:1-15; Proverbs 30:29-31
Focal Passage: Proverbs 30:29-31

LIVING BY FAITH

THE GREATEST KING OF ALL. If these created animals are stately, how much more a king. A king was made by the same creator. God. Let's take it to an even greater level. Sure, a human king deserves our awe and respect. Especially a good king who can lead his army to victory. But think of King Jesus. He came as a babe and grew to be a man. Even as a little boy Magi brought Him gifts. Gifts fit for a king. Gold, frankincense, and myrrh. There is no equal. The gates of hell will not prevail. In His humiliation on the cross, He conquered and subdued all enemies. His and ours. He arose and is alive. He sent forth the gospel to save the world. And in the latter day, He will come as a warrior and put an end to the enemy. HE will be coming indeed, and with great stateliness and majesty. Yes, this Jesus is the greatest king of all!

Enjoy family and friends today. Cherish the old memories from days gone by. But don't forget to create new ones. They will be ones that may even outdo the ones you're thinking of right now. Don't miss them! But be balanced in your celebration today of the birth of King Jesus. Make time to give praise to the divine King who reigns from heaven with the earth as His glorious footstool. Your time may be private. Ideally, your time will be with others in celebrating. There is none like Him. There never will be. He is why we enjoy this time of the year. He is THE reason. And do not fret about other leaders who may be contrary to everything Christ stands for. When we have King Jesus, we have victory. No matter what! Live by faith today...

DECEMBER 26

LIVING BY FAITH

POST-CHRISTMAS INSTRUCTIONS. For some, the day after Christmas is all good. There is a sense of relief from the stress that was caused in the weeks leading up to the big day. But for others, there can be a letdown. For example, listening to Christmas music may be odd now that the day is over. Someone has to take down the decorations. Maybe it's you. There may be a need to exchange presents to get the right size due to all the cookies eaten over the past few weeks. And the spirit we so often see at Christmas can begin to fade. So here we go again, what can you and I do to work through this transition? I believe David gives instructions here regarding the gracious provision of God. His desire is to help all mankind.

Call out to God. Pray. Pray every day and in every way. Whatever is on your mind, talk with Him about it before talking with others. He longs to hear from us, and He pays close attention to those with integrity. It matters how we live. Integrity is doing what's right when no one else is looking or may ever know. God knows if we fear Him. Respect for almighty God is paramount to those who pray with genuineness. God hears those cries and provides salvation. And God acts on behalf of all those who love Him. Don't worry, He will take care of those who have a wickedness about them. He knows their heart and their time is coming. Allow God to take care of it. You live your life with these instructions in mind going forward. It's going to be okay. The Lord is near. Live by faith today...

DECEMBER 27

LIVING BY FAITH

NEVER PUT YOUR TOTAL TRUST IN MAN. I am so grateful for the people whom the Lord has put in my path to influence me for good. Family, friends, teachers, coaches, deacons, and others have been used to point me to God. I'm sure many of you can say the same. If so, we are blessed indeed. But we cannot put our total trust in man. Our passage says they will come to an end. We will all return to the ground—die. It's just a matter of when. (Unless the Lord returns.) The psalmist is not saying our works for the Lord don't live on. They do. What we do for Kingdom purposes has a ripple effect, for they were done for eternal reasons. Just because my dad died when I was in my twenties does not mean he doesn't still influence me for good. Much of what he taught me came from God's Word. We should be grateful for their impact but never worship them. That's the main message of this passage.

God remains faithful forever. He is eternally trustworthy. He has no limitations. That's why when seasons change, He is still the same. When the leadership of our country changes, He is still there. When your favorite staff member changes, God is still in charge. And when someone close to you dies, God is with you. He is really with you—perhaps like no other time in your life. Our hope is in God alone. When we make Him our top companion, we have help. Always.

As you get ready to transition into a new year, allow these verses to encourage you. Maybe you had a difficult year. Maybe you had an overall great year. Maybe you just needed to be reminded that your faithful Lord will be with you no matter what next year brings. Live by faith today…

DAILY READING:
Zechariah 12:1-13:9; Revelation 19:1-21
Psalm 147:1-20; Proverbs 31:1-7
Focal Passage: Revelation 19:11

LIVING BY FAITH

THE ONE RIDING ON THE WHITE HORSE IS JESUS. Our passage today takes us back to the second coming. Jesus is coming again! Regardless of one's eschatological belief, we can all agree that the Bible clearly says that Jesus will return. Here it is! And He is on a white horse. (I think that's why I have always had an affinity toward big beautiful white horses.) HE will appear by heaven's visible opening. What an incredible sight that will be to behold! Can you see it? Take a moment and close your eyes and imagine the scene as much as possible. Yes, it's going to be one incredible experience. And for those who know Him personally, a victory like none other. You see, a white horse is a Roman symbol of victory. Jesus' primary task upon His returning to earth is making war against the enemies of God. The scene of a tiny baby, whom we all thought about recently due to the Christmas season, will not be the scene the next time He comes. No, no, no, not at all. The picture will be of a grown Jesus riding on a beautiful white horse as our Lord executing the final phase of life on earth.

It is not *if* your troubles on earth will come to an end, it's *when*. If you have a personal relationship with Jesus Christ, one day the trials you experience will be over. Name your problem right now. It's going to be over one day! Either at the second coming or your homegoing to heaven. If you do not have a relationship with Jesus, your trials will come to end as you know them. As a matter of fact, they will seem minute compared to what will happen to you upon Christ's return. I'm not trying to scare you. The Bible is clear. Please don't wait any longer. Repent of your sin and place your faith in Jesus alone. Lastly, let's all remember this verse the next time we encounter a white horse, and praise Jesus for always being faithful and true. Live by faith today...

DECEMBER 29

DAILY READING:
Zechariah 14:1-21; Revelation 20:1-15
Psalm 148:1-14; Proverbs 31:8-9
Focal Passage: Revelation 20:14-15

LIVING BY FAITH

WHAT DOES THIS VERSE DO TO YOUR HEART? If you are a Christian, it should hurt your heart. It hurts mine. Think about it for a moment. This is it for those who do not have a personal relationship with Christ. There are no second chances at this point. You see, the second death is just another way of speaking of eternal judgment. The first death was the physical death of the body. This one, the second death, is eternal separation from God. Forever. No more love, blessings, or benefits from God. When lost people are living, they receive benefits from the living God whether they realize it (or admit it) or not. Think about that too, and you'll surely agree. You see, in hell there is no God and so there is no good. None. It's over. It's over forever. As a believer, it should really crush us. Do you know any people who do not have a relationship with Jesus right now? Sure you do. I do too. It hurts my heart to think of them in hell forever. It hurts my heart that there are many I know who I've made no intentional effort to share Christ with. It hurts my heart that some I've shared with rejected Him. Not me, but Him. There's a difference. We can never let someone's unwillingness to trust Jesus be personal toward us. It's personal toward the God who made a way for them. We must keep sharing and praying for those lost without Jesus. I cannot stop. You cannot stop. One day it'll be over forever and there will be no more opportunities. Let's share while we can and trust God with the results.

If you are reading this and don't have a personal relationship with Christ, it should touch your heart. Here's what I mean. It should cause you to want to place your faith in Christ alone. Think about what He did for you by dying on the cross for your sins. Yours and mine. He arose and desires that you spend eternity in heaven with Him when you die. Better yet, He wants to know you now on earth and help you fulfill your God-given purpose. It's not too late. Admit that you are a sinner and believe in Him alone for redemption. Ask a mature believer to help you grow in your relationship and watch how your life changes. I dare you. Live by faith today...

DECEMBER 30

DAILY READING:
Malachi 1:1-2:17; Revelation 21: 1-27
Psalm 149:1-9; Proverbs 31:10-24
Focal Passage: Revelation 21:27

LIVING BY FAITH

ARE YOU IN THE BOOK? I'm not talking about just any book. I'm talking about the Lamb's Book of Life. Only those who have put their faith and trust in Jesus alone are in that book. While the invitation to dwell in this incredible city called *The New Jerusalem* is universal, the requirements to enter are very specific. Only those who have a personal relationship with Jesus Christ dwell there. So let me ask again, are you in the book? If not, I can't think of a better time to have your name written down than right now. When it's written down, it's in ink. It is not in pencil. It cannot be erased by your bad deeds because you weren't put there by your good deeds. It's only due to the blood of Jesus Christ shed on the cross for our sins that allows us the possibility of redemption as well as the blessing of being a resident of the holy city, Jerusalem. The New Jerusalem that we will dwell in forever one day.

In the meantime, how then shall we live? With purpose. With intentionality. With anticipation. With great expectations. With a Christlike attitude. With anticipation for what is to come. You see, we need to make every day count. Each day is a gift from God. And every day we live for Jesus here, we will be investing in a better forever life there. To be given a brand-new year ahead is a wonderful time to re-evaluate priorities. I'm not necessarily talking about New Year's resolutions. Those are fine and have a place. I'm talking about just thinking through the major areas of our lives. Spiritual, physical, emotional aspects, for example. It may be time to make some adjustments. Why? Because the more we have a Kingdom perspective for our future life, the more likely we are to maximize every day and every new year. Live by faith today...

DECEMBER 31

DAILY READING:
Malachi 3:1-4:6; Revelation 22:1-21
Psalm 150:1-6; Proverbs 31:25-31
Focal Passage: Malachi 3:10

LIVING BY FAITH

THIS ONE PRACTICE ESPECIALLY DEMONSTRATES IF OUR FAITH IS GENUINE. Tithing. I know, you may be thinking, *"Leave it to a Baptist preacher to write on tithing for the very last devotional of the year!"* That's funny. (If I had put smiling emojis in this book, there would be one right here.) I get it. Why not speak on one of the other magnificent truths from our reading today? They are certainly there! Well, because this entire year I have tried to write about what I sensed God wanted me to write about. And this is it. This year has been my most difficult year of my life to continue practicing the tithe. The pandemic has been a challenge for my family financially, like it has for many others. An unexpected surgery that absolutely wiped out the little savings we had. I could go on listing our challenges, but I will stop. By the grace of God, we never stopped tithing. I just can't. My parents taught me to tithe. And Kellie and I have always—I mean *always*—tithed to God's church where we belong. (Yes, I believe the storehouse is the church.) God has never let us down and He won't. This is the one place where He has asked believers to test Him. That's a big statement, folks. He means it and He will fulfill His promises.

Our level of daily faith shows up in our checkbook or bank statement. If I had always done the math, I would have freaked out! (Maybe it's good that I'm not good with numbers after all?) Did you know that the average church goer gives less than three percent of his or her income to God? It's really sad, but it's reality. Listen, we cannot accomplish Kingdom work for Jesus if we ignore this clear command. Jesus fulfilled it. He didn't do away with it. Somehow or another, we need to be sure we get this one right. Trust me, I know the temptation to justify not tithing. But it's just that—justification. Never define what "blessing" means, either. Let God do that. One can be wealthy and not be blessed. Some have no joy or peace but have multiple houses. Only an intimate relationship with Jesus Christ gives us joy and meaning. So go ahead and tithe. Based on this verse, I not only dare you, I double-dog dare you! Where I'm from that's called an "in your face" dare. (This would be another good place for a smiling emoji.) Perhaps this is exactly what God uses to change the trajectory of your life going forward. Live by faith today...

ACKNOWLEDGMENTS

Two-Penny Publishing has been everything I had hoped for in a publishing company. They are a consummate team of professionals I hope to partner with again in the future. A special thanks to Owner and Author Coach, Tom Goodlet, as well as Chief Executive Officer, Jodi Costa.

Thank you, Fifth Avenue Baptist Church, for supporting me in this endeavor. I want to especially thank the following staff members—Berniecia Edwards, and Cindy and Hope Lewis. You have been extremely patient. God bless you!

I had two proofers willingly invest their time and expertise in helping me provide a better product for the reader. Bonnie Brown and Jeff Spotts are a dynamic duo that I trust with my entire being. Well, almost. You know I love you. Thank you.

For all those that helped promote the book—THANK YOU! Your willingness to, in essence, attach your name in various ways to mine on this project blessed me beyond words. Thank you for your encouragement.

Thank you most of all to the wife of my youth—Kellie Kitchings, for yet again, providing what I needed to fulfill what I sensed God was calling me to do. She never complained about my taking time each morning for an entire year to write my devotional thoughts. Numerous times she would verbalize how excited she is about having her own copy to read one day. Kellie is a fantastic Pastor's wife and, in this case, author's wife. She is special and I love her.

ABOUT THE AUTHOR

Hal Kitchings has been in vocational ministry for forty years. He is a third generation Pastor and served in churches of various sizes. Although he has spent most of his adult years pastoring in Florida, he is a native of Mississippi. He has three earned degrees beyond high school (BA, MARE, and DMin) and written one book, *Three Mississippi*. Hal and his wife, Kellie, have two adult children and three grandchildren—so far.

Harold and Ann Kitchings, Hal's parents, modeled what it meant to grow spiritually. The Bible says, *"But grow in the grace and knowledge of our Lord and Savior Jesus Christ…"* (2 Peter 3:18) They did. And they did not just teach him, their lives exemplified what it means to bear the fruit of the Spirit as a result of an intimate relationship. He says they were as much like Jesus as anyone he has ever known and believes it was primarily due to the overflow of their time alone with God. Therefore, Hal has intentionally and regularly followed their example for decades and is passionate about teaching others how to do the same.

Made in the USA
Columbia, SC
13 January 2022